8-28

'For Hannah, who lives in Derbyshire'

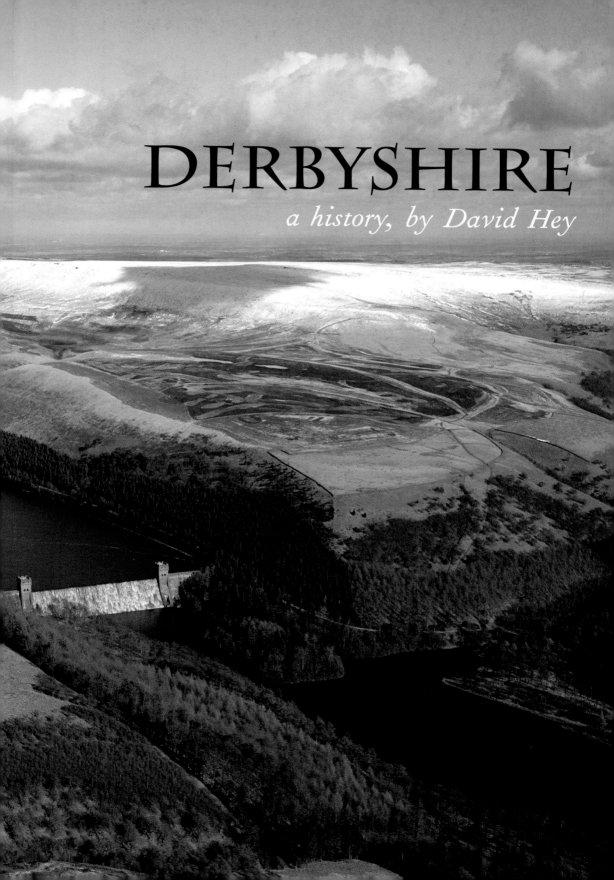

DERBYSHIRE

a history, by David Hey

Derbyshire: a history

Copyright © David Hey, 2008

First published in 2008 by
Carnegie Publishing Ltd
Chatsworth Road,
Lancaster LA1 4SL
www.carnegiepublishing.com

British Library Cataloguing-in-Publication data
A catalogue record for this book is available from the British Library

ISBN 978-1-85936-167-2   *hardback*

Designed, typeset and originated by Carnegie Publishing
Printed and bound in the UK by Cambridge University Press

FRONTISPIECE
An aerial photograph of Howden and Derwent dams. These reservoirs in the Upper Derwent valley were created between 1901 and 1916 to provide water for Leicester, Derby, Nottingham and Sheffield. The River Derwent formed the ancient moorland boundary between Derbyshire and Yorkshire. Medieval cattle pastures, or heys, are seen beyond the river, extending up to rough moorland that was used for grazing sheep and, in later times, for rearing grouse for shooting. Birchinlee Pasture (*foreground, left*) has the typical patchwork pattern formed by burning heather in rotation so that grouse can feed from fresh green shoots. Forestry Commission conifers line the valley.
WWW.WEBBAVIATION.CO.UK

Contents

BRONZE AGE
COLLARED URN
(p. 24)

THE REPTON
STONE
(p.60)

ROMAN LEAD PIG
(p.53)

ANGLIAN CROSS,
EYAM (p.85)

MAP OF
WORMHILL
(p.205)

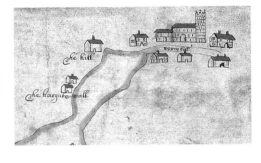

'T 'OWD MAN',
WIRSKWORTH
(p.168)

THE CRESCENT, BUXTON (p.328)

TABLEAU OF INNOCENCE (p.444)

WAR MEMORIAL,
GLOSSOP

WIRKSWORTH
FROM THE EAST
(P.325)

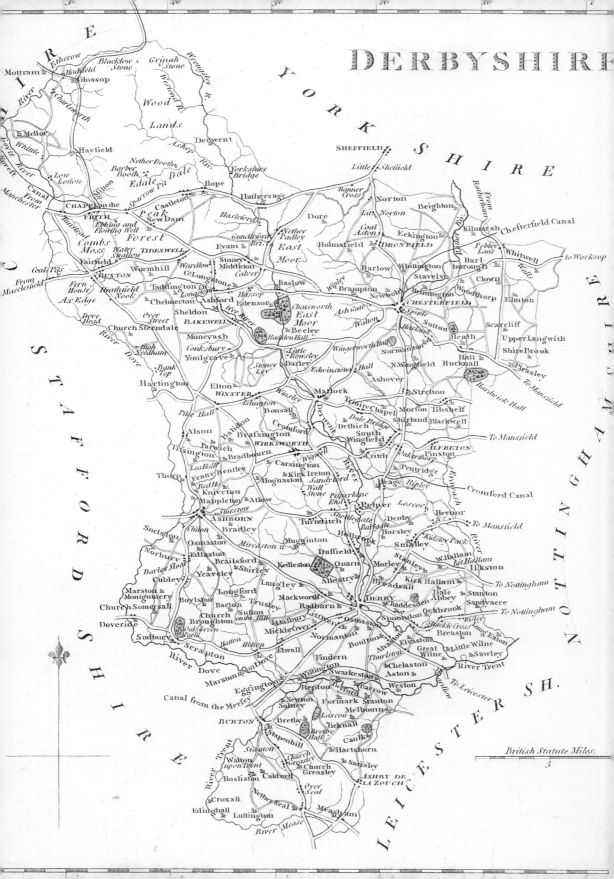

DERBYSHIRE

Preface

Although I am a Yorkshireman, I have now lived in Derbyshire for more than half my life. As a young man I got to know the Peak District well as a rambler; then from 1967 to 1969 I lived in Matlock when I was a lecturer at the College of Education, so I became familiar with the central parts of the county too. After that, I moved to Leicestershire, from where I often visited historic sites in south Derbyshire. Since 1974 my wife and I have lived at Dronfield Woodhouse, just inside the county's northern border. Walking remains my chief recreation and I have trod all parts of the county in search of 'history on the ground'. For many years I took Sheffield University extra-mural classes throughout north Derbyshire, and I am still a regular speaker at meetings of local history societies there. I have also been Chairman of the Derbyshire Victoria County History Trust and, many years ago now, I served as an elected member of the North-East Derbyshire District Council.

I have also been a diligent researcher among the literary and documentary sources which are available to the public at the Derbyshire Record Office and the Local Studies Library at Matlock, the Lichfield Joint Record Office, Sheffield Archives and the Local Studies section of Sheffield City Library, Chesterfield Local Studies Library, and The National Archives at Kew. My thanks go to all the helpful members of staff at these institutions over the years.

I have combined information gleaned from documents and maps with that brought to light from archaeological investigations and from the study of the historic landscape in order to write a history of Derbyshire and its people from prehistoric times to the present day. No one person can be an expert across the whole time range, nor in all of the different approaches which are now in use, but I have benefited greatly from the numerous books and articles that have been written by the authors whom I have quoted in the text or the bibliography. I hope that I have distilled their work in an acceptable fashion. They include many personal friends, for the study of the local past is a co-operative venture in which people with various skills and enthusiasms can add a great deal. I have learned a lot from fellow researchers and the members the university extramural and WEA classes which I used to teach. I hope that this book will provide an overview of the history of Derbyshire as we understand it at present and that it will encourage further research and writing.

I owe a particular debt to Alistair Hodge and Judith Franks of Carnegie Publishing, for their knowledge and enthusiasm in designing this book to their usual high standards and for obtaining so many superb photographs, many of which Alistair took himself on trips on his motor bike.

David Hey

Derbyshire in 1794, a map published in John Aikin's *A Description of the Country from 30 to 40 miles around Manchester.* Derbyshire is a county of rich diversity of experience and history.

Three Shires Head. Derbyshire's north-western boundary descends a clough from Axe Edge Moor to the river Dane, where it meets the boundaries of Cheshire and Staffordshire. The name was recorded in 1533 and is no doubt older. The packhorse bridge is one of many that were built of stone in this style in Derbyshire between the mid-seventeenth and the mid-eighteenth century, when the volume of traffic was increasing, even in remote moorland areas such as this.

Introduction

Derbyshire lies at the heart of England, about as far from the sea as it is possible to get in this small country. Visitors from the south obtain their first, spectacular views of the Pennines here; those from the north descend to the very different landscape of the clay vales of the Midland Plain. In 1870 *The Imperial Gazetteer of England and Wales* described Derbyshire as being nearly as distant from the eastern as the western seas and equally far from Scotland and the English Channel. It was never more than 52 miles long and 30 miles wide; its circuit was about 175 miles; and its area was 658,803 acres.

Derbyshire is first recorded by name in the *Anglo-Saxon Chronicle* for 1048, but by then it was well established as a county. Together with Leicestershire, Nottinghamshire and Lincolnshire, it seems to have been created in the late ninth or early tenth century, at a time when the Danes were firmly in control of the East Midlands. Its boundaries remained unchanged until modern times and even now they are mostly intact, except where Sheffield has sprawled over former countryside in the north or where modifications have been made to take account of population changes in the north-west. The ancient county boundary was reasonably clear on the ground, except in the south, where its line wove in and out of Leicestershire and Staffordshire in an inconsistent and shifting manner, with parishes and manors detached from the bulk of the counties to which they belonged. In the early eighteenth century William Woolley wrote of Great Appleby: 'The two counties are so mingled here that the houses, to an ordinary passenger, cannot be distinguished asunder, which be of either shire, there being no direct meer between them.' Such anomalies continued until as late as 1897.

In the west the deep limestone dale created by the river Dove still separates Derbyshire from Staffordshire as far north as the gritstone moors. There the boundary zig-zagged across to the Cheshire border at Three Shires Head, then down the Goyt valley and up the river Etherow to Woodhead. The moorland boundary with Yorkshire began at Saltersbrook and climbed up Far Small Clough to Swains Head before descending through Howden along the banks of the Upper Derwent, then climbing again past natural features and Stanage Pole, the ancient boundary marker between Mercia and Northumbria. The moors were left at Dore, which the *Anglo-Saxon Chronicle* twice recorded as a boundary point between the two kingdoms in the ninth and tenth centuries.

'... a waste and houling wilderness'

DANIEL DEFOE

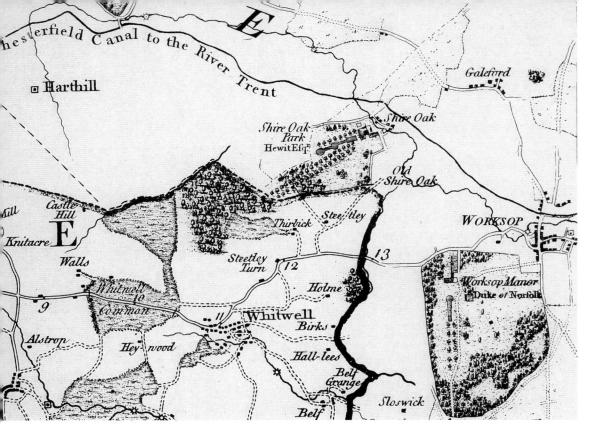

From there it followed the river Sheaf and the Meersbrook, both of whose names refer to their boundary status, then to Shire Brook and other streams as far as what the chronicler referred to in 942 as Whitwell Gap and so on to Old Shire Oak, an ancient tree that separated Derbyshire from Yorkshire and Nottinghamshire.

The boundary with Nottinghamshire followed streams such as the Millwood Brook, which flows through the magnesian limestone gorge known as Creswell Crags, continuing south to Shirebrook and west through Pleasley Vale, then turning south again at Hardwick Hall to follow the river Erewash on its meandering course down to the river Trent. This eastern boundary became far less obvious in the nineteenth century when great ironworks and collieries were opened on each side of the border.

Few English counties can boast of such varied and attractive scenery as Derbyshire. It is now hard to believe that the glorious views which draw huge numbers of visitors to the Peak District National Park once deterred all but a determined few. In the seventeenth and eighteenth centuries, before the Romantic writers and artists changed people's perception of rugged landscapes, Daniel Defoe saw 'a waste and houling wilderness', Edward Browne a 'strange mountainous, misty, moorish, rocky, wild country', and William Stukeley 'the poverty and horror of the Peak'.

Old Shire Oak. Burdett's map of Derbyshire (1767) shows how this ancient tree was a boundary marker for Derbyshire, Yorkshire and Nottinghamshire. In his survey of the manor of Worksop in 1636 John Harrison remarked: 'Ther is within this mannor a great Oake very remarkable (called "Shireoak") in regard the branches extends themselves into three Shiers.'

| DERBYSHIRE: A HISTORY

The oldest rocks in the county are those of the carboniferous limestone in what is now known as the White Peak. This part of Derbyshire stretches for ten miles or so from the Dove to the Derwent, much of it forming a plateau at about 1,000 feet above sea level. But this plateau is cut by the spectacular scenery of the dales, formed by deep river valleys, some of which are now dry because the water has found a different outlet through caverns and underground channels. Carboniferous limestone varies in colour according to its purity; the whitest and purest limestones are extracted from vast quarries near Buxton. Most of the lead veins, or rakes, that sometimes run for several miles from east to west, have been exhausted since Victorian times, but for hundreds of years they were the source of the White Peak's major industry. Some rakes were re-opened in the twentieth century to extract fluorspar for the chemical and metallurgical industries. Other, small mineral veins were exploited for the 'Derbyshire marbles' that adorned great country houses or for tourist trinkets made of 'Blue John'.

The Dark Peak is a very different landscape composed of the millstone grit series of rocks. Shales have produced the heavy clay soils of the Edale and Hope valleys, while hard sandstones underlie the high moorland district that is shaped like a horseshoe from Axe Edge in the west to the escarpments above the Derwent in the east. In the north, Bleaklow and Kinderscout rise to over 2,000 feet in some of the wildest countryside in England. Here, the bleakness of the moorland plateau contrasts sharply with the dramatic 'edges' that are partly shaped by the activities of the millstone hewers and quarrymen. The series starts with the Upper Derwent and Bamford edges and follows the skyline high above the east bank of the river as far south as Riber.

LEFT

The Derbyshire hills rise from the Cheshire plain to the west. Here Mellor parish church is picked out in winter sunshine. Around the church are the recently excavated remains of an Iron Age settlement site (see page 38). The church, which was formerly a chapel-of-ease in the parish of Glossop, was largely rebuilt in the nineteenth century, but within there is still a beautiful, carved stone font dating from the eleventh or twelfth centuries (see page 120), and what it thought to be oldest wooden pulpit in the country (see page 177), dating from the years just before the Black Death in the fourteenth century.

PHOTOGRAPH: CARNEGIE

Further east, the sandstones and shales of the coal measures produced a gentler, undulating landscape. Cereals were grown on the better soils, but the clay lands derived from the shales were laid down to grass. This was originally a district of hamlets and scattered farmsteads as much as villages and small market towns, and numerous deciduous woods were managed as coppices whose main purpose was to supply the ironmasters and lead smelters with fuel. Coal was mined anciently in shallow pits, but it was not until the canal and railway age that landlocked Derbyshire could compete successfully in the national market. The sinking of deep mines and the founding of large ironworks

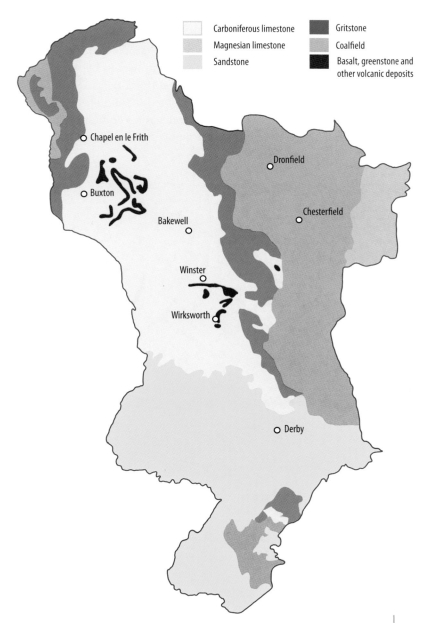

Carboniferous limestone	Gritstone
Magnesian limestone	Coalfield
Sandstone	Basalt, greenstone and other volcanic deposits

Chapel en le Frith

Dronfield

Buxton

Chesterfield

Bakewell

Winster

Wirksworth

Derby

The geology of Derbyshire.

in the nineteenth century transformed this eastern part of the county into an industrial, populous district that was very different in character from the Peak District and the agricultural lowlands, both of which lost population as the lead industry decayed and farming entered a prolonged depression. In Victorian times, Chesterfield, Alfreton, Ripley, Heanor and Ilkeston grew rapidly and new pit villages suddenly appeared in the landscape.

In the north-eastern corner of Derbyshire a small but distinctive district on the outcrop of magnesian limestone lost some of its individual character when deep mines were sunk far below the surface rocks in the late Victorian and Edwardian era. The escarpment rises from the valley of the Doe Lea to Bolsover Castle and the long dip slope beyond provided the most fertile arable soils in the county. This was a countryside of small, compact villages, once surrounded by open fields divided into strips, with farmhouses and cottages in cream-coloured limestone and red pantile roofs. This narrow belt of magnesian limestone stretched well into Yorkshire, as far north as Tadcaster.

Derby has always been the only town of national significance in the county, though it was overshadowed by Nottingham and was never high in any ranking based on the number of inhabitants or the amount of tax paid. But it was an

A map of Derby, from *The Beauties of England and Wales*, 1806.

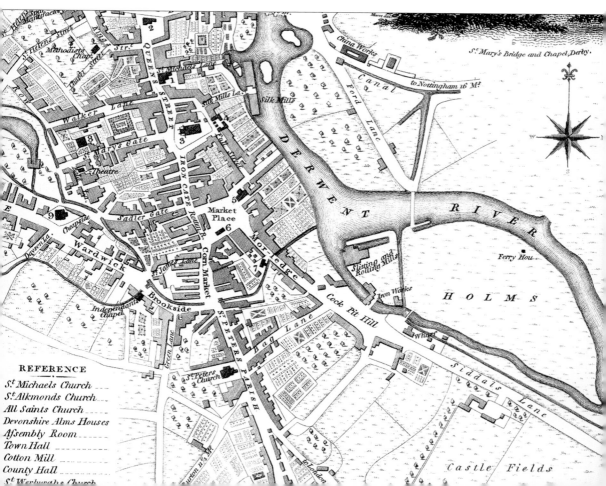

REFERENCE

St. Michaels Church ....
St. Alkmonds Church ....
All Saints Church ....
Devonshire Alms Houses ....
Assembly Room ....
Town Hall ....
Cotton Mill ....
County Hall ....
St. Werburghs Church ....

Red Lion Square, Heanor, 1885. The square formed the heart of the town, where the Derby Road joined Market Street and its continuation, High Street. The old hilltop settlement, which had once been a small market centre, was transformed in the nineteenth century by coal mining and iron manufacture. A new market place was laid out nearby in 1894.

'A strange mountainous, misty, moorish, rocky, wild country'

EDWARD BROWNE

important thoroughfare town, with numerous inns and a flourishing market. It occupied a key position between the northern uplands and the southern lowlands. The gently undulating landscape of south-west Derbyshire was formed by the Keuper marls that consisted of soft, limey clays and bands of sandstone known as 'skerries'. By the seventeenth century the farms on these marls and on the alluvial soils of the Trent and Dove valleys were noted for their excellent cheese. By then, the buildings were mostly of brick, though in some places Bunter sandstones were available. The geological structure also produced bands of gypsum that could be used for floors, while Chellaston acquired a wide reputation for its alabaster, which could be carved into monuments for the departed aristocracy and gentry. On Derbyshire's southern border, an isolated outcrop of coal measure sandstone around Swadlincote was developed into the South Derbyshire Coalfield, and in the twentieth century the substantial terrace deposits of sands and gravels of the wide Trent floodplain have been extensively quarried.

The history of Derbyshire is therefore not a unity, but one of contrasts between its component parts or natural sub-regions. The experiences of its sheep farmers on the fringes of the northern moors were different from those of the cheese-makers south of Ashbourne or the cereal-growers on the magnesian limestone, and the lifestyle of all these farmers was completely different from that of the coal miners in the eastern pit villages or the workers in the cotton mills of Glossop or the lace factories of Sandiacre and Long Eaton. Unlike the inhabitants of neighbouring Yorkshire and Lancashire, the people of Derbyshire never developed a strong sense of belonging to their county. Instead, they were attached – as were people all over England – to their neighbourhood, or what they called their 'country', and within that to the particular places where they lived. This sense of belonging to certain localities has weakened in recent decades but is still strong in many parts of the county. It is with this sense of attachment and the varied history of these different districts that we shall be concerned.

Prehistory

The Palaeolithic or Old Stone Age

The caves at Creswell Crags in the dramatic limestone gorge that separates Derbyshire from Nottinghamshire have long been famous as a prehistoric site of national importance. The caves have romantic names – Pin Hole, Robin Hood, Mother Grundy's Parlour and Church Hole – and they have attracted archaeologists since Victorian times. An engraving of a horse head on a bone found in Robin Hood Cave in 1876, a human figure engraved on a rib bone in Pin Hole Cave, and hatched lines on other pieces of bone were long recognised to be the earliest known art in Britain.

In 2003–04 all that changed with the astonishing discovery by Paul Bahn, Paul Pettitt, and their Spanish colleagues Sergio Ripoll and Francisco Muñoz of about 90 representations of Ice Age animals, mostly in the entrance chamber of Church Hole, where plenty of natural light illuminates the ceiling. The engravings and sculptures that use the natural curves of the rocks are of prime international importance. Images of deer, horses, bison, bears and birds, some of them superimposed on each other, have been recognised. Recent research that has found red ochre pigment in the lines of the horse head engraved by sharp flint tools on a piece of animal bone suggests that perhaps the rock art too was painted. The art at Creswell Crags is similar in style to that found in caves in France and Spain and is thought to be about 12,000 years old.

As the Ice Age came to an end, the British Isles were still physically linked to the Continent. A warm spell had allowed adventurous hunting parties to follow migrating animals through the gorge and to find shelter in the caves. Then about 11,000 years ago it grew colder again, forcing humans to retreat until the ice began to thaw about a thousand years later. Prehistorians call this warm interlude the Upper Palaeolithic period and speak of the 'Creswellian culture' when they find similar artefacts in other parts of Britain. It is likely that people had ventured into what is now Derbyshire in the long distant past during previous warm spells, but with the return of the ice all the evidence has been obliterated.

The excavations of the 1870s and the more careful ones of the 1920s unearthed bones of animals, such as reindeer, wild horse, hyena, bison, mammoth, woolly

Excavated bones at Harborough Cave, 1922. Caves in the limestone districts of Derbyshire have revealed animal bones dating from the time when the ice sheets retreated at the end of the last Ice Age and human settlement began. At Harborough Cave near Brassington Moor finds included the bones of wild horses, reindeer, woolly rhinos, hyena, bison, red deer and wild boar.

rhinoceros and arctic fox, which are now extinct in this country but which once roamed in an environment reminiscent of tundra and steppe. They were not all human prey; the hyenas, in particular, were scavengers that sheltered in the caves. After the final retreat of the ice, red deer, roe deer, aurochs, elk and wild pigs found the new landscape of woods and grassy clearings congenial. These were the prey of Mesolithic men in the succeeding era.

The Upper Palaeolithic hunter-gatherers paid repeated visits to their 'base camps' in the caves of Creswell Crags. They were mobile groups who obtained the flint for their tools and weapons from the Yorkshire and Lincolnshire Wolds. Creswell Gorge would have been an obvious place to trap herds moving from lowland pastures to summer feeding grounds in the hills to the west. Caves were also occupied during the Palaeolithic period nearby at Whitwell, and in Lathkill Dale, at Harborough, near Brassington, and in the valleys of the Dove and the Manifold. Tools and weapons made from flints and animal bones, together with the bones of animals that had been eaten, are all that survive, for wooden objects and skins and furs used for clothing have perished. Evidence for settlement outside the caves is far more difficult to find, but perhaps some of the Trent valley terraces, such as Beeston Terrace at Potlock, might have been occupied from time to time.

The Mesolithic or Middle Stone Age

As the ice retreated, the climate grew rapidly warmer and soon reached temperatures similar to those of today. No precise dates can be given to the various divisions of the Stone Age, but the Mesolithic period is generally thought of as lasting from around 8,000 BC to about 4,500 BC (give or take 500 years).

It is identified by the distinctive flint tools and flakes that have been found at summer camps and perhaps more permanent settlements. The painstaking task of classifying flint tools has suggested two general types in Derbyshire. The early broad blades, made of grey-white flints from the Wolds, were used for axes, barbed spears, and harpoons shafted with bone and stag antlers; examples have been found in caves near Earl Sterndale, Lathkill Dale and the Dove valley. The later 'microliths' were made from brown flints and local black chert and were far more numerous and sophisticated. They were shaped into triangles, crescents and points and were secured to wooden or bone shafts with birch pitch, for use as arrows, spears, harpoons, knives and edge-tools. They have been found in various parts of the Derbyshire countryside, particularly on the north-western moors, where they have been preserved in the sandy soils beneath the later covering of peat, especially on the edges of scarp slopes where the peat has eroded. In the Mesolithic period, these uplands, rising from 1,200 to 1,600 feet, were well wooded, with patches of grassland or heath. A good example is the Harry Hut site on Chunal Moor, near Charlesworth, which seems to have been occupied from time to time between the sixth and fourth millennium BC. An excavated site at Lismore Fields, Buxton, has found debris which has produced a radiocarbon date from the sixth or fifth millennium BC.

Mesolithic people lived in small groups in each type of countryside but they have left little mark on the landscape. On the limestone plateau their artefacts and the bones of animals that they had eaten have been found in caves and rock shelters, such as that at Stoney Low on Sheldon Moor, where traces of a hearth remain. Caves and rock shelters on the magnesian limestone in north-east Derbyshire also continued in use. On the coal-measure sandstones a number of Mesolithic sites have been identified at Unstone, overlooking the Drone valley, where excavations at Hardhurst Hill have revealed several hearths and evidence for the shaping of flint tools; the site seems to have been re-occupied over the generations. Fewer Mesolithic sites have been recognised in lowland Derbyshire, where evidence has been destroyed by thousands of years of farming or building, but systematic fieldwalking and excavations in the Trent valley, notably at Swarkestone Lowes, is beginning to suggest more activity than was once thought likely.

Mesolithic people have been traditionally regarded as hunter-gatherers, but prehistorians now place less emphasis on hunting and fishing and more on the abundant and varied plant foods that were available. The discovery of cereal pollen at Lismore Fields suggests a more settled way of life than was imagined, though it was probably still a seasonal one. Did people in the later Mesolithic period also keep domesticated cattle, sheep and pigs? It is not a great change of practice from herding prey to farming livestock. In the country at large, evidence for the management of woodland clearances through selective burning becomes more common from around 6500 BC onwards. But as the population of Britain numbered only a few thousands their impact on the countryside was minimal.

The Neolithic or New Stone Age

By the Neolithic period, between about 4500 and 2200 BC, men were definitely farmers rather than hunter-gatherers. But the transition was made gradually over numerous generations, when summer temperatures were higher than they are today. There is nothing in the archaeological record to suggest a sharp break with the past, but the population of Britain grew steadily to perhaps 100,000 as new people arrived from Iberia up the Atlantic coast or along different routes from north-west Europe. The people of the New Stone Age can be identified from the pottery that they began to make. Peterborough Ware is found commonly in Derbyshire, and in recent years Grooved Ware has appeared at excavated East Midlands sites. Often, the presence of early Neolithic groups is signalled only by sherds of these distinctive types of pottery.

Neolithic sites can also be identified from characteristic leaf-shaped flint arrowheads, spearheads, sickles, knives and scrapers. Stone axes were sometimes still shaped from flint, but most were now made from polished stones. Several hundred axe-heads that have been found in the Peak District have been identified as coming mostly from Great Langdale in the Lake District or from Graig Lwydd in North Wales. Some of those axes which remain in prime condition were perhaps status symbols or for ceremonial use, but the great majority were for felling or lopping trees, fighting, butchering animals, and perhaps for hoeing land to grow emmer wheat.

Botanical evidence in the form of pollen sequences suggests that although cereals were grown in clearings most of the landscape was still covered by trees. The cover varied considerably, from open woodlands of birch, hazel and ash in the higher districts to darker woods dominated by oak or native lime in the valleys. The rich, light, well-drained soils of the limestone plateau were not thickly wooded and so did not need a huge amount of arduous clearing. The White Peak became one of the most important areas of prehistoric settlement in Britain. It is here that the most impressive megalithic monuments in Derbyshire are found. Neolithic people were the first to make a mark on the landscape, yet they continued to live in small, scattered groups, which were usually little more than extended families that met other groups only on special occasions. They moved with the seasons between the limestone plateau and the gritstone uplands, along the paths that their Mesolithic ancestors had created. The continued use of caves as both temporary homes and burial sites is evident from finds of flint arrowheads and scrapers, polished stone axes, sherds of Peterborough Ware and sometimes human bones in caves and rock shelters in Ravensdale, Dowel Dale, Lathkill Dale, Hartle Dale, Dovedale, and near Brassington and Earl Sterndale. Similar discoveries have been made in caves on the magnesian limestone in north-east Derbyshire at Whaley and Whitwell and near Markland Grips.

In *The North Derbyshire Archaeological Survey* (1981) Clive Hart noted Neolithic occupation debris from at least 40 settlement areas in the White

Big Moor round barrow. The Big Moor to the west of the road that descends from Owler Bar to Baslow is one of England's major Bronze Age sites. Here, among the heather above the Bar Brook, is an extensive burial ground, preserved because these moors have not been cultivated since peat started to spread in prehistoric times. Round barrows seem to have been family graves; they are often hard to distinguish from the mounds which were simply clearance cairns.

PHOTOGRAPH: AUTHOR

Peak. For example, surface finds at Aleck Low included pottery sherds and flint arrowheads, scrapers and knives, and excavations revealed a polished stone axe and traces of four house floors, hearths and storage pits. Many more finds have been made in the two or three decades following his survey. It is now known that Neolithic flint scatters are also quite common in the valleys of the Wye and Derwent and on the gritstone moorlands to the east. The varied topography of Derbyshire offered different resources over the changing seasons. The uplands were used as summer pastures, while the thickly wooded valleys provided shelter in winter time and food in the form of fish, fruit and game.

In the mid-1980s Daryl Garton excavated a Neolithic site at Lismore Fields, near the river Wye to the west of Buxton. The site, which occupies a clayland plateau that had previously been occupied by Mesolithic people, is of national importance and has changed our thinking about the nature of Neolithic settlement. Nothing survives above ground level, but the postholes that were found are the best-preserved evidence for well-built, rectangular, timber-framed structures with central hearths that has so far been discovered in Early Neolithic Britain. Radiocarbon dates show that they were constructed in the centuries around 3500 BC. Several pits and nine small circular structures of unknown function and date were found close by, together with Early Neolithic pottery (including an almost complete vessel), a polished stone axe, flint and chert tools and a considerable quantity of charred cereal grains, hazelnuts and the fruit and seeds of crab apples. The acidity of the clay soils has destroyed any bones of domesticated livestock or wild animals that might have been hunted. The site was occupied over an unusually long time, though continuous use cannot be proved.

In recent years Neolithic occupation sites have also been identified by fieldwalking, excavations and aerial photography on the gravel terraces of the Trent valley, a district that was once thought to be so thickly wooded that Stone Age people avoided it instinctively. We now know that the middle Trent valley between Shardlow and Willington was occupied over a long period, despite the fact that at the beginning of the Neolithic era much of the district was undoubtedly covered with mixed oak woods or with alder carrs in the flood plains. Excavations led by Hazel Wheeler at Willington have found traces of scattered dwellings whose occupation is dated by sherds of pottery from the second half of the fourth to the early second millennium BC. At Aston-upon-Trent an excavation of what appears to have been a temporary site has revealed a hearth, pits and carbonised grains of emmer wheat dating from around 3680 BC. Aston and Potlock also provide evidence of those extensive, mysterious earthworks that prehistorians call cursuses. At Potlock evidence of food that complemented the fish and fowl from the rivers includes that of hazelnuts, seeds of blackberry, sloe, elder and hawthorn and plants that grew in grassy clearings. Aerial photography has revealed a high density of crop marks in some lowland areas, such as that between the Dove and the Derwent; organised fieldwalking has led to the discovery of extensive surface scatters of stone tools and weapons; and since 1990 excavations and watching briefs that have been carried out in advance of quarrying and highway construction have produced evidence of an unexpectedly large number of Neolithic and Early Bronze Ages sites, many of them preserved beneath alluvium. Isolated finds from the Neolithic period in other parts of south Derbyshire include a fragment of an adze at Cubley, a macehead at Chellaston and polished stone axes at Belper, Derby, Doveridge, Duffield, Etwall, Heanor, Sawley, Spondon and Sudbury. Neolithic people seem to have spread into many parts of Derbyshire.

CHAMBERED BARROWS

The earliest surviving monuments in Derbyshire are the distinctive Neolithic burial mounds that we call chambered barrows. Many of them were excavated in a quick and amateurish fashion by Thomas Bateman, Samuel Carrington, John Ward and other Victorian archaeologists; relatively few have been investigated in a systematic manner. Often, they (and other prehistoric mounds) can be spotted on Ordnance Survey maps by the place-name element -low (derived from the Old English *hlaw*), which survives in several Peak District place- or field-names. A striking example is Tideslow, a high point above Tideswell, which contains stone cists under the largest Neolithic mound in the Peak District.

Five Wells chambered tomb. Sited deliberately on the edge of Taddington Moor, on the skyline above the wide pastures that slope down to the river Wye, this chambered tomb was in use over a long period of time in the Neolithic period and the Bronze Age. The stones of one of the two chambers survive, but the limestone mound which eventually covered them has gone. Human bones, animal teeth, an arrowhead and a few potsherds, all dating from the Neolithic period, have been found here. Tombs such as this were more than burial mounds. They acted as shrines or temples and also marked a particular community's territory.

Over 20 chambered barrows and long mounds have been identified in Derbyshire, all of them in the White Peak. One of the earliest is that at Five Wells, sited at 1,400 feet on the north-western edge of Taddington Moor, with commanding views over the pastures descending to the river Wye. The site seems to have been deliberately chosen to lay claim to a territory that had long been used by the ancestors of the people who erected the monument. The massive stone slabs of one of the two chambers are intact, but the large, limestone-rubble mound that covered it has almost gone. To enter the chambers a person had to crawl through one of the low entrances on the east and west sides and along a dark, narrow passage to the heart of the mound. Here were stored the bones of ancestors, some of which were found by the amateur excavators in the nineteenth century, along with animal teeth, an arrowhead and fragments of Neolithic pottery. Sites such as this have long and complicated histories as communal burial grounds, stretching over 2,000 years from the Neolithic to the Bronze Age. Over such a long period of time, religious beliefs changed and the chambered barrows acquired new meanings. At Five Wells the chambers were eventually enclosed within a much larger mound, which

Trees at Minninglow
Hill surround the
Peak District's
largest surviving
burial ground from
the Neolithic period.
The original small
barrow was extended
over time until
the site consisted
of a mound of
stone with at least
four chambers.
Here we see the
excavation of the
south passage in the
1970s. But Minning
Low was more
than a burial site;
it acted as a focal
point or seasonal
gathering place for
a Stone Age tribe or
extended family.

PHOTOGRAPHS: AUTHOR;
MALCOLM DOLBY

effectively cut off access to the bones inside. In time, other bones were inserted
into a pit that was cut into the mound or placed in a cist on the outer edge.
Despite such changes, the barrows kept their significance as communal burial
grounds in prominent places. We must think of them as shrines or temples, not
just as tombs. They come in different shapes and sizes, with a variety of internal

arrangements, for they were the expressions of local communities or extended families. Now they are quiet places, remote from everyday life and venerated for their antiquity, but for all we know the ceremonies on the forecourts of the mounds may well have been loud with music, singing and dancing and the stones may have been brightly painted.

The chambered barrow that is now set in a beech plantation at Minning Low, high above the High Peak Trail between Pikehall and Longcliffe and close to the prehistoric and Roman road that heads north-west across the White Peak, is much larger and more complex than that at Five Wells. Excavations have proved that, at first, the barrow was just a small mound with a chamber, but later it was converted into a long cairn (a mound made of stone) about 35 metres long, with at least four chambers which were entered through low, stone-lined passages. Eventually, this too was enlarged into an oval mound measuring 45 metres across and about two metres high. Sherds of Beaker pottery dating from the end of the Neolithic era were found underneath the stones that blocked the passage of the central chamber. Standing high on a ridge overlooking watersheds, Minning Low was the most prominent focal point for a Neolithic community in the whole of the Peak District.

Two of the other chambered barrows are worthy of special attention. From Green Low, 1,020 feet above a gorge north of Aldwark, spectacular views include a sighting of Minning Low. The chamber is aligned on the rising sun at the winter solstice. When the site was excavated in 1963–64, human bones were found both in the narrow entrance passage and the chamber. Animal bones, late Neolithic potsherds, flints and a polished stone axe were discovered elsewhere on the site. Eventually, the passage was deliberately blocked by a slab and the chamber was sealed under a cairn. At Ringham Low, just north of

Neolithic axe head
from Arbor Low.

Lathkill Dale and east of Monyash, the five or six chambers which were set in a large mound did not have paved entrance passages. Two cists that contained bodies and jumbled human bones were surrounded by limestone paving, which had been laid on a flattened clay surface that contained earlier burials, animal bones and arrowheads. The mound that covers these earlier features was built in stages over a long period of time and was used for further inhumations. The barrow we see today is simply the final form that was achieved by the end of the Stone Age. We get a sense of the re-use and development of sites that had long been revered, perhaps as far back as the Mesolithic era. From time to time they were altered in different ways by local groups whose ancestors had long used the surrounding summer pastures. They were symbols in the landscape that acted as ceremonial points for the people who built them and as a warning to other groups to keep off the ancestral lands. As Mark Edmonds has emphasised, they bound communities together.

The chambered barrows on the limestone plateau were robbed of their contents well before they were first excavated in the nineteenth century. Enough evidence survives, however, both here and in other parts of the country, to show that they contained the mixed bones of several men, women and children. They were not the tombs of an elite group, but chambers that stored the bones of ancestors. Over a very long period of time, new bones were added, but what prompted this renewal and why a tiny minority of the population were commemorated in this way is beyond our understanding. It seems likely that the bones were periodically removed for ceremonies and that only priests or shamen crawled along the low passages into the dark chambers where the bones were kept. The Neolithic custom was to de-flesh bodies before burial by exposing them on open-air platforms after death. The only exposure platform that has so far been discovered in Derbyshire is that excavated by John Collis at Wigber Low, between Bradbourne and Kniveton. The remains of human bones from at least 30 individuals, many of them cremated, were scattered over a flat-topped, oblong cairn, encircled by blocks of limestone. The cairn cannot be dated precisely but it was preceded by at least two phases of Neolithic occupation, starting no earlier than 2500 BC, and it was no longer used after about 1700–1500 BC. We do not know where the bones that were exposed on this site were eventually buried.

The evidence for storing and mixing bones in this way dwindles in the later Neolithic period. The bodies that were placed in simple graves suggest that the average height of men was 5 feet 6 inches and of women 5 feet 2½ inches, that life expectancy was only about 40 and the level of infant mortality was high. Other ceremonies for which we have no material evidence probably took place at natural sites such as springs or spectacular rock formations, and the distinction between the spiritual and the everyday may not have been a sharp one. Then in the Late Neolithic and Early Bronze Ages, throughout Britain, the old chambered barrows began to give way to new types of communal monuments: the henges and the stone circles.

The dramatic monuments that archaeologists classify as henges needed much more communal labour than could be provided by the local groups that had built the chambered barrows. The ceremonies that took place there were probably on a much larger scale than the old seasonal gatherings at Five Wells or Minning Low and the people who attended them came from much further afield than before. The earthworks of two of these monuments survive in the Peak District; one that attracts visitors from all over Britain and abroad, and another of similar size that most people have never heard of.

Arbor Low (an Old English name meaning 'earthwork hill') stands at 1,225 feet on a limestone crest close to the ancient track that the Romans re-used as they headed across the White Peak to the baths at Buxton. It commands uninterrupted views in all directions, though when it was built the landscape would have been far more wooded than it is today. A tall outward bank and a deep internal ditch which enclose a circular area 76 metres in diameter still form an effective barrier, but when they were freshly made they were even more formidable. The ditches were dug into the bedrock between two and three metres deep and their spoil was thrown up on to the bank to a height of three metres. Visitors would not have seen the stones inside the circle until the last moment. Although they now lie on the ground, the stones probably once stood upright. Some are in fragments and so are difficult to count; originally they numbered about 40. At the centre of the circle four massive stones formed a cove or inner sanctuary, the focal point of ceremonies. Perhaps the whole of the area within the stones was restricted to the priests, while the visitors who attended the festivals stood on the bank? We can only speculate on the nature of these ceremonies, but scatters of Late Neolithic and Early Bronze Age material in the surrounding fields suggest that festivals were attended by large numbers of people. At such times, Arbor Low was far from the being the peaceful place that it is today.

Finds from excavations within the ditch suggest a date around 2500 BC for the original construction, though the stones were probably added later. But as with the chambered barrows, henges may have been erected on sites that had long had a special spiritual significance. Evidence of late Mesolithic camps has been found nearby. Across the fields south-west of Arbor Low, the five metre-high mound known as Gib Hill seems to have been the focus of the site before the henge was erected. It started as a long barrow built of clay, but in the Bronze Age it was converted into a round barrow with a cremation burial and a food vessel, similar in date and style to the round barrow that was placed on the outer bank of Arbor Low itself.

The valley of the river Wye separated the people who flocked to Arbor Low from those who turned instead to the Bull Ring at Dove Holes, alongside the same prehistoric track. Standing at 1,100 feet, high on the limestone plateau, the Bull Ring is not at all what we expect a prehistoric monument to be, for it lies close to a built-up area and a busy road, and no stones survive. Nevertheless,

it is roughly the same size as Arbor Low and the massive bank and ditch of the circular earthwork are readily apparent and can be walked around. As at Arbor Low, the approach to the inner circle is through two opposing causewayed entrances and a barrow south-west of the circle is similar in appearance to Gib Hill.

The White Peak has the most dramatic evidence from the Neolithic era, but the lack of upstanding monuments elsewhere may be misleading. Aerial photography has identified a high density of crop marks in the Trent valley that suggest the former presence of barrows, causewayed enclosures and cursuses. The great mound set within a circular ditch at Round Hill, Twyford, has been removed by the plough, but it may have been erected within a former henge. Old ideas have been overturned by recent discoveries and it is now recognised that the valleys of the Trent, Derwent and Dove may once have had a complex of monuments to rival those of famous wetland sites in other parts of the country.

Arbor Low from the air. A major henge monument of national importance, Arbor Low can be reached across a farm track and fields. The stones have fallen, but otherwise the earthwork is remarkably well preserved in a lonely part of the White Peak.

WWW.LASTREFUGE.CO.UK

GARDOM'S EDGE

The effectiveness of intensive field surveys and systematic excavations in changing our ideas about the final phase of the Stone Age is nowhere better shown than in the case of Gardom's Edge, high on a gritstone shelf above the road that descends steeply from Owler Bar to Baslow. The massive stone bank that stretches back form the precipitous edge to form a 15-acre, D-shaped enclosure has been known since it was revealed by a moorland fire in the 1940s, but its purpose was unclear. The bank is still 16–30 feet wide and 3–5 feet high in parts, with entrances spaced at intervals. As much of the boulder-strewn interior of the enclosure was unsuitable for settlement, it was probably used only for seasonal gatherings. Gardom's Edge occupies a commanding position overlooking the deep valley of Bar Brook as it joins the wider valley of the Derwent, with clear views of the limestone plateau in the distance. The site is now interpreted by the archaeologists from the Peak Park and Sheffield University who investigated it over several seasons as a major Neolithic ritual enclosure dating from about 3500–3000 BC, similar in age and purpose to the causewayed enclosures of southern England. These normally occupied sites that were peripheral to settlements and so appear to have served many different small communities that came together at certain times of the year for ceremonies, feasting and trade.

The surveys and excavations at Gardom's Edge revealed a complex landscape that was shaped in many periods, but the majority of the 1,300 archaeological features that were found are prehistoric. To the north and east of the edge-top enclosure, stretching up towards Birchen Edge, where the land was subsequently used for rough grazing, are extensive remains of prehistoric field boundaries,

Gib Hill. A striking landmark on the skyline close to Arbor Low, Gib Hill seems to have been a Neolithic long barrow that was converted into a round barrow during the Bronze Age. This suggests that this upland site had religious significance even before the henge monument was erected.

PHOTOGRAPH: CHRIS SMITH, TWENTY TREES PHOTOGRAPHY

Bull Ring. This spectacular Neolithic henge monument is not well known, for, unlike Arbor Low, it has no stones, and it stands by the quarrying village of Dove Holes, where lorries thunder past. But the massive circular bank and ditch are well preserved and public access is easy. Bull Ring and Arbor Low seem to have been contemporary henges that served groups of New Stone Age people whose territories were separated by the river Wye.

PHOTOGRAPH: AUTHOR

clearance cairns, house sites and monuments that were probably first laid out about a thousand years later. On the southern slopes, farming activities over numerous generations have probably destroyed similar evidence. The sites of prehistoric timber-framed houses amongst the fields can be recognised from their stone footings; some of these houses were erected on platforms that had been levelled into the hillside. Pottery discovered during excavations has proved that they were in use over a long period of time, extending from the Late Neolithic period into the Iron Age.

Gardom's Edge also has the best-preserved example of prehistoric cup-and-ring marks that has so far been found in Derbyshire. The exact purpose and date of these patterns and linear designs remain controversial, but this type of rock art often appears alongside important paths, perhaps as signs or markers of territories. Much has been found in northern England in recent years, but in Derbyshire these primitive designs are restricted to the gritstone areas, perhaps because it would have been difficult to carve limestone in this manner. Two fine examples were found in the year 2000 at Ashover primary school.

The Bronze Age

The transition from the Stone Age to the Bronze Age was not a clear-cut one. Such divisions are used by prehistorians for the sake of convenience, but the present trend is to dub the five centuries before 2000 BC as the Late Neolithic – Early Bronze Age, with the emphasis on continuity rather than change. Of course, far more implements continued to be made of wood than of metal, but

Cup-and-ring stone, Gardom's Edge, a fine example of this mysterious rock art. Only a few cup-and-ring stones have been found in Derbyshire, where they are restricted to the gritstones. The Gardom's Edge stone has since been removed for safe keeping and a replica installed in its place.

PHOTOGRAPH: AUTHOR

they have vanished whereas axes and swords cast in bronze have often survived intact. The discovery of an antler tool for digging in the abandoned Ecton Copper Mines, just beyond the Derbyshire border in Staffordshire, suggests that the copper that was combined with tin to make bronze weapons was mined there in prehistoric times; if so, mining was on a much smaller scale than at the great complex of mines at Great Orme, Llandudno.

The transitional period was marked by the deposit of beakers amongst grave goods that included finely worked flints or bones but rarely metal. Beakers have been found commonly in the White Peak and along the Trent valley at Aston-upon-Trent, Stenson, Swarkestone and other places nearby, but none has been found on the gritstone uplands. During this period many of our roads and trackways were formed, permanent settlements became far more common, and the national population grew to perhaps 250,000.

A photograph taken in 1996 during the excavation of the Gardom's Edge enclosure on the escarpment north-east of Baslow, overlooking the Bar Brook as it descends swiftly from the moors. The massive stone bank which forms a half-circle back from the steep edge has entrances at various points. The interior is strewn with boulders and so was not suitable for settlement. It is therefore interpreted as a seasonal gathering place for different groups, a trading, feasting and ceremonial centre dating from c.3500–3000 BC.

PHOTOGRAPH: AUTHOR

ROUND BARROWS

As in the previous era, much of our information about the Bronze Age comes from burial practices. Bronze Age people had many ways of dealing with their dead, some of which have left little trace on the surface of the land. Cemeteries such as that which was found near the Eagle Stone, on the East Moors high above Baslow, are discovered only when the chance to excavate arises. In this case, the cremated ashes of 15 people, all of them women and children, were either interred in pots that were placed in pits in the ground or placed straight into the earth. John Barnatt's excavation team found an intact funeral pyre, the remains of several other pyres nearby, and funerary goods that survived the fire, including stone tools, a perforated antler plate, faience beads and a bone whistle that had been placed in a small urn that contained the cremated ashes of a child. At least eight phases of occupation, extending over several hundred years, were identified over the whole site, in the form of clearance heaps, platforms and low field walls.

Neolithic chambered barrows, such as those at Bee Low (near Youlgreave) and Glebe Low (Great Longstone), were sometimes re-used by the insertion of a stone cist containing human bones, but by the Bronze Age the characteristic burial mound was round and unchambered. Well over 500 round barrows, dating from the Late Neolithic and Bronze Ages, have been identified in the Peak District and the original number was probably significantly higher. They are found mostly in the White Peak, but many more lie on the gritstone moors on either side of the northern section of the river Derwent. Sometimes, they stand alone in prominent positions, such as Crow Chin on Stanage Edge or

Lord's Seat, Rushup Edge. Some of the largest round barrows stand alone in prominent positions on dramatic edges, such as this fine example to the west of Mam Tor, overlooking Edale. They tended to acquire fanciful names in the Middle Ages or the early modern period. This one had come to be known as Lord's Seat by about 1620.

PHOTOGRAPH: AUTHOR

Lord's Seat on Rushup Edge, but on certain sites such as the East Moors (near Bar Brook) and below Carl Wark large numbers are found close together. The densities in the present distribution of barrows occur because the surviving mounds — many of which are on the tops of hills or ridges — have escaped destruction by later farming and building. It is significant that barrows can still be spotted in the relatively undisturbed landscape of Chatsworth Park but not in the surrounding farmland. Recent surveys have found evidence of barrows in places where they were once unknown, such as the Trent valley or the flanks of moorland rising from the upper Derwent.

Round barrows vary considerably in size, but most are only 10–20 metres in diameter. Excavations have shown that they were sometimes enlarged or modified at a later stage, often with the insertion of fresh burials. Many seem to have been left without cover for long periods of time before a mound was erected once several people had been laid to rest on or below the surface of the ground. Perhaps the building of a mound was a symbolic act that was intended to close the site down? Round barrows appear to us as grass-covered mounds of earth and stone, but originally they stood out more distinctly in the landscape, especially in the White Peak when the sun shone on the limestone boulders.

Many barrows in the White Peak, and occasionally beyond, were excavated in the 1840s and 1850s by Thomas Bateman and Samuel Carrington. The survival of bones in the alkaline soils of the limestone plateau has produced a large amount of information about Bronze Age burial practices. Round barrows appear to have been family graves. Five or more bodies — and sometimes up to twenty — were placed there, often on their sides in a foetal position, and sometimes under a stone cist. The dead were often accompanied by a few, simple grave goods, such as bronze and flint daggers or jet necklaces, but no-one received special treatment. Many barrows stand close to Bronze Age fields and settlements, marked by clearance cairns, low walls and building platforms. Some seem to have been sited deliberately next to stone circles.

Round barrows are numerous, but as they were in use for more than a thousand years they contain the bones of only a minority of those who died. Far more people were cremated or buried elsewhere. On the gritstone moorlands around the river Derwent, and in the Trent valley, cremated remains were often placed in a type of urn that was distinguished by its 'collared' or 'overhanging' rim and sealed with flat stones. Large numbers have been found among the barrows, ringcairns and stone circles on Stanton Moor, together with similar vessels that were used for storing food.

STONE CIRCLES

One of the puzzles of Peak District archaeology is that stone circles, ranging in diameter from 15 to 100 feet, are abundant on the gritstones but absent from the limestone plateau. They are found mainly on Stanton Moor, Beeley Moor, the Eastern Moors, Eyam, Abney and Offerton Moors, and Bamford Moor. They date from a few hundred years on either side of 2000 BC but are mostly

Barbrook I. Stone circles dating from a few hundred years either side of 2000 BC survive on several of the Peak District's gritstone moors. They have been interpreted as the monuments of family groups. The two which stand close together on the Big Moor, alongside numerous round barrows and clearance cairns, are known to archaeologists as Barbrook I and II. Barbrook I is a typical circle of small, upright stones of different shapes and sizes, standing close to a large round barrow.
PHOTOGRAPH: AUTHOR

from the Bronze Age rather than the Late Neolithic period. They are small in size and belong to a type of monument that is found throughout northern and western England and southern Scotland. A typical site has a ring of upright stones, no more than two or three feet high, set in a circle on the inner edge of a bank, with one or sometimes two entrances and perhaps a single stone standing beyond. The stones are of various shapes and sizes and are spaced irregularly. Many stones have been removed and some circles – known as ringcairns – have none at all; perhaps they never did. The interiors of the circles were often levelled and several have produced excavated evidence of human cremations, sometimes in urns.

Some stone circles have different designs from the rest, none more so than that at Nine Stone Close on Harthill Moor to the west of Birchover. Only four stones still stand in the circle, with a distant one incorporated in a field wall. The ring has no bank and each stone is six feet high. A circle at Stoke Flat on Froggatt Edge has two rings of stones on both the inner and outer edges of its bank, though few are still standing. The largest stone circle in the Peak District is that at Wet Withens on Eyam Moor, where ten of the original 16 or 18 stones remain in place and a cremation in a Middle Bronze Age urn was inserted in the centre. Two circles, known as Barbrook I and II, stand within

a large cairnfield on the Big Moor. The first one is overlooked by a substantial barrow. Barbrook II was carefully excavated in the 1960s and, after vandalism, was restored in 1989 to what is probably its original appearance. Unusually, the ring of standing stones is set in a dry-stone wall on the inner edge of a bank constructed of rubble, with a single entrance to the north-east. A little to the south of west (with no obvious astronomical explanation) stands a taller stone. Four human cremations were placed within the circle, one in a cist, another in a pit under a small cairn, and two more just in pits.

No doubt a variety of other ceremonies that have left no trace in the archaeological record also occurred within stone circles during the changing seasons. The evidence for prehistoric activities is heavily weighted towards the practices for burying the dead. Each local community or extended family seems to have had its own stone circle and barrow, sited close to home amongst the clearance cairns, though set slightly aside from everyday concerns. Stone circles were probably laid out by eye with rough alignments on the setting or rising sun at the solstices. The Nine Stone Close circle on Harthill Moor (where an impressive range of prehistoric earthworks survive) was sited to observe the full moon passing between the dramatic natural rock pillars of Robin Hood's Stride at midsummer.

One of the best-preserved prehistoric sites in the country stands a thousand feet high on Stanton Moor, a natural outlier of gritstone on the eastern edge of the White Peak, overlooking the cultivated valleys of both the Derwent and the Wye. Hidden from view are the numerous cremation urn cemeteries, but five stone circles or ringcairns and over 70 barrows can be found amongst the heather and bilberries and the spreading silver birch. The finds from numerous

Barbrook II has been excavated and restored to what is thought to have been its original appearance, with its standing stones incorporated into a circular, drystone wall on the inner edge of a rubble bank. Since this photograph was taken, rushes and grasses have re-grown and now partly obscure the site.

excavations by J. C. and J. P. Heathcote are housed in a private museum in Birchover. The best-known feature is the 'Nine Ladies' circle (a misnomer as a tenth stone has been found and another probably filled the remaining gap), with the 'King Stone' standing aloof 40 metres south-west. The bank on which the stones were placed and the central cairn depicted in old drawings have now been flattened by the feet of numerous visitors. Another circle just to the north is now difficult to find underneath the bracken and trees and yet another is disguised by heather. The largest of the circles, known as the 'Central', is classified as a ringcairn, for it is uncertain whether or not it ever had standing stones. The smallest stone circle at Doll Tor has six standing stones and a later cairn at the eastern end; cremation urns and simple grave goods were discovered during excavations and the site has now been restored after vandalism. The moor also has some striking natural rocks, notably the Cork Stone, which is over ten feet high and was once encircled by four standing stones, and the Andle or Anvil Stone, which dominates the landscape close to Doll Tor. The lack of evidence for settlement or agriculture, contrasted with the cremation cemeteries, the large number of circles and the barrows (many of which stand out on the skyline), mark Stanton Moor as an exceptional place that was set apart in memory of the ancestors.

Nine Stone Close on Harthill Moor. The circle now has only four stones, but others are known to have been removed since the mid-eighteenth century. These massive stones are very different in size and shape from those that were normally used in Derbyshire's stone circles, and the diameter of the circle is smaller than usual.

The whole area seems to have had particular religious significance in prehistoric times.

Robin Hood's Stride. This dramatic skyline seems to have had magical associations for prehistoric people. A sub-circular earthwork can be traced on the ground below it and the nearby Nine Stone Close stone circle on Harthill Moor was positioned so that the full moon could be seen passing between the rock pillars at midsummer.

PHOTOGRAPH: AUTHOR

At the height of the Bronze Age what are now the gritstone moorlands overlooking the Derwent valley from Hope down to Darley had a very different appearance from today. Peat had spread only in a few isolated areas and much light woodland remained between the pastures and fields. The population of this district cannot be estimated with confidence, but it was far higher than it is now. The soils consisted of light sands over the gritstones and heavier clays on the shales. They could be tilled by hand and were fertile and robust enough for growing cereals as well as for pasture, perhaps in rotation in small plots. Many 'ancient field systems' dating over a long period of time from the Late Neolithic to the Iron Age can be found in all sorts of shapes and sizes, enclosed by low stone walls and earthen banks. They are particularly evident on the moors to the east of the Derwent, amidst small clearance cairns which stand on patches of stony ground that is unsuitable for cultivation and veering around boulders that were too heavy to move. Numerous house platforms and the foundations of round, timber-framed houses were discovered during Stewart Ainsworth's careful survey of the Big Moor. Each extended family or kin group had its stone circle and barrow within or on the edge of its fields, with rough pastures stretching beyond.

Much has been learned from a site at Swine Sty on the Big Moor, below a shelf on the opposite side of Barbrook to the two stone circles. The excavation of one of a small group of farmhouses (or perhaps a shepherd's shelter) that were surrounded by small yards or plots no bigger than gardens revealed the stone footings of a dwelling that had probably been built of timber and roofed with thatch or turves. It was 20 feet in diameter and stood on the previous site of a larger timber building identified only by its postholes. The artefacts that were found showed that the inhabitants supplemented their farming activities with the manufacture of polished shale rings, some of which seem to have been bracelets.

The heaps of cleared stones in and around the small, irregular-shaped fields at Swine Sty and elsewhere point to a laborious process of woodland clearance, season by season. The complicated layout of the field walls suggests that they were added to and modified over a long period. It is not clear whether all the farms were occupied at the same time or whether old sites were sometimes abandoned in favour of new ones. The cereal fields could have been ploughed with primitive wooden ards and harvested with bronze sickles, but the considerable increase in the amount of grassland revealed by pollen analysis shows that farming was essentially pastoral. In summer time flocks and herds grazed the surrounding uplands. The type of settlement that has been unearthed at Swine Sty was probably typical of many others on what are now the East Moors, such as those on Stoke Flat and Birchen Edge, where the prehistoric earthen field boundaries that are still visible probably supported stock-proof hedges. Pollen analysis, radiocarbon dates and the presence of stone circles and barrows indicate that such fields were cultivated over a long span of time

LEFT
Nine Ladies stone circle. The best-known stone circle in the Peak District is found on Stanton Moor in a grassy clearance among silver birch trees. It had acquired its name by the late eighteenth century, though it is now clear that the circle originally consisted of eleven stones. Countless visitors have trodden down the bank and the central cairn which is shown on old drawings. A single standing stone, known as the King Stone, about 40 metres away, appears to be aligned on the circle.

PHOTOGRAPH: AUTHOR

Swine Sty. The excavation of this prehistoric site on the Big Moor has added greatly to our understanding of farming in the Bronze Age. A small group of buildings, marked now by their stone foundations, were probably timber-framed and thatched with turf or heather. The surrounding fields were no bigger than modern gardens, enclosed by sinuous stone walls. Clearing these fields and ploughing them with primitive ards must have been a strenuous but worthwhile task, for they remained in cultivation over a long period of time before the climate deteriorated and peat began to spread.

PHOTOGRAPH: AUTHOR

in the second and first millennium BC, but whether these farms were occupied throughout the year or just in the warmer months cannot be judged from the archaeological record. In his detailed surveys of all the available evidence, John Barnatt has argued that the sustained use of specific areas of land by small 'family' farms on the gritstones may have developed at an earlier date than in parts of lowland Britain and have continued in use long after the creation of planned landscapes in areas such as Dartmoor. The people who lived in these farms had 'family' monuments within easy access, including their own stone circle and numerous barrows with multiple burials and simple grave goods.

This settling-down in the landscape started in the Late Neolithic period and became usual during the Bronze Age. The settlement by the Neolithic ceremonial enclosure at Gardom's Edge flourished between 2000 and 1500 BC, but of course the fields may have remained in continuous use long after people stopped building distinctive ritual monuments. They may not have been abandoned until soils deteriorated and peat began to spread when the climate changed in the first millennium BC. A few modern farms may occupy sites that continued in use into the Roman period and beyond.

When the climate was still warmer than it is today, an extraordinary settlement gathered on the summit of Mam Tor. More than 100 platforms have

been cut into the hillsides and some have been shown by excavation to have supported circular houses. Even if the platforms are not all contemporary, the settlement was of unusual size, location and persistence. Charcoal from the foundations of some dwellings provided radiocarbon dates from the centuries around 1350 BC and many Late Bronze Age artefacts, including a mass of pottery, a polished stone axe and several shale bracelets have been found during excavations. A bronze axe and a cinerary urn came from the remains of two Bronze Age barrows on the summit edge. The exposed position and the lack of arable land nearby emphasises the special nature of this settlement, which must have drawn on a large catchment area, stretching down into the Hope and Edale valleys and on to the limestone plateau. The encircling ramparts have not been dated securely but are generally thought to be a later development in the Iron Age.

Much remains to be learnt about Bronze Age settlements in other parts of Derbyshire. A great deal of metalwork that has been recovered from wetland contexts in the Trent valley has been dated to the Middle and Late Bronze Ages, but no extensive field systems have so far been discovered, despite the obvious reduction of the wildwood to create a more open landscape in some districts. Elsewhere, fieldwalking has not turned up large spreads of artefacts, though possible Bronze Age settlements have been identified at a few places, such as Birken Lea Farm, Dronfield, or Scarcliffe Park on the magnesian limestone. But we are reminded of the archaeologist's adage: 'Absence of evidence is not evidence of absence'. The picture may change in future years.

THE LATE BRONZE AGE

About 1500 BC the rituals in the stone circles came to an end and the great cemeteries such as that on Stanton Moor fell out of use. Perhaps they were no longer needed to assert communal grazing rights once the population had grown to such an extent that the landscape was fully parcelled out between different owners? Yet there are no signs of tribal leaders or hereditary elites in the Peak District at this time and no great linear earthworks such as those that have been found in Yorkshire or Wessex. In fact, archaeological evidence for the Late Bronze Age is remarkably thin in Derbyshire. Relatively few burial sites are known, artefacts are usually found only in isolation and pottery cannot be placed in sequences of different types. Late Bronze Age metalwork is conspicuously absent on the limestone plateau, nor has much turned up elsewhere.

DERBYSHIRE: A HISTORY

The reasons for this apparent decline of economic, social and ceremonial activities are not clear, but climate change may have been the main one. Britain became significantly cooler and wetter, with average temperatures dropping to about 2° C lower than today. As the shallow soils on the gritstones lost their fertility, perhaps because of increased demands from the rising population, so the growing of cereals was abandoned and peat began to spread over the old arable fields. These uplands were now used only for pasture and many a settlement was deserted, perhaps in favour of new sites that were cleared from the woods in the river valleys.

In the Trent valley, too, not much is yet known about this period, though excavations at Willington by a silted-up river channel revealed a burnt mound and a remarkable rectangular trough with a capacity of 400 litres, made from a foundation of 13 timbers and with other, stacked timbers forming the sides. Tool marks show that the timbers were felled and shaped by metal blades. Prehistoric men had long ago learned how to manage coppiced underwood and how to ensure a continuous supply of timber for a variety of purposes, including the making of boats. In 1998 a remarkable discovery was made in a quarry at Argosy Washolme between Shardlow and Aston-upon-Trent. A log-boat that carried cargo along a former course of the river had been packed with large sandstone rocks that had been quarried two miles upstream and had collapsed under the weight. The stones were perhaps intended for the foundations of a trackway. The outer rings of the boat have provided radiocarbon dates of around 1115 BC. A second log-boat has recently been discovered about half-a-mile away. By the beginning of the Iron Age around 700 BC nearly all the ash, alder, birch, hazel and willow woods along the river valleys of south Derbyshire had been put to productive use. The great ceremonial landscapes had fallen out of favour and the land was farmed more intensely.

The Iron Age

Recent excavations such as those at Willington have revealed extensive settlement sites along the middle Trent valley during the Iron Age. Round dwellings, pits and granaries, all enclosed within rectangular ditches, were surrounded by fields and connected to the pastures by drove-ways. We get a strong sense of population growth and increased pressure on the available natural resources. But few Iron Age occupation sites, tools, implements and pottery have been identified in other parts of Derbyshire and the burial practices of this period have left little evidence on the ground. It is particularly puzzling that little has been found in the White Peak from the first millennium BC, when so much survives from earlier periods. Perhaps the climate worsened so badly that the farmers retreated from the limestone plateau to the surrounding valleys in the winter months and drove their livestock back up the pastures each spring? Banked enclosures on Tideswell and Harrop Moors are thought to have been stock enclosures from this period. On the gritstone East Moors many of

Prehistoric log boat. Found in Hanson's Shardlow gravel quarries by the river Trent, this boat, hollowed out of a tree trunk, has been estimated from carbon-14 dating to be well over 3,000 years old. At 10 metres in length, the surviving structure is nearly complete. It was packed with Bromsgrove sandstone, quarried a few miles upstream, and may have been intended to strengthen a causeway. It is on display in Derby Museum.

the old fields remained in use, but there too we know less about the Iron Age inhabitants than we do about their ancestors. As so few cereals are grown in either the White Peak or the Dark Peak and as much of the southern lowlands have clay or alluvial soils, aerial photographs do not reveal cropmarks that might have identified Iron Age settlements, such as those that have appeared so often on the magnesian limestone belt across the border in South Yorkshire. The iron artefacts and weapons that we might expect to find have been corroded by the acid soils and, of course, the dearth of pot sherds might be explained by a preference for wooden or leather vessels.

Few changes to the Late Bronze Age settlement pattern can be observed anywhere in Britain between 700 and 500 BC, but from then onwards sites and finds multiply. Pottery provides plenty of evidence of long-distance contacts and the national population seems to have grown quite quickly after about 300 BC. By then, the change from bronze to iron tools that were harder and sharper was complete. Evidence of iron-smelting in this late prehistoric period has been discovered on the Burbage Brook near Hathersage and elsewhere in north Derbyshire.

HILLFORTS

In searching for evidence of Iron Age occupation a disproportionate emphasis has to be placed on the puzzling collection of miscellaneous sites that are labelled 'hill forts'. They range from the magnificent, defended site at Mam Tor to small enclosures whose purpose may have been simply to protect stock. As few have been studied in detail, we do not know much about them. Nearly all are on prominent hilltops overlooking the main valleys, with ready access to a variety of resources where the limestone plateau meets the gritstone uplands.

Mam Tor, whose British name is derived from its distinctive breast shape, is the only Derbyshire hill fort to have a national reputation. As we have seen, this was a major site in the Bronze Age. Its ramparts have not been dated, but on stylistic grounds they appear to be Iron Age. A single, stone-revetted rampart, with a ditch and counterscarp bank, follows the contours around the hog-back of the hill, enclosing about 16 acres. Landslips on the eastern side

Castle Ring, Harthill Moor. The bank, ditch and wall to the left of the trees on the skyline enclose a small, circular site measuring no more than ¾ acre. Because of its striking position, close to prehistoric earthworks, it is normally classified as a small Iron Age hill fort, but as it has not been excavated, its date and purpose are uncertain.

PHOTOGRAPH: AUTHOR

Aerial view of Mam Tor. The ramparts of Derbyshire's finest prehistoric hill fort curve round the contours of the hill top which dominates the landscape above Winnats Pass (seen top left emerging from the Hope valley). The ramparts have not been dated but are in a style associated with the Iron Age. Excavations of the shallow depressions that were scooped out of the slopes have shown that they mark the sites of numerous circular dwellings from much earlier in the Bronze Age. The ramparts may have been constructed for prestige rather than actual defence, for Mam Tor was clearly an important tribal centre which could be seen for miles around.

of 'the shivering mountain' have destroyed the defences there, but elsewhere they are well preserved. At the main entrance at the south-west corner and at the smaller entrance at the northern end the rampart turns to form narrow passages. We do not know how long the site remained in use. It was obviously a major focal point for much of the first millennium BC.

The rampart and ditch of a 12-acre oval enclosure at Burr Tor, at 1,300 feet on the western edge of a steep escarpment about half-a-mile north of Great Hucklow, were recorded in a measured survey before their destruction in 1978. The defences were only slight, so the site was either abandoned early or used simply as a stock enclosure. A similar-sized enclosure at Fin Cop stands impressively on top of a precipitous slope that rises from a sharp bend in the river Wye. Several barrows were erected here and the site may have been used for various purposes from the Late Neolithic to the Iron Age. The 'fort' was defined by a double rampart that can be followed for part of its course on the eastern and southern sides that had no natural defences. Castle Naze, at the northern end of Coombs Moss, south of Chapel-en-le-Frith, is a much smaller fort of 2¼ acres. Steep natural slopes form two sides of this triangular site; the third is defended by a deep ditch and double ramparts, stretching for about 550 feet across the promontory, with a causewayed entrance in the middle.

Two other hill-top enclosures are even smaller and may have been merely fortified homesteads. Ball Cross stands at the highest point on the way from Chatsworth to Bakewell and measures just 1¾ acres. Away from the steep natural slopes, it was defended by an embanked stone wall, ditch and counterscarp bank that were eventually forcibly destroyed. Excavators discovered Neolithic 'cup-and-ring stones' and pottery that was similar in type to that found at Mam Tor. Nearby barrows add to the impression that the Calton Pastures area had been especially significant since the Bronze Age. A similar site at Castle Ring on the skyline where the Limestone Way now leads from Harthill Moor to Youlgreave, covers only ¾ acre. It too is enclosed by a bank, ditch and counterscarp bank, which has now been levelled on the south-east side where the original entrance may have stood. The remains of a barrow can be seen in the south-west corner and the site is close to the earlier ceremonial monuments on Harthill Moor. Castle Ring has not been excavated and its purpose remains puzzling.

That we still have much to learn about Iron Age hill-top enclosures became clear in 1998 when Ann Hearle noticed crop marks in her garden and the adjacent field near the parish church at Mellor, in a district where hillforts were thought to be absent. Excavation proved that a ditch six feet deep and four metres wide had been cut through the hard underlying rock. The top layers produced fragments of Roman tile, pottery and glass, but the lower levels turned up Iron Age potsherds and the shattered remains of crucibles that had

The remarkable discovery of a substantial Iron Age settlement around St Thomas's church, Mellor, began in the dry summer of 1995 when Ann and John Earle noticed cropmarks in their back garden at the Old Vicarage. Three years later, excavations by a team from Manchester University began to unearth evidence of a large settlement during the fifth and fourth centuries BC, enclosed by two systems of ditches. The ditches seem to have served as boundaries rather than for defence, so the term Iron Age settlement is preferred to hill fort. Large numbers of round houses were identified from their postholes. Other finds included Mesolithic and Bronze Age flints and Roman remains from about AD 180. This view shows an exposed section of the main ditch, cut into the bedrock around the church. In the background there is a reconstruction of a circular hut of the period.

PHOTOGRAPH: CARNEGIE

been used for casting bronze. Charcoal from near the base of the ditch gave a radiocarbon date from the fifth century BC. Further excavations in the middle of the field uncovered an almost complete Iron Age pot, an important find as so little pottery survives in the Peak District from this time. It was shaped in clay slabs without the use of a wheel and its charcoal radiocarbon date is 520–380 BC. Then what seems to have been an Iron Age round house was excavated on the front lawn and in 2003 a trench at the far end of the garden revealed another deep ditch, suggesting a double system of enclosures, one for defence the other for livestock. Perhaps the fort went out of use before it was reoccupied by the Romans from the first to the third century AD? The discovery of high-status Samian ware, glass and some fine brooches suggests that a Roman building stood nearby.

Another possible fort, recently mooted, is a site of just under ten acres near Conksbury, whose name means 'Crane's Fort'. No artefacts have been found and the levelling of the site by centuries of farming has obscured the possibility of limestone ramparts and an outer ditch. Its low-level setting adds to the uncertainty of its interpretation. Finally, just one Derbyshire Iron Age hillfort has been identified beyond the Peak District. This is the impressive promontory fort, covering 10½ acres, at Markland Grips, a mile-and-a-half to the east of Clowne on the magnesian limestone. Set between two wide ravines, or 'grips' that converge to the east, it was defended at the western end by three lines of ramparts. Fragments of Iron Age and Roman pottery have been found there.

We remain in the dark about the dating and purpose of these earthworks. Some of them occupied sites that were important long before the Iron Age. The defensive ditches and ramparts indicate that population growth – perhaps reaching 1 million in England by the end of the first millennium – had produced a more aggressive, hierarchical society at a time when the deterioration of the climate reduced the supply of fertile land and good pastures. Yet the lack of complex earthworks such as those in Wessex suggests that the Derbyshire hillforts and other defended enclosures had been abandoned long before the arrival of the Romans.

When they arrived the Romans found a landscape that in many ways would have been familiar to us. Pastures, meadows and arable land had long been cleared from the wildwood that had become dominant after the end of the last Ice Age and the remaining woods either provided grazing and fuel or were managed carefully to supply timber and coppiced underwood. As yet, Derbyshire had no towns and perhaps few villages, but the countryside was filling up with conical farmhouses that were timber-framed and thatched and surrounded by ditches. They were connected by winding holloways, many of which are still in use as roads and lanes. Most of the population were descended from the Stone Age inhabitants of the British Isles, as indeed is still the case today.

Romans, Britons and Angles

The Roman advance

When the Roman army landed on the south coast of Britain in AD 43, the whole of what is now Derbyshire lay within the territory of a British tribe known as the Corieltauvi (whom we used to call, mistakenly, the Coritani). Their tribal capital was at Leicester and they controlled most of the East Midlands until they were defeated by the Romans two years later. But it was not until the early 60s that the Roman army crossed the Trent and built a timber and turf fort for 500 soldiers on the west bank of the Derwent in what is now the residential area of Strutt's Park on the northern side of Derby. Archaeological finds there have been dated from the reign of Nero (54–68) to the governorship of Agricola (78–84), when the fort was abandoned in favour of a new one that was built nearby at Little Chester and which was known to the Romans as *Derventio*. The line of the main approach to this new base is now followed by Old Chester Road, but most of the fort site was built upon in the nineteenth century. Modern excavations have confirmed the accuracy of the plan drawn by William Stukeley in 1721, which shows a rectangular fort, about 600 feet long by 500 feet wide, enclosed by a stone wall and outer ditch. A civilian settlement, or *vicus*, grew up on both sides of the present Sawley Road, with an industrial area where this road changes course on entering Racecourse Park. Here, in the late first and early second centuries pottery kilns produced jars, bowls and dishes made from the local clays; a cemetery lay nearby. *Derventio* occupied a strategic position in the network of Roman military roads that soon linked the Trent and Derwent valleys to the lead fields of the White Peak. It was always the largest and most important Roman fort in Derbyshire. Just as *Deva* and *Eboracum* laid the foundations of Chester and York, so *Derventio* established the primary importance of the site that eventually became the county capital.

Once *Derventio* was secure, the Roman army advanced further north towards the territory of the Brigantes, whose southern boundary seems to have been the

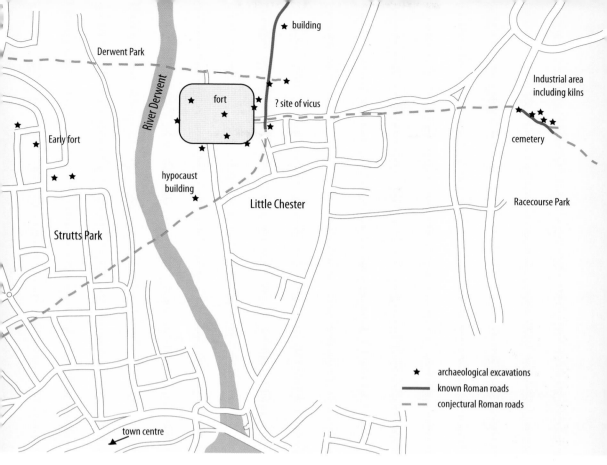

Roman Derby. Excavations in recent years have increased our knowledge of the successive stages of the Roman fort of *Derventio* and have identified the site of the civilian settlement, or *vicus*, and an industrial area and cemetery beyond.

river Don. The Roman name for Chesterfield is not known, but excavations in the 1970s confirmed the existence of a fort on the knoll that is now occupied by the parish church, overlooking the rivers Rother and Hipper. Later excavations have shown that the Romans took over a site that had been occupied in the Iron Age. The turf and timber fort of the 60s was replaced by a fort on a new alignment about AD 79–80. The ramparts of this later fort followed what are now Station Road and Holywell Street, then crossed the present churchyard and ran northwards from the angle of Church Way. St Mary and All Saints church stands in the centre of the complex on the site of the Roman headquarters, and St Mary's Gate seems to follow the line of the principal road. During the first quarter of the second century the fort was reduced in size on its eastern side and new ditches and ramparts defended the southern and eastern approaches. By then, it was similar in size to the forts on the south bank of the Don at Templeborough (Rotherham) and Doncaster. No evidence of a *vicus* has yet been discovered and the fort was never reoccupied after it was abandoned about AD 150, but enough survived in much later times to determine the layout of the medieval town and to explain the place-name, which was recorded in 955 as *Cesterfelda*, 'the Roman fort in cleared countryside'.

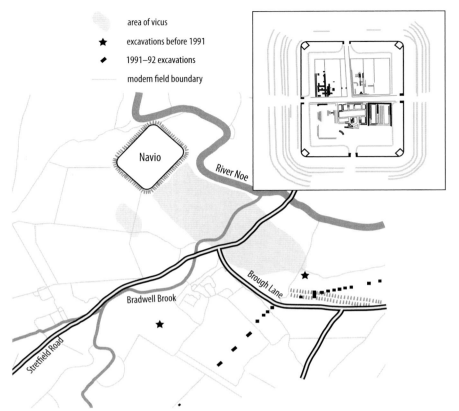

area of vicus

★ excavations before 1991

✦ 1991–92 excavations

—— modern field boundary

Navio. The typical 'playing-card' plan of the Roman fort at Brough has long been known, but more recent excavations have revealed a large *vicus* extending over seventeen acres on both sides of the Bradwell Brook. This was the second most important Roman fort in Derbyshire.

The Roman advance in the 60s continued as far as Templeborough, then in AD 71 the invasion of Brigantia began. Some historians have argued that, as Roman forts were not built in the Peak District until the late 70s or early 80s, that area belonged to the Brigantes, but this seems a tenuous theory that lacks firm evidence. A fort known as *Navio* was built at Brough, at the confluence of the river Noe and the Bradwell Brook, perhaps deliberately close to Mam Tor, the former native stronghold and guardian of the route down Winnats Pass into the Hope valley. *Navio*'s strategic importance grew with the development of lead mining in the High Peak. The name of the fort was derived from *Nava*, the British name for the river, whose present form is Noe. The site is now grassed over, but the outline of the fort as it was reconstructed in the second century remains clear. Excavations have revealed that it was enclosed by a clay rampart, which was about 30 feet wide and surmounted by a wooden palisade. Two large ditches (the innermost eight feet wide and two feet deep, the outer 24 feet wide and five feet deep) surrounded the ramparts. This three-acre site was the second most important Roman fort in Derbyshire. It was occupied until the garrison was moved to the newly built Hadrian's Wall in the 120s, but the soldiers returned to quell an insurrection 30 years later. The *vicus* that stretched across the Bradwell Brook grew considerably in the second and third centuries.

The other fort in the northern part of the Peak District was erected on a spur of land covering 3½ acres and overlooking the confluence of the river Etherow and the Glossop Brook, so as to guard the road from *Navio* to Manchester and the approaches to the Pennine crossing through Longdendale. The name Melandra Castle appears to have been an eighteenth-century antiquarian's invention (like Templeborough). The Roman name is uncertain but may have been *Erdotalia*, meaning 'on the edge overlooking the Etherow' (whose British name was *Edera*). The ground falls away steeply on three sides, so the main

Melandra Castle. Here again, the outline of the fort and some of the internal arrangements have been revealed by excavation, but the *vicus* has been obscured by modern housing.

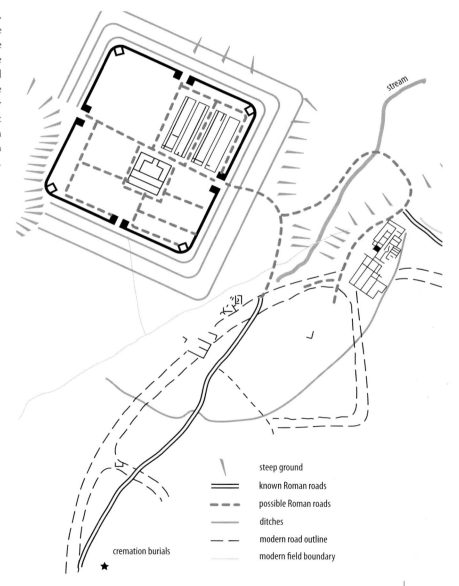

stream

steep ground
known Roman roads
possible Roman roads
ditches
modern road outline
modern field boundary

cremation burials

approach was from the south. A turf-covered earth rampart, surrounded by a ditch, was pierced on each side by timber gateways. The wooden buildings of the early fort were replaced with stone ones when the fort was rebuilt in the 120s. Recent excavations have uncovered a bath house outside the north-west corner of the fort, but much of the *vicus* is now covered by an estate in Gamesley.

The Peak District's other important Roman site was very different in character. The warm thermal springs of Buxton were known to the Romans as *Aquae Arnemetiae*, from a Celtic cult-site, and were valued for their medicinal properties. A votive deposit to the Celtic goddess *Arnemetiae* that was found during building work near St Anne's Well (the likely successor of the Roman springs) consisted of 232 Roman coins dating from the first century to around AD 400, three bronze bracelets and a wire clasp. Pottery and coins from the late first or early second century and part of a Roman milestone recording the distance from *Navio* have been found in the Silverlands area of the town. No fort has been identified, though Buxton occupied a strategic position in the High Peak, but the civilian settlement grew into a small spa centre that was second only to *Aquae Sulis*, Bath.

A few smaller sites may have been fortlets during the early stages of the Roman occupation. In the Trent valley, a 1½ acre, rectangular earthwork to the south of Sawley church, has produced Roman pottery of indeterminate date. Castle Hill Camp at Pentrich, where a Roman road heads north on the high ground overlooking the Amber valley, was an earlier earthwork that was converted for a brief period by the Romans. A nearby small earthwork at Higham may have been linked to it. And at Highstones, overlooking the Longdendale reservoirs, a rampart and ditch, with a causewayed entrance, enclosed a defensive site. None of these was of lasting importance.

Later Roman forts

Roman troops were recruited from many different parts of Europe and northern Africa. Their numbers in Derbyshire fluctuated according to the political situation on the Empire's northern frontier. When Hadrian's Wall was built, Little Chester and Chesterfield were reduced in size and Brough was abandoned. Then when the Antonine wall was errected in Scotland in the 140s, Melandra Castle and Chesterfield too were abandoned and the garrison at Little Chester became a mere token. A native insurrection in the 150s prompted the Romans to re-garrison their Derbyshire forts and rebuild Brough in stone.

At the same time, the entirely new timber fort that was built at Little Chester was enclosed with a clay rampart, an inner ditch, and an outer ditch some 30 metres beyond. Archaeologists have unearthed a complicated sequence of rebuilding. At the end of the second century, the inner ditch was re-dug further away from the rampart, the outer ditch was abandoned, and the internal timber buildings were demolished. In the second quarter of the third century

Aerial view of Melandra Castle. The square plan and hill-top position of the fort are remarkably clear from the air. The fort was rebuilt in stone in the 120s, but there are few signs of activity in later times.

a thick layer of dark soil was laid over part of the internal area of the fort, then in the late third century the rampart was cut back so that a new wall of mortared sandstone rubble could be built three metres high and the old ditch was replaced by a broader ditch (6.6 metres wide) some 20 metres from the wall. The fort and its *vicus* were occupied until the mid-fourth century, but the site was abandoned long before the final withdrawal of the Romans in 410. During the twentieth century a large collection of Roman material was found in or near the fort and *vicus*, including coins and pottery, glass, pewter, bronze and iron objects, various brooches and other bronze ornaments, and an unusual bas-relief about 20 inches high.

Immediately to the east of the industrial area lay a walled Romano-British cemetery. The remains of 61 inhumations and 39 distinct cremation deposits have been recovered, but originally many more people were buried there. The cemetery was opened in the mid-second century and continued in use to the end of the period of the occupation of the fort and the *vicus* in the mid-fourth century. A sample of the skeletons shows that the average male height was 5 feet 6¾ inches and the average female 5 feet 2¼ inches. Their bones and teeth indicate that they were reasonably healthy; over 20 per cent of the sample died before the age of 20, but of the survivors about half lived beyond 25 and some to well over 40. Grave goods were sparse and gave no indication of Christian influences. As was common at the time, the typical grave goods in the cremations were pots, pottery lamps and joints of pork.

A datestone records the rebuilding of Navio in the 150s by the First Cohort of Aquitanians, whose prefect, Quintus Sittius Caecilianus, also dedicated the altar to the local god *Mars Braciaca* which was found near Haddon Hall. As the defences by the river Noe had eroded badly, a radical rebuilding was necessary. The earlier ramparts and interior buildings were demolished and heavy clay soil was spread evenly over the entire site. A new rampart was surrounded by a ditch 22 feet wide and eight feet deep and by a double wall 20 feet in width; then 20 feet beyond, a final outer ditch measuring at least 16 feet across provided an additional defensive barrier. The interior of the fort was reduced to about 2¼ acres and re-orientated by 180 degrees so as to face north-east. The barracks, granaries and other buildings were all rebuilt in timber.

At the end of the second century, perhaps in response to another insurrection by the Brigantes further north, the headquarters and granaries at *Navio* were rebuilt in stone and the barracks were remodelled, with their roofs covered with diamond-shaped stone tiles. The regimental shrine had an elaborate semi-circular apse in which perhaps a statue of the emperor was placed. The defensive gritstone wall of the fort, which was 5½ feet thick and at least 15 feet high to the parapet walk, was faced with dressed stone backed by the earlier clay rampart. Then, early in the fourth century, the barrack buildings, stables and granaries were rebuilt again, the two inner ditches filled in, and the garrison reduced to about 250 men, whose principal duty may have been to protect the lead trade. The finding of gritstone balls, between 1½ and 6 inches in diameter, shows that the fort's defences included the projection of missiles. Evidence from pottery and coins indicates that *Navio* was occupied until at least the mid-fourth century. Meanwhile, the *vicus* had expanded during the second and third centuries until it sprawled over some 17 acres on either side of the Bradwell Brook.

Melandra Castle was rebuilt in stone during the 120s or not much later. An outer wall of dressed millstone grit was erected against the earlier rampart and the defences were strengthened by a stockade and two additional ditches around the southern half of the fort. The northern half needed only one new ditch because the slopes provided natural defence. Stone gateways, with guard chambers above their arches, replaced the timber gateways of the earlier fort. Three of them had double archways, each eight feet wide, that allowed wheeled vehicles to pass through, but because of its exposed position the southern gateway had a single archway that was ten feet wide. Little is known about the interior of the fort, except that the headquarters was rebuilt in stone. A carved altar stone has been found beneath the courtyard and other finds include an inscribed stone indicating the presence of the First Cohort of Frisiavonians, who were also based at Manchester. Unlike *Navio*, Melandra Castle does not seem to have been reoccupied in the 150s, but some coins have been found which date from the end of the third century to the end of the fourth. The *vicus* that covered five acres on the southern and south-eastern sides of the fort was protected by its own rampart and ditch, beyond which lay the cemetery, alongside the road to Buxton. Another road linked the fort with *Navio*. The timber-built dwellings included a guest house measuring 150 by 60 feet, which seems to have been demolished about 140, when all signs of occupation come to an end.

Roman roads

The most famous Roman road through Derbyshire is Ryknield Street, which was noted about 1400 as a road running all the way from St David's in Pembrokeshire through Worcester and Lichfield to York. It seems to have been named after the famous Icknield Way, for it is first mentioned as *Ykenild* in a Burton Abbey charter of *c.*1200. It is generally supposed to have passed through Little Chester on its way to Chesterfield, Templeborough and York, but although the lines of Roman roads can be traced at certain points on this course, no evidence of the use of the name in Derbyshire has been found. The presence of Ricknieldthorpe, near Kiveton Park in South Yorkshire, and numerous other *stret* names along the crest of the magnesian limestone suggests that Ryknield Street in fact followed an entirely different course, or that more than one road bore this name on the way to York. In north-east Derbyshire Pleasley, Scarcliffe, Elmton and Ault Hucknall each have a a field called Street Close, which mark this ancient highway as it headed towards the crossing of the river Don at Strafford Sands, near Conisbrough. Much of the line of the Roman road that headed eastwards from the fort at Wall, near Lichfield, is today followed by the A38 Burton–Derby road, and its Roman origin has been confirmed on its approach to Little Chester as far as the Markeaton Brook. The Roman road heading north-eastwards from Little Chester can be followed along the ridge through Pentrich, Higham and Stretton ('the farm on the Roman road', recorded with this name about 1002) to Chesterfield. The continuation of this road to Templeborough, via Tupton, has been confirmed by aerial photography and excavation at Hagge Farm, Staveley. This was undoubtedly an important Roman route but we have no evidence that it was called Ryknield Street.

Another important road from Little Chester, known simply as 'The Street', headed for Buxton and Manchester. The line is speculative as far as Brassington, but from there its course can be followed across 18 miles of the limestone plateau to Buxton. It probably followed a prehistoric route, for it passes close to Minninglow and Arbor Low, and it remained well defined in later times, for even now it often serves as a parish boundary. Little Chester was also linked with Rocester, following the present Long Lane, and with a crossing of the Trent at Sawley.

The other well-evidenced Roman road in the Peak District linked Brough and Buxton along Batham Gate, a name that refers to the medicinal baths at *Aquae Arnemetiae*. Stretches of modern lanes still bear this name on modern Ordnance Survey maps. Other claims need to be treated with suspicion. The

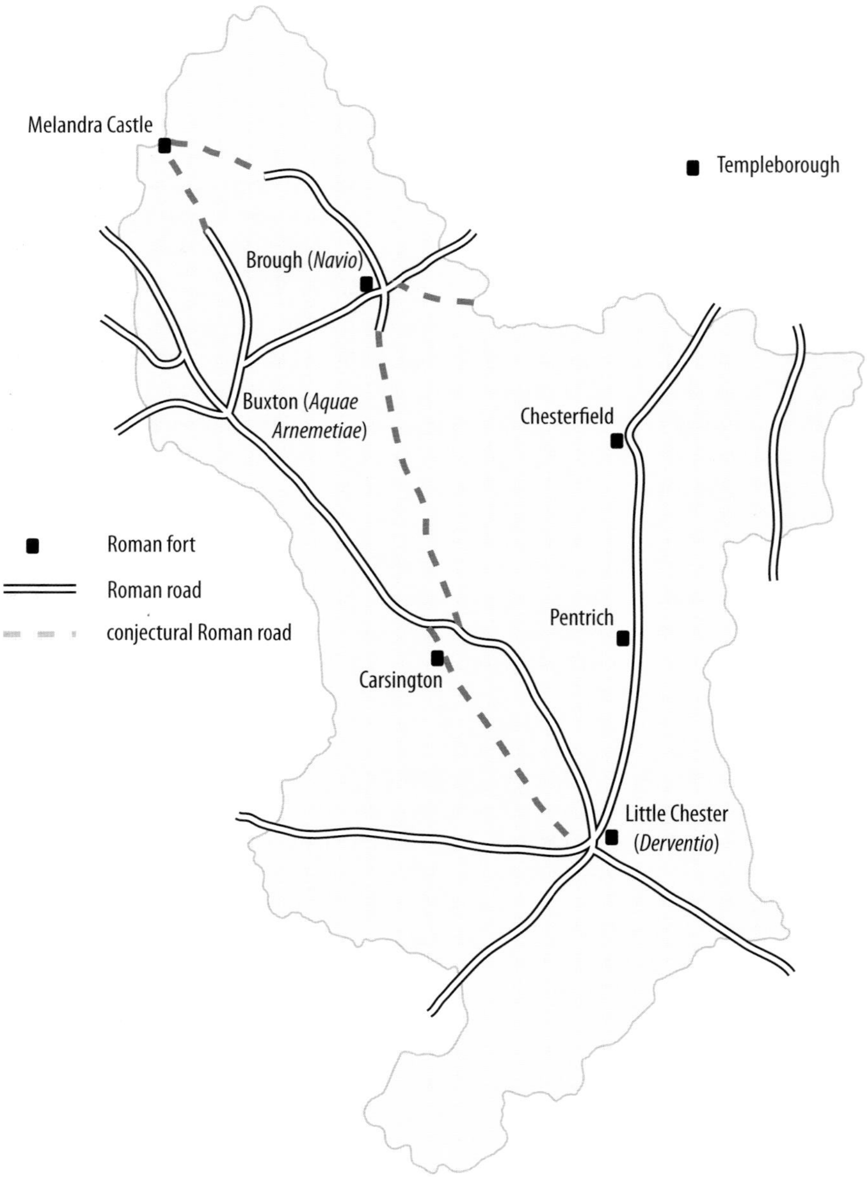

The Roman military roads which connected these forts to each other and to the wider world have not left a great deal of physical evidence in Derbyshire. Such roads were usually hard-core, raised causeways or 'aggers', with drainage ditches on either side. They were built in short straight stretches, but in Derbyshire needed frequent changes of angle to negotiate the difficult local countryside. Excavations at Derbyshire's forts have located roads heading in the general direction of other forts, but most of them can be traced with certainty only in short sections. Great reliance has to be placed on place-names incorporating 'street', which are derived from the Anglo-Saxon word *stret*, meaning a Roman road. However, it is not always clear where these 'streets' were heading. Rumbling Street near Barlow, known as 'Rombellowe stryt' in 1590, is one example that appears to have been unconnected to any of Derbyshire's forts.

Melandra Castle

Templeborough

Brough (*Navio*)

Buxton (*Aquae Arnemetiae*)

Chesterfield

Roman fort

Roman road

conjectural Roman road

Pentrich

Carsington

Little Chester (*Derventio*)

precise course of the road over the moors from Templeborough to *Navio* is not known, Doctor's Gate is a later route than the Roman one from *Navio* to Melandra Castle, and the supposed place-name evidence for long-distance routes known as Hereward Street and the Portway does not stand up to rigorous examination. It is also clear that the military roads formed only a small part of the network of routes that connected the scattered farms of the native British. Although we cannot prove that a particular footpath, lane or road has been in continuous use since at least Roman times, we know that the national population level was high enough to require a network of tracks comparable with that of modern times.

Rural settlements

The Romans made little impact on the way of life of the native people of Derbyshire, except where they exploited the lead reserves of the White Peak. The forts and their attendant civilian settlements were modest in size and urban life was almost non-existent. Nor were great villa estates, comparable with those of southern England, developed in the countryside. The fourth-century stone dwelling that has been excavated at Carsington may have been a small villa, for it had two wings, one of which had a bath suite with a hypocaust heating system, but even that was exceptional. Most native families continued to live in thatched round houses, surrounded by yards, garden plots, small fields and paddocks, with droveways to lead the livestock to the pastures beyond. Some produced food for the Roman garrisons, and the better-quality pottery and

In 1957 three Roman pottery kilns were discovered at Overlane Farm, Hazelwood. A few years later excavation revealed the typical 'Derbyshire Ware' pottery that was distributed widely across central and northern Britain during the second and third centuries AD. The pitchers shown here were dated to about AD 260. 'Derbyshire Ware' was a hard, gritty pottery with a pimply surface which varied in colour from buff through brick-red to dark blue-grey or purple. (See also the photograph on page 53.)

BY COURTESY OF BROMBY COLLECTION AND WWW. PICTURETHEPAST.ORG.UK

jewellery that have been found suggest a more buoyant economy during the first and second centuries, when the growing numbers of country people in Roman Britain exported their cereals and wool to Continental Europe. Many native families, however, were little affected by the Roman presence and continued to farm in the manner of their Iron Age ancestors.

The population of the Trent valley seems to have risen considerably as the climate became warmer and drier in the early Roman period. Excavations at Willington in the 1970s and elsewhere in more recent times with the growth of developer-funded projects, together with systematic fieldwalking and aerial photographic surveys, have overturned old ideas and have shown that some parts of the Trent valley became more densely settled under the Romans as woodland was cleared progressively on the floodplain and gravel terraces. At Willington, where two second-century farms have been identified, farming activity seems to have started in Neolithic times and to have continued into the Anglo-Saxon era and beyond. At Breaston at least three circular dwellings within a rectangular ditched enclosure of nearly four acres has been interpreted as a peasant family holding.

In north-east Derbyshire the fertile soils that overlie the magnesian limestone district were attractive to native farmers. The foundations of oval and rectangular dwellings within a ditched enclosure, dated by pottery to the second or third centuries, have been revealed at a site in Scarcliffe Park and the traces of lead smelting in the south-east corner of the park may also date from the Roman period. A similar group of dwellings have been found in Scratta Wood, near Whitwell, and a small, third-century aisled building has been recognised in Stubbin Wood, near Shirebrook. Most of the magnesian limestone district has been tilled continuously from the Roman period, so finds are restricted to woods that have grown since then or to special, undisturbed sites such as Creswell Crags and the Markland Grips hill fort.

Evidence of cultivation on the coal-measure sandstones and the southern clays in the Roman period is much harder to come by. This is partly because of the destruction of sites by later farming and by the great expansion of industry and housing in the last two centuries, but it is probably also due to the lack of surveys and excavations that are funded by developers, such as those that have transformed our understanding of the Trent valley. Our main clues are the hoards of Roman coins that have been discovered at Alfreton, Chesterfield, Ripley and Shipley, as well as at numerous other places further west on the carboniferous limestone.

The fullest evidence for the Roman period comes from the Peak District, where about 50 hamlets or farms, consisting of several circular or rectangular buildings, constructed with timber or stone and roofed with thatch, have been identified in places where they have not been obliterated by later activities. Surrounded by yards, gardens, small fields and holloways, these farms were probably settled at the margins of cultivation, for the better land had long been occupied. Population growth meant that younger sons had to clear more woodland to bring fresh land into cultivation. One such site in the Dark Peak that can still be recognised on the ground is at The Warren, Outseats, up the slope towards Stanedge from Hathersage, where a group of houses was erected on terraces that had been cleared of boulders. Most of the surviving examples, however, are found in the White Peak.

The majority of the native field systems from the Roman period that were recorded by Bill Bevan in his survey of the Peak District were sub-rectangular in shape and defined by banks, walls or cultivation terraces known as lynchets. Field sizes varied enormously. The spectacular site at Chee Tor, near Blackwell, was largely saved from destruction by later farming because on three sides it descends from a rocky spur to the deep gorge of the river Wye. The foundations of the settlement are marked by a series of lynchets and low stone banks, which define several rectangular yards and house sites, separated by short lanes and adjacent small fields or garden-plots. Limited excavations have unearthed artefacts dating from the third or fourth centuries and a burial under a small cairn in the corner of one of the enclosures. In later times, extending up to the seventeenth or eighteenth century, the area immediately east of the settlement formed part of the open arable fields of Blackwell and so the lynchets were ploughed out, but even further east the remaining terraces (which were created in the Roman period to grow crops) became part of the wastes and commons of Blackwell township and so stayed intact. Similar 'Celtic fields' that are square in plan with substantial boundary lynchets created by arable production can be found at Cow Low, near Buxton.

Other prominent native settlement sites and field systems that date from the Roman period can be seen in the White Peak on high ground such as The Burrs, north-west of Chelmorton, or Staden Low, near Buxton, and in valleys such as Deep Dale Head, Taddington. All seem to have been a natural development from the housing and farming systems of the Iron Age. Their remote situations suggest that mixed farms of cereals and livestock had been established not only on the better soils throughout Derbyshire but on many poorer soils as well.

Lead mining and smelting

It is very difficult to tell which of Derbyshire's lead mines were worked as far back as the Roman period, for the techniques used in the Middle Ages were probably little different from those of earlier times. The accidental discovery of cast ingots or pigs, some of them stamped with Roman inscriptions, proves that some mines were indeed active at this early period. They are the only source of evidence to show that the Romans exploited the rich lead veins of the White Peak. The earliest ingot with an imperial stamp dates from the reign of Hadrian (117–38). Altogether, 28 ingots have been found in Derbyshire and 20 of them have an abbreviated form of the name *Lutudarum* stamped on them. The location of *Lutudarum* is contentious, but the general opinion is that it was

somewhere in the Wirksworth district, the major lead field in the Middle Ages, and recent opinion tends to favour Carsington, where traces of a settlement and a modest villa were found during excavations in the 1980s before the construction of the reservoir. Here, lead might have been weighed and stamped by a Roman administrator before it was sent on its way. Many of the Derbyshire ingots have been found at Carsington, Cromford, Darley Dale, Matlock and Yeaveley; the only one from the High Peak lead field was discovered at Bradwell. Lead was used for cisterns, baths and water pipes in civic and military buildings and for pewter vessels, trade seals, coffins and various military purposes, but the silver content of Derbyshire lead was generally too low to have been of much use for making coins. The export trade flourished in the second century but declined when fewer monumental buildings were constructed. The discovery at Carsington of two unstamped ingots dating from the late fourth century, however, suggests that lead mining and smelting continued under private ownership long after most of the troops had left.

The site that has been investigated most thoroughly is that at Roystone Grange, near Ballidon, where Richard Hodges' team identified two small settlements near the valley bottom, dating from the second to the fourth century. Five farms have been located but others may await discovery. The largest of the house platforms that

Roman pig of lead. Discovered at Yeaveley and bearing the official stamp SOCIURVM LVTVD, BRIT EX ARG, this ingot was smelted and moulded in the lead field centred on the unidentified *Lutudarum*, not far from the later lead-mining centre of Wirksworth. EX ARG is thought to denote 'from the lead-silver works'. Such ingots weigh about 144 lbs (65 kg).

PHOTOGRAPH BY CARNEGIE, WITH PERMISSION OF DERBY MUSEUMS AND ART GALLERY

were terraced into the slopes supported an unusual farmstead (some 20 metres long by 12 metres wide) in the form of an aisled building of at least three bays with a roof supported by timber posts and drystone wall sides. Finds of the typical pottery known as Derbyshire Ware date its foundation to the early or mid-second century. Other finds included a Roman trumpet brooch of about 100–150, some Samian Ware, and a disc-headed pin from the second or third century, while traces of lead working nearby suggest that the Romans employed miners (or perhaps forced them to work as slaves). The house seems to have been demolished in the second half of the third century.

Derbyshire ware pot. During the second and third centuries AD, and a little later, native craftsmen made this utilitarian pottery in and around the Derwent valley, at sites such as Holbrook, for export all over Roman Britain. These very hard, gritty jars were made for storage or transport.

PHOTOGRAPH BY CARNEGIE, WITH PERMISSION OF DERBY MUSEUMS AND ART GALLERY

Two large enclosures took in the valley side and higher land above, giving the settlement and its fields an unusual butterfly shape when viewed from the air or on a map. One of the enclosures was divided into a series of narrow fields that were seemingly dug by spade-work to grow oats and perhaps barley (as the climate was more favourable then), while the other may have ben used for open grazing. Roystone Grange is the only known Romano-British site in the Peak District with such a distinctive field system. Martin Wildgoose's survey has shown that the field walls that were constructed around these enclosures during the Roman period were at least three feet thick and were formed by double lines of upright stones known to field archaeologists as orthostats. The space between the parallel lines of orthostats was filled with small boulders and rubble. Although they do not survive above foundation level, their outline is clear. The presence of double othostatic walls elsewhere in the White Peak has since been used as an indicator of a Roman date. They have been found, for instance, at Rainster Rocks, Carsington Pastures and Chee Tor. So far, 29 sites have been identified by field surveys and excavations as having such walls, while another 29 sites have possible examples. Double orthostats were not used in all the Roman settlements of the Peak District, however, for only ten per cent have them.

Richard Hodges interpreted the lack of Iron Age material at Roystone Grange and its absence in most of the Peak District as an indication of population collapse before the Romans recolonised the area in order to exploit the lead and sheep pastures of the area. This combination of two cash crops would, he speculated, have attracted an entire community from the Trent valley or further south to set up home at Roystone on favourable terms offered by the Roman administrator. The community withered when the recession during the later years of the Roman Empire meant that they no longer had sufficient cash to buy their food. But this view has not been widely accepted. It has stimulated debate but much more work remains to be done on the White Peak settlements of the Iron Age and the Roman period before a consensus can be reached.

Coal was mined too during the Roman era, but only for local use, for it was too costly to transport long distances in this landlocked part of the country. It fuelled the pottery kilns that in the second and third centuries made coarse Derbyshire Ware for the troops and local markets. Kilns producing this ware have been excavated at Little Chester, Hazlewood, Holbrook and Shottle, near good supplies of potter's clay, fuel, water and military roads, but probably other sites were just as productive. For those who could afford high-quality products, Samian Ware was imported from Italy or Gaul; large quantities have been found during excavations at Little Chester. Stone was quarried in the Dark Peak to make beehive querns, and marble from the Hopton Wood quarries was transported as far as the baths at Godmanchester (Huntingdonshire). Other trades that must have flourished, notably textiles and woodworking, have left no physical reminders of their former importance.

The remaining Roman forts at *Derventio* and *Navio* were reconstructed in the early fourth century, but by 350 the troops had been withdrawn. It is unlikely that the adjoining *vici* were able to survive without the demand for goods from the troops. Buxton probably declined as a small spa town, though votive offerings to the goddess Arnematiae continued for the rest of the century. The Roman military presence in Derbyshire disappeared long before the army finally left Britain in 410. They did not leave an impressive legacy.

Britons

The abandonment of the Roman forts and the collapse of the civilian settlements and markets associated with them had a severe effect on the general economy. Even in the countryside, numerous sites were abandoned. Throughout Britain, some of the cultivated land reverted to wood, heath or fen and as sea levels rose coastal areas and river basins were flooded. Perhaps too, a major outbreak of plague swept through the country, for the native population seems to have shrunk and settlement to have retreated in a manner similar to that following the Black Death in the Middle Ages. The economy did not recover to the level that had been achieved under the Romans until the late Anglo-Scandinavian period. Nevertheless, it is clear that in some parts of the Derbyshire countryside the pattern of land use that had been established by the Romans and the native farmers survived for centuries with little change.

Under the rule of the Roman Empire the native Britons farmed their land in much the same way as their Iron Age ancestors had done, but as they were illiterate the only written records that we have are those of their conquerors. After the Roman withdrawal, the literary evidence is sparse and uncertain. Even Bede's magnificent *History of the English Church and People*, written in 731, has to be read as a hostile account of the British from the point of view of the triumphant English. Faced with the collapse of Roman forts and towns and with the scarcity of surviving British place-names, historians long held the view that the weak and divided British were eventually driven out of the country that became England by Anglo-Saxon armies, followed by a large-scale migration of settlers from across the North Sea. But neither archaeological nor genetic evidence supports the theory of mass invasions. Life in the countryside seems to have continued much as before, though on a reduced scale of activity. The widespread adoption of English place-names indicates not the driving out of the native population but merely the replacement of one ruling class by another and the gradual adoption of the new language, just as English is now widely spoken in the former British Empire though the conquering force was small and migration from Britain was limited. As the documentary and archaeological evidence for the post-Roman period is thin, different interpretations of this era can be offered, but it is generally agreed that after the Roman withdrawal native warriors re-emerged as tribal leaders and that their lack of unity made them vulnerable to attack.

British place-names

Experts in ancient languages tell us that the oldest surviving names in our
present landscape are those of rivers. Some of these names probably go back
to prehistoric times, others are what linguists classify as Celtic, the language
of the Britons. Kenneth Cameron's analysis of the river-names of Derbyshire
shows that the names of the main rivers – Derwent, Dove and Trent – and
of some of the smaller tributaries – Amber, Dane, Goyt, Noe, Rother and
Wye – are either Celtic or pre-Celtic. He adds to this list four place-names

– Clowne, Clownholme, Cown Edge and Umberley – which were derived from ancient river-names.

Other Celtic words are preserved in topographical features, such as woods or hills. Morley Lime and Lime Farm in south-east Derbyshire and Limb Brook and Limb Hill on the county's northern boundary at Dore seem to be derived from the British *lemo*, meaning an elm wood. A variety of words for hills of different shapes have produced such diverse names as Chevin, Crich, Crook Hill, Kinder, Mellor and Pentrich. Intriguingly, the use of *torr*, a Celtic word for a hill that passed into Old English, is found isolated in Derbyshire, well away from south-west England, where it is used commonly. Derbyshire has 14 examples, most notably Mam Tor, and as some of them were recorded well back in the Middle Ages the word seems to have been part of the local vocabulary and not imported. The series of 'bar' names applied to gritstone edges such as Baslow Bar are apparently derived from a very old word meaning the crest of a hill, though in time 'bar' came to mean a horseway up a steep hill. Most of Derbyshire's Celtic names are in the upland parts of the county, with about half in the north-west; only Barr Hall, near Walton-upon-Trent, is in the extreme south of the county. This village, and the Walton near Chesterfield, take their names from an English word for a small settlement of native Britons.

Most interesting of all are the three *eccles* names in the Peak District, which point to the location of churches that were established by groups of priests sometime after Constantine made Christianity the official religion of the Roman Empire in the early fourth century and which survived the withdrawal of the Roman troops. The name was derived from Latin *ecclesia* and has a shared origin with the Welsh *eglwys*. First, the river Ecclesbourne rises close to Wirksworth church, at the centre of the major lead field in the Low Peak. Second, Eccles House stands half-a-mile from Hope church and close to the Roman fort at *Navio*, which guarded the northern lead field in the High Peak. Third, and less obvious as an early centre, the dramatic landmark of Eccles Pike rises sharply to the west of Chapel-en-le-Frith, with another Eccles House just below it. These names provide important evidence of continuity through the centuries for which we have few documents and only a patchy archaeological record.

Angles

No British leader had sufficient authority to rule the whole of the land that had been abandoned by the Romans. Legend has it that, after the Roman withdrawal, a British tribal leader called Vortigern invited Anglo-Saxon mercenaries from across the North Sea, who subsequently rebelled and seized eastern territories for themselves. The group of warriors who eventually invaded Derbyshire and who gave their name to England were the Angles, who came from the Schleswig-Holstein peninsula between modern Germany and Denmark. Between the fifth and seventh centuries intermittent war was waged between small bands of warriors, while the native population continued their immemorial way of life mostly undisturbed. The victorious English fighters replaced the British leaders, but they did not kill or drive away the families who worked the land, produced the food and paid the taxes. Genetic studies have shown that the English farming families that crossed the sea after the success of the invading armies were greatly outnumbered by the native population.

Pollen analysis and other evidence indicates that the climate deteriorated from the late Roman period onwards. Increased rainfall and frequent floods made the Trent valley more difficult to farm. The Angles did not penetrate this far west in a major way until the sixth century, so a huge gap appears in the archaeological record. When the organised production of the Roman Empire came to an end, farmers perhaps returned to subsistence agriculture and the use of organic and perishable materials. The boundaries of the Romano-British farms on the gravel terraces along the Middle Trent valley and its fringes nevertheless provided a broad framework for the development of Anglian settlement. At Willington they influenced the alignment of the ridge-and-furrow patterns in the open fields that were developed much later. The earliest Anglian farms seem to have been scattered across the countryside, but so far only a few early Anglian settlements have been discovered in the Middle Trent valley and they are hard to place within a broader landscape context. The sites that have been examined remained in use until the Anglo-Scandinavian period, when they were apparently abandoned in favour of the new villages that were appearing at that time.

The heathen burial sites that have been found from Newark to Burton-on-Trent and beyond indicate that the Trent valley was the route by which the Angles came into Nottinghamshire and Derbyshire. These pagan cemeteries include two Derbyshire examples to the south of the river at King's Newton and Stapenhill, which probably date from the mid-sixth century. The King's Newton cemetery contained several hundred cremation urns covered with flat stones and placed in rows on stone flags about two feet below ground level. The place-name evidence has few pointers to early settlement, except that Repton, 'the hill of the Hrype', contains a tribal name that is repeated as far away as Ripon (Yorkshire) and possibly Ripley in east Derbyshire. Repton rises above the south bank of the Trent, in a region where pagan cremation cemeteries are found. This type of cemetery fell out of use in the Trent valley in the early seventh century.

Mercia

The Mercians were the 'boundary folk', and the general consensus now is that this border was shared with the British to the west. Until the ninth century, when they were defeated by the Vikings, the Mercians were the most successful of the peoples who are known to us collectively as the Anglo-Saxons. Their original heartland consisted of much of modern Staffordshire, Leicestershire and

Nottinghamshire and of south Derbyshire and north Warwickshire. According to Bede, their kingdom was divided in two by the river Trent. Repton may have been the original capital of South Mercia, for here in 653 Peada, son of King Penda of Mercia, married the Christian daughter of King Oswy of Northumbria and St Wystan's church later became the mausoleum for the kings of Mercia. In 669, however, St Chad was installed at Lichfield as bishop of Mercia and Lindsey and by 691 Tamworth was the chief residence of the Mercian kings. Both Lichfield and Tamworth were better situated than Repton for communication with other parts of the kingdom. The capital of North Mercia was probably Derby, whose earlier name was Northworthy. As the successor of the long-abandoned Roman fort at Little Chester, it occupied the high ground on the west bank of the Derwent, at the hub of communications by road and river.

The Repton stone. This fragment of an Anglian cross, perhaps dating from the eighth century, shows a man riding a horse, carrying a shield and a dagger. It has been suggested that this may be a representation of Aethelbald, King of Mercia, who was murdered, then buried at Repton about 757.

PHOTOGRAPH BY CARNEGIE, WITH PERMISSION OF DERBY MUSEUMS AND ART GALLERY

Mercia emerged as a mighty political power in the first half of the seventh century under Penda, whose prowess as a warrior enabled him to unite the various tribes in the Midlands. Bede wrote that, at his last battle in 655, Penda was supported by 30 tribal rulers. With his ally, the British king Cadwallon, he ended the supremacy of the kingdom of Northumbria by defeating Edwin at Hatfield in 633 and Oswald near Oswestry in 642. After his death in 655, the Northumbrians annexed North Mercia but allowed Penda's son, Peada, to rule South Mercia, where he became the first Christian king. Peada was murdered within a year but in time his younger brother Wulfhere recovered the whole of Mercia and eventually became overlord of most of the southern English. Penda's dynasty and Mercian strength were continued by Aethelred, then by Aethelbald, who was murdered in 757 after a successful reign of 47 years and buried in the crypt of the church at Repton. After a brief civil war the Mercian throne passed to his cousin, the war lord Offa, under whom the kingdom of Mercia reached its widest extent, stretching across the Midlands from his famous dyke that marked the border with Wales. Mercian influence declined sharply after his death in 796, and though it survived as a kingdom until 870 it then became part of Wessex.

The Peak District

A seventh-century list known as the *Tribal Hidage* names the tribes or small kingdoms that paid tribute to the Mercians (or perhaps with Mercia to the Northumbrians). One of the groups on the northern edge of the Mercian heartland were known as the *Pecsaetan*. Their territory was recorded as *Pecsaetna lond*, 'the land of the settlers of the Peak'. Historians long thought that these settlers were Angles, but it is more likely that they were native people, like their northern neighbours in the small kingdom of Elmet, which remained independent until it fell to the Northumbrians in 617. As recent DNA studies have shown that the majority of present-day British people are descended from the prehistoric inhabitants of Britain, it is likely that the post-Roman inhabitants of the Peak District were from the same stock that established the first farms there in Neolithic times. And just as the memory of Elmet lasted in later medieval place-names, so the *Pecsaetan* retained their identity in succeeding centuries. Three hundred years after the *Tribal Hidage*, the *Anglo-Saxon Chronicle* for 920 referred to Bakewell as being in *Peac lond* and a charter of 963 described Ballidon as being 'in the district of' the *Pecsaetan*. Their territory therefore extended over both the High Peak and the

The Benty Grange helmet. Discovered in 1848 by Thomas Bateman upon an excavation near Monyash, this chieftain's helmet is nationally famous as one of just three of its kind that have been discovered at Anglo-Saxon sites in England.

Low Peak to include the whole of what we now know as the Peak District. The *Pecsaetan* seem to have been the ancestors of the *Peakrills*, the derogatory name given to the local inhabitants a thousand years later.

The Angles penetrated the Peak District by the mid-seventh century. Although pagan cremation cemeteries are not found there, some White Peak place-names go back to the heathen period. The clearest example is Wensley, 'the grove or clearing dedicated to Woden'. Another possibility is Friden, recorded in 963 as Frigdene, the valley perhaps named after the heathen goddess Frig (who, like Woden, has given us the name of a day in the week). A large number of place-names and field-names contain the element *hlaw*, which could mean simply a mound or a hill, but in Derbyshire it usually has the more precise meaning of burial mound. Ten examples have a short Old English personal name as their first element: Atlow, Baslow, Hawks Low, Hucklow, Knotlow, Ows Low, Shacklow, Snelslow, Spark Low and Tideslow; Cadley (a corruption of Cadlow) is the only such name from south of the Trent. Kenneth Cameron's opinion was that some of these names probably belong to the pagan period, as do Hurdlow (Hartington Middle Quarter, 'the treasure mound') and the lost *Heathen's Low* (Bakewell). The warriors who led the Angles into the Peak District chose prehistoric burial grounds for their tombs, perhaps in a deliberate symbolic attempt to claim possession of this ancient landscape from the leaders of the *Pecsaetan*.

As in earlier periods, much of our evidence is restricted to burial sites. Many of these were excavated in a quick and amateurish fashion in the nineteenth century by Thomas Bateman and other antiquaries and the finds were placed in museums. At Lapwing Hill, near Brushfield, Bateman excavated the burial of an Anglian warrior within a shallow cist covered by a barrow 17 yards in diameter. Then, in 1848 he made his most famous discovery: a chieftain's helmet at Benty Grange, near Monyash. The helmet was made of iron bands that radiated from the crown of the head to a circle of iron round the brow and of plates of horn that were fastened to the iron frame by silver rivets. A silver filigree cross decorated the rib that protected the nose and a small figure of a bronze and silver-gilt boar with eyes of garnet was fixed to the crown. This helmet is one of only three of its kind which have so far been discovered in England; the others are from the major sites at Sutton Hoo in Suffolk and Coppergate, York. The boar crest was commonly worn by Teutonic warriors in honour of the goddess Frig, but in the Benty Grange helmet it was combined with a Christian cross. The grave also contained the remains of a leather cup, decorated with silver edges, four wheel-shaped silver ornaments and two silver crosses. The survival of fragments of three hanging-bowl escutcheons in yellow enamel on a red background dated the grave to the second half of the seventh century. Most of the decorative items found in the Derbyshire barrows can be dated to this period by comparison with similar finds in other parts of the country. Contemporary shield bosses have been found at The Low (Alsop), at Boar's Low (Tissington) and at Hilton.

High-ranking women were buried with their necklaces and brooches; some also had iron knives and occasionally spears. In the eighteenth century a silver-gilt brooch with garnets set on gold foil, a garnet and gold filigree pendant cross, a silver collar and other precious articles were found at White Low on Winster Moor. At Galley Low on Brassington Moor, Bateman unearthed a fine seventh-century gold necklace with garnet pendants from within a Bronze Age barrow. At Cow Low near Buxton the remains of the head dress of another noble lady interred in a Bronze Age barrow included two gold pins, set with ruby glass and linked together with a gold chain. Her box, which was made of ash wrapped in a woollen cloth, had two brass hinges and a hasp, fastened by an iron padlock; it contained an ivory comb, a silver pendant necklace, a blue glass bead and other personal possessions. The grave goods that have been found in these Peak District mounds suggest pagan beliefs, yet the bodies were placed facing east in the Christian manner.

When John Lucas excavated the communal grave of members of another noble Anglian family in 1869 at the Bronze Age barrow at Wigber Low, near Kniveton, he deposited his finds of gold, silver, and other objects in

The massive earthwork known as the Grey Ditch which descends the steep hillside north-east of Bradwell cuts across Batham Gate, the Roman road from Navio to Buxton, and so must date from after the retreat of the Romans. The most likely explanation is that it was constructed to mark the boundary between the Britons and the advancing Angles. It consists of a high rampart erected on a wide base, with a V-shaped ditch on the northern side. Such linear earthworks are a rarity in Derbyshire.

the British Museum. John Collis's modern excavation of the site showed that these ornaments belonged to a group of six or more burials that had been placed in or around the ancient barrow. They may have been members of an important household over two or three generations, perhaps even relatives or descendants of Wicga whose name has been attached to the site? In this total excavation over many seasons, every stone was plotted and thousands of bones and objects were recorded, so that by using computer graphics the barrow has been reconstructed at each of its stages and then rebuilt to give an impression of how it would have appeared in the seventh century.

Derbyshire does not have major dyke systems to define boundaries, like those in Yorkshire, except for the Grey Ditch that descends the hillside north-east of Bradwell and cuts across Batham Gate, the Roman road from *Navio* to Buxton, and across the main route from the Hope valley to the limestone plateau. A section cut through this linear earthwork showed that the rampart was 2.5 metres high and seven metres wide at its base and and that the ditch on the northern side was roughly V-shaped, 1.80 metres deep and seven metres wide. The Grey Ditch is clearly post-Roman, but it seems to be well inside the territory of the *Pecsaetan*. Perhaps it was a temporary, agreed boundary between the advancing Angles in the south and the surviving British stronghold in the north?

Most of the British place-names in the Peak District were gradually replaced with Mercian ones. The clearest evidence comes from names derived from the Mercian word *waella*, meaning a spring, such as Bakewell, Bradwell, Blackwell and Tideswell. In Derbyshire, they are found most frequently in the Peak District. The linguistic evidence suggests that, north of the Trent, the original Mercia did not extend east of the Derwent, except in the north-east near the Yorkshire border, where Anglians may have penetrated from the Humber and the Don. Place-names in the north-west, beyond the highest points of the Peak

District, have a different character from those elsewhere in Derbyshire: Milton is the only example of a *tun* name; and Buxworth, Charlesworth, Chisworth, Hollinworth, Ludworth and Rowarth form as many *worth* names as in the rest of the county put together. The Angles probably entered this remote district from Cheshire, perhaps a little later than elsewhere, for here we have the survival of the largest group of British place-names in Derbyshire.

The final decades of the Roman Empire and the thinly recorded centuries that followed are the most contentious in British history. National origin myths that are based largely on the writings of Bede have been challenged by archaeologists who say there is no excavated evidence to support the theory of mass migrations from Europe by the people whom we know as the Anglo-Saxons. And now geneticists tell us that the immigrants who followed the warriors across the North Sea amounted to no more than 5–10 per cent of the population. The Ancient Britons were not driven out. Rather, they continued to form the bulk of the population who farmed the land much as before. The military leadership had changed, but tribes such as the *Pecsaetan* continued a way of life that had long been familiar to their ancestors.

Detail of the Benty Grange helmet. The boar crest symbolised the pagan goddess Frig, but this warrior also adorned his helmet with a Christian cross.

The origins of Derbyshire

Place-names and settlement

The old idea that the Anglo-Saxons lived in villages from the time of their arrival in England has been discredited. The archaeological evidence is that most of the new settlers lived in scattered farmsteads, much like the native British, and that villages were unknown in the places whence they came. These dispersed settlements seem to have been founded within a framework of large units, known to historians as 'multiple estates' or 'folk territories', some of which were perhaps already ancient when the invaders arrived. Villages were formed much later; in Derbyshire they date perhaps from the second half of the ninth century onwards, though we have no firm evidence.

Some of the place-names of our present towns and villages were recorded in the two or three centuries before the Norman Conquest, but most made their first appearance in Domesday Book in 1086. This means that we cannot date the origins of settlements with any confidence, nor can we be certain of the original forms of their names. It was once thought that the ubiquity of Old English place-names meant that the native population of Britain had been driven out by thousands of Anglo-Saxon warriors and settlers, but archaeo-logical and genetic evidence has shown that this did not happen. Bryan Sykes's Oxford Genetic Atlas Project estimates that in southern England the combined Anglo-Saxon and Viking population amounted to no more than 10 per cent of the whole and that in the northern half of England it was no higher than 15 per cent. In remote places like the Peak District the proportion of immigrants from the Continent of Europe and Scandinavia must have been even lower, despite the names imposed on settlements by the new lords. Derbyshire has few place-names that are thought to have been of a very early Anglo-Saxon type. The Angles were not triumphant here until well into the seventh century. They replaced the old rulers but the great majority of the people who farmed the land were descended from the native Britons.

Throughout England the largest group of place-names that were recorded by 731, when Bede wrote his great history, refer to features of the landscape, such as hills, valleys, fords and springs. Judging by their names, some of the places that lay at the heart of the great estates that we know about in later times, notably Ashbourne, Ashford, Bakewell and Hope, may already have been significant by this time. So may Chesterfield and Duffield, whose large territories were centred on settlements within extensive pastures in woodland landscapes, for this was the original interpretation of the place-name element -*feld* before it evolved into its modern meaning of field. Domesday Book records 11 examples of this type of name n Derbyshire, six of them in the High Peak. It also lists 13 examples of -*dun* 'hill', 11 of -*waella* 'spring', eight of -*halh* 'nook' and seven of -*ford*. Another interesting group of Old English place-names is that containing the element *ofer*, meaning 'a flat-topped ridge with a convex shoulder'. We can usually see what was meant when we visit Ashover, Birchover, Bolsover, Calver, Codnor, Edensor, Heanor, Littleover and Mickleover, or when we view Cobnor Wood at Barlow from the dual carriageway between Sheffield and Chesterfield.

By far the largest number of Anglian place-names in Derbyshire, however, are those that end in -ton or -ley. These are thought to date from after 750, indeed some minor names ending in -ley are not recorded until after the Norman Conquest. A -*tun* was a small settlement that eventually became a village surrounded by arable fields. A -*leah* was a clearing in a wood, or a wood pasture, including some grassy spots that had been denuded of many of their trees and shrubs well before the arrival of the Angles. The first element of these types of place-name was often the personal name of the man who in later times would be known as the lord of the manor. The lowlands of south Derbyshire and the coal-measure sandstones in the east of the county have numerous -*tuns* and another group can be found in the eastern part of the Peak District. Derbyshire has over 100 examples recorded in Domesday Book or shortly afterwards. The -*leahs* were found amongst the numerous managed woods where the farmers pursued a more pastoral economy than those who lived and worked in districts whose fertile soils had long been used for growing cereals. Both types of name were given to settlements that emerged within an older framework of large estates. Bakewell, for instance, was surrounded with small places such as Beeley, Longstone, Pilsley, Rowsley, Sheldon and Taddington, while Chesterfield's outliers included Brampton, Brimington, Tapton, Temple Normanton, Walton and Whittington and a number of minor places with -*leah* names.

Place-names ending in -*worth*, meaning an enclosure, are essentially Mercian in origin. Tamworth was the capital of the kingdom of Mercia. The most important example in Derbyshire is Wirksworth, 'the enclosure of Weorc or Wyrc', a well-documented Old English personal name. Wirksworth was recorded in 835 when a Mercian nobleman, Humbert, was granted land there by the Abbess of Repton in return for an annual rent of lead payable to the Archbishop of Canterbury. This, incidentally, is the only firm evidence that we have for the working of lead in the White Peak during the Anglian period. A group of -*worth* names in the far north-west of the county form as many of this type as in the rest of Derbyshire put together.

The *Anglo-Saxon Chronicle* records that in 828 the king of Northumbria submitted to Egbert of Wessex immediately beyond their boundary at Dore and that in 942 Edmund, son of Edward the Elder, conquered the Danes of Mercia 'as far as where Dore divides'. The place-name means a 'narrow pass' or literally a door at the boundary. The border between Mercia and Northumbria was defined clearly, with no overlapping secular estates or parishes. The *-burh* endings in the names of both Mosborough and Barlborough, on either side of the river Rother at the northern edge of Derbyshire, suggest fortifications, but no earthworks have been found there and no firm date can be assigned to the names. Pilsbury, Norbury and Sudbury, which seemingly guard passages across the river Dove at the opposite side of the county, pose a similar problem.

Minsters

As we have seen, the *eccles* names near Brough, Chapel-en-le-Frith and Wirksworth show that at least some Christian communities continued to worship after the withdrawal of the Romans. The invading Angles were pagans and those in Mercia did not turn to Christianity until King Peada married the daughter of the Christian king of Northumbria in 653 and invited four priests as missionaries from Lindisfarne. As in other parts of England, the Mercian royal family imposed Christianity on their subjects. Our evidence is derived mostly from Bede and the other English monks who wrote the biographies of early saints, kept the *Anglo-Saxon Chronicle* up to date, and generally underplayed the role of the native British church.

Diuma, the Irish leader of the four Lindisfarne missionaries, was based in Repton, the early capital of South Mercia, where the king founded a double monastery for men and women. The site was probably already a high-status one, for large timber buildings have been discovered by excavation underneath the monastery. At that time, the river Trent flowed below the cliff that forms the northern edge of the monastic church and alongside Monsom Lane which led to the ferry at Twyford, but its course is now half-a-mile to the north. Repton soon became the favourite choice of burial ground for the royal family of Mercia. Merewalh, the third son of Penda and king of the *Maegonsaetan* tribe, was buried there in or about 686; then a succession of Mercian kings – Aethelbald (757), Wiglaf (840) and Wystan (849) – were buried in the same eighth-century chamber or mausoleum. Soon after his canonisation, the shrine of the murdered St Wystan at Repton began to attract pilgrims.

Harold Taylor has shown that the chamber, much of which now lies below ground level, was probably built for Aethelbald's burial in 757 and covered with a timber-framed roof. The internal recesses on three of its sides are thought to have contained shrines for each of the royal burials. Then, about the time of Wiglaf's burial in 840, the sanctuary of a new church was erected over the chamber and extended to the west by a central tower and nave, perhaps replacing an earlier church that may have stood immediately to the west of the chamber. Following the burial of St Wystan, stairs leading down from the north and south *porticus* of the new church were cut into the chamber, so turning it into a crypt through which pilgrims could wind their way. Pilgrims kept coming to Repton until Wystan's remains were removed to Evesham by King Cnut. The later reconstruction of what became the parish church of St Wystan obliterated much of the Mercian building, but the crypt, chancel, eastern angles of the crossing and part of the north transept survive from the eighth and ninth centuries. The crypt was rediscovered in 1779 and exactly 200 years later part of the top stone of a high cross shaft, with carvings on both sides, was found just outside its east window. Martin and Birthe Biddle, who led the modern excavations, interpreted the image as a carving of Aethelbald as a rider (see the photograph on page 60).

Repton church was severely damaged by the Danish army when they wintered here in 873–74, but it was eventually restored, at least in part, and continued to be used throughout the remaining Anglo-Scandinavian period; a collegiate community was recorded there in Domesday Book. Repton parish had dependent chapelries at Bretby, Foremark, Ingleby, Measham, Milton, Newton Smisby, Solney and Ticknall, all of which were given to the Augustinian priory that was established next to the old church in 1172. The compactness

The interior of the crypt at Repton church, reached by a narrow staircase from the transept of the church. This became a celebrated place of pilgrimage to the shrine of St Wystan.
PHOTOGRAPH: CARNEGIE

LEFT
St Wystan's church, Repton. The chancel of this important and ancient church was erected in the later Anglo-Saxon period in a characteristically tall and narrow design with a string course and pilaster strips in the upper section; the original windows were replaced by the present larger ones later in the Middle Ages. The walls are clearly of more than one date. The darker stones at the bottom mark the crypt which was built as a mausoleum for King Aethelbald of Mercia in 757 and which became a popular shrine for pilgrims after the murder of St Wystan in 849.
PHOTOGRAPH: CARNEGIE

of this group of chapelries suggests that Repton parish originally covered most of that part of Derbyshire which lay south of the Trent. Nevertheless, it soon lost its ecclesiastical pre-eminence to Lichfield, which is where St Chad established his see in 669 when he was appointed bishop of Mercia and Lindsey (north Lincolnshire). Three Derbyshire churches – Barton Blount, Longford and Wilne – are dedicated to St Chad. By the eighth century the bishops of Lichfield had become substantial landowners within the Derbyshire part of their diocese.

Another important early minster, or mother church, was St Alkmund's, Derby, whose nineteenth-century successor was demolished in 1976 to make way for a ring-road. Excavations led by C.A. Ralegh Radford proved that the church, which was situated close to the north gate of the later borough, was in existence by the eighth, perhaps even the late seventh century. Its original dedication must have been different, for St Alkmund, the younger son of the king of Northumbria, was killed about the year 800. His remains were moved later from Lilleshall to Derby and pilgrims were attracted to his shrine. The discovery of a richly decorated, stone sarcophagus in which his body is believed to have been laid was made during the excavation of St Alkmund's; the grave that was found alongside it was that of a high-status individual. Fragments of two high crosses (similar to another found in 1844) were also recovered. The excavators demonstrated that the earliest church on the site consisted of a nave (44 feet × 19 feet) with a sanctuary at the east end (14 feet × 12 feet). Towards the eastern end of the south wall of the nave a *porticus* (nine feet × seven feet) was entered through a wooden-framed internal doorway, probably opposite a similar one on the north wall. This simple plan was adopted by many early Anglo-Saxon minsters. The reputation of St Alkmund's church must have peaked in the mid-ninth century, just before the Danes invaded Mercia. In 871 the body of the Mercian ealdorman Aethelwulf, who was killed near Reading, was brought by stealth and buried here.

The Domesday Book entry for Derby recorded a collegiate church, which can be identified as that of St Alkmund, in the time of King Edward the Confessor. By then, the nearby church of All Saints (now the cathedral) was a wealthier, secular collegiate church, or royal free chapel as it was known in the twelfth century, but as no archaeological investigation of this site has taken place we cannot date its foundation. Derby was the only place in the county with more than one parish church. In the Norman period it had five parishes that included not only a share of the town but which stretched over the neighbouring countryside. Taken together, these large parishes probably define the limits of a large royal Mercian estate, typical of those that covered much of Derbyshire but very different from the small, urban parishes in the rest of the Five Boroughs of the East Midlands.

Minster churches on other large, royal estates can be identified or inferred from various scraps of evidence at Ashbourne, Bakewell, Chesterfield, Hope and Wirksworth. Dawn Hadley's analysis of the evidence for mother-parishes in Derbyshire and Nottinghamshire suggests that the minster churches of Ashbourne and Bakewell were formed before some outlying townships became small, independent estates, though not independent parishes, during the tenth century. Whether all these royal estates supported minster churches before the Viking invasions is unclear as we simply do not have enough evidence.

Ashbourne church was probably the original focus of the settlement there, for it is sited well to the west of the market town that was laid out after the Norman Conquest. The dedication is to Oswald, king of Northumbria, a popular saint in the North who was killed in battle in 642. The conversion of Mercia from Lindisfarne began not long after his death; perhaps Ashbourne was one of the earliest of the new Christian centres? The size and splendour of the present church demonstrates its importance, but the earliest architecture dates from the thirteenth century and just one fragment of sculpture survives from before the Norman Conquest. Nor is there any documentary record of Ashbourne before Domesday Book, when a priest and church were recorded. When William II gave the dues of Ashbourne parish to Lincoln Cathedral in 1093, his gift included the dependent chapelries and thus provided a clue to Ashbourne's early importance. Ashbourne was the mother church of Alsop, Bradley, Edlaston, Fenny Bentley, Hognaston, Kniveton, Mappleton, Parwich and Thorpe, and as this enormous parish was partly bisected by the parish of Bradbourne, which included the townships of Atlow, Ballidon, Bradbourne, Brassington and Tissington, it is likely that they too belonged to Ashbourne originally.

St Mary's, Wirksworth, was founded on another large and ancient royal estate beyond the north-eastern border of Ashbourne. As we have seen, the name of the river Ecclesbourne, which rises nearby, suggests the presence of a Christian community there in the Roman period. The large, circular churchyard, encircled by town houses looking inwards, hints at an unusual foundation. A church and priest were recorded in Domesday Book. When Henry I gave the dues of the church to Lincoln Cathedral in 1100–07, Wirksworth parish included the chapelries of Alderwasley, Alton, Ashleyhay, Biggin, Callow, Cromford, Hopton, Ible, Idridgehay and Middleton-by-Wirksworth. It was also the mother church of the later independent parishes of Bonsall, Carsington and Kirk Ireton and probably also Matlock and Tansley. Perhaps at one time Darley and its dependencies of Wensley and Snitterton were also included within its territory? In other words, Wirksworth's minster church may have served the whole of the central part of Derbyshire that lay between the royal estates of Ashbourne to the south-west, Duffield to the east, and Bakewell to the north. A spectacular figure sculpture, one of the best from the whole of Anglo-Saxon England, was discovered in the church in 1820 and is now displayed on the wall of the north aisle. Its date is uncertain but is thought to be not later than 800. As it must have been the cover of the tomb of an important saint who was buried here, the sculpture provides striking confirmation of Wirksworth's early importance.

St Alkmund's sarcophagus. Discovered during the excavations at St Alkmund's church, Derby, in the 1970s, this is thought to be the original tomb of the patron saint, who was murdered about the year 800 in Shropshire and whose body was brought to Derby, at that time known as Northworthy. St Alkmund's shrine became an object of pilgrimage.

PHOTOGRAPH BY CARNEGIE, WITH PERMISSION OF DERBY MUSEUMS AND ART GALLERY

The ancient parish church of Wirksworth occupies a circular churchyard with town houses facing into it. St Mary's was the minster church for the hundred or wapentake of Wirksworth. It stands large and proud with a crossing tower and is mainly in the Perpendicular Gothic style of the late middle ages, much restored by Sir George Gilbert Scott in the 1870s.

PHOTOGRAPH: CARNEGIE

This remarkable coffin lid, now displayed on the north wall of the nave of St Mary's church, Wirksworth, was found during alterations in 1820. It has been dated on stylistic grounds to about AD 800, and is thought to have marked the burial of a saint. The church seems to be the successor to the *eccles* that stood hereabouts in Roman times and which has given the Ecclesbourne its name. St Mary's was an important minster church in the Anglo-Scandinavian period. The scenes carved on the slab depict stories from the life of Christ: washing the disciples' feet; the Crucifixion with the Lamb of God on a Greek cross; the burial of the Virgin Mary; the presentation in the Temple; the descent into Hell; the Ascension; the Annunciation; and St Peter receiving a scroll from the Virgin and Child. It is one of the most important pieces of pre-Conquest sculpture in England.

PHOTOGRAPH: CARNEGIE

The evidence for Duffield having been a minster church is less clear-cut, but the church is dedicated to St Alkmund and it occupies a now isolated position on the right bank of the river Derwent, well away from the site of the Norman castle and the medieval settlement, but easy of access from those parts of the large parish that lay on the opposite side of the river. The manor of Duffield covered an extensive estate which after the Norman Conquest became a royal forest known as Duffield Frith.

The enormous territory that was served by the minster church of All Saints, Bakewell covered the royal estates of Bakewell and Ashford. It stretched as far west as the old Roman road that crossed the White Peak from Derby to Buxton, as far north as the deep valley of the river Wye, and even beyond

During the extensive restoration and rebuilding of Bakewell church in the 1840s, a unique collection of Anglo-Saxon cross fragments, medieval carved grave slabs and floor tiles were discovered in the foundations. Most of these are now assembled in the south porch. They form the largest and most varied collection of this kind in the country. The grave slabs with carvings of foliated crossings, which are stacked on the west side of the porch, date from the twelfth and thirteenth centuries. As was usual, they are not inscribed with any name, but some bear symbols, such as a sword for a knight, shears for a wool merchant, a bugle horn for a Peak Forest warden, a bow and arrow for an archer, or a chalice for a priest. Such men would have been benefactors of the church and were buried inside the building. The decorated tiles on the east side of the porch (*below*) can be dated on stylistic grounds to the thirteenth century.

this valley in the north-east. The river Derwent formed its eastern boundary, except where Beeley was taken in, and in the south it included Youlgreave. Long after the Norman Conquest, the parish of Bakewell included the chapelries of Ashford, Baslow, Beeley, Buxton, Chelmorton, Hassop, Longstone, Monyash, Over Haddon, Rowland, Rowsley, Sheldon and Taddington, all of which were expected to contribute towards maintaining the fabric of Bakewell church and the upkeep of the churchyard. A remarkable collection of pre-Conquest fragments of sculptured crosses and grave covers, most of which were found when All Saints was rebuilt in the 1840s, are displayed in the south porch, together with some later ones. They form the largest collection of fragments of free-standing Anglian and Viking sculpture in the land. Standing in the churchyard is the decorated shaft of a cross that is eight feet high even with the cross-head missing. The carvings on the side facing the church depict the Crucifixion, Annunciation, and other Christian scenes that are now indecipherable, but the figure and vine-scroll ornamentation on the eastern side may be pagan. It has usually been regarded as an eighth-century Mercian sculpture, but may be as late as the early tenth century. Other crosses in the churchyard include one that was moved from Blackwell, a few miles up the Wye valley. Bakewell was the wealthiest manor in the Peak District at the time of Domesday Book and a church and two priests were recorded there, as at Repton. From 1192 the Dean and Chapter of Lichfield acquired most of the church's income.

Further north, St Peter's, Hope stood at the centre of an enormous royal estate in the High Peak, close to the Roman fort and *vicus* at Brough and the *eccles* that is commemorated by Eccles House. The estate and minster territory stretched from the county boundary in Longdendale to the north as far south as the Wye valley and thus included places that became independent parishes after the Norman Conquest: Castleton, Chapel-en-le-Frith, Tideswell, and their chapelries. In 1192 it too was given to the Dean and Chapter at Lichfield. No pre-Conquest architecture can be seen in the later medieval church, but a tall Anglo-Scandinavian cross stands in the raised, circular churchyard.

Another Derbyshire church that seems to have had minster status in its early days, though we have no firm evidence to prove it, is St Mary and All Saints, Chesterfield. The earliest surviving architectural features in this imposing building date from the thirteenth century and no crosses or other pre-Conquest sculptural fragments survive. The first documentary evidence dates from 1093, when the church in the 'manor of Chesterfield' and its dependent chapelries were given to Lincoln Cathedral. This parish was over 45 square miles in area and its chapelries included Brampton, Brimington, Calow, Hasland, Newbold, Tapton, Temple Normanton, Walton, Whittington and Wingerworth. Chesterfield was the only large royal manor in Scarsdale and it is tempting to think that the minster once served the whole of the wapentake. The church stands on the site of a Roman fort, and a nearby holy well was guarded by St Helen's chapel.

This important cross in Bakewell churchyard stands eight feet high, even though its cross-head has been removed. Most sides are carved with animals and vine-scroll ornamentation, but the side facing the church (*right*) has rather worn human figures. Scholars disagree as to whether it is a Mercian sculpture of the eighth or ninth centuries or whether it dates from the 920s, after Edward the Elder's northern advance against Viking forces. It is thought that it originally stood in the countryside and was brought to the churchyard for safe keeping.

PHOTOGRAPH: CARNEGIE

Vikings

Occasional raids on England by Scandinavian pirates began in the late eighth century, but it was not until 865 that what the *Anglo-Saxon Chronicle* described as a 'great heathen raiding army', led by Halfdan, landed in East Anglia and conquered that kingdom within a year. We do not know the size of this army, but even if it consisted of just two or three thousand men it would have appeared enormous in the sparsely populated country of that time. After moving north to capture York, Halfdan's army invaded Mercia and during the winter of 867–68 established a base at Nottingham, where they were joined by a second invading force under Guthrum. The Mercians had to appeal to the kingdom of Wessex for help. After an uneasy peace, the Danish army moved south into Berkshire, where they were thwarted by forces led by Aethelwulf, an ealdorman, whose Mercian origins were commemorated after his death in battle in 870 by the removal of his body 'to the province of the Mercians, to the

RIGHT
Excavations at Repton, 1976. The excavations at St Wystan's church, Repton, revealed the external walls and the plinth of the eighth-century crypt which had become obscured by the rising ground level over the centuries.
PHOTOGRAPH: AUTHOR

| DERBYSHIRE: A HISTORY

Cross shaft, St Peter's church, Hope. The dating of these Anglo-Scandinavian crosses is controversial, with suggestions varying between the late ninth and the early eleventh century. Most were defaced as idolatrous structures at the Reformation, but the surviving parts were re-erected in the nineteenth century. This one has typical interlace designs and pairs of figures.

place called Northworthy, but Derby in the Danish tongue'. In 872 the Danes moved back north into Mercia and in 873, under the leadership of four kings – Halfdan, Guthrum, Oscytel and Anund – they sacked and burned the town and monastery of Repton and stayed there over the following winter.

The excavation of the area around St Wystan's church and Repton Priory has been a major research project directed by Martin and Birthe Biddle. They believe that the massive, D-shaped ditch and bank, which they discovered there was the winter headquarters of the Viking Great Army in 873–74. It enclosed 3½ acres, incorporating the church and stretching as far east as the Repton Brook and as far north as the old course of the river Trent. After the Vikings had inflicted considerable damage on the Mercian holy site, they recognised its symbolic importance and established themselves alongside it. The graves included that of a warrior buried with his sword, a boar's tusk and a Thor's hammer pendant. Beneath a low mound to the west of the church, the Biddles also discovered a small, stone building with two rooms, aligned east-west, which they interpreted as another mausoleum of the royal family of Mercia, that was re-used for the burial of a Viking chief.

Until the Danes were driven back in the early tenth century by Edward the Elder and his sister Aethelflaed, the old Mercian Christian centres were subdued. St Wystan's church was eventually restored, but the monastic community was reduced to a small collegiate community of priests. St Alkmund's, the minster church at Derby, seems to have been severely damaged in the same Viking invasion, but it too was repaired and by the late tenth or early eleventh century it had recovered some of its former glory.

Two-and-a-half miles south-east of Repton, Heath Wood, Ingleby, contains the most important pagan burial site in Viking England. It consists of 59 barrows arranged in four distinct clusters and as long ago as 1855 it attracted the attention of Thomas Bateman. Some of the mounds were excavated more thoroughly in 1941 and in recent years Julian D. Richards has re-examined the old finds and has excavated two mounds and the area between them in a modern, scientific manner. The finds from the 20 barrows that had been excavated earlier were unspectacular and badly burnt. They included the remains of swords and their attachments, numerous iron nails, part of a spur and some finer items, all of which were entirely Viking in style, and the bones of domesticated animals. It seems that the cemetery was used only for a short time and by a distinctive group of people who burned their dead on pyres and celebrated funerals with feasts.

From this cemetery, St Wystan's church can be seen in the distance. From the opposite point of view, the funeral pyres would have dominated the skyline, especially at night time. Richards suggests that the dual composition of the Great Army that spent the winter of 873–74 in this neighbourhood provides an explanation for the contrast between the pagan cemetery in Heath Wood and the Christian burial ground at Repton, which contains many Viking graves. He proposes that Halfdan's army, which had been in England for nearly ten years, had converted to Christianity and had buried their dead around the Mercian royal mausoleum, which stood at the heart of their winter camp, whereas Guthrum's army were still pagans whose barrows in Heath Wood were an aggressive statement of their beliefs. His recent excavations there were mostly concerned with the excavation of just two neighbouring barrows and the area between them. One of the mounds provided evidence for a cremation hearth, large quantities of ash, charcoal and burnt bone, but the other contained nothing to suggest extreme heat; indeed, the cremation deposit appeared to have been brought to the site from somewhere else. Richards concluded that about 20 barrows had clear evidence for funeral pyres and that the rest were 'token barrows' which commemorated people whose funerals had taken place elsewhere, perhaps men who had died during the campaigns against Wessex. The cemetery must therefore date from the earliest period of Danish settlement. In 877 the victorious Great Army retained the northern half of Mercia and the warriors settled down as farmers. We know that their families had already joined them, for the skeletons of women and children have been found in the barrows. Peace with Wessex was agreed the following year, when Alfred and Guthrum agreed to a division of England.

Guthrum's share – the Danelaw – was divided into four new shires that were named after their military strongholds: Derbyshire, Nottinghamshire, Leicestershire and Lincolnshire. These new shires were occupied by separate divisions of the Danish army, each of which had taken over the territory of an existing administrative unit. The new county of Derbyshire used the Lichfield diocesan boundary, which stretched as far as Nottinghamshire in the east, Leicestershire in the south and the kingdom of Northumbria in the north. The Danish settlers in each of these counties long continued to regard themselves as distinct 'armies'. Their headquarters at their fortified strongholds became the county towns and, together with the Danish *burh* at Stamford, they were eventually known as the Five Boroughs. Derbyshire's capital was the old Mercian centre at Northworthy, which was now re-named Derby, the successor to the old Roman fort at Little Chester.

Viking place-names

Distinctive Viking place-names within Derbyshire are found principally in the Trent valley (where the Danes first invaded) and in the north-eastern wapentake of Scarsdale, not far from the border with Nottinghamshire and Yorkshire. The total number of such names, however, is significantly lower than in the rest of the East Midlands The Viking place-name element *-by*, the equivalent of the Anglo-Saxon *-tun*, occurs only ten times in the Derbyshire folios of Domesday Book, compared with 22 in Nottinghamshire, 60 in Leicestershire and 225 in Lincolnshire. As Staffordshire, too, has few examples of *-by* names, the infiltration of the Danes obviously weakened considerably as they moved west. The Derbyshire *-bys* comprise Appleby Magna, Blingsby, Bretby, Derby, Denby,

Herdby (a lost name whose site may be marked by Coxbench, Holbrook), Inglesby, Smisby, Stainsby and Wingby (a lost vill in Walton, near Chesterfield). The first element in what are now small or lost sites in Scarsdale wapentake, at Blingsby, Stainsby and Wingby, is a Scandinavian personal name; in Derby it is a Viking word for deer; in Smisby ('the settlement of the smiths') the first element could be either Old English or Scandinavian. The use of English elements in Appleby and Herdby suggests that an existing settlement was re-named by the Danes. Bretby was where a group of Britons lived, Inglesby was an English colony surrounded by the Danes who had conquered Repton, whereas Denby was different from its neighbours in belonging to the Danes. No settlement was named or re-named Kirkby or Kirby, after its church, though such names are common in other parts of the Danelaw. (However, Kirk Hallam. Kirk Ireton, Kirk Langley and Kirksterndale use the Viking version of Church to distinguish themselves from places of the same name.)

The re-naming of Northworthy as Derby and the many Danish names with English first elements suggests that many of the -bys were not new settlements. Like Nottinghamshire and Leicestershire, Derbyshire also has a considerable number of place-names in which a Scandinavian personal name is followed by Old English -tun: Foston, Kedleston, Ravenstone, Roston, Scropton, Stenson, Sturston, Swarkestone, Thulston, Thurvaston and Tupton; all except Foston are mentioned in Domesday Book. Kenneth Cameron has shown that they are found chiefly to the north of the Trent and west of the Derwent in Appletree wapentake, where distinctly Scandinavian names are absent. This pattern suggests an extension of Danish lordship over existing Anglian settlements when the large estates began to break up or when more marginal land was brought into cultivation. The frequent use of personal names in the -by and hybrid forms of place-names indicates that in some parts of Derbyshire in the late ninth and tenth centuries a great deal of land was coming into private ownership for the first time. But no -by names are found in the Peak District, where the inhabitants remained chiefly the descendants of the *Pecsaetan*, nor, more surprisingly, around Derby or any other of the Five Boroughs of the East Midlands.

The other common place-name element that points to Viking settlement, or at least ownership, is *thorp*, an outlying farmstead or hamlet. The English used a similar word, but as *thorps* are much commoner in the Danelaw than in the southern half of the country they are assumed to be mainly Viking. In south Derbyshire these secondary settlements are found near villages with English names, on poor soils, or on the edges of more fertile patches of land in the valleys of the rivers and streams that flow into the Trent. In at least nine examples the first element of a *thorp* name is a Scandinavian personal name. Many were not recorded in Domesday Book, either because they were included silently within a larger estate or sometimes because they were not founded until after the Norman Conquest, by which time many Viking words had passed into common speech in the former Danelaw. Of the 17 *thorps* in Scarsdale wapentake, only Boythorpe (Chesterfield) was recorded in Domesday Book. They were mostly clustered in and around the large parish of Chesterfield and its chapelries: at Algarthorpe (a lost name), Bagthorpe, Boythorpe, Cutthorpe Hackenthorpe, Harlesthorpe, Ingmanthorpe, Jordanthorpe, Millthorpe, Netherthorpe, Northorpe (lost), Oakerthorpe, Waterthorpe, Williamsthorpe and three Woodthorpes. Few *thorps* were established in the Peak District, where Scandinavian place-names of any kind are scarce.

We should add to the -*bys* and -*thorps* the place-names (mostly minor ones) that contain various other Scandinavian elements, whether Danish or Norwegian. Gillian Fellows Jensen's list comprises Brackenfield, Carnfield, Cutholme, Flagg, Foremark, Griffe, Hardstoft, Hasland, Hazlebadge, Holmesfield, Holme Hall, Hoon, Langwith, Lathkill, Loscoe (2), Lund (the earlier name for Heath), Rowland, Scrater, Shirland and Thurlowbooth. The last example combines a Danish personal name with booth, meaning a cattle-rearing farm, such as those which are scattered along the valley bottom in Edale. Brackenfield and Carnfield were originally Brackenthwaite and Carlingthwaite, the only Derbyshire examples of -*thwaite*, a common Norse name for a clearing, meadow or paddock in areas of Viking settlement in northern England, especially in Cumberland; most of the houses at Brackenfield are arranged around a large green which may have been the original *thwaite*. The various holmes were either low-lying meadows by rivers and streams or, in the case of Holmesfield, an 'island of open land on a ridge surrounded by moors', the equivalent of the Anglo-Saxon -*eg*, as in Abney. Langwith was derived from the Norse word *wath* for a ford, and Lund is from the Old Norse word for a grove. Numerous minor topographical names and field names show that Scandinavian words were absorbed into English vocabulary, particularly Old Norse words that have given us beck (stream), carr (marsh overgrown with alders or other brushwood), gate (road), grain (a small valley forking off another in the Upper Derwent valley), and slack (small, shallow valley).

The 13 Normantons in the East Midlands, including three in Derbyshire, commemorate Norwegian farmers who had settled on the outskirts of areas where Danish -*bys* are common. A small group of names, which are not found in Nottinghamshire and Leicestershire, indicate that men of Irish-Norwegian descent settled in Derbyshire in the later Viking period. Kirk Ireton and Ireton Farm (Weston Underwood), both recorded in Domesday Book, mean 'the farm of the Irishman or Irishmen'. The first element is Old Norse *Iri*, the term used of a Viking who had been in Ireland before moving to England, or of an Irishmen who joined the Vikings on their new adventure across the sea. The first element of nearby Mercaston is a British personal name that is recorded in north-west England, so perhaps a Briton accompanied the Vikings into Derbyshire in the tenth century; Mercaston lies within the area of the main group of hybrid Anglo-Scandinavian names.

The Viking invasions and settlements may have helped to create the flourishing land market of the tenth century. The old 'multiple estates' were breaking up and some of their components, especially those in marginal areas, passed to the Danes. Most of the Viking settlers in the East Midlands probably arrived before the advance of Wessex during the reign of Edward the Elder (died 924). Others came across the North Sea after Cnut's conquest of England at the beginning of the eleventh century, and some of his troops remained in England after the army was disbanded in 1018. The place-names that all these settlers have bequeathed to us are our main source of information about Viking settlement in Derbyshire.

The advance of Wessex

The campaign of the royal family of Wessex against the Danes began in 917 under Alfred's son and daughter, Edward the Elder and Aethelflaed, the widow of the Mercian ealdorman Aethelred. Edward occupied Towcester while, according to the *Anglo-Saxon Chronicle*, Aethelflaed, the 'Lady of the Mercians', regained Derby in 917, 'together with the region which it controlled', a phrase which implied that the county of Derbyshire was already in existence. The positions of the minster churches of St Alkmund's and All Saints on the main route through the borough suggest that the Anglo-Scandinavian settlement at Derby was sited alongside an ancient trackway above the river Derwent and the Markeaton Brook. Expansion of the settlement to the south of the brook is suggested by the positions of two other pre-Conquest churches, dedicated to St Werburgh and St Peter.

When Aethelflaed died in 918 the Mercian lords accepted Edward as their king. Edward had taken Nottingham without a fight and in 920 he built a second fort, or *burh*, there and re-fortified Manchester. In the same year, in order to strengthen his frontier half way between Manchester and Nottingham, he ordered the construction of a *burh* near Bakewell. The *Anglo-Saxon Chronicle* records that Edward went from Nottingham 'to Bakewell in the Peak of Derbyshire and had a fortress built in the neighbourhood and garrisoned'. Jan Stetka's fieldwork and documentary research has pinpointed the linear bank and outer ditch of the *burh* in the meadows at Burton, a mile south of Bakewell, on the eastern bank of the river Wye. The sub-rectangular enclosure covers about 35 acres and could therefore have accommodated large numbers of troops. But the *burh* lasted no more than 20 years before the Vikings returned under Olaf, who got as far south as Tamworth.

For most of the tenth century the Wessex kings were triumphant. Athelstan's policy of purchasing land from the Danes is demonstrated by a charter that he granted in 926 to Uhtred, an ealdorman and younger son of the Earl of Northumbria, of the large estates of Hope and Ashford 'which he had bought with sufficient money of his own ... from the pagans'. In 942 King Edmund regained full control of Derbyshire. Seven years later, when his brother Eadred was king and Uhtred was now an earl, a royal charter allowed Uhtred to reinforce the ancient importance of the church at Bakewell by founding a

Burdett's map of Derbyshire, 1767, a detail of Derby. This shows the town still largely confined within its medieval limits.

religious community there; though Eadred was careful to keep in his possession the town and the bridge over the river Wye.

The next charter, which dates from 963 when King Edgar sold an estate in Ballidon to a thegn named Aethelferth, is the most revealing of the handful that survive for Derbyshire in the Anglo-Scandinavian period. The similarity between the boundaries described in this charter and those of the present-day civil parish show that the small territories known as vills or townships which are recorded in medieval taxation returns were already in existence by the mid-tenth century; they remained the basic unit of local government for hundreds of years. But it is the description of Ballidon as being *in pago Pecset* ('in the

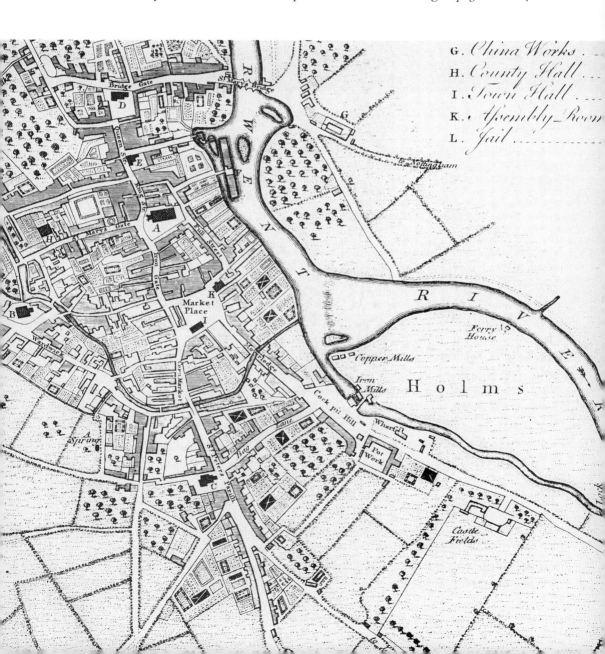

district of the *Pecsaetan*') that has excited most interest, for this second reference to the tribe is about three centuries later than the first. It implies that the people who inhabited the Peak District were still a distinctive group with a recognised territory long after the county boundaries of Derbyshire had been established. The southerly position of Ballidon within the Peak District suggests that the *Pecsaetan* occupied the whole of the upland area.

In 966 Edgar gave a large estate at Parwich to his thegn Aelfhelm, a large landowner in northern and midland England. Unfortunately, the bounds were not described in the charter, but it is clear that several outlying units, known as berewicks, belonged to the estate. In Domesday Book these included Alsop, Cold Eaton and Hanson. Two years later, another charter of King Edgar recorded the grant to Bishop Wulfric of an estate at Stanton-in-Peak. The boundaries in the charter are those of the townships (or modern civil parishes) of Stanton and its dependent berewick at Birchover.

The loyal service of high-ranking Mercian thegns continued to be rewarded with generous grants of land. In 942, once he had regained control of the Upper Trent valley, King Edmund gave Wulfsige Maur a large block of territory on either side of the river, including the Derbyshire estates of Caldwell, Coton-in-the-Elms, Drakelow, Linton, Roslinton and Walton-upon-Trent. Likewise, in 1009 King Aethelred granted Morcar land along the Trent and in eastern Derbyshire: at Crich, Ingleby, Kidsley, Morley, Smalley and Weston-upon-Trent. Morcar received further lands in the Mickleover–Littleover area in 1011 and at Eckington in 1012, which enabled him to consolidate estates that he had already inherited in north-east Derbyshire from his kinsman through marriage, Wulfric Spot, the Mercian thegn who founded Burton Abbey on the Staffordshire–Derbyshire border.

Bakewell viewed from Burton. In the distance, the spire of Bakewell church marks the site of the ancient minster, which in Norman times became a small borough and market centre. When, in 920, Edward the Elder strengthened his frontier zone by constructing fortified burhs at Nottingham, Bakewell and Manchester, he chose a site in the broad meadows of the Wye valley (*foreground*). This acquired the name of Burton, but it was used as a fort for only 20 years or so. Burton was recorded in Domesday Book and the name is commemorated in Burton Closes.
PHOTOGRAPH: AUTHOR

The Anglian cross in Eyam churchyard has lost two feet at the top of the shaft, but its cross-head has been re-fitted to what remains of it. It is carved with figures, vine scrolls and interlace patterns in a style that is usually thought of as eighth or ninth century, but may be as late as the 920s. This sculpture is of national importance because of the survival of the cross-head.

PHOTOGRAPH: CARNEGIE

The will of Wulfric Spot, which dates from between 1002 and 1004, is a rare piece of documentary evidence to fit alongside this small collection of charters. Spot bequeathed a large group of estates in north-east Derbyshire, at Barlborough, Beighton, Clowne, Duckmanton, Eckington, Glapwell, Morton, Mosborough, North Wingfield, Ogston, Palterton, Pilsley, Scarcliffe, Snodeswick (a lost place-name near Morton), Stretton and Whitwell, together with many adjoining lands in South Yorkshire. He also left scattered possessions in south Derbyshire at Alvaston, Breadsall, Morley, Newton Solney, Sutton-on-the-Hill and Ticknall. Had it not been for this will, we would not have heard of most of these places before Domesday Book was compiled in 1086. The medieval pattern of settlement in the Derbyshire countryside had been well established long before the Norman Conquest.

Crosses and churches

Another type of evidence for the Anglo-Scandinavian period, albeit an enigmatic one, is provided by the numerous stone, carved crosses that are now found in churchyards, but which were sometimes moved there in the nineteenth century for safety reasons. Three outstanding examples of crosses that show no Scandinavian influence, and which have therefore been dated traditionally to the decades around 800, stand erect in the churchyards at Bakewell (see page 76), Bradbourne (page 88) and Eyam (page 85), within the former territory of the *Pecsaetan*. That at Eyam is remarkable for the survival of the head of the cross, though the top two feet of the supporting shaft are missing; as we have seen, that at Bakewell is eight feet high even without its cross head. We do not know where or when the cross shaft that was re-erected in Bradbourne churchyard in 1886 was originally constructed. After the cross was uprooted at the Reformation, a large fragment of it was partially buried under the west wall of the porch and two other pieces were placed in the churchyard wall. The carvings are of a crucifixion scene on one side and an archer on the other. The style of the carvings on all three stones, especially the dominant use of a naturalistic vine-scroll, is similar to that used on Northumbrian crosses.

Other Derbyshire crosses have Scandinavian design elements, which have usually been dated between the ninth and eleventh centuries, with the simplest designs classified as 'debased' and late. But as very few stone crosses can be dated from independent evidence, their interpretation remains controversial. Philip Sidebottom, who has surveyed almost 300 stones in seven counties centred on Derbyshire, concludes that all of them were erected in one short phase after Edward the Elder's advance in 920. He believes that the different styles of carving reflect different groups of carvers rather than changes of fashion through time and that their purpose was to symbolise group identities and to stake a claim over particular districts. He attributes the so-called 'late' monuments to the poorer, marginal communities where Norwegian-Irish settlers arrived during the early tenth century. Other scholars believe that crosses were raised over a much longer period and for a variety of reasons: as objects of veneration, statements of the faith, memorials for the dead, markers of places of prayer or of boundaries, and sometimes to commemorate significant sites in the life of a saint or to mark the route taken by his funeral party. The most elaborate ones were often erected at the centres of old estates and by minster churches, though this is not true of the outstanding example at Eyam.

Parish churches other than the ancient minsters were still rare in 900 but they became common during the tenth century as the old multiple estates were broken up. The favoured men who were granted small estates followed the national fashion of building a church next to their hall, or manor house as it would become known. The few charters that survive from before the Norman Conquest show that estate boundaries coincided with those of the new parishes. The pattern of landownership also explains why many parishes had detached portions. For example, Stoke was an outlying member of the royal estate centred on Hope and so it retained its link with Hope parish even though it was separated from the mother church by the parish of Eyam, and Stoney Middleton remained a detached chapelry of the parish of Hathersage because both places were owned by the same lord. What is now the parish of Barlow was, until Victorian times, divided between the intermingled properties of Great Barlow (which belonged to Staveley parish several miles to the east, because they had the same lord) and Little Barlow (which was part of the neighbouring parish of Dronfield). The boundaries of the new landed estates that became parishes were sometimes ancient features of the landscape. For instance, parts of the Roman roads from Derby to Buxton and from Derby to Lichfield marked parish boundaries. On the other hand, the course of the Roman road from Derby to Chesterfield was rarely used as such.

The rebuilding of Derbyshire's parish churches after the Norman Conquest means that hardly any of their original architectural features remain, except of course at the ancient minster at Repton. At Bradbourne and Stanton-by-Bridge some quoin stones are arranged in the characteristic 'long-and-short' manner of eleventh-century Mercia, while at Sawley the herringbone pattern of the masonry can be dated either side of the Conquest. So can a window in the west wall at Ault Hucknall, but that is about all.

Shire, wapentakes and hundreds

We have noted that, although the first reference to Derbyshire occurs in the *Anglo-Saxon Chronicle* entry for 1048, the county had probably been created soon after the first Danish invasions. The deep valley of the river Dove divided Derbyshire and Staffordshire in the west; elsewhere, except for the detached townships in the south, the county boundary coincided with that of the diocese of Lichfield. If the diocesan boundary had been followed upstream from the junction of the Seal Brook with the river Mease, those parts of

LEFT

The cross shaft which now stands near the entrance to the churchyard of All Saints, Bradbourne dates from the late eighth or ninth century, judging by the vine scrolls and the crucifixion scene. It was smashed into three pieces at the Reformation; two pieces then formed a churchyard stile and the other was buried under the west wall of the church porch. It was re-erected in its present form in the late nineteenth century. We do not know where the cross was originally located.

PHOTOGRAPH: CARNEGIE

RIGHT

Cross shaft at Brailsford church. The figure of a warrior and the interlace decoration on the cross standing on the south side of All Saints church places it in the Anglo-Scandinavian period. An ancient yew grows nearby. Both cross and tree pre-date the Norman work inside the church. The church stands alone, on the slope above the ford which provided the second element of the place-name, for at some point in the Middle Ages the village migrated half a mile to a crossroads on the busy route from Ashbourne to Derby. The first element of the name comparable to that at Brailes (Warwickshire) seems to be derived from an old British name for a hall or the chief place in a district, sited on a hill.

PHOTOGRAPH: AUTHOR

St Helen's church, Darley, is the focal point of a small settlement known as Churchtown within a large medieval parish. The yew tree which stands opposite the south porch is one of the largest and oldest in the country. Ancient yews lose much of the growth in their trunks and therefore cannot be dated by their tree rings. Various estimates of their date have been based on their circumferences, but these remain controversial. There seems little doubt that the yew tree at Darley is older than the earliest architecture in the church. In many parts of the British Isles ancient yews are associated with early Christian sites. The dedication to St Helen is another indicator that Christianity was established early in Darley. Other Derbyshire churchyards which contain ancient yews close to the south-west corner of the church include Brailsford, Kniveton, Muggington and Radbourne.

Appleby, Chilcote, Donisthorpe, Measham, Oakthorpe, Stretton-en-le-Field and Willesley, all of which lay within Derbyshire until 1897, would have formed part of Staffordshire, whereas the Derbyshire parts of Packington and Ravenstone would have been in Leicestershire. These anomalies may have arisen when the heathland which extended from Appleby Wolds to Desford was colonised from neighbouring villages or perhaps because landownership was so fragmented in this border area in the Anglo-Scandinavian period. In Domesday Book some manors, such as Appleby, Donisthorpe, Linton, Ravenstone and Stretton-en-le-Field, were listed under both Leicestershire and Derbyshire, such was the confusion in people's minds.

The shires of the Danelaw were divided into wapentakes, the equivalent of the Anglo-Saxon hundreds. Such divisions in Derbyshire were all referred to as wapentakes in the earliest records but were usually known as hundreds in

LUDWORTH

Glossop

MELLOR

HIGH PEAK

BEAUCHIEF
TOTLEY
DORE
NORTON

Buxton

Dronfield

Bakewell

Chesterfield
Bolsover

SCARSDALE

WIRKSWORTH
Matlock

Wirksworth

Belper

MORLEYSTON
AND LITCHURCH

Modern county
Old county boundary
Wapentake boundaries

APPLETREE

Derby

WINSHILL

STAPENHILL

REPTON AND
GRESLEY

EDINGALE

CROXALL

CHILCOTE

STRETTON EN LE FIELD

OAKTHORPE / DONISTHORPE
WILLERSLEY

RAVENSTONE

PACKINGTON
MEASHAM

APPLEBY

Wapentakes. Derbyshire's wapentakes are shown in their final form after the Norman Conquest. Those in the south of the county had several detached parishes. These Viking wapentakes were known alternatively by the Anglo-Saxon term 'hundred'.

later years. They were governed through open-air assemblies that met at some prominent natural feature or a specially erected stone in order to settle matters of law and order, to raise armies and to collect taxes. Wapentakes were probably introduced shortly after the Vikings reconquered the East Midlands in 942. The five that were recorded in Domesday Book were named Appletree, Hamston, Morleystone, Scarsdale and Walecros. Hamston was divided later between the wapentakes of High Peak and Wirksworth, but it originally covered the whole of the ancient territory of the *Pecsaetan*, stretching up on to the high moors east of the river Derwent. The meeting place was probably Hamston Hill in the parish of Thorpe, near Wirksworth. Walecros is another name that disappeared after the Norman Conquest, when the district became known as Repton wapentake and later as Repton & Gresley hundred. The meaning of the name Walecros is uncertain and the site of the meeting place is unknown. Nor can we locate the tree and stone where the wapentakes of Appletree and Morleystone (later Morleystone & Litchurch) held their meetings. The identity of Scarsdale, too, remains elusive, but the concentration of the Scandinavian place-names Hardstoft, Blingsby, Stainsby and Temple Normanton close to the upper reaches of the Rother, which divides the wapentake into two parts, suggests that Scarsdale was not far from Chesterfield (which in the thirteenth and fourteenth centuries provided the alternative name for the wapentake). The boundaries of the post-Conquest wapentakes coincided with those of the ecclesiastical deaneries, except where complications arose from some detached portions in the south of the county; the whole of Derbyshire comprised the Archdeaconry of Derby.

Place-names that Kenneth Cameron identified as commemorating early meeting-places for smaller districts include Matlock, 'the oak where the moot was held', and the minor names Moatless (Edensor), Moatlow (Newton Grange and Youlgreave), the lost name Mootlow (Brassington), the field-name Motlhaue (Hartshorne), Spellow (Brassington), the lost name Spellowe (Newton Solney), and Speetley (Barlborough). Dethick and Treak (Castleton) both got their names from oak trees on which criminals were hanged, an earlier usage than the numerous gallows names of later medieval times. Old legends and memories of haunted sites have also produced names such as Drakelow (dragon), Eldon (elves), and Thirst House (giant's house; a cave in Chelmorton in which prehistoric and Roman remains have been found). Shucstonefield (Crich) and Shuckton (Hulland Ward) acknowledge fear of demons, various worm names in Baslow, Hassop, Ticknall and Wirksworth indicate beliefs in serpents, and many later references to hobgoblins occur in numerous minor names and field-names. Supernatural forces were felt to be an ever-present threat.

Domesday Book

The Derbyshire folios of Domesday Book, compiled 20 years after the Norman Conquest, provide our first documentary record of the whole of the county. The clerks noted the changing fortunes of each vill or township since the time of Edward the Confessor (for they did not acknowledge the legitimacy of Harold's brief reign). The terse entries, however, conceal as much as they reveal and do not list all the minor settlements that were in existence by that time. David Roffe has shown that Domesday Book's record of livestock and the resources of each manor is nowhere near complete. Vast tracts of upland pasture, moorland, and inter-commoned woodland hardly interested the

commissioners, who were content to include remote parts of manors silently as integral parts of an estate. And though the churches on the huge estates of Henry de Ferrers in the southern half of Derbyshire were recorded consistently, elsewhere they were not. For example, no mention was made of Eyam church, despite the evidence of the substantial cross in its churchyard that Christianity had long been established there.

The inhabitants of each vill were so under-recorded that it is impossible to give a realistic estimate of the population of Derbyshire at a time when England's population was between 1.5 and 2.25 million. To take but one example, only 18 families were noted in the huge manor of Ashford and its 12 outlying settlements or berewicks. Surviving early twelfth-century surveys of the manors of Burton Abbey list a whole class of rentpayers, the *censarii*, who were unrecorded in the same places in Domesday Book. In the whole of Derbyshire only 20 serfs were counted, and the numbers of tenant farmers – villeins (1,776) and bordars (734) – were unrealistically low. Nevertheless, some 350 Derbyshire estates were named, very often for the first time in the written record. Most of the county's present towns and villages, except

Linacre woods. The deciduous woods on the coal-measure sandstones of north-east Derbyshire are at least as old as recorded history. Extensive woods were recorded in this part of the county in Domesday Book. They were valued not only for their timber but for their underwood, which in later centuries became the prime source of fuel for the lead smelting mills and iron furnaces that were erected in the river valleys. By the sixteenth century, the Linacres of Linacre Hall in the parish of Brampton, were leasing 'All those wodes trees and underwodes growinge and beinge of in and upon one woode grounde commonly called over Linacre wood or Linacre great woode lyinge and beinge within the Lordshipe of Linacre'.

those that were creations of the Industrial Revolution, were mentioned in the Domesday survey.

The lowlands of south Derbyshire had acquired much of their present character before the Norman Conquest. The typical settlement was a village, surrounded by its communal open fields where cereals were grown and with a large amount of valuable meadow and pasture land beyond. The origins of this system of farming await detailed investigation in Derbyshire, but evidence from other parts of the East Midlands suggests that it began in the Anglo-Scandinavian period but was not completed until long after the Norman Conquest. Most of Derbyshire's 50 or more corn mills were strung out along the fertile valleys of the Trent, Derwent, Dove and lower Erewash. Three fisheries were recorded at Derby, Markeaton and Sawley and a fishpond was a feature of the royal manor of Weston-upon-Trent. Very little woodland remained in the southern lowlands, nor in the Dark Peak above 800 feet. Yet, overall, some 26 per cent of the county was woodland in 1086, compared with the national average of only 15 per cent. Most of Derbyshire's woods were situated at 400–500 feet, either in Scarsdale wapentake, the Pennine foothills, or the south-eastern part of the county around Morley. The wood-pasture landscape of scattered villages, hamlets and farms, linked by deep, winding lanes in large parishes and farmed as much in closes of many shapes and sizes as in the strips of the open fields, was very different in character from the lowlands of south Derbyshire that formed part of the Midland Plain and from the exposed villages high in the White Peak, where work tending the crops in the open fields and the livestock in the pastures or on the extensive commons was often combined with toil in the lead mines. Domesday Book recorded lead works or smelting sites at Ashford, Bakewell, Crich, Matlock Bridge and Wirksworth (which remained the foremost lead-mining district, as it had been since Roman times).

The county town was a prosperous borough and market centre on the eve of the Norman Conquest, the only one in Derbyshire. It had no fewer than 243 resident burgesses, the principal 41 of whom held a considerable amount of land and 14 mills in and around the town. But two-thirds of the borough's revenues, in the form of dues, fines, tolls and customs, went to the king, and the remaining third passed to Earl Hugh of Mercia. Domesday Book records six churches in the borough, two of them collegiate with seven and six priests and four that had been founded by laymen on their own estates in the late Anglo-Scandinavian era.

The breaking up of large estates

Domesday Book is informative about the nature and structure of large estates. In 1066 the Crown was the major landowner in Derbyshire and its possessions included almost all the ancient 'multiple estates'. Two thegns, Leofnoth and Leofric, held a large estate in Scarsdale wapentake and several other dispersed lands, but the other Anglo-Scandinavian nobles had relatively small properties. Many Derbyshire manors, especially in the south of the county, were identical with vills or townships, but it was equally common to find that a vill contained more than one manor. Barton Blount and Etwall each included as many as eight small manors and Hilton had four. In other cases, manorial and township boundaries did not coincide; for example, the vills of Codnor, Heanor, Langley and (the lost) Smithycote contained six manors between them. The fragmentation of the old estates over the previous two centuries had produced complicated patterns of ownership.

The survival of large multiple estates, which had once covered most of the county, is best seen in the Peak District, where most of the land was still included within them. The centres of these estates can be recognised from the services that were owed by the inhabitants of outlying territories. For example, the Ashford estate covered a huge district that included Baslow, Birchills, Blackwell, Bubnell, Calver, Flagg, Hassop, Little Longstone, Priestcliffe, Rowland, Sheldon and Taddington. Similar estates in the Peak District were centred on Ashbourne, Bakewell, Darley, Hope, Longdendale, Matlock Bridge, Parwich and Wirksworth. The lords of these multiple estates did not own their land in the modern sense, but were entitled to certain money payments, the provision of food and labour, and a tenant's commitment to serve as a soldier when called upon; Domesday Book records renders of honey and lead.

As we have seen, some of the multiple estates had a parallel ecclesiastical organisation as minster churches, whose vast territories were breaking up into smaller units, sometimes into a new parish but more often, as yet, a chapelry. The process intensified after the Norman Conquest, so that, for instance, by the mid-thirteenth century all but two of Ashbourne's Domesday Book berewicks had chapels. In the thirteenth century the church of Bakewell received pensions that acknowledged former dependent status from the parishes of Youlgreave and Edensor, and the church of Hope received similar payments from Chapel-en-le-Frith, Tideswell and probably Eyam, in right of their superior status. The apparent independence of Glossop, Darley and Hathersage may have been masked by the grant of each of them to religious houses in an earlier, poorly documented period. The fragmentation of royal estates was perhaps hindered by the strategic importance of the Peak District, the continued semi-independence of the *Pecsaetan*, and the pastoral nature of a farming system that did not produce enough of a surplus to support a large number of local lords.

Judging by the few surviving charters, in other parts of Derbyshire the great estates were being split into sub-manors by the ninth century, especially after the arrival of the Danes. By the time of Domesday Book the process was almost complete in the wealthier, fertile southern lowlands. Repton and Melbourne retained some of their old character, but they were exceptional. In Appletree wapentake manors were rarely much larger than a single township and often smaller. A hint of an older system there is provided by the manor of Mickleover, which still had property in Bearwardcote, Dalbury, Hilton, Hoon,

Rodsley, Snelston, Sudbury and Sutton on the Hill. The estate of Siward Barn, centred on Duffield but extending eastwards across the river Derwent, both as a manor and a parish, seems to have been another important early centre.

In Scarsdale a few small manors such as South Wingfield and South Normanton had become independent before the Norman Conquest, but the wapentake was dominated by two great estates. The royal manor of Chesterfield was at that time administered from a new building, which has given us the name of Newbold, now a Chesterfield suburb. It contained 18 townships, including Dronfield, whose large parish extended to the Yorkshire boundary and might therefore have once been incorporated within that of St Mary and All Saints, Chesterfield. Even without Dronfield, Chesterfield's medieval parish covered over 45 square miles. The other great estate belonged to the brothers Leofnoth and Leofric and was the successor of that once held by Wulfric Spot. It stretched over the coal-measure sandstones and the magnesian limestone to the county boundaries with Nottinghamshire and Yorkshire. These two estates defended a crucial frontier zone and so resisted the process of fragmentation that transformed landownership in the southern half of the county.

The county of Derbyshire came into being in the Anglo-Scandinavian period over a thousand years ago, with boundaries that are mostly still recognisable. The borough of Derby occupied the site between the river Derwent and the Markeaton Brook that remains the heart of the modern city. In the countryside, the present settlement pattern of villages and scattered farmsteads had begun to take shape, with names that we still use. A communal farming system, based on open fields, divided into strips, and common meadows and pastures beyond was becoming widely adopted. And as the ancient 'multiple estates' were broken up, manorial lords built churches for the new parishes that were often identical in size and shape with their manors. Many of the familiar features of the present Derbyshire landscape had been shaped by countless generations of families long before the Norman Conquest.

RIGHT

The Bronze Age settlement and Iron Age fort on top of 'the shivering mountain' of Mam Tor were the first to dominate this area and to control the key route down Winnats Pass into the Hope valley.

PHOTOGRAPH: CARNEGIE

The Normans

The new landowners

The Norman Conquest and settlement of Derbyshire did not bring about a radical reorganisation of society in the reign of William I; it merely replaced one ruling class by another. The structure of Derbyshire estates remained intact as the new Norman lords took over the lands of the men they had vanquished. Few Anglo-Scandinavian lords held on to their property, though perhaps some became under-tenants. We cannot be certain about this, for the under-tenants of 70 per cent of the county's manors were not recorded in Domesday Book. William the Conqueror became the major landowner in Derbyshire by succeeding Edward the Confessor as lord of an important group of ancient and extensive manors: Ashbourne, Ashford, Bakewell, Chesterfield, Darley, Hope, Matlock Bridge, Melbourne, Parwich and Wirksworth. The Domesday Book entries make it clear that before the Conquest five of these manors – Ashbourne, Darley, Matlock Bridge, Parwich and Wirksworth – had been managed by a tenant as a single estate. The Crown had a strong presence in Derbyshire, particularly in the Peak District.

We have no direct evidence of military conflict within the county at the time of the Norman Conquest, but in 1086 over ten per cent of Derbyshire vills were recorded as 'waste' and more than a third had dropped in value by a half or more. The whole of Derbyshire had fallen in value by one-third since King Edward's reign and in the borough of Derby the number of burgesses had been reduced dramatically, 103 of its tenements were unoccupied, and four of its mills were no longer in use. This seems at first sight to point to severe disruption, yet no meaningful pattern can be discerned in the distribution of 'waste' vills and no archaeological evidence for the destructive effects of a rampaging army can be found. As in Yorkshire and Cheshire, 'waste' may have meant loss of revenue to the Crown rather than total destruction; indeed, some 'waste' vills were given a value by the commissioners, whose concern was to find what was owed to the king. It is very unlikely that the relatively small Norman army could have caused such carnage in a part of England that was not heavily involved in the Conquest. Nor was it in their interest to do so, for they needed the native population to provide the food and pay the taxes.

LEFT

Viewed from the hillside of Cave Dale, William Peveril's castle occupies a steep, rocky site high above the huge cavern that was recorded in Domesday Book as Peak's Arse. Now it was the turn of the Normans to build a fort that would guard the route through the Hope valley, like its predecessors: the prehistoric hillfort of Mam Tor and the Roman fort at *Navio*. Known at first as Peak Castle, Peveril's stronghold was strengthened in the 1170s by the addition of King Henry II's keep. Throughout the Middle Ages the castle's main role was not military but that of the administrative centre for the Forest of the Peak.

PHOTOGRAPH: AUTHOR

The Normans consolidated their acquisition of the north midlands by building castles with forced labour and creating compact lordships to support them, especially at the major sites at Nottingham, Tickhill and Tutbury. Derbyshire was not of great strategic importance to them, nor was it prosperous, so there was less need for castles to dominate its landscape than in border regions such as Yorkshire or the Welsh Marches. The greatest landowners in the county lived for most of their time beyond its boundaries and Norman Derbyshire lay constantly within the shadow of Nottinghamshire. The Domesday Book entries for the two counties were compiled together; a single shire court (held at Nottingham) served both counties until 1256; and the sheriff of Nottingham had jurisdiction over Derbyshire until the sixteenth century. Derby's castle was small and rather insignificant in comparison with that at Nottingham.

After the king, Henry de Ferrers, the son of the lord of Ferrières-St Hilaire, Eure, in Normandy, was by far the greatest landowner in Derbyshire when the Domesday Book was compiled. His lordship formed a compact bloc in eastern Staffordshire and western Derbyshire within the newly formed honour of Tutbury, where his castle was reared on the south bank of the Trent. Before the Conquest, much of this territory had belonged to Siward Barn, but he lost all when he was involved in the revolt at Ely in 1071 with Edwin, Earl of Mercia, and his brother Morcar. Domesday Book names Henry as the tenant-in-chief of 256 manors in 14 English counties. Over 150 of these manors lay in Derbyshire, including almost the whole of the wapentake of Appletree. He built two castles in Derbyshire, one at Duffield overlooking an important crossing of the river Derwent and the other at Pilsbury high above the middle reaches of the Dove valley on the border with Staffordshire. Henry and King William owned between them nearly all the manors in the western half of the county. When he died about 1101, Henry was buried at the Benedictine priory that he and his wife Bertha had built at Tutbury, alongside his castle. Most of his English property passed to his third son, Robert, who in 1138 was created Earl of Derby. In the early thirteenth century King John granted William de Ferrers II the royal manors of Ashbourne, Matlock Bridge, Parwich and Wirksworth, with their outlying berewicks. For 200 years after the Norman Conquest seven generations of the de Ferrers family were the major baronial landowners in Derbyshire, but after Robert de Ferrers III had joined the barons' rebellion in 1266 the family's estates were confiscated and granted to Edmund 'Crouchback', Earl of Lancaster, the son of King Henry III. Thereafter, they formed part of the Duchy of Lancaster.

The origins of William Peveril or Peverel are obscure and the unproven story that he was the illegitimate son of the Conqueror dates only from Tudor times. He may have been related to Ranulf Peveril of Essex, for both men held estates in west Normandy. He was made governor of the castle that was built at Nottingham in 1068 and may have served as joint sheriff of Nottinghamshire and Derbyshire; in 1102 he founded a great Cluniac priory at Lenton, on the outskirts of Nottingham, and endowed it with the tithes of his major manors.

Domesday Book lists the 23 manors that he held in Derbyshire. One group stretched along the county's eastern border from his castle at Bolsover as far south as Codnor, the second formed a fairly compact group around Castleton, where Peak Castle was firmly established by 1086. The north-western manors of Ashford, Bakewell and Hope were also placed in his charge by the Conqueror and in the first decade of the twelfth century Henry I granted him the lordship of Longdendale. His other small, scattered estates included Beeley, Chatsworth, Eyam, Mapperley and Tibshelf. But the Peveril estate lasted less than 100 years, for it was forfeited to the Crown in 1155 when a later William retired as a monk to avoid the charge of poisoning Ranulph de Gernon, Earl of Chester. The Peverils then died out in the male line.

King Henry II kept both Peak and Bolsover castles in his own hands and in the 1170s he rebuilt both of the keeps. The eastern manors that supported Bolsover Castle were all tenanted from the start, mostly by Frenchmen, such as Serlo, the ancestor of the lords of Pleasley and Glapwell. In 1157 Henry II granted the manor and church of Glossop to Basingwerk Abbey in Clwyd, about 1170 the berewicks of Nether and Over Haddon were granted to Richard Vernon, and in the 1190s Bakewell was given by Richard I to Ralph Gernon. Richard entrusted his brother, the future King John, with large estates in the East Midlands, including Bolsover and Peak Castles. John took a personal interest in the region, which he visited a number of times. Several of the constituent manors of the honour of the Peak, including Ashford, Bakewell, Beeley, Eyam and Tideswell, were subsequently granted to various lords, but the greater part of the estate remained within the Duchy of Lancaster.

Castles

The Normans introduced castles to England in order to intimidate the local population and to act as secure bases from which troops could move to quell any revolt. The earliest were hastily erected earthworks that were surmounted by timber buildings. They were constructed in a variety of sizes and designs and, having served their purpose, were abandoned unless they were chosen for rebuilding with stone defences. The simple ringwork style was often favoured for minor castles that were erected soon after the Conquest, though in this poorly documented period we cannot be certain that some were constructed as late as the civil war years of the mid-twelfth century. Good examples can be seen near the parish churches of Hathersage and Hope. At about 80 metres in diameter, Camp Green, Hathersage, is the largest of the local ringworks; it was constructed in at least two phases, with a wide, deep ditch; on the western slope of the knoll St Michael's church is aligned at 45° north-east so that it could stand alongside it. At Hope, St Peter's church stands 100 metres away from the ringwork, part of which is still enclosed by a wide ditch. Other ringworks have been identified at Parwich, Stoney Middleton, Tapton and Tissington. Motte-and-bailey castles were built to a more elaborate design. The motte was

ABOVE

Castle Gresley
motte. Nigel de
Stafford (*alias* de
Gresley) was the
tenant-in-chief of
nine manors on the
south Derbyshire
border at the time
of Domesday Book.
His son, William de
Gresley, is believed
to have built the
castle whose mound
still rises above the
village of Castle
Gresley, and to
have founded a
small priory at
Church Gresley.
This William was
the ancestor of a
long line of Gresleys
of Gresley and
Drakelow.

PHOTOGRAPH: AUTHOR

an earthen mound which supported a timber building and was encircled with a ditch and bank, while the bailey had a separate ditch and rampart surrounding the outbuildings. Fine examples can be found at Castle Hill, Bakewell, on a spur on the opposite side of the Wye valley from the town at Morley, and at Mouselow Castle, between Dinting, Glossop and Padfield, high above the river Etherow. The castle at Derby, on a site known in 1266 as Copecastel, just south-east of the borough, was probably of this type.

Derbyshire's outstanding example of a motte-and-bailey castle is found in a remote location near the shrunken medieval village of Pilsbury, just over a mile north of Hartington, high above Dovedale, near the Derbyshire–Staffordshire border. The natural knoll on which the motte stands was defined more sharply by a deep ditch and heightened by the spoil. Unusually, the motte has two baileys, one to the east and one to the south, which make good use of the natural features. A well-defined holloway descends to the Dove. The castle has not been excavated and no contemporary documents survive, but the visible earthworks are clearly Norman, for the castle was not rebuilt in stone. Another motte occupies a prominent position at Bank Top nearby and Pilsbury's name points to an earlier, undiscovered fortification, perhaps one that was re-used when the Normans built their motte-and-bailey.

Few Derbyshire motte-and-baileys were enlarged into substantial stone castles during the twelfth century. Nothing remains above ground of Henry

II's castle on the magnesian limestone ridge at Bolsover, though its motte determined the extent of the Little Castle and its bailey defined that of the Fountain Garden which Robert Smythson designed for Sir Charles Cavendish in the early seventeenth century. Royal records for 1172–73 record the costs of provisioning Bolsover Castle with corn, bacon and cheese, the spending of £20 for the wages of 20 knights and the minor sum of £2 on the building. Much more was spent on pay for the knights and their retinues and on building works in 1174. New domestic buildings and additional towers went up during the thirteenth century, but by the fourteenth century the castle had become ruinous. It remained in royal hands until it was granted to George, sixth Earl of Shrewsbury in 1553.

William Peveril's other north Derbyshire castle was erected on a naturally defensive site high above Cavedale and the gaping entrance of the cavern that was recorded in Domesday Book by the name of Peak's Arse. It was the successor of the hill fort at Mam Tor and the Roman fort at Brough in guarding the route into the Hope valley down Winnats Pass, though its main role turned out to be that of administrative centre for the royal forest that covered much of the High Peak. Originally named Peak Castle, in time it became known as Peveril Castle. Masonry laid out in herringbone patterns can be seen in the lower courses of the original, eleventh-century curtain wall on the north side of the bailey and in the early twelfth-century west wall. The foundations of a chapel and a small hall also date from the Peveril era. After its confiscation by the Crown, Henry II spent substantial sums on rebuilding the castle between

1173 and 1177, particularly on erecting the keep. In the following century a new hall and kitchens were built in the north-west corner of the bailey. Its role in supervising the Forest of the Peak kept it going throughout the Middle Ages, but by the seventeenth century the buildings had fallen into ruin.

Derbyshire's most intriguing castle has, alas, left little evidence on the ground or in the documentary record, though its plan is known from excavations that took place in 1886 and 1957. This is the substantial tower that a member of the de Ferrers family erected at Duffield as the headquarters of his extensive hunting district known as Duffield Frith. Just one course of foundations can now be seen in two places, together with a bit of the motte and a fragment of the ditch in the grounds of Castlehill House. The excavations in 1957 showed that Henry de Ferrers' eleventh-century castle had a timber keep surrounded by a dry ditch, on a site that had been first occupied in the third century AD. At some unknown time in the twelfth century one of the de Ferrers family replaced this timber building with a square stone tower that was matched in size only by those of the White Tower in London and Colchester Castle. The walls were about 15 feet thick, 95 feet long and 93 feet wide. Duffield Castle was clearly designed as a magnificent ceremonial building, comparable with that at Castle Hedingham (Essex), which was built for the Earl of Oxford in 1142. It did not last long, for it was probably one of the castles that were destroyed after a rebellion in 1173, in which William de Ferrers II was involved. Nor do any surrounding landscape features survive, for the turnpike road and the railway passed through the site in Victorian times and much has been subsequently built over. Duffield Castle was one of Derbyshire's most important medieval buildings and its destruction is a major loss from the county's heritage.

In south Derbyshire traces of a motte-and-bailey castle were discovered during excavations at Repton and similar earthworks may have preceded the later castles at Codnor, Horsley and Melbourne. Some ancient estate centres, however, were not fortified by the Normans. Castles do not seem to have been erected at Ashbourne, Ashford or Wirksworth, Hope was now overshadowed by Castleton, and although the Chesterfield estate had a motte-and-bailey at Tapton the main castle within Scarsdale wapentake was at Bolsover. A new pattern had emerged under the Normans.

Knights

Henry de Ferrers kept only one-third of his Derbyshire manors under direct management; the rest were tenanted by knights, most of whom had accompanied him from Normandy. Gladwyn Turbutt's analysis of the earliest known tenants of these Derbyshire manors suggests that five families – those of Wakelin (Radbourne), Nigel de Albini (Catton), Saswalo (Etwall, Hoon and Hatton), Henry de Chambrais (Burnaston and Bearwardcote) and Wazelin de Boscherville (Sutton-on-the-Hill) – either were, or may have been, Henry de Ferrers' close relations; that four – Curzon (Croxall, which at that date lay within Derbyshire), Bagpuize (Barton), Montgomery (Cubley) and Dun (Breadsall) – were feudal tenants of his Normandy barony; that at least ten were other neighbours in his native land; and that at least another ten were of English or Scandinavian descent.

Many of the descendants of these knights remained large landowners in Derbyshire through the Middle Ages and beyond and some flourish to this today. An outstanding example are the Curzon family from Notre-Dame-de-Courson, Calvados, a component of the de Ferrers' estate. Giraline de Courson was in Henry de Ferrers' retinue at the time of the Conquest and was rewarded

Fragments of Norman sculptures from an earlier building than the present one have been incorporated into the walls of the transepts and nave of Wirksworth parish church. Prominent among these is the 'King Stone' shown here.

PHOTOGRAPH: CARNEGIE

by King William with the manor of West Lockinge (Oxfordshire). His son, Roger, held Croxall and part of Fauld (Staffordshire) from Henry de Ferrers in 1086, and soon afterwards Roger's son, Richard, became lord of Kedleston. In the reign of Henry I (1100–35) Richard held four knight's fees of the Ferrers family, at Croxall, Edingale, Kedleston and Twyford-Stenson. Kedleston has been owned in unbroken male descent by the Curzons ever since, the present representative being the 30th lord.

Another prominent knightly family during the three centuries after the Conquest were the Bagpuizes, who came from Bacquepuis, Eure, some 22 miles from the de Ferrers' stronghold at Ferrières-St Hilaire. In 1086 Ralph de Bagpuize held eight manors in Barton (which became known as Barton Bagpuize), a manor in Alkmonton, and another in Hungry Bentley. His son, Robert, founded a leper hospital at Alkmonton and the family were benefactors of Tutbury Priory. Barton Bagpuize remained in his family until the death of the last male representative, William de Bagpuize, about 1381, when the greater part of the property was purchased by Sir Walter Blount, a member of John of Gaunt's retinue. Barton Bagpuize then became known as Barton Blount.

The only manor house of a Derbyshire knight to retain some late Norman work is Haddon Hall, which was acquired through marriage about 1170 by Sir Richard de Vernon, the descendant of a family from Vernon, Eure. A royal licence of 1195 allowed him to fortify his house by building the tower that stands in the north-east corner of the present complex. Enough masonry survives elsewhere, in the south, west and chapel walls and in the 'King John's wall' that has recently been brought to light, to show that Sir Richard's manor house was as large as the later medieval one.

Forests

The Norman kings and barons turned extensive areas of the English countryside into royal forests and private chases, where they had exclusive rights to hunt deer and other game. The term 'forest' was used not in the present sense of a dense wood, but as a legal term for a district that was subject to a special set of harsh laws imposed by forest courts and officers of the Crown. Forests were wooded only in parts and they often covered moors, heaths and fens rather than woodland. They stretched over much of the Pennines, as far south as the Forest of the Peak and the adjoining Macclesfield Forest. But as hunting was only an occasional activity, suitable parts of forests were set aside for cultivation or for grazing cattle, sheep, pigs and horses. Forests contained villages, hamlets, farmsteads and cottages within their bounds, but forest laws prohibited the clearing of new land for farming, prevented the peasants from fencing their crops to keep out the game, imposed harsh penalties on poachers, and ordered the maiming of dogs so that they could not chase the deer and wild boar.

Three extensive forests were created in Derbyshire, two of whose names are still well known – the Forest of the Peak (with the place-names Peak Forest and Chapel-en-le-Frith) and Duffield Frith. A short-lived one that covered the whole of Derbyshire east of the river Derwent as far as the county boundary with Nottinghamshire has been rescued from obscurity by David Crook.

THE FOREST OF THE PEAK

The *foresta de Pecco* was first recorded in 1223, long after its creation, and its boundaries were described in 1286. It covered about 180 square miles of the north-western uplands in the most remote and thinly populated part of Derbyshire. Much of it was rough moorland that had belonged to the royal manors of Hope and Longdendale before the Conquest, so perhaps parts had been used for hunting before the Normans took control. In the west and the north the forest boundary followed that of the county, marked by the rivers Goyt and Etherow, as far as Saltersbrook, where it turned due south, climbing up a footpath along the present county boundary to Swains Head and down to the river Derwent just below its source. It followed the Derwent to the river Noe just below Mytham Bridge, which at the time was a ford whose name meant 'at the meeting of the streams'. The boundary continued westwards up the Noe to Brough, then up the Bradwell Brook through the deep valley that was at that time known as 'the great dell of Hazelbache'. Here it turned abruptly to the west along the line identified by Eric Heaf from a deed of 1698, where a property boundary followed 'the Ancient King's fence' up Hartle Dale to Castleton Lane. The forest boundary then turned due south along this lane, passing Poynton Cross (which is mentioned in a description of the boundary c.1600). The cross has gone but Poytoncross Barn stands on the brow where the townships of Great and Little Hucklow, Litton, and Tideswell converged. The boundary continued along the present green lane to Litton and down Litton Dale and Tideswell Dale, up the river Wye to the west of Buxton and across the moor to the head of Goyt's Clough.

The forest was divided into three wards: Longdendale, Hopedale, and Campana. Their precise boundaries are unclear, but they seem to have met at Edale Cross. Campana (the 'champion' or open country) covered the lower,

'perhaps the most desolate, wild, and abandoned country in all England'
DANIEL DEFOE

Edale Cross. The boundaries of the three wards of the Forest of the Peak – Longdendale, Hopedale and Campana – are thought to have met at Edale Cross, at the summit of a bridleway below the Kinderscout plateau. This medieval cross was half-buried in the peat until 1810, when it was re-erected by John Gee of the Ashes, Kinder, and four friends, all of whom are commemorated by their initials and the date carved on the cross. The base is missing.
PHOTOGRAPH: AUTHOR

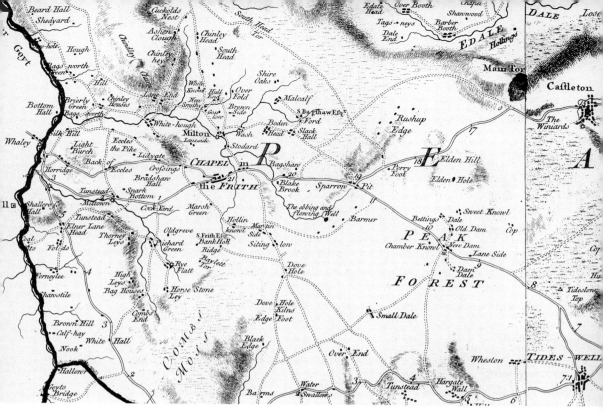

Burdett's map, 1767: detail showing Peak Forest and Chapel-en-le-Frith. In the early eighteenth century Daniel Defoe thought that this was 'perhaps the most desolate, wild, and abandoned country in all England'.

mostly limestone district that extended south to the river Wye. It provided the best feeding for the deer and was enclosed by a low wall with a ditch wide enough to keep out cattle or sheep but not to prevent deer from leaping over it to roam throughout the rest of the forest.

Peak Castle was the residence of the forest bailiff, the administrative and legal centre of the forest and the prison for local offenders, but the hunting lodge for the forest was on or near the site of Chamber Farm, 'the chamber in the forest', which stands on a knoll just north of the present village of Peak Forest. A chapel that was built nearby (the ancestor of the present church at Peak Forest) was a 'peculiar jurisdiction' that lay outside the parish system. Gervase de Bernake, who was bailiff of the Peak Forest in 1255–56, presented it with vestments, an altar cloth, chalice and missals. Regular 'swainmotes', or minor courts, for Campana ward were held at the Chamber in the thirteenth and fourteenth centuries, while those for Longdendale Ward were held at Bowden, near Chapel-en-le-Frith, and those for Hopedale Ward at Hope.

The chief officers under the authority of the bailiff were the four verderers, who usually held their jobs for life and were occasionally succeeded by a son. They held inquests into forest trespass, presided over the swainmote courts, presented cases at forest eyres, and were responsible for looking after the deer. They were substantial figures, whose symbol of office was an axe. Below them were the regarders, a body of twelve or more knights who enquired into offences. Then came the woodwards, whose symbol was a small hatchet, the agisters who collected rents for feeding cattle or pigs, and the rangers, who were responsible for the observance of forest law in the remote, outer parts.

The forest has left little evidence on the ground, but minor place-names offer clues to former hunting and farming activities. Stodhart (Chapel-en-le-Frith) and Dogmanslack (Peak Forest) are derived from the occupational names of the stud- and dog-keeper; Wildboar Clough (Charlesworth), the lost Boare Cloughe (Chinley), and Swint Clough (Hope Woodlands) recall pigs; numerous booths in Edale and to a lesser extent in Hayfield speak of cattle rearing; and wolves are commemorated in Woolow (Green Fairfield), Wolf's Pit (Abney), and Wooler and the lost Wolfstone (Hope Woodlands). References to deer in place-names are uncommon but include Buxton, Roeside (Chapel-en-le-Frith) and the lost Derstones (Great Hucklow).

LEFT
Old Glossop Cross. The cross in a small square in Old Glossop to the east of the parish church may date from 1290, when the Cistercian monks of Basingwerk Abbey (Wales), lords of the manor since 1157, obtained a royal grant of a weekly market and an annual fair. The cross stood nearer the house in the background until 1910, when it was moved and given a new head. This ancient market space was replaced by a new one in Norfolk Square in 1844, at a time when the population was shifting away from the old centre towards the new mills.

PHOTOGRAPH: CARNEGIE

Grants of land within the Peak Forest were made to religious houses in the twelfth and thirteenth centuries. In 1157 Henry II gave the Cistercian abbey of Basingwerk (Clwyd) the manor and church of Glossop, which enabled later abbots to claim that their estates lay outside the forest's jurisdiction. Merevale Abbey (Warwickshire) had land near Chinley that is still known as Monk's Meadows and a house and land at Fairfield, a large area of pasture (the finest in Peak Forest) that lay north-east of Buxton. The nuns of King's Mead, Priory, Derby, who were also granted rights of pasture on Fairfield in 1223, are remembered by Nun Brook and Nunsfield Farm. Two Nottinghamshire monasteries also obtained royal grants of land within the forest. Lenton Priory established a grange in Monk's Dale, in the parish of Tideswell, and Welbeck Abbey acquired an extensive tract in the Upper Derwent valley, in particular the pasture known as Crookhill and woodland pastures rising up to Derwenthead. Welbeck also benefited from grants made by Derbyshire lords: William de Ferrers gave them land in Ashop and Matthew de Hathersage donated the site that became known as Abbey Grange. By the fourteenth century the Welbeck Abbey estate in the Upper Derwent was named Hope Woodlands and it had acquired extra-parochial status exempt from the payment of tithes.

DUFFIELD FRITH

Duffield Frith had probably long been in existence as a private chase of the de Ferrers family when it was first recorded in late twelfth-century charters. A survey of 1540 said that it was 30 miles in circumference. Brian Rich and his colleagues have established that its northern boundary followed Holehouse Brook and Mere Brook ('mere' meaning boundary) as far as the river Derwent. There it turned south to the confluence with the river Amber, which it followed upstream eastwards to the old Roman road from Derby to Chesterfield. After turning southwards along the road for a short distance, it descended again along the course of the Bottle Brook and turned sharply in a westerly direction towards Duffield church. Another short stretch of the Derwent was then followed before the boundary turned up various brooks and Brunswood Lane to its furthest point west.

The Frith was managed through four Wards: Duffield (south), Hulland (west), Colebrook (north), and in the east Belper, where it covered all that part of the parish of Duffield that lay beyond the Derwent. Belper's name is a corruption of *Beaurepair*, meaning 'beautiful retreat', the same Norman French word that has changed to Bearpark in County Durham. After the demolition of Duffield Castle, Belper became the administrative centre of the Frith and the other Derbyshire estates of the honour of Tutbury. The high-status manor house that was built there probably stood in the area now known as the Coppice car park above the Coppice Brook.

The Abbey, Darley. Now a pub, this medieval building is thought to have been the guest house to the Augustinian abbey that was founded about 1146 on the banks of the Derwent just north of Derby. Very little survives of what was once Derbyshire's premier monastic house.

The upland parts of the attractive countryside of Duffield Frith are mostly on shales that would have supported gorse, bracken, bilberry, bramble and thorn, with managed woods of holly, oak and ash, and alder in the wetter patches. The wards contained small villages with open arable fields, meadows and pastures, coppices and open woodland, fenced parks and hays for deer and other livestock, and vast commons. Plots of land beyond the farming settlements were allotted to the forest officers and to specialist workers, such as the *conigers* who looked after the rabbit warrens; a Coneygreave Farm stands in Colebrook Ward just north of Shottle Park and another is located in Hulland Ward. Bowbearers Piece and Bowmerlane Farm are other possible examples. Encroachments from the wastes were allowed upon payment of a fine and rent, as they provided an extra source of income to the lord.

THE FOREST OF EAST DERBYSHIRE

The whole of Derbyshire east of the Derwent (except Belper ward) was designated as another royal forest by Henry II, sometime between the start of his reign in 1154 and the first recording of fines for forest offences in 1167. This eastern forest covered an enormous area of some 250 square miles in the most wooded part of the county. At the Nottinghamshire boundary it joined Sherwood Forest to form a continuous, near 30-mile stretch between the Derwent and the Trent; at its greatest extent it was also 30 miles from north to south. The Cauz family of Laxton Castle (Nottinghamshire) were appointed hereditary keepers, but little is known about this forest as it lasted for only two generations before its abolition in 1225. The barons' hostility to royal forests was one of the grievances that led King John to sign the Magna Carta in 1215, after which much land in different parts of the country was 'disafforested'. The East Derbyshire forest was not of lasting consequence like the Peak Forest and Duffield Frith, both of which survived into the seventeenth century, and it left no imprint on the landscape.

Religious houses

The Normans demonstrated their dominance of England not only with castles and manor houses but with abbeys and priories. But as Derbyshire was of little strategic or economic importance at that time, no monasteries were established within the county by the Benedictines or Cistercians and the sole Cluniac foundation was a small priory in Derby. This absence of major religious buildings contrasts starkly with Yorkshire, where Benedictine and Cistercian abbeys are among the county's greatest medieval glories. The post-Conquest religious houses of Derbyshire were few in number and were endowed rather poorly. They were not established until well into the twelfth century, by the preaching orders of Augustinian and Premonstratensian canons.

The largest and most prosperous of the Derbyshire monasteries was Darley Abbey, a house of the Augustinian or Black canons that was founded about

1146 as a joint venture by Derby burgesses and Robert de Ferrers II. It took over a site beside the river Derwent, two miles north of Derby, that had served since 1137 as an oratory of St Helen within the borough. A large number of endowments were made by people from many walks of life. By 1159 the abbey possessed the Derby churches of St Peter, St Michael, and St Werburgh, and the churches of Ashover, Bolsover, Crich, Pentrich, South Wingfield and Uttoxeter (Staffordshire). Gifts of the churches of Brailsford, Scarcliffe, Shirley, and the chapel of Osmaston soon followed. The estates that were donated by lay people were so numerous and scattered that the abbey had to establish 11 outlying granges to administer them: at Aldwark, Alvaston, Burley, Crich, Normanton, Osmaston, Pentrich, Scarcliffe, Thulston, Wessington and Wigwell. Valuable woodland rights were acquired in Duffield Frith and in Bolsover, Crich, Pentrich and Ripley. Very little of the abbey has survived. The only standing building on the site, believed to have been the guest house, is now a public house known as 'The Abbey' and some medieval work can be seen in the rear elevation of numbers 7, 8 and 9 Abbey Lane.

Between 1115 and 1120 a small Augustinian priory was founded at Calke by Richard, Earl of Chester, but in 1172 the prior and most of the canons moved to Repton and Calke became a dependent cell. The buildings have disappeared under the house that in 1808 was given the erroneous name Calke Abbey by Sir Henry Crewe. The Augustinian priory at Repton, dedicated to the Holy Trinity, had been endowed in the 1150s by Matilda, the widow of the fourth Earl of Chester. It was built symbolically close to the east of the parish church and the former Mercian Benedictine double monastery that had been destroyed by the Vikings. The priory consisted of a church, cloister, chapter house, refectory, and the prior's lodgings and hall with cellars beneath; various outbuildings stood a little away from this compact group. The earliest surviving work from the late twelfth century includes part of the original undercroft, which has deeply splayed windows and a rib-vault in the late Norman style.

The Augustinians (or Austin canons, as they were known for short) had three other small houses within Derbyshire. Gresley Priory was founded during the reign of Henry I (the royal sponsor of this order in England) by William de Gresley. It received further endowments by his descendants, but in 1339 it had only a prior and four canons, the same number as were there at its dissolution in 1536. The nave of the church and the lower part of the tower survived the dissolution as it belonged to the parish of Church Gresley, but the cloister, refectory and chapter house were reduced to their foundations. A house of Austin canonesses, which became known as the nunnery of St Mary of King's Mead, was founded in the 1150s by an abbot of Darley on a site in the meadows to the west of the borough of Derby, but its endowments were modest and it has left no trace above ground. Finally, a member of the Curzon family founded a priory in Breadsall Park, about 1½ miles north of the village, sometime before 1266, for a prior and two canons. It remained small and poor

St George and St Mary's church, Church Gresley. Most of the building dates from the nineteenth century, but the lower part of the tower was built by the Austin canons of the small priory that was founded by William de Gresley in the early twelfth century. After the dissolution the western half of the building continued as a parish church.

PHOTOGRAPH: CARNEGIE

Beauchief Abbey. After the dissolution in 1536 the buildings and surrounding 260-acre estate in what became known as The Liberty of Beauchief were bought by Sir Nicholas Strelley. The estate passed through marriage to Edward Pegge, who converted the base of the church tower into a private chapel; the interior is still furnished as it was in the 1660s. In 1727, when Samuel Buck made this sketch, the church still retained its top storey and 'the beautiful headland' that gave Beauchief its Norman-French name was still surrounded by rolling countryside.

COURTESY OF DERBYSHIRE LOCAL STUDIES AND WWW. PICTURETHEPAST.ORG.UK and only an arch and a drain survive in the basement of the Jacobean house that succeeded it.

The Premonstratensians or White canons, who were named after their original site at Prémontré in northern France, built two medium-sized abbeys at Beauchief and Dale. Beauchief was the Norman French name for the 'beautiful headland' in a remote corner of the parish of Norton, by the river Sheaf on Derbyshire's border with Yorkshire. The abbey, dedicated to St Mary and St Thomas the Martyr (otherwise known as Thomas Becket) was founded between 1173 and 1176 by Robert FitzRanulf, the former sheriff of Nottinghamshire and Derbyshire and lord of Norton and Alfreton. The first canons came from Welbeck Abbey (Nottinghamshire), which had been founded in 1153. The estate granted by FitzRanulf extended from the river Sheaf as far as Abbey Brook and Chancet Wood in the north and to a spring and stream by the present Twentywell Lane in the south-west. Twentywell is a corruption of St Quentin well, named after the abbey of St Quentin, not far from Prémontré. Further grants soon extended the abbey's estate up the hill to the south, as far as the hamlets of Greenhill and Birchitt. The earliest charters also record the gifts of Norton mill, some small properties in Norton Lees and Meersbrook, and all the rights of the churches of Norton, Alfreton, Edwalton (Nottinghamshire) and Wymeswold (Leicestershire). The abbey soon began to attract grants from the lords of other manors in Derbyshire, Yorkshire and Nottinghamshire and eventually received substantial donations from the Chaworths, who succeeded the FitzRanulfs in 1269. The surviving architecture at Beauchief is dominated by the great fourteenth-century tower, but excavations have shown that buildings were laid out to the standard Premonstratensian plan in several stages between the late twelfth and the fifteenth century.

Little now remains of the other Premonstratensian abbey that was founded on an attractive, peaceful site at Dale in south-east Derbyshire, nor is there much evidence from medieval sources. The legend of its chequered beginnings is that,

following a vision, a baker left Derby to become a hermit in Depedale, where the site of his dwelling and oratory cut out of the soft sandstone cliff is still visible; William Stukeley drew the interior of the cave, furnished as a chapel, on a visit about 1710. In the 1150s Serlo de Grendon invited some Augustinian canons from Calke to establish a priory here, supported by a gift of all his land at Boyah, which afterwards became a grange, but after about 30 years the canons were sent back to Calke by Henry II for infringing the laws of his Forest of East Derbyshire. Serlo's son, William de Grendon, thereafter invited a prior and six Premonstratensian canons from Tupholme (Lincolnshire) to re-found the priory about 1185, with the endowment of Stanley Park instead of Boyah, but their poverty forced them to leave seven years later. William de Grendon then invited the Premonstratensian abbey at Welbeck (Nottinghamshire) to send five canons, but they too soon withdrew. Success finally came when William FitzRanulph, an important royal official, founded an abbey in Stanley Park, adjacent to the former monastic settlement in Depedale, and persuaded his nephew William de Grendon to donate Depedale and Boyah. An abbot and nine canons arrived from England's senior Premonstratensian house at Newhouse in January 1200 and permanent buildings were completed four years later. The first abbot, Walter de Toteneye, who was there for 31 years, was a driving force who obtained many more endowments until Dale was the second richest abbey in Derbyshire.

Masses for the donors' families were sung in the chapel of Depedale, which became the Grendon chantry and is now the parish church of All Saints, Dale. It is one of the most curious historic buildings in the county, for it is only 26 feet long and 25 feet wide and shares the same roof as a dwelling house that was once the village inn. The nave is Norman and the aisle was added soon after, though most of the architectural details are in the Perpendicular Gothic style of the late Middle Ages, when an upper storey with an open timber roof was added. The interior is packed with post-medieval box-pews, gallery, pulpit and altar and is one of 'the churches the Victorians forgot'.

As for the abbey church, the chief surviving architectural fragment is the late thirteenth-century arch of the east window, which rises over 17 feet high and which seems to have once had similar geometrical tracery to that of Newstead Abbey (Nottinghamshire). Excavations have proved that the church had transepts 100 feet in length, a crossing tower, a chapel attached to the south chancel, and a nave that has not been fully identified. The other abbey buildings were laid out to the standard Premonstratensian pattern. An 80 feet-square cloister has been excavated, the outline of the chapter house on the east side of the cloister can still be recognised, and the remains of a gatehouse survive to the north-west.

The income that might have supported the foundation of splendid abbeys and priories in Derbyshire was diverted instead to monasteries beyond the county's borders and to the cathedrals at Lichfield and Lincoln. Numerous monastic granges were set up, especially in the Peak District, to administer the estates that were granted to religious houses in neighbouring counties or from even further away. Just across the border in Staffordshire, Burton Abbey had lost much of its Derbyshire property before the Norman Conquest, but William I gave it important manors and a church and mills in Derby. Then, in 1080, the Conqueror's largest tenant-in-chief in Derbyshire, Henry de Ferrers, founded a Benedictine priory near his castle at Tutbury and endowed it with the manors of Marston-on-Dove and Doveridge. Both these religious houses subsequently received grants and bequests from other Derbyshire landowners, as did Staffordshire houses at Brewood, Croxden, Dieulacres, Hulton and Trentham. The principal Nottinghamshire monasteries that acquired estates in Derbyshire were the Cluniac priory at Lenton and the Premonstratensian abbey at Welbeck, but smaller grants were also made to houses at Newstead, Rufford, Shelford, Thurgaton and Worksop. The other religious houses that benefited were: in Leicestershire, Garendon, Launde and St Mary's Leicester; in Cheshire, Combermere and Vale Royal; in Shropshire, Buildwas and Lilleshall; in Lincolnshire, Louth and Sempringham; and Basingwerk (Clwyd), Dunstable (Bedfordshire), Merevale (Warwickshire) and Roche (Yorkshire).

Little or nothing survives of the various properties of the military orders within Derbyshire. The preceptory of St Lazarus of Jerusalem that was founded at Locko about 1120, from England's principal Lazarite house at Burton Lazars (Leicestershire), primarily for the care of lepers, has disappeared without trace, but part of the chapel of the preceptory of the Knights Hospitaller at Yeaveley, south of Ashbourne, survives as a wall lit by lancet windows. The Yeaveley preceptory was founded about 1190 by Ralph Foun, who donated a former hermitage at Stydd, together with lands, woods and mills. Later Founs and Meynells made further grants in Yeaveley and different families made bequests in other parts of the county. In 1312 Yeaveley became the owner of the suppressed Knights Templar estate at Temple Normanton.

The hospitals that were founded in the twelfth century were also run by the religious. Nothing survives of the Hospital of St Helen, which was founded in 1137 by the Derby burgesses on the northern outskirts of the borough as a hospital for the poor under the care of a group of brethren led by a master or warden, nor of the leper hospital dedicated to St Leonard, which seems to have been founded by Henry II by 1171 to the south of the medieval borough. Leper hospitals were often dedicated to St Leonard. That at Chesterfield, which stood beyond the town alongside the road to Calow, where it is commemorated by various Spital place-names, was founded by King John between 1189 and 1194 and survived until the Dissolution. There are no remains of the Hospital of St Leonard at Alkmonton, which was established for female lepers by Robert de Bagpuize of Barton c.1100 and dissolved in 1548, but the site of the Hospital of St Mary in the Peak at Castleton is marked by prominent earthworks at the north-eastern edge of the medieval town (opposite the entrance to Losehill Hall). It was endowed for the infirm poor by the wife of one of the William Peverils and survived until the Dissolution.

Parish churches and chapels-of-ease

The process of creating new parishes and chapelries that had begun in the Anglo-Scandinavian period was completed by the Normans. Within the old minster territory of Chesterfield, for instance, a charter of 1121–38 informs us that the chapel at Wingerworth had recently been erected by Nicholas de Wingerworth. In the same parish, Brampton had become a chapelry by about

The interior of the nave, All Saints church, Youlgreave. Youlgreave church's impressive tower can be seen for miles around. At first glance, the church seems to date from the Perpendicular Gothic period of church architecture in the late Middle Ages, but closer inspection reveals that it is much older. The wide nave is late Norman, with the south arcade (*right*) finished before that on the north side. The circular piers are topped with capitals in styles which can be dated to the close of the twelfth century. The font is also late Norman. Youlgreave was anciently a chapel-of-ease within the huge parish of Bakewell.

PHOTOGRAPH: CARNEGIE

St Peter and St Paul's church, Old Brampton. Topped by its broach spire, Old Brampton church has a Norman south doorway and one small Norman window in the tower. It was founded as a chapel-of-ease in the huge parish of Chesterfield and did not have its own burial ground until the late thirteenth century. Until then, the inhabitants of Brampton were obliged to maintain that section of the churchyard wall at Chesterfield that enclosed the part of the graveyard that was reserved for their burials.

PHOTOGRAPH: AUTHOR

1100, though it was not allowed its own burial ground until the late thirteenth century; in or about 1260 the inhabitants of Brampton were still maintaining that part of the churchyard wall at Chesterfield that enclosed their burial plot. Brimington, Whittington and Walton also became chapelries of the large parish of Chesterfield. Former allegiances such as these are often revealed by the payment of annual dues or by who had the right to appoint ministers and chaplains. Thus the vicar of Bakewell received a pension from Youlgreave and he chose the clergymen who served the numerous chapels-of-ease of his enormous parish. Likewise, as rector of Ashbourne the dean of Lincoln remained the patron of the former chapelries of Bradley, Edlaston and Fenny Bentley.

Derbyshire had been part of the diocese of Lichfield since the seventh century, but in 1102 the see was moved to Coventry, and from the 1220s or 1230s it was known as Coventry & Lichfield. The Norman kings made generous grants of the tithes and other ecclesiastical dues of the minster churches on their enormous Derbyshire estates to the cathedrals at Lichfield and Lincoln. In 1093 William II gave Ashbourne and Chesterfield, together with their chapelries, to Lincoln. A decade later Henry I gave Lincoln the two Derby collegiate churches of All Saints and St Alkmund, as well as the minster church of Wirksworth and its chapelries. Henry also gave Melbourne to the bishop of Carlisle when his see was founded in 1133. In 1192 the future King John gave the major part of the income (including the valuable tithes of lead) of Bakewell and Hope and their extensive chapelries to the bishop of Coventry &

Lichfield, who in the first half of the thirteenth century also received Sandiacre. In these ways, much of the wealth generated in Derbyshire drained away across its borders. Meanwhile, the county's religious houses acquired the rights and dues of some of the smaller parishes – Darley 9, Dale 4, Beauchief 3, Repton 3, Gresley 2, King's Mead 1 and Breadsall 1 – and monasteries from outside the county obtained others.

The Norman origins of many Derbyshire churches, or perhaps the rebuilding of an earlier pre-Conquest church, may be recognised in architectural features or pieces of sculpture that were not replaced later in the Middle Ages. Although grand rebuilding schemes in the fourteenth and fifteenth centuries have obliterated such evidence in many parishes, notably Ashbourne, Chesterfield and Tideswell, no fewer than 55 of the 140 or so Derbyshire churches and chapels that were founded by 1200 still retain at least a doorway, a splayed window, or a plain stone font from the Norman period. Such features are often discovered in the churches of the smaller parishes, such as Alsop, Beeley, Stanley or Thorpe, where the population failed to grow or even declined in later centuries, thus reducing the need and the resources to rebuild.

Most Norman work in Derbyshire dates from the middle or later years of the twelfth century and is instantly recognisable as a rounded arch, perhaps decorated with a zigzag pattern, or a row of circular piers supporting the arcade between the nave and its aisles, with capitals carved with scallop or waterleaf designs. The strangest carvings to modern eyes are those that are placed over the main door on the south side of the nave. Those at Ault Hucknall have been interpreted as the lamb and cross, St George fighting a dragon, and a centaur.

St Leonard's church, Thorpe. Tucked away at the end of the village of Thorpe, close to the entrance to Dovedale, St Leonard's is one of a small group of Derbyshire churches that have retained their Norman towers. It has the characteristic twin belfry openings, slit windows, and quoin stones instead of buttresses. The battlements were added in the late Middle Ages.

PHOTOGRAPH: AUTHOR

Norman carvings, Bradbourne. The Normans added the west tower of All Saints, Bradbourne to the Saxon church, part of which remains. This detail of the carvings on the south door of the tower shows a typical range of mythical beats and human figures whose moralising meaning is now largely lost to us.

PHOTOGRAPH: CARNEGIE

RIGHT

St Michael's church, Alsop-en-le-Dale. Although the west tower is a Victorian imitation of the Norman style, the south door is original twelfth-century work, and the building gives a sense of what a small medieval church looked like. It was not enlarged during the Middle Ages because the population of the village shrank, so that it now serves only a tiny settlement. Alsop is a common surname that spread well beyond Derbyshire as people left the parish.

PHOTOGRAPH: CARNEGIE

Other curious carvings over Norman doorways can be seen at Hognaston and Parwich (re-set in the west door of the tower) and to a lesser extent at Ashford, Findern, Kedleston and Willington. The earliest wall-paintings inside a Derbyshire church, indeed the only ones to survive from the Norman period, are the late twelfth-century murals at Wingerworth, which depict the head of Christ and four saints in roundels. The most remarkable fonts are those at Ashover (made of lead and decorated with the figures of the Apostles beneath a continuous Romanesque arcade), Wilne (made from a circular, carved Anglo-Scandinavian cross), and Youlgreave (decorated with animals and fleurs-de-lis, with a projecting side stoup).

Norman towers are uncommon and have usually been given a new crown and sometimes buttresses in the later Middle Ages, but they can be recognised at Aston-upon-Trent, Bradbourne, Brassington, Mugginton, Norton, Thorpe, Tissington and Whitwell. The rest of St Lawrence's church, Whitwell, has Norman walls, reaching up to a corbel table above the clerestorey; the masonry can be distinguished readily from the ashlar stone that was used in the rebuilding in the Decorated Gothic style of the first half of the fourteenth century. The whole church of St Giles, Sandiacre, was another substantial Norman building until it was restyled in the mid-fourteenth century and the arcades of the nave of All Saints, Youlgreave, show that there too a large Norman church is incorporated within the impressive Perpendicular Gothic building that was reared in the fifteenth century.

Norman font, All Saints church, Ashover. This, the finest Norman font in Derbyshire, is encased in lead and decorated with ten pairs of standing figures, each about eight inches high, under Romanesque arches. The figures, probably represent the Apostles. The font is only about two feet in diameter.

PHOTOGRAPH: CARNEGIE

BELOW LEFT

Eyam parish church is very unusual in having two Norman fonts. It has been argued that this one, now in the north aisle, is Saxon; but it looks primitive not because it is so ancient, but because it is made of millstone grit, which is difficult to carve. Its simple Norman arches, and a comparison with other Derbyshire fonts, most of which are plain, suggest that it is more likely that it was made after the Norman Conquest, although we cannot be certain. On a visit to Eyam church in 1864 Sir Stephen Glynne made no mention of this font, but noted that the one by the main entrance through the porch was, 'a circular bowl on [a] stem of Norman character'. The font shown here is said to have been recovered in the later nineteenth century from the garden of Brookfield Manor in Hathersage, where it had served as a flower pot, and given a new base. Perhaps this font was originally used in St Michael's church, Hathersage, before it was replaced it in the mid-fifteenth century by the font still in use there.

PHOTOGRAPH: CARNEGIE, WITH THANKS TO EYAM CHURCH

Three photographs of the fine Norman carvings to be found on the arches of the tower within the parish church of Melbourne. Rita Wood has argued recently that these remarkably well-preserved carvings on the capitals seen from the chancel and beneath the tower of Melbourne church were inspired by passages from the Bible and a sermon of St Augustine and were teaching aids favoured by Austin canons.

The font in St Thomas's church, Mellor. The font is probably Norman rather than late Saxon. The carving is cut into the sandstone bowl in a similar manner to the incisions on the fonts at Tissington and Thorpe. On this side we see a helmeted warrior mounted on a horse. Out of sight are two other horses biting the tails that curve over their bodies and a small naked man between them. Such figures are mysterious to modern eyes. The bowl is lined with lead.

St Michael and St Mary, Melbourne, is known throughout the land as one of England's finest and most enigmatic Norman churches. For a start, it has no churchyard and its original dedication was just to St Mary. The explanation for both these puzzles is that Melbourne's original parish church, which was dedicated to St Michael, stood further north at the end of Castle Street, where its graveyard continued in use as the parish burial ground until 1860. At the Reformation, St Michael's was partly demolished and St Mary's became the parish church under a joint dedication. Why then was such a grand building as St Mary's erected not far from a parish church that was adequate for local needs? The old explanation was that, as it was presented by Henry I to Adelulf, the first bishop of Carlisle, when his see was created in 1133, it must have been built as a secure base for the bishop, just south of the Trent, in face of frequent Scottish invasions, but this idea has been discredited by the research of Richard Gem and Rita Wood. It is now clear that the church was begun, and perhaps finished, in the 1120s, when the first King Henry was lord of the manor. The gallery in the upper storey at the west end of the church seems to have been designed as a distinctive viewpoint for the king, modelled on the gallery where Charlemagne sat in his chapel at Aachen. Eight large, carved capitals that can be seen from the chancel and crossing were inspired by passages from Jeremiah, Luke, Hebrews, and a sermon of St Augustine, each of which concern preachers and teachers. They have therefore been interpreted as visual aids or basic texts for a small group of Austin canons and their pupils. Henry I was a patron of the Augustinian order, and his confidant, Adelulf, was prior of the Augustinian community at Nostell (Yorkshire) before he became a bishop. The canons may have left Melbourne after Henry died, but they have left their mark on the iconography of the church.

Melbourne church is remarkable for its size and grandeur and its unusually elaborate, two-storey arrangement. The west front is unique amongst English parish churches in having twin towers that enclose a public space, or narthex, at the entrance and a royal gallery above. Passages or walkways at clerestorey level connect the west gallery to the crossing tower (which was heightened in the seventeenth century) and to a (demolished) upper room of unknown purpose above the chancel. Only the side walls of the chancel remain Norman, but traces of three former apses can be seen inside and outside the eastern end of the church. All these features point to strong influence from Rhineland churches. The slow, solid rhythms of the great circular columns in the nave suggest strength and dignity and the vigorous carvings in many parts of the church reinforce the sense that this is a very special building, a royal foundation that was far removed in status from an ordinary parish church. Curiously, it is constrained at the west end by the high wall of a substantial medieval barn. Perhaps the site was originally that of the royal manor house, giving quick and easy access to the gallery?

A similar plan was mooted for the west end of Bakewell church. Excavation has proved that walled-up arches at the western ends of the aisles led into towers that were never completed. Instead, the present outer west wall was built 15 feet further back than the planned façade, in the form of a blank arcade of intersected Norman arches above a decorated doorway. Other Norman work includes the first bay of the nave arcades (unless they are pre-Conquest), the outer wall of the south aisle, and some of the masonry of the chancel, including an apse. In 1852 the Norman nave arcades, except the westernmost arches, were 'rebuilt in a lighter style'. It was during the mid-nineteenth-century restoration of the church that the Norman and Anglo-Scandinavian cross fragments that are displayed in the porch were discovered in the foundations.

Bakewell was planned in a similar style to Melbourne, with twin towers at the west end, but these never materialised. Instead, the west door is the most striking Norman feature.

This representation of St Michael in a south window of the nave of All Saints, Dalbury, was thought to date from about 1200 but has now been attributed to the late eleventh century, making it possibly the earliest example of glazing *in situ* in England. It was restored and conserved by the York Glaziers' Trust in 1980. The saint is identified by his wings.

BELOW

The church at Dalbury stands inside an enclosure marked by a bank and a ditch, seen here just beyond the path. The etymology of Dalbury is 'Dalla's fortification'. Was this the *burh* or fort that gave the village its name?

PHOTOGRAPHS: CARNEGIE

LEFT

The nave of St Michael and St Mary's, Melbourne. This view looking through the nave arcade into the north aisle, shows one of the finest Norman church interiors in the country. The building was erected in the 1120s, when Melbourne was a royal manor, in an unusually grand style for a parish church. It has long been accepted that it must have had a special purpose, but what that was remains a matter for debate.

PHOTOGRAPH: CARNEGIE

Far lower in status than these enormous churches, Steetley chapel delights visitors to its hidden site in the north-eastern tip of Derbyshire, tucked away in a remote corner of the parish of Whitwell. The style is that of the mid-twelfth century, but we do not know the name of the lord who built it nor to which saint it was dedicated. Steetley is a deserted medieval village and for a long time the chapel stood forlorn and abandoned as a roofless ruin. It was restored to its present condition between 1876 and 1880 by the ecclesiastical architect, J.L. Pearson, who gave it a new roof and bellcote and an extravagant portal above the carved doorway into the nave. The chapel consists of an aisleless nave, a chancel and the only Norman apse to survive in Derbyshire. A corbel table of carved heads encircles the church and the apse is decorated with pilasters, a string course and three splayed windows. Inside the chapel, elaborately ornamented arches separate the nave from the chancel and the chancel from the apse. Their capitals are carved not only with the usual zigzag and scallop designs, medallions and foliage scrolls, but with animals (including a double-headed lion), signs of the Zodiac, and depictions of St George and the Dragon and Adam and Eve. Sir Nikolaus Pevsner's conclusion was that, 'There are few Norman churches in England so consistently made into showpieces by those who designed them and those who paid for them.'

Steetley Chapel. One of England's finest small Norman churches, Steetley chapel stands almost alone in the north-eastern tip of Derbyshire, within the ancient parish of Whitwell. The original dedication is not known; nor do we know the name of the Norman lord who founded it in the middle years of the twelfth century. Steetley became a deserted medieval village and the chapel fell into ruin. By the time that it was illustrated in Daniel and Samuel Lysons, *Magna Britannia*, V (1817), and probably long before, the nave roof had collapsed. As interest in old churches grew in the nineteenth century, the chapel was recognised as an outstanding example of Norman architecture. It was painstakingly restored in 1876–80 by the leading Victorian architect, J. L. Pearson. His over-elaborate south door has been rightly criticised and he chose to place the bell turret curiously between the nave and the chancel, but otherwise Pearson sought to restore the church to its original appearance. This view from the east, taken from the churchyard path, shows the apse, once a characteristic feature of small Norman churches. The pilaster buttresses, string course, decorated heads of the corbel table, and small splayed windows all date the chapel to the middle decades of the twelfth century. Ashlar stone from local magnesian limestone quarries gave the chapel a high-quality appearance. The interior view is from the nave, looking through the two chancel arches into the vaulted apse.

Towns

At the time of the Norman Conquest Derby was the only borough in the county and no other place showed any sign of developing into a market town. Domesday Book recorded that the number of burgesses in Derby had fallen to 140 since the reign of Edward the Confessor and that 103 tenements were unoccupied. Nottingham was far more prosperous and easily the most important place in the Trent valley. But Derby was still a mint town, for two moneyers are known to have been striking coins there between c.1075 and 1087 and Domesday Book noted ten corn mills on the river Derwent and the

Markeaton Brook. The original area of the Market Place and the Corn Market, north of the brook, was reduced in later centuries by the encroachment of the surrounding stalls and shops. On the other side of the confluence of the brook and river, Morledge may have been another Norman market site, for it was situated below Copecastel Hill (whose name means 'market-castle'). For many years this was where the borough's cattle market was held. Weekly markets in the town were eventually established on Sundays, Mondays, Wednesdays, and from Thursday evenings to Friday evenings, and four fairs were held each year.

As yet, the town was not divorced from the surrounding countryside. Derby's open fields, where cereals were grown, lay mostly on the west side of town, but also across the Derwent to the east and north-east. Low-lying meadows occupied the river valley and the common pastures stretched beyond. The burgesses' earliest royal charter dates from 1155–60, but this confirmed the rights and customs that their predecessors had enjoyed since the reign of William II. A charter of 1204 granted the burgesses the same liberties as those of Nottingham, including freedom to elect their own reeve or bailiff and the right to have a merchant guild, which became an influential governing body for the weavers, fullers, dyers, tanners, glovemakers and later the potters. Medieval Derby flourished as a trading centre in wool, lead, wood, foodstuffs and other merchandise. In the reign of King John ships and boats were still able to sail all the way up the Derwent to the borough.

At the time of Domesday Book the large royal estate at Chesterfield was administered from Newbold, 'the new building' in what is now a suburb of the town, but the centre of influence soon moved back to the area of the Roman fort, dominated by the parish church. Chesterfield became a market town long before it received its first charter in 1204, which allowed weekly markets on Tuesdays and Saturdays and an annual fair of eight days at the feast of the Exaltation of the Holy Cross. A market was recorded in 1164–65 and a fair in 1196. The old market lay partly in the churchyard to the north of the church and partly in Holywell Street, where Saltergate brought Cheshire salters into town. In the twelfth century the present Market Place was laid out to the west of the church at what was then the edge of the town, in the space still bounded by Packers Row, Low Pavement and High Street, with the long, narrow plots of the burgesses stretching back from the houses and shops that fronted on to the Market Place. William Senior's map of Chesterfield c.1635 shows how little the shape of the town had altered nearly five centuries later. A grid pattern of narrow lanes gave a special character to the Shambles, or the Butchery as it was known in the Middle Ages, at the eastern edge of the Market Place where each lane was given over to some special trade. West Bar was one of the two bars where market tolls were collected and immediately beyond lay the fields, meadows, pastures and commons.

The 1204 charter from King John was a grant to William Brewer, a Devon man who was an outstanding royal officer in the reigns of both Richard and

John, and one who had a particular interest in founding boroughs. After the suppression of John's rebellion in 1194, the custody of Richard's many possessions in the Midlands was given to Brewer. He was in charge of the honour of Peveril until 1196–97 and remained sheriff of Nottinghamshire and Derbyshire until 1200. His 1204 charter allowed the burgesses of Chesterfield, through the lord of the manor, to enjoy the same liberties and customs as those of Nottingham. In other words, Chesterfield became what historians call a seigneurial borough, like Sheffield or Bawtry, where the burgesses were not entirely free from the jurisdiction of the manor court. In time, four medieval guilds were established in the town: those of St Helen (based on the chapel on the Sheffield road, by the ancient holy well); the Blessed Mary (founded in the parish church in 1219); Holy Cross (which merged with that of the Blessed Mary in 1540); and the guild of the Smiths (which merged with Holy Cross in 1387). Chesterfield's principal medieval trade was in cloth, based on wool from the Peak District that was spun, woven, fulled and dyed in the town. Another thriving group were the tanners on the banks of the river Hipper and the leather workers who used their products.

At the other side of the county, Ashbourne had a market long before it became necessary to obtain a royal charter to hold one. This was perhaps held in the churchyard of the ancient minster until a new town was planned further east in the thirteenth century. The present Market Place, which was created on the hillside alongside the road to Buxton, has since been reduced in size by the encroachment of permanent buildings. Large-scale nineteenth-century maps show that the main highway, Church Street, had a regular pattern of burgage plots laid out along both sides, as far north as a parallel minor road that led to the top of the Market Place and as far south as the brook that separates Ashbourne from Compton and still divides the Uppards from the Downwards at the annual Shrove Tuesday football match. In the thirteenth century the new town was referred to as 'the royal borough of Ashbourne', for the estate was still held by the king. Like Chesterfield, it was a seigneurial borough, subject to the manorial courts but without a castle to dominate it. Ashbourne flourished as a market centre, where the Peak meets the Dove valley, and as a thoroughfare town at the junction of the Derby–Buxton–Manchester road with roads to Uttoxeter and Leek.

The church at Wirksworth was another ancient minster, situated in an ideal position for the development of a market where the hills of the High Peak descend to the Midland Plain and at the centre of the Derbyshire lead industry. The town was granted a charter for a weekly market and annual fair in 1306, probably as a confirmation of ancient rights. The market place extends from the churchyard up the slope to the west and is much infilled, but it does not seem to have been surrounded by burgage plots and we have no documentary evidence of any attempt to found a borough.

Bakewell was yet another minster church and the wealthiest manor in the Peak at the time of Domesday Book. By ancient custom, it held a Monday

Ashbourne in the 1890s. The Ordnance Survey map shows how the Victorian market town was still largely confined within its medieval limits. The Norman lords had created a small borough that was separated from the village of Compton by the Henmore Brook, to the east of the ancient parish church of St Oswald. A triangular Market Place (that was later much encroached upon by stalls, shops and pubs) stretched up the hill at the eastern end of the town, as far as Back Lane and King Street, which appear to follow the line of the original through route towards Wirksworth. The pattern of medieval burgage plots was partly retained in Victorian times by the buildings fronting both sides of Church Street and their long gardens up to this old track or down to the boundary stream. The medieval plan of the town is still evident on the ground.

COURTESY OF DERBYSHIRE RECORD OFFICE

market and a three-day fair on 13–15 August, then from 1254 a chartered annual fair lasting 15 days from 1 May. Henry I granted Bakewell to William Peveril in the first decade of the twelfth century and it was probably one of this family that founded the seigneurial borough on the opposite side of the valley to the motte-and-bailey on Castle Hill. Richard I granted Bakewell to Ralph Gernon, the first of eight generations of a family who held the manor for nearly 200 years but who were absentee landowners who lived in Essex. Firm evidence for the existence of a borough comes from the second half of the thirteenth century. Ralph Gernon III, lord of the manor from 1258 to 1274, addressed 'my Burgesses' when he appointed a chaplain in a chantry chapel in the parish church; a near contemporary charter of Beauchief Abbey mentions 'a burgage in Bakewell'; and in the Derbyshire Eyre of 1281 a widow claimed a third of a burgage in Bakewell. At the same court, Ralph le Wyne, the queen's bailiff, argued that Bakewell was a free borough where tenements could be bequeathed, but the knights and stewards of the shire affirmed definitely that it was not a borough, by which they may have meant that it did not have the status of a chartered borough such as Derby. The uncertainty about the precise status of the Bakewell burgesses was resolved in 1286, when the 'Burgesses & Free Servants' of Bakewell had their liberties set down in a charter from their lord, Sir William Gernon; these rights included the freedom to sell or give away their burgages and for their heirs to inherit. The references to burgages in records from the late thirteenth century onwards show that all the plots lay in 'Upper Bakewell' towards the church and the present Buxton Road, by the original market place. The records of the 1281 eyre also note that 'Henry de Langedon erected 20 shops on the king's highway in Baukwell' and that four more shops had been erected by others. Bakewell was obviously a thriving commercial centre.

Very many English medieval towns were seigneurial boroughs such as Bakewell rather than fully fledged corporations. William Peveril I founded seigneurial boroughs, which he arranged around market places alongside his castles at Bolsover and Castleton and enclosed with defensive ditches. Bolsover obtained a market charter in 1256, but this may have just confirmed ancient rights. The town has a linear grid plan along the limestone ridge, extending from the castle to St Mary's church. The six-inch Ordnance Survey map of 1883 marks 'Intrenchments' along part of the northern boundary of the town and to the south-east, just beyond the church. It also shows the Market Place, which had been much reduced by encroachments, and the pattern of former burgage plots extending back from narrow frontages in Castle Street, Middle Street and Church Street.

Castleton was referred to as the 'borough of the High Peak' in 1196, so its market grants of 1223 and 1245 must have confirmed and extended existing privileges. The outline of the market place between St Edmund's church and the steep hill on which the castle is placed is still recognisable, despite infilling, as are traces of the town's defences (especially on the north-eastern side of the present car park and alongside a stream in the north-west). These defences form a huge rectangle and consist of an earth rampart and ditch, which probably date from the twelfth century. A survey of properties in 1255 recorded 43⅝ burgages and 71 stall holders in the borough, but it seems that the space within the defences was never fully occupied. Deeds relating to burgages continued to be drafted in the late-medieval and Tudor periods. For example, in 1455 'a burgage in Castleton' lay 'between the mill and lands of Richard Cademan west and east and the ditch of the town and 2 large stones south and north'. The arable townfields, their strip pattern partly preserved by later stone walls, stretched to the north and east of the town ditch, with extensive pastures and commons beyond.

The countryside

Most of the population of England under the Normans lived in the countryside. In Derbyshire, the various rural settlements ranged from populous villages in the river valleys of the south to numerous scattered hamlets in the Peak District. On the whole, the names of the settlements that were recorded in the Derbyshire folios of Domesday Book have survived, but Blingsby, Cowley, Cottons, Hearthcote and Wallstone are now just single buildings and others have disappeared from the map altogether. The approximate locations of Uluritune, Ludwell and Upton are known, but a few other lost names, such as Bolun, Tunstall and Langley, have gone without trace. Some new settlements do not appear until local records become much fuller from the late twelfth century onwards. For most of the Norman period we have few documents and little archaeological evidence to guide our understanding of life in the Derbyshire countryside. Occasionally, we are provided with clues which suggest that some villages were moved to new sites after the Norman Conquest, though we have no means of discovering precisely when this happened. For example, Domesday Book records two small places that lay close together within the manor of Stainsby which were both called Lunt, Lund or Lound, from the Old Norse word for a grove or small wood. Several centuries later, these are marked on a William Senior map of 1609 not as settlements but as field names to the west and east of the village of Heath and the isolated position of the parish church is shown in the eastern one. On the current Ordnance Survey 'Explorer' map, the former church site is marked as 'Church (rems of)', close to Junction 29 on the M1 motorway, a quarter-of-a-mile to the east of the parish church that was built to replace it in 1853. Senior referred to 'the Heathe' and this was how the village was first recorded in the thirteenth century. The regularity of the houses and crofts stretching back from the village street to the open fields suggests that a planned village replaced the two Lounds and took its name from the heath upon which it was sited.

With this example in mind, we might consider other places where the parish church now occupies a remote position in relation to the village that it served.

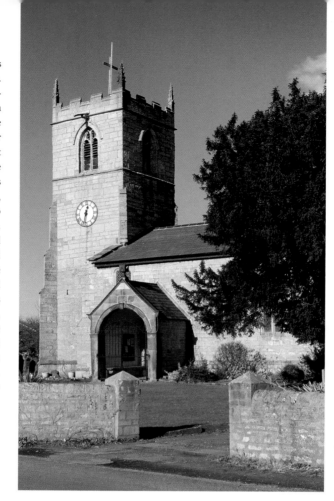

St John the Baptist's church, Clowne. Like many medium-sized medieval parish churches, Clowne has a Perpendicular Gothic tower, but the interior of the building reveals much earlier work, going back to Norman times. The church is sited intriguingly, well away from the village centre and alongside what is now a minor road, suggesting that the settlement has moved since the twelfth century.

PHOTOGRAPH: AUTHOR

Brailsford, Clowne, Duffield and South Wingfield are prime examples, where an isolated church perhaps marks the original nucleus of a settlement. Great Longstone is not as immediately obvious, but St Giles's church stands at a bend of the road from Hassop on a knoll above the rows of houses that on a Senior map of 1617 were arranged in a regular pattern on both sides of the village green and the road descending to the east, with long, narrow crofts extending back to the open arable fields. On Senior's map Great Longstone looks to be a planned settlement. But Derbyshire has few such examples compared with some other parts of the country, notably North Yorkshire and County Durham.

Most families in Norman England earned their living by the cultivation of small farms of 10–15 acres, sometimes more, of land in the open fields, with rights to cut hay in the meadows and to graze livestock on the common pastures. The services that the unfree peasants, or villeins, of Derbyshire owed their lords, such as helping with ploughing, hoeing, harvesting and carrying, were lighter than those that were customary in southern England, but they were still burdensome at times. It helped if a farmer had another source of employment, such as weaving cloth, mining coal or hewing millstones. In the White Peak families were often able to supplement their farming income by mining and smelting lead. Domesday Book recorded three lead smelting works on the royal manor of Wirksworth, one each on the royal manors of Ashford, Bakewell and Matlock Bridge, and one on Ralph FitzHubert's manor

Peveril Castle and Castleton. Castleton is now thought of as a village, but in the Middle Ages it was a small town or borough. This new town was laid out by the Norman lord, William Peveril, below his castle, on a site defined by wide ditches and ramparts which can still be followed in part today, particularly the section near the car park. St Edmund's church was built in the centre of the town, as a chapel-of-ease of the parish of Hope, and a market place was created alongside it. Much of this old trading space has been lost to buildings over the centuries. The leading townsmen, or burgesses, held their property in long, narrow 'burgage plots' within the town and in the strips of the open-fields beyond the defensive earthworks. The town failed to thrive. Only its market, its burgess privileges and its hospital on its north-eastern boundary distinguished it from a large village.

at Crich. The High Peak mines were granted to William Peveril, but in 1154 they reverted to the Crown. The principal duties that were payable on lead were known as lot and cope. Lot was paid by a miner to the lord of a mining liberty at the rate of every thirteenth dish of lead ore, whereas cope was a money payment of 4*d*, later 6*d*, for every load of ore. The Crown got a large income from these dues, and the tithes of the parishes of Bakewell, Hope and Tideswell produced substantial revenues for the dean and chapter of Lichfield Cathedral, for lead was in great demand far and wide for building works of all kind. Pigs of lead were transported down the Trent and the Humber wherever possible, for water transport was much cheaper than land transport for heavy, bulky goods, but it may have been economical to use the highways when heading south. The foundations of a bridge that crossed the old course of the Trent just north of Hemington (Leicestershire) have been dated to about 1100. It is the only surviving example of such an early bridge across a major English river.

Deeds and accounts that survive from the late twelfth century show that lead was mined actively on the High Rake near Great Hucklow and on a branch that passed through Tideslow, Wardlow and Stoney Middleton. In 1195 the output from the Tideslow mines reached 2,600 loads of ore, but as we shall see, periods of boom such as this were often followed by slump. The simple technology of the medieval lead industry remained broadly unchanged from Roman times to the Elizabethan era. Lead ore was dug from trenches or 'groves' that were cut into the mineral veins or 'rakes' which outcropped near the surface. Each rake was divided into sections or 'meers' that were worked by groups of free miners. The miners sold the ore to lead burners or 'brenners' who dressed, washed and graded it for smelting. The medieval method of extracting lead was to burn the ore with wood fuel in a specially constructed hearth or 'bole', sited on a high ridge in the prevailing wind. Many of these smelting sites are commemorated by the minor place-name Bole Hill, but no site has yet been excavated.

The Norman Conquest was achieved by a relatively small army that stamped its authority on the land by the building of castles, the foundation of religious houses and the creation of extensive stretches of hunting forests. During the twelfth and thirteenth centuries new towns were laid out around market squares, many villages were planned anew and the parish system that survived until Victorian times was completed. Parish churches up and down the land still contain some Norman work. The barons and knights who accompanied William the Conqueror replaced the old Anglo-Scandinavian aristocracy and remained in power throughout the Middle Ages and sometimes far beyond, but the majority of the population were from the ancient stock of these islands who continued to earn their living in the time-honoured way in small family farms.

Samuel and Nathaniel Buck's engraving of the ruined Peveril Castle.

THE NORTH-

To the most Noble
f Hartington Earl of D

Growth and recession

During the two-and-a-half centuries between the Norman Conquest and the early years of the fourteenth century the population of England more than doubled and may have trebled. We do not have firm figures, but estimates based on Domesday Book suggest that in 1086 the national population was between 1.5 and 2.25 million. By 1300 this number may have risen to as much as 5 or even 6 million. This sustained growth came to a sudden end in the crisis years of 1315–22, when dearth produced by cattle plague, sheep murrain and harvest failure caused the national population to decline by at least 15 per cent. A generation later, the Black Death brought unparalleled disaster and the population plummeted back almost to its Domesday Book level.

VIEW OF CASTLETON CASTLE, & THE DEVILS ARSE IN THE PEAK

M Duke of Devonshire, Mary.
ron Cavendish of Hardwick Lord

THIS Castle in Derbyshire is a very antient Building, and by

Great landowners

During the twelfth and thirteenth centuries, upon the forfeiture of the great baronial estates of the Peveril and de Ferrers families, the Crown again became the largest landowner in Derbyshire. In the south of the county, the royal manor of Melbourne was developed into an impressive stronghold. In 1133 this manor was divided into two parts when Henry I gave his splendid new church and its land to the recently created see of Carlisle. Nothing remains of the residence that was erected for the first bishop, for the site is now occupied by Melbourne Hall, nor can we be certain of the whereabouts of the original royal manor house. If it had stood immediately west of the church, it must have been replaced on a new site by the castle. A market was established in 1230 in the Old Marketstead, now known as Castle Square, where Potter Street joins Castle Street, immediately west of the former castle gates; the present triangular Market Place further west at the junction of High Street, Church Street and Derby Road, was not laid out until 1789. Both the castle and the bishop's residence had large deer parks attached. In the early fourteenth century, the royal manor was acquired by Thomas, Earl of Lancaster, who in 1311–22 replaced the castle with a magnificent new one. A high wall, covered with ivy, behind the buildings of Castle Farm is all that remains of it, but we know that it was extensively repaired in 1483–85 and was still in good condition in 1562 when a drawing was made to accompany an Elizabethan survey. Eighteen chimneys and numerous towers rose around the gabled louvre of the central hall, high

above the nearby village houses and the medieval parish church. It remained a royal property until 1604, when James I sold it to the Earl of Nottingham, who demolished it. Melbourne must have been one of the most impressive places in medieval Derbyshire, with its castle, bishop's residence, two churches, two parks and a thriving market.

Meanwhile, two new castles had been erected in the eastern part of the county. At the time of Domesday Book, Ralph de Buron from Calvados held a small Domesday Book barony of five manors in Derbyshire and eight in Nottinghamshire. In the first half of the twelfth century, his son and heir, Hugh de Buron, built Horston Castle, one mile south-west of Horsley and about three miles east of Duffield Castle, on the opposite side of the river Derwent. On the death of Roger de Buron in 1194 the male line failed and the estate passed to the Crown. King John made substantial improvements to the castle between 1202 and 1205, before giving it to his trusted servant, William Brewer. Horston Castle was an important stronghold in the baronial wars of the thirteenth century, but now only the lower courses of some of the walls survive. These comprise the north wall of the keep, the sloping plinth of corner towers and a small, square chamber. The rest of the castle was destroyed by quarrying in the eighteenth century. The medieval park is recalled by the names of Horsley Park Farm and The Warren.

By the mid-1190s the estate of the knightly de Codnor family had been granted by King Richard I to his loyal officer, Sir Henry de Grey of Thurrock

(Essex). Sir Henry's eldest son, Richard, settled at Codnor; his second son, John, moved to Shirland; his third son, William, to Sandiacre. Richard de Grey of Codnor was an active Crown servant as governor of the Channel Islands, sheriff of various counties and a crusader. Later members of the family were soldiers in Wales, Scotland and France until the line became extinct in 1496. The castle that the Greys built one mile east of the village of Codnor is now an impressive ruin, with fragments rising 18 feet high, but its plan is difficult to follow on the ground. It seems to have been built in three stages between the thirteenth and the fifteenth centuries. The upper court contained the most important buildings, which rose three storeys high. The later, lower court, which now extends west and north-west of the seventeenth-century farmhouse, was separated from the upper court by a wall between two circular towers and by turrets at each side of the gateway. The castle was surrounded by a 1,500-acre park.

An early manor house, on a much smaller scale than these castles, survives in part in the south-western tip of Derbyshire, where the Fitzherberts had acquired the manor of Norbury from the Prior of Tutbury in the early twelfth century. About 1250 they erected a type of building that was fashionable at the time, which architectural historians call a first-floor hall. Part of it can still be seen to the rear of the seventeenth-century Norbury Manor which stands to the west of the church that the Fitzherberts endowed so liberally in the later Middle Ages. The main room on the upper floor has blocked thirteenth-century windows in the west wall and an original entrance to the north. It was enlarged c.1305 by Sir Henry Fitzherbert and restored in 1970.

Forests

By the early thirteenth century, many of the officers of the Forest of the Peak lived in and around Bowden, three miles north-west of their headquarters at Chamber Farm. About 1225 they were numerous and substantial enough to build their own chapel, perhaps symbolically near the old Christian centre commemorated by the names of Eccles House and Eccles Pike. It was given the Norman name of Chapel-en-le-Frith, the chapel in the forest. An extensive district within this part of the forest was divided into two townships: Bowden Middlecale (which consisted of the hamlets of Beard, Brownside, Bugsworth, Chinley, Great Hamlet (north of Hayfield), Kinder, Ollersett, Phoside, Thornsett and Whitle); and Bowden Chapel (i.e. the township and the southern half of the chapelry of Chapel-en-le-Frith).

Some of the foresters held their land in return for discharging specific duties. In 1285 they claimed that their offices had been hereditary since the time of the Peverils. They included families with the distinctive surnames of Archer, Forester and Wolfhunt. Wolves remained at large in the Peak District until Tudor times; the Wolfhunts set traps for them in March and September and hunted them with trained mastiffs. Among the forester families that lasted for many generations and rose to gentry status were Archer, Bagshaw, Balguy, Eyre, Foljambe and Woodroffe. The Robert the Archer who witnessed a deed dating from before 1214 was the ancestor of the lords of Abney, Highlow and Hucklow until the family died out in the male line by the fifteenth century. The Bagshaws, who had taken their name from a local hamlet, became lords of Wormhill and Abney. The Balguys lived at Aston in the twelfth century, but a junior branch moved down the valley to Hope and at the end of the seventeenth century Henry Balguy built Derwent Hall. The Eyres of Thornhill and Hope acquired the manor of Padley through marriage and became one of the most prolific gentry families in Derbyshire. The Foljambes owned property in Wormhill and Tideswell and became knights of the shire from the end of the thirteenth century; after the marriage of Sir Thomas Foljambe with the heiress of Darley the family split into two branches, one based at Tideswell, Wormhill and Elton, the other at Darley and Walton. Finally, the Woodroffes became a gentry family with properties in Wormhill, Hope and Great Hucklow.

The kings of England were infrequent visitors to the Forest of the Peak and so the leading families from Derbyshire and neighbouring counties hunted there with impunity. Nor were the officers slow to enrich themselves at the Crown's expense by taking deer, pilfering the woods, breeding large numbers of horses on stud farms and grazing their own livestock on the royal pastures. In the thirteenth century the Crown had a stud farm at Hope and some monastic houses had studs elsewhere within the forest. The Duchy of Lancaster rented out considerable areas of waste or commons but retained one-third of the 1,500-acre common pasture at Fairfield, north-east of Buxton, and 100 acres of waste in Mainstonefield, a name commemorated by that of Mainstone Farm, east of Chinley Head. The wastes were constantly encroached upon by both the foresters and local peasant farmers as the population rose in the thirteenth century. These assarts were allowed by the Duchy, which benefited from entry fines and rents once a new clearing had come to the attention of officials, but many people escaped paying for years on end. At an enquiry in 1251 it was reported that 131 people had built new houses without licence in the forest since the previous enquiry in 1216 and that 127 new houses had been erected with a licence. Parts of the Peak Forest, especially in the south, now had villages surrounded by open fields and even a few market centres. Royal charters were granted for weekly markets and annual fairs at Tideswell (1251), Chapel-en-le-Frith (1254), Glossop (1290) and Charlesworth (1328).

After the Earls of Lancaster acquired Duffield Frith in 1266 the administration of the forest was made more business-like and forest officials were obliged to draw up annual accounts. These are particularly informative for 1313–14 and, together with an *inquisition post mortem* for Edmund, Earl of Lancaster, in 1297, they provide information about the several deer parks that were enclosed with ditches, banks and palings in different parts of the forest. Belper was still a wild place in 1266, when a man was appointed to drive wolves away, but the manor house there had replaced Duffield as the administrative centre of the frith. The small deer park, only about one mile in circuit, that was created alongside it, has been encroached upon by modern housing for about half its area, yet its outline can still be traced on the map and on the ground. The names of the other parks within the frith were Mansell, Morley, Champion, Postern, Ravensdale, Shottle and Shining Cliff.

Surviving accounts for Duffield Frith mention many other activities, including fishing and fowling, the quarrying of stone at Alderwasley and small-scale mining of coal, ironstone and lead. Holly trees, which provided winter fodder for the deer, and numerous coppice woods were carefully protected with banks, ditches and temporary fencing, but the local farmers were allowed to clear assarts from the waste, for the new fines and rents were a welcome source of income to the lord. These new fields often appear in the records as intakes or riddings.

Other medieval parks and moats

Derbyshire still has traces of about 60 medieval moats, many of which probably mark the sites of early manor houses. Good examples survive at Atlow, Hough (Hulland), Hungry Bentley, Shirley, Stainsby and immediately west of Farnah Hall, Windley, on the northern boundary of the former Champion Park within Duffield Frith. The moated manor house to the west of the church at Cubley belonged to the Montgomerys, whose effigies may still be seen in the church. That at Callow Hall (Wirksworth) retains the medieval stone undercroft that belonged to the de la Laund family.

In a series of charters in the year 1200 King John granted hunting rights to several Derbyshire lords who were prepared to pay handsomely for the privilege. They included Hubert fitz Ralph, lord of Crich, and William fitz Walkelin, lord of Stainsby, who was specifically allowed to hunt beasts of the warren, together with wolves, wild cats, hares and otters. David Crook has calculated that between 1227 and 1257 Henry III granted similar rights of free warren to 37 lords, 30 of whom were laymen, for at least 121 places in Derbyshire. These figures are probably not complete because some charter rolls are missing or have damaged entries. Of the 121 places, about 42, that is over a third, lay within the former royal forest area between the rivers Derwent and Erewash. A similar pattern of grants can be recognised in Nottinghamshire. In 1252, according to Matthew Paris, the St Albans chronicler, warrens were effectively sold to whoever wanted them. All but four of the Derbyshire grants from Henry III were made after 1250 and over half were dated between 1252 and 1257. A particularly important grant in 1251 to William de Ferrers III covered 80 places in three counties, 45 of them in Derbyshire. This grant made him the greatest lay holder of chartered hunting rights in the whole of England. In Derbyshire, as in Yorkshire, lords often used their grants of free warren to enclose a deer park.

The medieval manorial landscape of the north Derbyshire township of Holmesfield can be reconstructed by a remarkable sequence of surviving earthworks and buildings. The earliest feature is the Norman motte that the Deincourts erected on Castle Hill; half of the mound and part of the surrounding ditch survive on the sky-line. In time, this site was abandoned in favour of a moated manor house, which remained the residence of the lords of Holmesfield until they built a timber-framed hall near the Norman motte in the 1450s. The moat is still a well-defined feature, square in shape and with slight evidence of two building platforms on the central island. It was originally fed by springs and one of its roles was to act as the fishpond. It may date from about 1252, for it stands within the southern border of the deer park that was probably created in that year, after a grant of free warren to John Deincourt. The park and a deer-leap were certainly well established by 1330, when William Deincourt asserted that his ancestors had enjoyed hunting rights at Holmesfield time out of mind.

The boundary of Holmesfield Park is marked by one of the best surviving linear earthworks in north Derbyshire and is nearly as well defined today as it was in the thirteenth century. It can be recognised immediately on the Ordnance Survey map and be followed on the ground as a ditch and earthen bank all the way round Park Wood and some fields bordering a housing estate to the south. The park was the setting for an organised illegal hunt one night in 1343. William Deincourt complained before a court that several men, including a chaplain and a tailor from Crookes, broke his close, drove away 20 oxen, 30 cows and 200 sheep, fished his stews, carried away his fish, broke his park, hunted therein, took and carried away deer and assaulted his men and servants.

His complaint is all we know about this riotous event. The deer park seems to have remained in use until the sixteenth century, when it was converted into a coppice wood.

Towns

The towns that the Normans had established thrived in the thirteenth and early fourteenth centuries as the national population grew, but they were very small by modern standards. In each case, the surrounding countryside could be seen from the heart of the market place. In a ranking of urban wealth based on a national taxation return – the lay subsidy of 1334 – Derby was 28th in the country at large, but no other town in Derbyshire was of any importance. Derby was similar in size and prosperity to the other former Five Boroughs of the East Midlands, except Lincoln, which was England's 5th wealthiest town; Stamford came 21st, Nottingham 24th and Leicester 34th.

Little of Derby's medieval past remains above ground. Its parish churches have been rebuilt or demolished, though All Saints acquired a magnificent new tower late in the Middle Ages. The small priory of St James, which had only a prior and two monks in 1279, and the two hospitals were destroyed at the Reformation and no buildings survive on the site of the Dominican priory that the Black Friars established by 1238. The friars were granted a site to the west of the town, beyond the Markeaton Brook and St Werburgh's church. It stretched between Friar Gate and the Bramble Brook to the south and is marked by the present Friary Hotel. About 26 friars were housed here in 1324, but their numbers had declined to six at the Dissolution in 1539. We know nothing about the layout of the convent buildings and only a few artefacts have survived. A map of the friary estate in 1733 shows that it still covered nearly 77 acres, including a 19-acre meadow, closes, an orchard, a large house where the friary had been and a row of buildings along the brook. This was the only friary in Derbyshire, whereas Yorkshire's towns had 19.

Derby's most picturesque, remaining medieval building is St Mary's chapel, one of the few surviving chantry chapels that were commonly built on bridges across England's major rivers. A bridge chapel was served by a priest who relied on his small endowment and the offerings of travellers. The ruins of another Derbyshire chapel can be seen by the medieval bridge on the south-western bank of the river Derwent at Cromford. At Derby, the original fourteenth-century chapel was built of stone and the springing of the first arch of the medieval bridge can be seen below the east end. The building has a late-medieval, straight-headed, Perpendicular Gothic east window and a half-timbered gable above and has been much repaired in brick. St Mary's bridge was the only crossing of the river into the town. Travellers then proceeded westwards as far as St Alkmund's church, before turning south along the main thoroughfare to the Market Place and 'the Guildhall of the town called the Moot Hall'. Medieval street names that are still in use include those named after the

Bridge chapels, where travellers said prayers for a safe journey and made a contribution to the upkeep of the bridge, were a common feature in the Middle Ages. Few survive today, for after the dissolution of chantry chapels in 1547 only those which were adapted to other uses remained standing. The Derby chapel was built of stone in the thirteenth or fourteenth century, with a timber-framed gable above. The springing of the first arch of the old bridge across the river Derwent can be seen below. Since 1547 the building has been used variously as a Nonconformist meeting place, a carpenter's shop and domestic cottages. It was extensively repaired in brick in 1873, and in the 1930s was restored for public worship. On 25 July 1558, at the time of the Spanish Armada invasion scare, three Roman Catholic priests were hanged, drawn and quartered in Derby and their bodies displayed at the chapel entrance.

PHOTOGRAPH: CARNEGIE

parish churches and the friary, and Iron Gate (where the smiths congregated), Sadler Gate (saddlers and perhaps other workers in leather), Walker Lane (fullers), Full Street ('foul'), Newlands Street and The Wardwick, which was originally 'Walda's dairy farm' just across the Markeaton Brook.

Derby remained the only town in the county with more than one church. Derbyshire's finest medieval parish churches are those that served the market towns which had been ancient minster centres. They were built in their present form in the Early English and Decorated Gothic styles during the boom years of the thirteenth and early fourteenth centuries, a time of considerable economic prosperity. The outstanding ones are the cruciform churches of Ashbourne, Bakewell, Chesterfield and Wirksworth, together with the large, fourteenth-

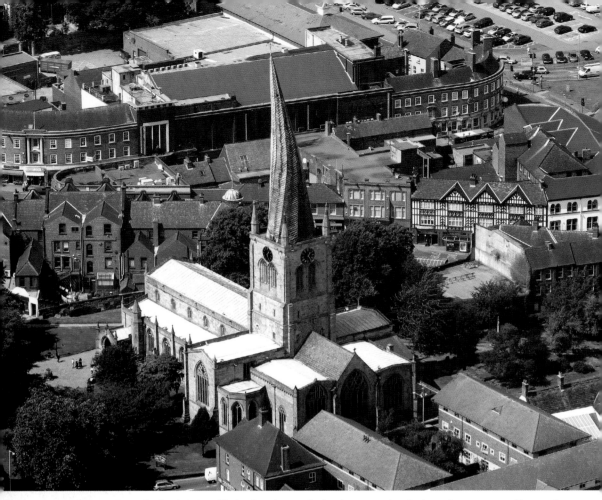

Famed throughout the land, it is unlikely that the crooked spire was twisted when observant travellers such as Celia Fiennes and Daniel Defoe came in the late seventeenth and early eighteenth centuries, for they do not mention it. No comments on the strange shape of the spire were made until the late eighteenth century. The twist occurred after the supporting timber-frame cracked, probably because of the great weight of the lead which sheaths the spire.

century church in the new market town of Tideswell. Each served large parishes that included scattered villages and hamlets in the surrounding countryside.

In 1330 Chesterfield, Derbyshire's second most important town, was granted another fair, lasting for eight days from the eve of Palm Sunday. Distinctive medieval street names that were derived from occupations include Draper Row, Fisher Row, Gluman Gate ('the street of the glee men' or minstrels), Iron Row, Knifesmith Gate, Mercer Row, Potter Row, Saltergate, Souter Row and Soutergate (shoemakers). St Mary's Gate was known as South Gate until the sixteenth century. From the outside, St Mary and All Saints church is an ashlar stone building entirely in the Decorated style of about 1325–50, without battlements and pinnacles, and renewed in Victorian times. But older work survives inside, starting with the Early English piscina in Holy Cross chapel and the supports of the crossing tower, dedicated in 1234, and continuing with the lower portions of the transepts and chapels, which date from about 1300, and a nave of six bays and aisles that was rebuilt about 1350–75. Beyond the south and north transepts, the east end consists of a chancel, flanked by four chantry chapels that were endowed by the town's guilds. The only medieval roof to survive is the late Perpendicular one in the south transept. Needless to say, Chesterfield's famous crooked spire was not intended to lean so dramatically. Early travellers do not remark on its peculiar shape and it was not until the late eighteenth century that visitors such as John Byng, the future Viscount Torrington, found it 'curiously awry'. The problem seems to have been caused by the use of green timbers, which have twisted and turned a few degrees, but the visual effect is made more peculiar to the eye by the herringbone pattern of the lead plates that cover it. The spire looks channelled, but its eight sides are in fact perfectly flat.

As we have seen, in the late thirteenth century Bakewell flourished as a small seigneurial borough and market town and its church continued to serve an enormous parish. The sturdy bridge across the river Wye is thought to date from about 1300. During the thirteenth and early fourteenth centuries All Saints was redesigned as one of Derbyshire's finest churches. The south transept, known as the Newark, or 'new work', with an east aisle like that at Ashbourne, was erected in the 1220s or 1230s (but was completely rebuilt in 1841–52). Late thirteenth-century work is evident in the chancel windows,

BELOW

Medieval bridges cannot be dated precisely, but the low arches of Bakewell's bridge over the river Wye suggest that it may have been built as early as about 1300, making it contemporary with the bridge and causeway at Swarkestone (see photograph on page 301). It has been widened on its upstream side to twice its original width. It led into the market place and the small borough by the ancient minster church.

PHOTOGRAPH: CARNEGIE

sedilia, piscina and south doorway, in the north aisle of the nave, and in the south and north doorways. Then, in the first half of the fourteenth century, a new octagonal bell tower, with a peal of eight bells, was raised ingeniously above the square, thirteenth-century crossing and an elegant, octagonal stone spire soared precariously above. They stood for nearly five centuries before they had to be taken down in the 1840s and rebuilt in a similar but not identical style.

Ashbourne, too, prospered as a small borough, market town and parochial centre and so the combined wealth of the parishioners enabled them to rebuild St Oswald's church in the new Gothic style. The church's low-lying position reduces the impact of the 212 feet-high spire until one approaches the churchyard. The oldest part above the Norman crypt (which was rediscovered during excavations in 1913) is the long chancel, which must have been completed by 1241 when the church was dedicated. The south doorway is richly designed in the Early English fashion and narrow lancet windows, set close together, rise high in the north and south walls. The transepts have impressively tall and wide arches and broad aisles on the east side, which in the fifteenth century were converted into chapels by the Bradbourne and Cockayne families. The crossing tower is a spectacular piece, with early fourteenth-century tracery. The nave has a wide and tall south aisle, but no aisle to the north, perhaps because the recession brought on by the Black Death curtailed building activities.

Some of the medieval wealth of Wirksworth was also channelled into the rebuilding of the parish church. After 1272, when the Dean and Chapter of Lichfield appointed their first vicar, St Mary's was reconstructed in an ambitious scheme, with a crossing tower and spire, transepts, and an aisled chancel. The lancet windows in the chancel and north transept were perhaps inspired by those at Ashbourne. The crossing tower is thirteenth century below and early fourteenth above, but much else was replaced during restoration in the nineteenth century. Nothing else survives of the medieval town, which never reached the status of a borough, except the outline of the market place, much encroached upon.

Two attempts were made to found new Derbyshire boroughs during the first half of the thirteenth century, but neither met with long-term success. At Chapel-en-le-Frith tradesmen were offered the usual burgess privileges around the market place that was laid out to the west of the chapel that the foresters had built in 1225. By 1254 a weekly market and three annual fairs were well established and 14 burgage plots extended back from the Market Place, but in 1281 only nine burgages were recorded alongside the ten shops and 14 stalls. We hear nothing more about them and must assume that they fell victim to the recession brought on by the Black Death. The outline of the original rectangular Market Place (whose cross dates from 1636) can be traced from Church Row in the east to Cross Street in the west, and from Eccles Road and the Market Place in the north to High Street and Market Street in the south. The infilling of the extremities of this space by later buildings is evident

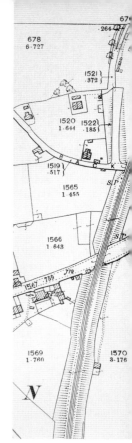

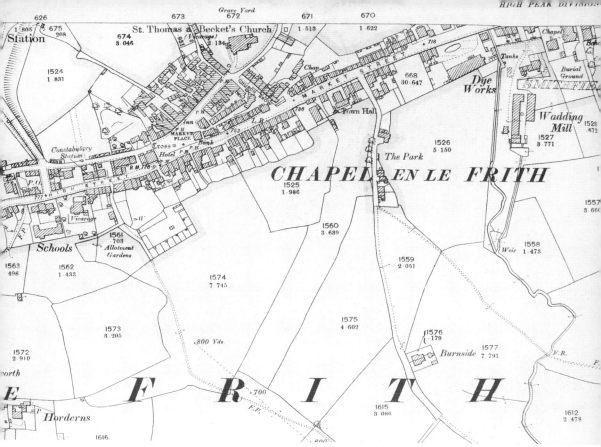

Chapel-en-le-Frith in 1883. The medieval plan of this small market town remains evident to this day. In 1225 the foresters of the Peak built their chapel and dedicated it to St Thomas Becket. By 1254 they had obtained a royal grant which allowed them to hold weekly markets and three annual fairs. The Market Place extended westwards from this chapel and was much bigger than it is now, but by Victorian times it had been encroached upon by buildings at its eastern end. The 14 burgage plots around the Market Place did not survive the recession following the Black Death.

COURTESY OF DERBYSHIRE RECORD OFFICE

immediately west of Church Row, where the encroaching properties have few or no gardens. Perhaps some of the boundaries of the former burgage plots were retained as the property divisions that were marked on the first edition, six-inch 1883 Ordnance Survey map on the south side of Market Street?

Brief documentary references to burgages have also been discovered at Higham, where the Grey family obtained a market charter in 1243. Sited on the highway from Derby to Chesterfield that followed the line of the old Roman road, the new borough seems to have been a speculative venture that was unable to compete with the market at Alfreton, three miles away. The planned nature of the settlement is immediately apparent from an inspection of the six-inch Ordnance Survey map of 1884, which shows that the properties on either side of the street had continuous boundaries to the rear. Higham resembles the planned medieval villages of Yorkshire and County Durham, which are conspicuous by their absence in most of Derbyshire, but it never grew into a town.

In the thirteenth and early fourteenth centuries lords of manors in all parts of England purchased royal charters that gave them the right to hold weekly markets and annual fairs. Many of these speculative ventures did not last long, but some of Derbyshire's best-known market towns date from this time. None aspired to the status of seigneurial borough. The county's earliest market charter was that granted by King John in 1203 to William de Ferrers II for Hartington, down the valley from his castle at Pilsbury. A large market place was laid out to the west of the original settlement around St Giles's church, at the junction of several roads or lanes. It eventually fell out of use, but a Wednesday market and three annual fairs were revived in Victorian times.

The most successful of the new market centres was that established at Tideswell, just inside the Forest of the Peak. Here, in 1251, Paulinus de Brampton, who had inherited the manor of Tideswell in 1232 from his father-in-law, obtained a grant for a market each Wednesday and an annual fair on the vigil, feast and morrow of St John the Baptist, the patron saint of the parish church. The original market was probably held immediately south-west of the church, in a space now infilled, before a large, irregular Market Square was laid out at the northern end of High Street and Pursglove Street. By the time that the market was founded, Tideswell church had become independent of the old minster territory of Hope. The rebuilding of the parish church proceeded slowly and without major breaks for about 75 years. The window tracery of the nave and its aisles can be dated to between 1320 and 1350. The nave roof is original and tall piers divide the five bays of the nave from the aisles and the transepts. The two-storeyed porch looks contemporary, though all have been given later battlements. A start was made on a new chancel about the same time, as is evident from the old roof line, but it was either abandoned because

of the Black Death or was soon judged unsuitable, for about 1360 work began on a new, higher and wider chancel which, when it was finished, turned out to be one of the finest in the county.

Numerous grants for markets and fairs were made throughout England during the period of expansion in the thirteenth and early fourteenth centuries before the disaster of the Black Death. The laying out of market places and fair grounds has sometimes had a lasting effect on the local landscape. At Alfreton (1252) a triangular market place slopes down the hill on the Chesterfield–Derby road, with another road coming in from the east at the top. Square or rectangular market places survive at the hearts of Ripley (1251) and Ilkeston (1252) and the old, prescriptive market at Repton is marked by a cross mounted on several circular steps at the cross-roads to the south of the priory, where the roads broaden and properties have encroached on the old trading space. The infilling of old market places is also evident at Glossop (1290) and at the irregular crossroads at Aston-upon-Trent (1257) and the triangular village green at Monyash may be a relic of former market activities that began with a grant in 1340.

A striking feature of the Derbyshire charters is that they were mostly granted to places that stood within a few miles of the county boundary, especially in the south and the south-east. This reflects the status of the lords who obtained the grants and the speculative nature of many of these ventures. So, the Grey family paid for charters at Higham (1243), Sandiacre (1252) and Denby (1334) and ecclesiastical lords founded markets close to the river Trent: the bishop of Carlisle at Melbourne (1230) and King's Newton (1231), the bishop of Coventry and Lichfield at Sawley (1259), and the abbot of St Werburgh's, Chester, at Aston-upon-Trent (1257). Many of these ventures failed to get going; indeed, an enquiry in 1330 found that no market or fair had been held at Sandiacre from the time of its grant in 1252. Others withered during the recession in the years after the Black Death. Little or no evidence, either from documents or on the ground, suggests much activity at at King's Newton (1231), Cubley (1255), Sawley (1259), Mapperley (1267), Doveridge (1275), Pleasley (1285), Overseal (1311; now in Leicestershire), Charlesworth (1328) or Denby (1334). Most of these markets probably disappeared early, overwhelmed by competition. They were certainly not all in existence at the same time. Some of the markets and fairs that were discontinued were revived or their market days were changed in Victorian times; only about one-third of the original foundations continued into the twentieth century.

Rural parish churches

In the countryside too church rebuilding continued in the thirteenth and fourteenth centuries as the population grew and the economy expanded. The transition from the late Norman style to the Early English Gothic is best observed at Eckington, where the big, square tower, topped by a fourteenth-century spire, the tall nave arcades and the chancel arch all date from around 1200 or shortly after. Breadsall has a slim, thirteenth-century tower, surmounted by an early fourteenth-century recessed spire, and a chancel and north arcade that were also built in the thirteenth century. Lancet windows, such as those that are seen in the chancel and transepts of St Giles, Hartington, provide the usual clue to the adoption of new styles in thirteenth-century Derbyshire.

In the fourteenth century, wealthy tithe owners paid for fine new chancels in the Decorated Gothic style at Norbury (c.1300–07, where the Fitzherberts were rectors as well as lords of the manor), Sandiacre (c.1342–47 by Bishop Northburgh of Lichfield) and Chaddesden (c.1357 by Henry Chaddesden, Archdeacon of Leicester). The chancel at Dronfield is comparable in scale, though the original tracery of the great east window fell out in 1563 and was replaced by straight mullions and transoms. At Whitwell the chancel and transepts of the Norman church were re-designed in the first half of the fourteenth century when their windows were provided with geometrical or flowing tracery. Other churches, such as those at Doveridge, Hartington, Kedleston and North Wingfield were partly re-styled at that time and St Werburgh's, Spondon was rebuilt after 1340, when a disastrous fire destroyed the old church and part of the town. The few outstanding church monuments include the early thirteenth-century effigy of a lady and child in Scarcliffe church, believed to represent Constantia de Frecheville, and the late thirteenth-century sculptured panel of the Nativity at Bolsover. In the smaller churches the new styles are represented only by a carved piscina, sedilia or font, or perhaps by a window or two with ogee arches and flowing tracery.

Derbyshire churches often have spires, even though the local sandstones prevented the masons from matching the elegant work on the oolitic limestone belt further east in Rutland and Lincolnshire. The earliest ones are the plain, unsubtle broach-spires of Baslow, Brampton, Breaston, Hope, Ockbrook, Rosliston and Taddington, where an eight-sided spire rises from a square tower, the joints masked by the semi-pyramid broaches at each corner. The earliest may be late thirteenth century, but most were erected after 1300. Derbyshire's later medieval spires are slimmer and the method of joining them to their towers is masked by battlements.

Monastic granges

Derbyshire's monasteries and priories also rebuilt their churches and living quarters in the thirteenth and fourteenth centuries. Beauchief Abbey got a sturdy tower that is still intact and excavations at Dale Abbey have revealed an early or mid-thirteenth-century south range, which comprised a ground floor undercroft and a first floor refectory, with a kitchen at the south-west corner. The most striking survival at Dale is the huge frame of the thirteenth-century east window of the former church. At the time of the death of Abbot Henry of Kedleston in 1287, Darley Abbey had a courtyard and garden, 240 acres of land and six acres of meadow around the convent, two corn mills, properties in Derby and estates at Aldwark, Alport, Butterley, Crich, Glapwell, Hartshay, Normanton, Pentrich, Ripley, Scarcliffe, Wessington, Wigwell and Youlgreave.

As the properties that had been granted or bequeathed by the faithful were so scattered, the usual practice of the monasteries was to administer them from the granges that they built in the countryside. These granges were superior farms that accommodated a small group of lay brothers and farm servants; a chapel was often attached. Dale Abbey's chief grange at Stanley, which was built or rebuilt shortly after 1291, had a chapel of St Cross, and a 'stone chamber' was added during the abbacy of William Horsley (1332–54). The abbey's other granges were at Boyah, Littlehay (on the outskirts of Ockbrook), at an unidentified site in the parish of Spondon that was known variously as Southwood, Southeridge, Sowters or South House, and later as Locko Grange, and at Griffe to the west of Wirksworth. The Dale cartulary also records that in 1240 quarries in Stanton-by-Dale and Kirk Hallam were granted to the abbey by Ralph of Hereford.

Monastic granges were of great importance in the more remote areas of the Peak District, both on the higher reaches of the limestone plateau and on the moorlands of the Dark Peak. In most cases, they were established on new or abandoned sites, though occasionally, as at One Ash (a small Domesday Book vill whose name distinguished it from the many ash trees of Monyash), they took over existing settlements. The Cistercians, who owned about half the granges in the Peak District, were particularly keen to exploit isolated sites and had a reputation for driving away their neighbours. One Ash Grange belonged to the Cistercian abbey at Roche in South Yorkshire.

Several monasteries from beyond the county's borders, notably Basingwerk, Buildwas, Combermere, Dunstable, Garendon and Merevale, kept large flocks of

St Mary's church, Norbury. Set in a delightful, secluded position among the woods around the old manor house, the parish church at Norbury is a showpiece of the Fitzherbert family, lords of the manor. The finest part of the church is the glorious chancel (right), which was erected in the first decade of the fourteenth century with large Decorated windows that retain their original stained glass. The tower, nave and chapels on either side of the tower were built by successive members of the Fitzherbert family in the Perpendicular Gothic style in the fifteenth and early sixteenth centuries. The tower is not in the usual position to the west because of sloping ground. Norbury manor house (see the photograph on page 137) lies to the left of this view.

PHOTOGRAPH: AUTHOR

Judging by the armorial glass in the windows, the chancel of St Mary's church, Norbury, was erected in the first decade of the fourteenth century. An exceptionally large amount of fourteenth- and fifteenth-century glass survives. The chancel has several monuments to the Fitzherberts, lords of the manor, ranging from an early fourteenth-century stone effigy of a cross-legged knight to two of the finest fifteenth-century alabaster tomb chests in the country and to incised slabs and brasses from the fifteenth and sixteenth centuries.

ABOVE

Stone effigy of Sir Henry Fitzherbert, who died in 1315; alabaster effigy and tomb chest of Nicholas Fitzherbert, who died in 1473.

BELOW

Alabaster effigy and tomb chest of Sir Ralph Fitzherbert (died 1483) and his wife. Sir Ralph's feet rest on a lion and the tomb is adorned with figures holding large shields under ogee arches.

PHOTOGRAPHS: CARNEGIE

St Peter's church, Hope, was the minster church for much of the northern part of the Peak District and the successor of the ancient *eccles*, commemorated in a nearby minor place-name. An Anglo-Scandinavian cross-shaft stands in the raised churchyard (see photograph on page 77). The early fourteenth-century tower rises to a broach spire, a style favoured in a number of Derbyshire churches. The battlements and pinnacles around the nave, porch and chancel date from a re-styling in Perpendicular Gothic in the late Middle Ages. The porch is two-storeyed with an upper room.

PHOTOGRAPH: AUTHOR

St Peter and St Paul's church, Eckington. In the nineteenth and twentieth centuries Eckington spread a long way up the hill towards Dronfield, so the parish church is now near the edge of the settlement. Its sturdy tower was built about 1200; the spire was added more than 100 years later. The south aisle and the porch were remodelled in 1763 to the designs of John Platt of Rotherham, the leading local architect of his time, but the spacious interior is evidently contemporary with the tower. The church served a large parish, which stretched from Mosborough to Renishaw and as far west as the three hamlets of Handley.

PHOTOGRAPH: AUTHOR

sheep on their granges in the Peak District. In 1284, for example, the Augustinian priory at Dunstable owned a flock of 1,200 sheep on their Bradbourne estate. On the limestone plateau high above Hartington, the Cistercians of Garendon Abbey had a specialised sheep farm at Heathcote, whose place-name is derived from the sheepfolds on the heath. But sheep farming was not the only activity, even in such remote spots. At nearby Needham fossilised open-field strip boundaries, with characteristic reverse-S shapes, can be traced alongside the grange of the Cistercian abbey of Merevale.

On the limestone plateau, granges had large pastures and arable areas that were defined by boundary banks or walls, but which were not sub-divided, except near farm buildings. Good examples of boundaries associated with medieval granges have been identified by Peak Park archaeologists at the Merevale Abbey granges at Cronkston, Needham and Pilsbury and at Cotesfield, which belonged to the Cistercians of Combermere Abbey in Cheshire. The sheep flocks grazed on the outfields and the unenclosed commons that lay beyond. The lead mining rake that was respected by the boundary of Cotesfield Grange provides a rare example of a site where medieval or earlier mining can be identified.

Medieval granges are poorly documented and as their buildings are now mostly covered by later structures the earthworks of stock enclosures are the only evidence to remain above ground. A series of enclosures and paddocks of several phases, surrounded by a ditch and a bank, are still well defined in the landscape at Cronkston Grange, north of Pilsbury. The only site to have been excavated systematically is that at Roystone, one of the three granges that the Cistercian abbey of Garendon possessed in the Peak District. It was established in the late twelfth or early thirteenth century, following a grant by Richard de Harthill, and was run as a 400-acre sheep farm, exporting wool to Flanders and elsewhere on the Continent. Surviving wall foundations of grange buildings have been identified by Richard Hodges' team in the sheltered valley, a little downslope from the Roman-period dew pond, but as no chapel has been discovered it is thought likely that the lay-brothers and servants walked to Ballidon church for their services. The original building consisted simply of a living room and a small dairy, but this was soon replaced by a first-floor hall, with the ground floor used for storage. This new building had to be abandoned in favour of a drier position when the climate deteriorated in the late thirteenth century. By the standards of the time, the granger and his men lived well. Amongst the finds at the grange were fine glazed jugs from the potteries at Burley Hill (near Derby), Brackenfield and Chesterfield, gilded buckles and catches for boxes, and even a fragment of a glass urinal.

The Premonstratensian canons of Beauchief Abbey owned at least seven granges. The largest one was sited on the eastern edge of Beeley Moor, where a farmhouse still bears the name of Harewood Grange. The original grant by Warin of Beeley allowed pasture on the moors for 100 oxen and cows, 20 horses with their young and 100 sheep. Another grange at Strawberry Lee, Totley, can be identified by an extensive green area on the edge of the moors and the boundary of its pastures is marked by the stump of the Lady Cross a mile or so away. Cattle were more important than sheep on the Beauchief Abbey estates, both on the moors and on the coal-measure sandstones further east, and like the religious of Basingwerk, Merevale and Welbeck, they also had studs for rearing horses. In the 1250s Welbeck Abbey owned 20 horses and 20 mares on their estates in the Peak District.

Like the great lay landowners, the abbeys and priories had extensive estates,

Stained glass drolleries, Dronfield. Fragments of medieval stained glass, dating from the first half of the fourteenth century, survive in three windows in St John the Baptist's church, Dronfield. Here we see three drolleries or grotesques, typical of the humour expressed in medieval art: a bird eating berries; a satire on quack doctors, depicting an ape with a urine jug; and a composite figure of a bird, beast and man.

PHOTOGRAPHS: PETER SHELTON

substantial capital and knowledgeable staff who introduced the latest ideas and technology. The Premonstratensian canons of Welbeck Abbey, for instance, were instrumental in opening up the Upper Derwent valley to farming and industry. At the end of the twelfth century King John granted them 'the pasture of Crookhill, the woods of Ashop up to Lockerbrook and from Lockerbrook up the valley of the Derwent and ascending up to Derwenthead'. The grange that they founded at Crookhill Farm had common pasture rights for 80 cattle in Derwent township, within the parish of Hathersage. The grange that they established in the 1250s at One Man's House, a former hermitage on the east bank of the Derwent, was given extensive pasture rights within Yorkshire. This border landscape of mixed moorland and woodland was divided between the large manors and parishes of Hope and Hathersage and the chapelry

Medieval wall, Roystone Grange. The systematic surveying of the drystone field walls at Roystone Grange resulted in a classification of styles according to period, ranging back in time to the Romans. This wall is judged to have been constructed in the Middle Ages, when the site was farmed by the lay brothers and servants of the Cistercian monks of Garendon Abbey (Leicestershire).

PHOTOGRAPH: AUTHOR

Lady Cross, Big Moor. Originally erected by the Premonstratensian canons of Beauchief Abbey to mark the boundary of their moorland grazing rights, this stone later served as the boundary between the manor of Baslow (marked on this side as MB) and the manors and townships of Totley and Holmesfield. In the days before detailed and accurate Ordnance Survey maps, such boundary markers were erected on many local moors. This one was known as the Lady Cross as far back as 1263.

PHOTOGRAPH: AUTHOR

BELOW

Crookhill Farm. The modern farm stands on or near the site of the medieval grange that the Premonstratensian canons of Welbeck Abbey erected on land granted to them by King John, high above the Upper Derwent valley. The first element of the place-name is an ancient one going back to prehistoric times that meant 'hill'. The meaning of the word became lost and so 'hill' was added much later. The canons were allowed to graze up to 80 cattle on the pastures and in the woods. The Cavendish family bought this grange upon the dissolution of the monasteries. In 1627 the farm amounted to 447 acres, including 165 acres in 'The great pasture'.

PHOTOGRAPH: AUTHOR

of Bradfield within the manor of Hallamshire. In the thirteenth century the Welbeck canons built a chapel at Derwent, a corn mill, a bridge on the highway from Sheffield to Hope, and reputedly two more chapels, one near Birchinlee and the other on the Hope–Glossop packway, though neither of these has been dated definitely to the Middle Ages. The canons were probably also responsible for introducing the smelting of lead with charcoal fuel into the Upper Derwent valley. Bill Bevan's survey has revealed numerous charcoal platforms and hearths and three smelting boles in the valley bottom, one of which stood near the Welbeck grange at One Man's House.

Farming and rural settlement

The thirteenth century was a period of 'high farming' when both lay and ecclesiastical lords employed stewards to manage their estates directly, rather than lease them to tenants, as they did later. Prices for agricultural produce were high and the demand for wool for export to the clothiers of Flanders and Italy was buoyant. In 1284 Dunstable Priory kept 1,200 sheep at Bradbourne; at the end of the century a flock of about 5,000 sheep grazed the upland pastures of the Duchy of Lancaster's ranch at Hartington, close to the sheep-cotes of the monastic granges; and at Shirland in 1325 the Greys kept 170 wethers, 122 ewes and 44 hogs, as well as 16 oxen, 14 dairy cattle and other livestock. The organisers who profited from the trade in wool included Alexander the merchant and Elias the merchant who witnessed charters at Ashbourne in the second half of the thirteenth century.

The breeding of horses for riding or pack animals was another speciality that appealed to large landowners. In 1293 the Crown's stud at Hope consisted of a breeding stallion, 21 mares, five fillies, 13 two-year-olds and 14 yearlings and in 1322 the Earl of Lancaster's stud at Duffield contained 113 mares and 112 other horses. The officers of the Forest of the Peak also grasped the opportunities that came their way. For instance, in the early 1250s the bailiff, Ralph Bugge, who was also a prosperous High Peak lead merchant, was fined for keeping 60 cart horses and four yoke of oxen on the pastures of Campana and Hopedale Wards, to the detriment of the royal herds of deer.

In the Middle Ages livestock were far smaller than now and disease was a constant worry. The fleece of a typical medieval sheep weighed less than half that of today and milk yields were less than one-sixth of the present ones. Cereal yields varied between manors and different soils, but they too were low by modern standards. In the century before the Black Death, yields of wheat and barley were less than one-third of present-day returns on seed sown, and oat yields were less than one-fifth. Oats was often the chief crop, followed by peas, rye, wheat and barley (which was sometimes mixed with oats to form dredge).

The lord of the manor's holdings were commonly spread amongst the open fields of the peasant farmers, though sometimes he enclosed a block of strips

Ridge-and-furrow, Tissington. The ridge-and-furrow patterns that were created by the plough in the medieval open-fields are still evident on the ground in many parishes in the White Peak. At Tissington they are particularly extensive and their slightly curving nature is quickly recognised. They follow the slope of the land to provide drainage via the furrows.

PHOTOGRAPH: CARNEGIE

into a 'flatt' or 'furlong'. Every Derbyshire town and village and many a hamlet once had its 'townfields' where cereals were grown for local consumption or, in the more favoured districts, for sale at the market. As we shall see, in most parts of Derbyshire, especially in the uplands, these open fields were often enclosed by the agreement of the farmers or because of the dominant ownership of the lord long before the parliamentary enclosure movement of the eighteenth and nineteenth centuries. The documentary evidence is thin, but the visual evidence in the form of ridge-and-furrow is impressive, especially in the White Peak. As these patterns were created by ploughing with teams of oxen that needed to be turned round on the headlands that served as access routes and borders, they are shaped like a long reverse S. Their main purpose was drainage and so they run down the slopes in blocks at different angles to each other, often continuing well beyond the present field patterns. Sixteenth- and seventeenth-century estate maps show that this type of ridge-and-furrow pattern matches exactly the strips of the open fields. (The other type, where the ridge-and-furrow is narrow and straight and does not extend beyond hedges or walls is much later, dating mostly from the Napoleonic Wars.)

The ancient ridge-and-furrow patterns in the White Peak confirm that the open fields of the villages stretched from behind the crofts as far as the common pastures and occasionally right up to the township boundaries. Sometimes, as at Litton, Tideswell and Wheston, the open fields of one township bordered those of another. The White Peak has long been devoted to the grazing of livestock, but in the Middle Ages each village grew its own cereals, even if the land was over 1,000 feet above sea level. Sufficient scraps of documentary references survive to support this conclusion. At Monyash about 1275 nine acres of land were spread equally between the three open fields. In Bradwell, about the same time, 1¾ acres were divided into 'separate pieces of which half an acre lies in the field called Braddale ... and half an acre beyond the ditch ... one rood on the claypit and a half land in the field called the Midilfurlong'; a land was the usual farmer's term for a strip. Other Bradwell documents from the late thirteenth and early fourteenth centuries refer to lands in various

parts of the South Field, including half an acre abutting towards the boundary that separated the Townend of Hazlebadge from the Townend of Bradwell. Contemporary records mention lands 'lying in the field of Wheston', an acre of arable land there divided into three strips, and three acres of land in the field of Wheston, 'two acres of which lie below the Brocwalclif … and one acre lies above'. Derbyshire strips were originally about a rood (quarter of an acre) in size, measuring 220 yards in length and 5½ yards in width, but even in the Middle Ages many had been amalgamated or sub-divided. Their pattern upon enclosure in later centuries was sometimes preserved by the stone walls that were erected along their boundaries, as at Castleton or Litton. The White Peak landscape also offers many examples of flights of terraces known as lynchets that at certain times are picked out by snow or low sun along the contours of steep hillsides. The best examples are to be seen at Wensley and Snitterton, at Priestcliffe and Taddington, and at Bakewell, though small groups can be found in many townships, such as Hassop. They provide a clear indication that new land had to be brought into the open-field system as the population continued to grow. Terraces offered the best way of creating reasonably level surfaces for the plough-team.

The limits of the communal open fields were defined by a ditch and a bank, such as those which can still be followed on the ground at Chelmorton, Wheston and Wormhill. The most common form of village in the White Peak is that where the farms are spaced along a single street between a Townhead and a Townend, as at Flagg or Wardlow, but other villages, such as Ashford, are arranged haphazardly, for reasons that are not obvious. A small group that are arranged around greens include Brackenfield, Foolow, Great Longstone, Litton, Wessington and the deserted village of Cold Eaton. Villages surrounded by open fields were also the usual form of settlement on the magnesian limestone

The long strips in open arable fields curved at their ends to allow a team of plough oxen to turn on the headland. When blocks of strips were enclosed by the agreement of local farmers in the seventeenth and early eighteenth centuries, it was a common practice to build drystone walls along the strip boundaries. The old strip pattern is well preserved here by ridge-and-furrow patterns at Pindale, Castleton. These plough patterns helped with drainage as well as defining the individual strips in the communal open fields.

PHOTOGRAPHS: CARNEGIE, AUTHOR

belt in the north-eastern corner of the county. Barlborough, for example, had its West Field, North Field and Mill Field, a town ditch and a common pasture. The southern lowlands formed part of the great Midland Plain and so were normally farmed under a three-field system, but on the coal-measure sandstones and the edges of the Dark Peak one or two townfields of modest extent usually sufficed for the growing of cereals.

In the Middle Ages the rents of hay meadows were three or four times the value of those that were paid for arable lands. Meadows provided an essential source of winter fodder. The largest were found alongside the Trent and the Dove and by the Derwent, the Wye and the lower Erewash. At some unknown point in the Middle Ages they began to be managed so that water could be channelled into them in springtime, to stimulate the early growth of grass for sheep to graze, then again to promote the growth of the grass that was to be cut as hay. The water was brought along dikes from rivers and springs or was run off the neighbouring arable fields, bringing nutritious silts and manures. Just a thin film of water was needed to raise the temperature, but it was not allowed to stagnate. Bakewell's warm springs were particularly effective in promoting an early bite in the meadows on the right bank of the Wye, which stretched as far as Holywell (now flowing in the recreation ground alongside the A6) and the Burton Meadows beyond. These springs were ducted underground in the nineteenth century and the channels in the town's meadows are no longer visible, but those at Burton can still be seen in low sunshine. Most medieval manors had some common meadowland, which was divided into doles like the strips of the arable fields, and sometimes reallocated to different tenants on a rotation basis every year. At Hilton, for example, in the thirteenth century the doles were shared by lot and were usually enclosed from Candlemas (2 February) to Lammas (1 August), when they were cut and then turned over to communal grazing.

As the population grew in the thirteenth century, the inhabitants of neighbouring townships became increasingly fractious over the boundaries of their commons and the definition of their rights where the wastes were inter-commoned. The Derbyshire Eyre of 1281 listened to many different claims from local lords. John of Newbold, for instance, claimed common of pasture on 100 acres of moor in Whittington, where he was accustomed to graze all his beasts throughout the year. Ralph de Crumwelle brought Geoffrey de Boyhawe and Richard de Sauney to court to justify their demand for common of pasture in 160 acres of wood in West Hallam for all kinds of beats throughout the year and with pigs from Michaelmas to Martinmas. And Roger Durdent and Oliver de Langeford came to an agreement about Roger's rights in Brandwood and and Oliver's park in Langford, whereby Roger was allowed common of pasture for all kinds of beasts in the wood pastures after the hay and corn had been harvested and to dig turf and peat on Langford common. Arguments over rights on the moors were increasingly fierce, especially where no natural features could be used as markers and claims had to be asserted by the erection of boundary stones in the form of a cross shaft set into a sturdy base. Elsewhere, deep ditches and high banks marked township boundaries. In the Dark Peak, for instance, the township of Outseats (which was based on the Domesday Book berewick of Hirst) was separated from that of Hathersage by a wall constructed of 'cog', or wattle and mud, a Cogwall whose name has been corrupted into the present Cogger Lane.

The Domesday Book survey showed that about a quarter of the Derbyshire landscape was covered by woods, though very little woodland survived in the lowlands to the south of Derby, nor on the magnesian limestone in the north-east of the county, and it was absent in the Dark Peak above 800 feet. In 1086 these woods were mostly in the form of wood pastures, but by the late thirteenth century the majority were managed carefully for their coppiced underwood as much as for their timber. In a period of population growth, wood became an increasingly valuable resource.

Barlow's wood pastures were estimated by the Domesday Book commis-sioners at 4½ leagues long and 12 furlongs wide. The scattered nature of settlement was typical of those townships that came down from the Pennines on to the coal-measure sandstones between Chesterfield and Sheffield. The small village of Barlow, dominated by the lord's hall, was surrounded by two open fields, which together covered only 200–220 acres on the best soils of the township. Beyond lay a 75½-acre common on the thin soils of the steep, north-facing slope, descending from the lead-smelting site at Bole Hill to Crow Hole by the Barlow Brook. The townfields were of modest size compared with the numerous closes and the extensive pastures. Field names suggest that the slopes down from these fields to the Sudbrook (Barlow's southern boundary) were brought into cultivation during the late twelfth and thirteenth centuries. About 100 acres of land, climbing up the side of the brook, were known as the Riddings and the neighbouring closes were often called Intakes or Intacks,

Brindwoodgate, Barlow. The wood-pasture character of Barlow township was well established by the Middle Ages. Brindwood means 'burnt wood' (as in 'Brentwood', found elsewhere in the country). A reference to 'Brendwood Spring' in 1610 shows that by then Great and Little Brindwood were coppice or spring woods. The sunken bridleway that descends from Cartledge past Great Brindwood was known as Brindwoodgate, either because of a gate into the wood or from the Viking word 'gate', a way. It gave its name to this small settlement at the bottom of the track. A survey in 1630 recorded six small houses or cottages there.
PHOTOGRAPH: AUTHOR

typical medieval names for land that had been laboriously cleared of wood, scrub and thorns. In summer time Barlow farmers could graze their cattle not only on their common pasture but on the moors high on the western skyline at almost 1,000 feet above sea level. Oxton Rakes takes its name from the paths along which oxen were driven on to these summer pastures and the moorland boundaries of the township were marked by crosses and ditches. In the twelfth century the Cistercians of Louth Park Abbey (Lincolnshire) were granted a compact estate on the very edge of cultivation, on or near the site of the present seventeenth-century farmhouse known as Barlow

Grange (the 'Barley Grange' of 1306), with the right to mine and smelt iron. About the same time, the Cluniacs of Lenton Priory (Nottinghamshire) were granted similar rights in the wood that covered the hillside on the opposite side of the Barlow Brook. The present name Monk Wood was in use by 1327, but for management purposes the wood was divided into sections; Grasscroft Wood was recorded in 1310, Ferny Lees and Cobnor Wood in 1324, and Brearley Wood in 1353. The Cluniacs administered their share from Monkwood Farm, on a shelf high above the brook, but the major part remained in the ownership of the lord of the manor. Other woods, such as Great and Little Brindwood

LEFT

Whibbersley Cross still marks Barlow's moorland boundary. It was perhaps erected by the Cistercian monks of Louth Park Abbey (Lincolnshire), who were granted estates here and who established a grange nearby. However, the name is not recorded until 1721.
PHOTOGRAPH: AUTHOR

(the 'burnt wood') covered much of the northern parts of the township, though freeholders were allowed to set up home in clearings on or near the boundaries. Barlow Woodseats and Barlow Lees were first recorded in 1269, but are probably older. This was a typical wood-pasture landscape with the scattered settlements of the freeholders and the possessions of the monks at the extremities of the township. The present boundaries of the woods and many of the fields date back well into the medieval period.

The lords of manors that had extensive woods or moors were very willing to allow younger sons of peasant farmers to make new clearings – or assarts as they are known in medieval documents – for they brought in extra income and helped to solve the problem of accommodating the growing population. A remarkable example of how the most unpromising land was brought under the plough, almost in desperation, can be found at Lawrence Field near Longshaw on the moors of the manor of Padley, more than 900 feet above sea level. Now largely hidden under heather, a large, oval area, divided into strips by merestones, is enclosed by a ditch and a bank with stones mounted on edge. On the eastern boundary of this enclosure are the stone foundations of a medieval longhouse, divided by a cross-passage through opposing doorways into separate quarters for the farmer and his animals. A smaller version of this boat-shaped building stood nearby. The low walls of medieval assarts of a similar nature can also be traced on the opposite side of Burbage Brook near Sheffield Plantation.

The Welbeck canons were not the only ones to carve new settlements from the woods and moors of the Upper Derwent valley. Sherds of medieval pottery, dating from the mid-thirteenth century onwards, have been found at 11 farmsteads and at Derwent hamlet. By 1285 the jurors of the forest courts were expressing concern about the diminishing woodlands. These new farms were all built on small terraces of relatively level ground on the sides of the valley, many of them just above the flood levels of the Derwent and its tributaries, but with ready access to the moorland pastures above. Five farms – One Man's House, Ronksley, Shireowlers, Tinkershouse and Nether Ashop – stand out from the rest in the numbers of potsherds and the range of vessels that Bill Bevan has found. Most sites were occupied until the construction of the Howden reservoirs in the early twentieth century, so the only structural remains to survive from the Middle Ages are those at the abandoned sites at Westend and in Dovestone Clough. There, platforms were terraced into sloping ground to support longhouses that were constructed with stone foundations, timber frames and roofs covered with thatch or turves and bracken. Along the valley bottom and its sides, walls enclose small, irregular fields between the woods, and holloways mark the ancient routes up to the peat grounds and the common moorland pastures.

Unlike their predecessors, peasant houses built in the thirteenth century were surrounded by trenches and drains and their crofts were enclosed by boundary ditches, perhaps because of worsening weather. Stone paths and cobbled thresholds also became common. Our knowledge of medieval peasant housing in Derbyshire is limited, but a simple dwelling house dating from the late thirteenth to the late fourteenth century has been excavated at Thurvaston to the west of Derby. A central hearth was used for domestic purposes, including cooking. Such buildings generally had a short life. They were replaced every generation or two, often on new sites within the surrounding toft.

Medieval field walls near Sheffield Plantation, Longshaw. On the opposite side of Padley Gorge from Lawrence Field the foundations of field walls dividing medieval clearances can be seen. They seem to date from the late twelfth or thirteenth century when families were hungry for land. These assarts, as they are described in medieval documents, were abandoned after the Black Death, when a severely reduced population no longer needed to farm marginal land such as this.

PHOTOGRAPH: AUTHOR

Even at a higher social level, few timber-framed houses survive from before the Black Death. Barbara Hutton has identified a smoke-encrusted, crown-post roof over the medieval hall at Sudbury Home Farm in the parish of Doveridge, which has been dendro-dated to 1319. Such high-status carpentry is very rare in medieval Derbyshire; only two other crown-post roofs have so far been discovered in the county, one at Repton and part of another at Etwall. Another superior building from this period was the (dismantled) tithe barn at Sandiacre (now in store at Elvaston Castle), which has a dendro-date of 1330 ± 10 years for the felling of its timbers. It was erected on the order of Roger Northburgh, Bishop of Coventry & Lichfield and the builder of the chancel of the nearby church of St Giles.

Industry

The cloth industry that was the basis of prosperity in many English medieval towns was established in Derby and Chesterfield from at least the twelfth century and seems to have provided employment throughout the Middle Ages. Early water-powered fulling mills were also recorded in the thirteenth-century at Hartington and Wirksworth and in the fourteenth century at Ockbrook. The best Derbyshire wool, however, was sold to Flemish and Italian merchants, who were prepared to pay high prices. Most of this wool was probably exported through Boston, which by the end of the thirteenth century was England's leading wool port, but no records of this trade survive. Dyestuffs such as alum and woad were imported into Derby and Chesterfield all the way overland from Southampton as back carriage in the lead wains.

In 1232 a confirmation of the privileges of the burgesses of Chesterfield assured them that only they were allowed to 'cut or shear linen or woollen cloths' and to buy tanned hides or 'hides or skins which are untanned, raw, fresh or salted in the market'. Chesterfield's tanneries were located along the river Hipper below Beetwell Street, so that unpleasant odours would not spread into the heart of the town, but their chief customers, the shoemakers, were gathered together in Soutergate and Souter Row. Leather workers were numerous, for the range of goods that they produced included clothes and bottles as well as saddles and straps or belts and bags. The importance of the various metal trades is also clear from names such as Iron Gate in Derby and Knifesmith Gate in Chesterfield.

Wirksworth was the most important town for the growing trade in lead, though some merchants were based further east. Ralph Bugge of Nottingham was a leading lead merchant between about 1210 and 1240 and his son and namesake, the bailiff of the Forest of the Peak, leased the Wardlow mine and delivered lead to Boston. As the miners went deeper, so they encountered problems with water levels; in the late 1240s, for instance, the Hucklow mines were flooded. Production in parts of the High Peak declined, but elsewhere new mines were opened in the late thirteenth century to meet rising demand. They

included the Hard or Mandale Rake between the rivers Wye and Lathkill, within the manors of Ashford and Bakewell, and the Hard Rake, which belonged to Leicester Abbey's Meadow Place Grange in the parish of Youlgreave. By the 1340s, annual output from these mines reached 2,300 loads of ore. Production levels were much higher than this in the Coast Rake in the Low Peak, between Hartington and Winster, which had been worked for much longer. To the east of the White Peak mining areas, an increasing number of windy escarpments were used as smelting sites or Bole Hills and the woods were coppiced for making charcoal. For example, about 1240 the woods of Kirk Hallam and Stanton were sold for this purpose.

Lead ingots were exported along the holloways that were deepened by the wheels of the oxen-drawn wains. From the late twelfth century onwards, many loads of lead were taken by wain through Derby to Colwick (Nottinghamshire), which was then the highest navigable point on the Trent, where it was shipped downstream to Torksey and Lincoln and along the river Witham to Boston. But merchants dealing in lead from northern fields found it easier and more economical to take loads overland to the inland port of Bawtry, then by boat down the river Idle to Stockwith and by larger vessels down the Trent to Hull. Alternatively, as early as 1245–51 Derbyshire lead was being carried by wains more than 150 miles overland via Derby, Coventry and Oxford to the port of Southampton.

Coal was mined for local markets only, for the Derbyshire collieries could not compete in the export trade with those in Northumberland and Durham that had immediate access to economical transport by the sea. Scattered references show that coal was mined in the thirteenth century at Denby, Duffield Frith, Little Hallam, Morley, Smalley and Swadlincote and no doubt small-scale mining was commonplace elsewhere in east Derbyshire. The associated seams of ironstone were mined in bell-pits and smelted in primitive charcoal-fuelled bloomeries. The best-recorded ones were those on the estates of great lords or abbeys and priories. For example, in 1257 four forges were recorded in Belper Ward and one in Hulland Ward within Duffield Frith. These large landowners also profited from their quarries for building stone or millstones. A millstone quarry was being worked at Alderwasley within Duffield Frith about 1257 and a neighbouring quarry provided fine roof slates. The gritstone ridge along the eastern side of the Derwent valley was exploited for its high-quality building stone, especially at Duffield Bank and at Rowcliff in Belper, and in north-eastern Derbyshire the magnesian limestone quarries of the Bolsover/Whitwell district produced another highly valued building stone.

Recession

The rapid growth of the national population came to an abrupt end in the early fourteenth century, long before the Black Death, because of an unprecedented series of harvest failures and livestock disasters between 1315 and 1322. The

Known locally as 't'owd man', this delightful medieval carving of a lead miner now adorns the west wall of the transept of St Mary's church, Wirksworth. It was reputedly brought from Bonsall church (within the ancient parish of Wirksworth) in the 1870s, yet it looks similar in execution to other Romanesque stones incorporated in the same transept walls. The miner is shown with his pick and basket, or 'kibble'.
PHOTOGRAPH: CARNEGIE

poor summer of 1314 was followed by exceptionally wet ones in the following two years, when the heavy, persistent rains that fell from May until autumn ruined the hay and con harvests and weakened people's resistance to disease; the harvest failed again in 1321. During this horrendous period sheep murrain devastated flocks and cattle plague had a similar effect on oxen and cows.

Long before these disasters, many of the great landowners had looked at their declining profits and had decided to lease their demesne farms if tenants could be found. All the Crown demesne lands in the High Peak were leased as early as 1256–57 and the Bolsover estates followed in the late thirteenth century. By 1313 the earls of Lancaster had leased all but one of their Derbyshire properties. Only in the valleys of the Trent and its tributaries did demesne farming continue until the end of the fourteenth century.

We have only patchy records of the reaction to the crises of 1315–22. Manorial rental income from the Derbyshire manors of the honour of Tutbury, including Duffield Frith, fell by 30 per cent between 1313–14 and 1321–22 and some lands were no longer tilled because of the poverty of the tenants and the

shortage of livestock. The Grey estates at Shirland and Higham were short
of tenants and so rents fell; in south Derbyshire 40 acres of demesne land at
Bradbourne, 40 acres at Hoon and 200 acres at Dalbury lay uncultivated; and
on the county's north-eastern border 194 acres at Eckington had fallen in value
by a third and much of the arable land was no longer sown. Monastic accounts
reveal a similar bleak picture, yet some Scarsdale manors, such as Morton, seem
to have escaped the worst effects of these harsh times.

In 1334 Derbyshire was one of the poorest English counties. Its taxable
wealth was rated 31st in a list of 38 counties and it paid less than half the tax
of Nottinghamshire. The inhabitants of Derby were assessed at £30, those
of Chesterfield, Ashbourne or Tideswell at over £6, but Derbyshire's other
market towns were hardly distinguishable from the better-off villages: Glossop,
Bolsover, Bakewell and Chapel-en-le-Frith each paid over £5 in tax, Repton,
Melbourne and Castleton (with Bradwell) paid £3 and £5, but Wirksworth was
languishing and paid only £2 12s. 0d. The lead trade in the Low Peak seems
to have been in difficulty at that time, but it was flourishing in the High Peak,
which paid far more tax than any other wapentake (if Derby is excluded).
Twelve High Peak townships or parishes were amongst the top 23 that paid
more than £3 in tax: Tideswell (4th), Glossop (5th), Hathersage (6th), Bowden
Middlecale (7th), Taddington and Priestcliffe (8th), Bakewell (10th), Bowden
(i.e. Chapel-en-le-Frith; 11th), Hope and Shatton (13th), Wormhill (14th),
Castleton and Bradwell (16th), Chelmorton (20th) and Litton (23rd). This list
includes that large area of scattered settlement that lay in the north-western
uplands beyond the lead mining district, from Chapel-en-le-Frith to Glossop,
whose apparent wealth may be partly explained by the large size of its taxation
units (though much of the district was wild moorland). However, it is clear that
the wealth of a group of townships on the limestone plateau on either side of
the upper Wye valley must have come chiefly from the lead trade. Otherwise,
Chelmorton, Taddington, Priestcliffe, Wormhill and Litton would have been
unlikely candidates for such a list. The flights of lynchets at Priestcliffe reflect
the hunger for land at this time and deserted house platforms nearby point
to the later shrinkage of settlement when some lead rakes were worked out
or when demand for lead was poor. Local industries in other parts of north
Derbyshire might help to explain why Scarsdale wapentake was assessed at the
next highest rate of tax. The purely agricultural townships of the central and
southern parts of Derbyshire fell way behind; Spondon (17th), Sudbury (18th)
and Ambaston (21st) were the only rural townships that paid more than £3.
Some townships had already been weakened during the crisis years of 1315–22
and were vulnerable to the devastation that lay ahead.

Wheston cross. The date and purpose of this cross are contentious, but Mr R. Taylor has argued that it was erected by the Cluniacs of Lenton Priory (Nottinghamshire) to mark a boundary of their Peakland estates in the first half of the fourteenth century. It stands by the roadside at the north-western edge of the village of Wheston, within the ancient parish of Tideswell. Its remarkably well-preserved carvings include Christ on the Cross and the Virgin Mary. It is over 11 feet high.

PHOTOGRAPH: CARNEGIE

RIGHT

Foolow cross. The design of the cross head is similar that of the medieval cross at Wheston, four miles away, though it is less refined. It has been suggested that both crosses mark the boundary of lands belonging to Lenton Priory in the first half of the fourteenth century. The base and steps are also of the same date, but in 1868 a new shaft was provided when the cross was re-erected on its present position on the village green. It previously stood about 35 yards away across the road by the present Wesleyan Reform chapel.

PHOTOGRAPH: AUTHOR

CHAPTER SIX

The end of the Middle Ages

The Black Death

We have seen that the great period of population growth throughout England shuddered to a halt during the crisis years of 1315–22. Some recovery was made during the next generation, but then in 1348 the Black Death arrived with devastating effects in all parts of western Europe. In the early twentieth century it became accepted that this deadly disease was bubonic plague, spread by fleas on the backs of black rats during the summer months, but rats are not mentioned in contemporary accounts and modern studies of epidemics in other parts of the world have shown that bubonic plague has a different pattern of development from the Black Death and that mortality rates are much lower. The disease that was endemic in England from the 1340s to the 1660s was known simply as plague or the pestilence. Recent research concludes that it was caused by an unknown, but deadly virus that was spread through droplet infection. Whatever its nature, it killed at least a third and possibly a half of the people of England. Together with further eruptions, especially in 1360–62 and 1369, it reduced the national population to between 2.2 and 3 million. During the next hundred years the number of deaths continued to exceed that of births, so that by the third quarter of the fifteenth century the English population may have sunk to barely 2 million. This demographic reversal had a fundamental effect on the economy of the late Middle Ages. It brought about the shrinkage and desertion of settlements, but in the wake of disaster fresh opportunities arose for some of the fortunate survivors. In the fifteenth and early sixteenth centuries most families were better fed and better housed than before.

The Black Death reached Derbyshire by May 1349, but we have only a few scraps of information to indicate the scale of the calamity. In the next two years 77 of the county's beneficed clergy died and 22 resigned their livings. When Sir William de Wakebridge lost his wife, father, and nearly all his brothers and sisters he established chantries to pray for their souls in his parish church at Crich. Tithe records from various parts of the county show a dramatic fall in the value of receipts. In 1351, for instance, the Ashford lead mine, which was usually worth £20 per annum in rent was worth only £1 that year because of a lack of workers. Ralph de Frecheville's manor at Palterton lay uncultivated because he had no tenants, at Drakelow so many tenants died that the harvest had to be gathered by hired labour, and at Walton-upon-Trent whole families appear to have succumbed to the disease. Mortality rates varied across the country and some places perhaps escaped altogether, but it is estimated that within a generation or two the population of Derbyshire had fallen to below 40,000. Such was the scale of the catastrophe.

Deserted medieval villages

The Black Death weakened village communities so severely that the old methods of communal agriculture sometimes had to be abandoned for lack of people. The minority of villages that eventually became totally deserted shrank to extinction over several generations, particularly in the middle decades of the fifteenth century, a hundred years or so after the Black Death, but some settlements lingered on in a reduced state until much later. Faced with less demand for cereals from the reduced population and unable to find enough tenants to work the arable land, lords converted the open fields of their manors into cattle or sheep pastures. The more ruthless landlords hastened the process of desertion by evicting the remaining families and pulling down their houses, while ambitious or grasping survivors from the ranks of the peasantry were able to prosper by farming more land of their own and by leasing on favourable terms the demesne land of absentee landowners. Amongst those who rose to yeomen and minor gentry status during the fifteenth century were the Bullock family, who held lands in Unstone and a 60-year lease of the demesne lands of Norton manor, and the Lowes who bought lands in Offcote, Underwood and Ashbourne, and later in Cold Eaton and Denby.

Over 3,000 medieval English villages were eventually deserted and many others shrank in size. The scattered nature of settlement in parts of the uplands and on the coal-measure sandstones, where hamlets and isolated farmsteads are more common than villages, makes it difficult to arrive at a firm figure for Derbyshire. The evidence lies on the ground in the form of the grassy mounds of former house platforms, the sunken tracks between individual plots, and the ridge-and-furrow patterns of the former open fields. Sometimes, as at Steetley, a small church or chapel survives, much patched up in Victorian times. At Ballidon, north of Ashbourne, the Norman and later church of All Saints stands amidst earthworks that tell of desertion but which do not indicate precisely when the villagers left. Ten deserted crofts have been recognised, but Ballidon still had 16 households at the time of an ecclesiastical enquiry in 1563 and the number had risen to 21 when hearths were taxed in 1670. Many of the settlements that were ultimately deserted were always small and sited on the more marginal lands and as they did not form townships of their own

Barton Blount. The earthworks of Derbyshire's best known deserted medieval village are seen clearly in this aerial view. Barton was a flourishing village before the Black Death, but by the fifteenth century all the houses but the lord's had gone. The holloways that once served as lanes and paths and the regular outlines of the crofts are picked out by the shadows formed by the low sun. The ridge-and-furrow patterns of the former arable lands show that the open-fields stretched out from behind the houses to the parish boundary. Dating evidence from the four crofts that have been excavated suggests that the village was established well before the Norman Conquest.

they do not appear separately in the taxation records that enable us to estimate population levels at various points in time. Shrunken villages such as Rowland, with house platforms in open plots between the present buildings, are almost as numerous as deserted ones, but are harder to spot on the ground or in the records. Other villages recovered in later times, so the gaps between their houses have been filled.

The only deserted medieval village in Derbyshire that has been excavated is Barton Blount in the former corn-growing claylands to the west of Derby. In 1334 the inhabitants paid £1 2s. 4d. tax, a typical rate for a village at that

time, but by 1563 all that remained were the hall, set within its moat, and the medieval church of St Chad (which was to be rebuilt in 1714 and again in 1845 as a private chapel). Guy Beresford's team identified a large village south-west of the hall and church with 43 crofts, four of which were examined in detail. The excavations showed that the village was occupied from the late Anglo-Scandinavian period until the fifteenth century. The ridge-and-furrow patterns of the surrounding open fields are well preserved in the present pastures. As some of the crofts had been abandoned between the late fourteenth and the early fifteenth centuries, the impact of the Black Death may have weakened the village community and begun the process of desertion. Visitations of plague started the long process of decline for many settlements, but they rarely wiped out an entire village at a single blow. Many villages withered in the late Middle Ages but lasted in their reduced state well into the Elizabethan or Stuart era, when a local lord decided that converting the land to sheep or cattle pastures paid better than growing crops.

A large proportion of the villages on the heavy soils in the lowlands of south-west Derbyshire either disappeared or shrank in the late Middle Ages. They lay at the northern edge of the Midland Plain, which was one of the worst-affected districts in the country. Neighbouring Leicestershire, for example, lost 60 of its 370 medieval settlements and many places in both counties are now smaller than they were before the Black Death. The Ordnance Survey map for Derby (259 in the 'Explorer' series) marks the sites of deserted villages at Barton Blount and Osleston and, to the west of the city, reveals a landscape where villages

All Saints church, Ballidon. The small, restored church stands alone in the fields, amidst the mounds and depressions of a deserted medieval village and the ridge-and-furrow patterns of the open fields. The church contains some Norman and late-medieval architecture, but it was heavily restored in 1882. Deserted medieval villages were rarely destroyed by one violent blow, such as the Black Death. Ballidon was a small settlement that lingered on until at least the late seventeenth century.

PHOTOGRAPH: AUTHOR

are generally small or absent. We can see immediately that townships such as Hoon or Mercaston no longer contain a village and that other places, such as Meynell Langley are thinly populated. In 1334 Mercaston paid £1 2s. 0d. tax, Osleston 19s. 6d., Meynell Langley 12s. 6d. and Hoon only 11s. 0d, so they were already small. Three centuries later, the hearth tax returns of 1664–70 have no record of Meynell Langley; Osleston and Mercaston had been swallowed up by their neighbours; and 'The Towneshipp of Hoone' had just three hearths, possibly all in the same building. A little further west, house platforms and holloways can be seen in a large pasture field at Alkmonton, a township that paid £1 2s. 6d. tax in 1334. A Norman font was unearthed at the point where the six-inch Ordnance Survey map marks the site of a chapel; later, a small settlement re-grouped around a new church to the west. Former village streets and house platforms are also defined clearly in the neighbouring landscape at Hungry Bentley, which was only a poor village paying 13s. 5d. tax in 1334; its place-name distinguishes it from Fenny Bentley by the poor quality of its soils. Some of the other 13 townships in Appletree wapentake that contributed less than £1 tax in 1334 were weakened even further by the Black Death. However,

Medieval pulpit, St Thomas's church, Mellor. Dating from about 1340 and carved from the trunk of an oak tree, this is the oldest surviving wooden pulpit in England, possibly the world. When a new, three-decker pulpit was installed in its place in 1783, the old one was placed in the tower, where it was used to store the gravedigger's tools; later, it was kept in the chancel. Finally, in 1885, the three-decker was removed and the old pulpit was re-installed.

PHOTOGRAPH: CARNEGIE

Sapperton, which paid the lowest rate of 6s. 0d., still had 11 hearth tax payers three centuries later. Other small places in the Trent valley, notably Arleston (£1 2s. 6d. tax in 1334) and Sinfin (14s. 8d.), were each reduced to a single farm and Willington (19s. 0d.) had just three households in 1563, though the village had grown again to 23 by 1670.

South of Ashbourne, the Old Hall is now the only house in Eaton-on-Dove in the parish of Doveridge, whereas in 1334 the payment of £1 12s. 0d. tax suggests a fair-sized village. Further north, Cold Eaton, near the shrunken village of Alsop, was still a thriving place in 1334 when £1 19s. 4d. tax was paid, but by 1563 the number of houses had been reduced to six. The wide triangular green at the end of the village street was probably once encircled by farmhouses but now their number has been reduced to two. The houses and cottages that were strung out in line along the street of the former village of Lea, between Bradbourne and Tissington, were probably abandoned by the early sixteenth century, when a charge that the landowner had ejected tenants was heard at the Court of Exchequer. In 1670 Robert Ensor paid tax on eight hearths 'for the Lea', which by then lay within Tissington township.

Clive Hart's archaeological survey of north Derbyshire noted that the majority of deserted sites in that part of the county had been small settlements before the Black Death. In the White Peak, where arable land was readily turned to pasture, the best examples that can be seen on the ground or from aerial photographs are at Conksbury, Nether Haddon, Smerrill and Snitterton. Eighteen crofts have been identified at Conksbury, high above the river Lathkill as it winds its way through its attractive gorge. A further 17 crofts have been recognised at Smerrill, near Middleton-by-Youlgreave, close to a former monastic grange. At Snitterton, near Matlock, the lynchets on the hillside show how the growing population brought new land under the plough in the decades leading up to the Black Death, before the number of inhabitants was reduced drastically and the township was absorbed within Wensley. And at Nether Haddon, as the hall increased in size the village on the opposite side of the present A6 road withered away. The Vernons were ruthless landlords who probably hastened this process, which ended with them turning the parish church into their own private chapel. The main holloway of the deserted village can be followed as it winds its way between the rectangular crofts up to the extensive remains of ridge-and-furrow and lynchets in the large fields on the hillside above.

In the decades after the Black Death, settlements also decayed on the shales and gritstones of north Derbyshire, particularly the relatively new ones such as Lawrence Field which had been cleared from the woods and the moors above Padley by hungry families desperate for land. The earthworks of a once-substantial medieval settlement at Uppertown, Birchover, have been destroyed by ploughing and the stones re-used in field walls, but the local archaeologist, J.P. Heathcote, recovered several carved stones from a twelfth-century chapel that was still being used in 1413. Elsewhere in this area of scattered settlement, it is difficult to judge the extent of the retreat of settlement, but the suspicion is that in some cases what are now isolated farms were once hamlets. Much more fieldwork and documentary research needs to be carried out before we can obtain a clearer picture.

The villages on and just off the magnesian limestone belt in north-eastern Derbyshire were reduced in size in the late Middle Ages but some of them grew again when the concealed coalfield was exploited in the late nineteenth and twentieth centuries. Quarrying and intensive ploughing have removed the evidence on the ground at Steetley, around the lonely Norman chapel, which was restored in Victorian times. Clive Hart has identified 11 abandoned crofts at Blingsby Grange, by the pale of the deer park surrounding Hardwick Hall. Recorded in Domesday Book as Blanghesbi – a Viking place-name preserved by the rare local surname Blanksby – it appears on a map of 1610 as a large, empty field of over 38 acres as 'Blingsbie'.

Decayed towns

Plague probably spread quickly in the congested towns and a much smaller population in the surrounding countryside meant far less demand for the goods produced by urban craftsmen. We do not have firm figures, but it seems that Derbyshire's towns, in common with those throughout the land, were much reduced in size. By 1377 Derby had only 1,046 taxpayers and it ranked 37th on the national scale in terms of the amount of tax paid. Amongst those who paid poll tax in the borough in 1377–79 were men whose surnames denoted their origins in Wales, Ireland, London, Lancaster, Liverpool, Ludlow, Nottingham, Pickering, Stafford and many of the south Derbyshire market towns and villages, but relatively few tradesmen had risen above the ranks of those who were taxed at the basic rate of 4*d*. In the fifteenth century more properties were abandoned, so by 1524 Derby was no longer amongst the top 42 English towns. Nevertheless, a small group of well-to-do merchants – the Liversages, Stringers, Walkers and Bainbrigges – were prosperous enough to frequently fill the office of bailiff. Derby remained far more important than any other town in the county.

Unfortunately, John Leland, whose *Itinerary* late in the reign of Henry VIII is a prime source of information about urban decay throughout England, did

A sturdy, sixteenth-century timber-framed building in the Shambles, Chesterfield. The narrow passages between the buildings preserve the ancient plan of this eastern part of the market place. Derbyshire's towns do not have many surviving timber-framed buildings, yet this was the common form of vernacular architecture before the seventeenth century, in town and countryside alike.

PHOTOGRAPH: CARNEGIE

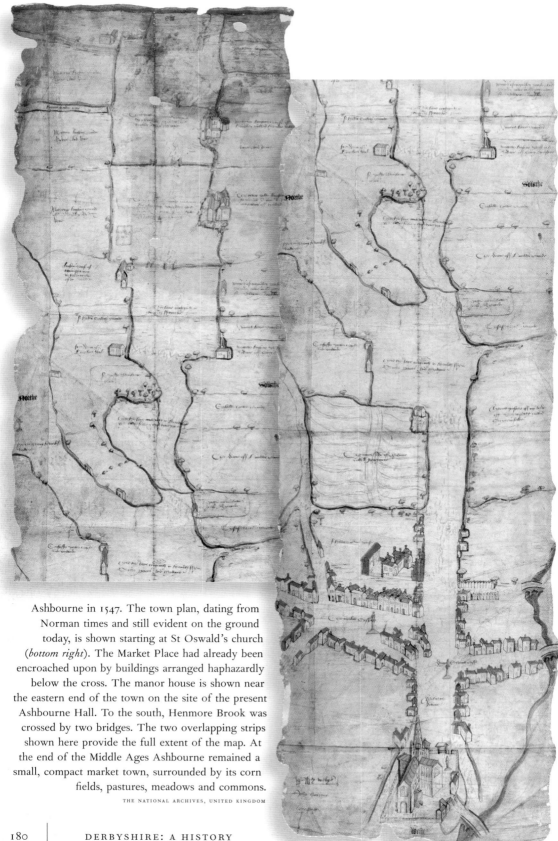

Ashbourne in 1547. The town plan, dating from Norman times and still evident on the ground today, is shown starting at St Oswald's church (*bottom right*). The Market Place had already been encroached upon by buildings arranged haphazardly below the cross. The manor house is shown near the eastern end of the town on the site of the present Ashbourne Hall. To the south, Henmore Brook was crossed by two bridges. The two overlapping strips shown here provide the full extent of the map. At the end of the Middle Ages Ashbourne remained a small, compact market town, surrounded by its corn fields, pastures, meadows and commons.

not tour Derbyshire, presumably because it had no great monastic remains or much else of note to attract his attention. But he was told that the county's market towns were Derby, Wirksworth, Chesterfield, Bakewell and Ashbourne. None of these appears to have been thriving. The accounts of the borough of Chesterfield show that rents fell during the fourteenth and fifteenth centuries and a map of the town in 1635 shows that it had not grown beyond its medieval limits. A similar story at Ashbourne can be deduced from a map of 1547, which shows that the shape of the town was unchanged except for the partial infilling of the market place by two rows of buildings. The 16 burgage plots that were owned by the Cockaynes of Ashbourne Hall, the tenants of the Duchy of Lancaster, were a distant memory of the time when the leading townsmen were semi-independent burgesses. Nor do we hear any more about burgesses in Bakewell. Wirksworth's fortunes went up and down according to the state of the lead trade, Bolsover and Castleton stagnated when their castles were reduced in importance, and all the other attempts to found markets when the economy was expanding in the thirteenth and early fourteenth centuries had floundered during the long years of recession.

The Duchy of Lancaster

From the middle of the fourteenth century onwards the Crown lands in Duffield Frith and the Peak District were administered through the Duchy of Lancaster. The duchy was created in 1351 when Henry, Earl of Lancaster, was made a

duke, and was revived in 1377 by a grant to John of Gaunt, second Duke of Lancaster, the father of the future Henry IV. Even after it became a Crown estate again in 1399, the duchy kept its distinctive judicial system and administrative structure. In the late Middle Ages the Duchy of Lancaster was by far the largest landowner in Derbyshire, with estates extending from the Dove to the Derwent and from the Cheshire border to the Trent valley. The county no longer had huge baronial estates and, although the cathedrals at Lichfield and Lincoln profited handsomely from the payment of tithes and numerous abbeys and priories benefited from their cattle farms and sheep ranches, great ecclesiastical estates were absent. Gentry families owned many small manors in south Derbyshire, but their individual estates were relatively small and were confined mostly within the county's borders.

During the fifteenth century the Duchy of Lancaster gave up stock farming and rented out its cattle and sheep farms and horse studs to local gentry families, notably the Vernons, Bradburnes, Okeovers, Babingtons and Knivetons. Duffield Frith, however, continued to be administered much as before. Its most remarkable feature was the 450-acre park at Ravensdale in Hulland Ward, which was probably enclosed from the wastes in 1251, when William de Ferrers obtained a grant of free warren. A 1614 survey noted that it:

containeth in circuit by estimation about three myles being full of hills and dales. And from the soil thereof that is very barren ground and the most part of it covered with ferne and the rest boggy ground and not above ten timber trees growing … the rest of the trees are Rampickes not fit for pale or rale.

Detailed records from the fourteenth century onwards show that the Ravensdale Park pale was inspected and repaired regularly. The remains of the high bank on which this pale was raised can still be followed for 88 per cent of the circuit, but quarrying has destroyed the rest. A high status building, with a chapel attached, which lay within the southern boundary of the park, was occupied from the thirteenth to the seventeenth century and was described alternatively as a Manor House or a Lodge. The park also contained a mill and was crossed by Ravensdale Park Road, the highway from Belper to Tutbury.

Ravensdale is unique amongst the parks of Duffield Frith in having a deer course along its valley bottom. Christopher Taylor thinks that it is by far the best and at present the earliest known example in England of this complicated, well-organised, spectator sport. It may have been established in the fourteenth century, possibly by John of Gaunt, who was a keen hunter and a frequent visitor in the 1360s and 1370s during August and September, when the bucks were in the best condition. Maps and aerial photographs show a double-hedged trackway curving down the central dry valley of the park for almost exactly a mile. This feature is 70 to 80 metres wide, narrowing to 60 metres before opening up into a triangular area in the south. It pre-dates the field boundaries that abut on either side. Deer were driven from their collecting point and funnelled into the course, whereupon greyhounds, hunting by sight, were released from their holding pens and the chase began, with men on horseback in hot pursuit. Spectators on the natural slopes and artificial banks high above the valley had a thrilling view of the whole proceedings. The deer were killed by bow and arrow or by the hounds, unless they reached the finishing point, where they were allowed to escape.

Knights and gentlemen

By the end of the fourteenth century the former Derbyshire Domesday Book baronies had been much subdivided. Susan Wright has shown how in the late Middle Ages a broadly based social pyramid of gentry families, consisting of knights and 'gentlemen', had became prominent throughout the county. A tax return of 1436 reveals a small elite, headed by Derbyshire's two resident peerage families, Grey of Codnor and Blount of Barton Blount. The Greys' estates lay mostly in the north and east midlands, particularly Nottinghamshire. The castle that they had built at Codnor remained their main Derbyshire seat until 1496, when it passed to the Zouche family. The Blounts had lands in seven counties and Walter Blount's elevation to the peerage in 1465 recognised the family's long-standing importance.

Derbyshire was a poor county with relatively few men wealthy enough to take on a knighthood. Susan Wright has calculated that between 1430 and 1509 the Derbyshire gentry formed a group of 50 or so families of widely ranging incomes below the level of the peerage but above that of the lesser or parochial gentry. The leading knights, who occasionally took their retainers to war in France, were from the families of Gresley, Vernon, Chandos, Frecheville, Fitzherbert, Foljambe, Solney, Dethick, Twyford, Montgomery, Longford, Brailsford, Shirley, Curzon, Meynell, Bagpuize, Savage, Chaworth and Tuchet. They could depend on baronial patronage and lucrative senior appointments. For example, the Foljambes were deputy stewards of Chesterfield, the Curzons were appointed as stewards to the Greys of Codnor and to the Audleys at Markeaton, and the Vernons acted as stewards for the Dukes of Norfolk at Bretby and elsewhere.

The Vernon estates were far more extensive and scattered than those of any other Derbyshire gentry family. The Vernons were easily the largest gentry stock rearers in the Forest of the Peak, their flock in 1418–19 consisting of 249 wethers, 263 ewes and 176 hogs, and, as we shall see, they profited hugely from the revival of the Derbyshire lead trade. In the 1360s or 70s Sir Richard Vernon IV decided to turn his Norman hall at Nether Haddon into a large manor house whose splendour would reflect his family's standing. The new hall stretched 220 feet between the outer walls and separated two courtyards on a sloping site. The view from the lower courtyard reveals the original tall windows and the gargoyles that adorn the external walls of the buttery

Haddon Hall from the south-west. Derbyshire's finest medieval manor house grew at the expense of the village of Nether Haddon on the opposite bank of the river Wye. The village was abandoned in the late Middle Ages. The parish church, which stood on a rock close to the house, was incorporated within the manorial complex of buildings and became a private chapel. The former arable fields of the village became cattle and sheep pastures. Fierce battles broke out over the right to mine lead, but the Vernons emerged victorious.

PHOTOGRAPH: CARNEGIE

and the hall, but the porch, battlements and chimney stack were added about 1450. Haddon Hall was laid out in the classic medieval manner. An off-centre porch leads into a passage that goes right through the house and divides the kitchen, buttery and other service rooms from the living quarters. The massive fireplaces, log boxes, ovens, stone floors, chopping boards, troughs and other simple furniture in the kitchen provide England's most authentic picture of the working environment of the men and boys whose task it was to prepare the meals. The kitchen was originally higher and perhaps free-standing with a louvred roof; the low ceiling was inserted in the sixteenth century. The heat

A View of HADDON HALL *in Derbyshire, the Seat of the Duke of Rutland.*

The medieval manor house at Haddon was added to in the reign of Henry VIII by Sir George Vernon, the last of his line, though not in as regular a fashion as is shown in this idealised view, by an anonymous artist, in 1779. The bridge over the river Wye, which provided the sole access to the hall, dates from 1663.

and smells from the kitchen were kept away from the hall, as far as possible, by a huge, ornate screen, dating from about 1450, which graced the hall from the opposite side of the cross-passage; it is one of the best survivals from this period in the country. The lord and his family, and special guests, sat at the long table on the slightly (but symbolically) raised dais on the other side of the hall from the screen, while their retinue and servants ate at trestle tables in the main body of the hall, and afterwards slept on the floor. A log fire in the centre of the hall provided warmth, its smoke rising to blackened beams and partly escaping through a louvre in the roof; the present roof dates from the restoration work of the 1920s. The lord's private parlour was entered through a door at the dais end of the hall. This too was originally open to the rafters, but about 1500 a ceiling was inserted to make the present two levels. The lower part, now known as the Dining Room, retains its painted ceiling and its walls and panelling with an ornamental top frieze.

Sir Richard also added a north aisle and widened the south aisle of the church of Nether Haddon, which in time became incorporated into the manor house complex as the Vernon family's private chapel. Its chancel was rebuilt in 1427 with a large east window in the Perpendicular style and the picturesque turret dates from about 1450. In the late fifteenth century the walls of the chapel were painted with the popular image of St Christopher carrying the Christ child across a river, scenes from the lives of St Nicholas and of St Anne, and a gruesome depiction of the moral of the 'Three Quick and the Three Dead'. In the sixteenth century Haddon Hall was altered and enlarged further by Sir George Vernon, until it had acquired its present, rambling and romantic appearance. The north-west gate tower dates from c.1530, the apartments to its east from about the same time, and those to its south towards the chapel from a few years before.

Noble patronage also helped the Eyres to prosper. An Eyre had been a forester in Hopedale in 1285 and by the fifteenth century numerous Eyres were established in the Peak District and several were manorial officers. Robert Eyre II was the steward of Holmesfield manor by 1480 and the Earl of Shrewsbury's steward in Derbyshire a few years later; meanwhile, his youngest brother Stephen was bailiff of Ashford manor. The Eyres who had acquired Padley manor through the marriage of Robert, third son of Nicholas Eyre of Thornhill, and Joan Padley, were the most successful branch of the family. The foundations of the north and west ranges of the fourteenth- and fifteenth-century manor house at Padley, arranged around a quadrangular courtyard as at Haddon, were revealed in 1933 when the site was cleared and part of the substantial gatehouse was converted into a Roman Catholic chapel. The original chapel lay above the main entrance to the south range, which contains two ancient doorways and parts of a hammerbeam roof, carved with angels. The west part of the upper floor may have been the lord's private room, or solar. Sections of a five-feet thick wall, thought to have been that which enclosed Robert Eyre's park in 1499, are said to have been destroyed

Padley Hall. The Eyres of Padley built a fine manor house in the parish of Hathersage during the fourteenth and fifteenth centuries, of which only a portion is still standing. When the site was cleared in 1933, the foundations of the rest of the manor house were revealed, arranged around a courtyard the same style as, but on a smaller scale than Haddon Hall. The Eyres were a prolific and successful family in the High Peak. Their brasses in the Eyre Chapel at Hathersage parish church provided the name of the heroine in Charlotte Bronte's most famous novel, when she stayed with her friend Ellen Nussey in the vicarage.

PHOTOGRAPH: AUTHOR

Wingfield Manor. Access to this majestic ruin on a hill side overlooking the village of South Wingfield is difficult, and so the site is not much visited. This elaborate manor house was built as a showpiece by Ralph Lord Cromwell, Lord Treasurer of England and much else besides, who was one of the wealthiest men in the land in the 1440s, when work began. It was completed during his lifetime and little was added by the Earls of Shrewsbury who inherited it. When it decayed, it was turned into a farmhouse.

during the construction of the railway four centuries later. Memorial brasses of prominent members of the Eyre family are to be found in Hathersage church, where they had a private chantry chapel.

Derbyshire's other major medieval manor house at South Wingfield was built by a newcomer, Ralph Lord Cromwell, Lord Treasurer of England, Warden of Sherwood Forest and Constable of Nottingham Castle, the owner of over 100 manors in various parts of England, especially Derbyshire, Nottinghamshire and Lincolnshire. Descended from a Nottinghamshire family, he became extremely rich in the service of Henry V and Henry VI. He inherited South Wingfield and began building there in 1442. Work proceeded quickly and was finished in 15 years, a rapid rate of progress in an age when walls rose only two or three feet each season. Hardly any alterations were made by later owners, so this complex house survives as a picturesque and dramatic tall ruin, seen in the distance from the railway line to London, half-a-mile from the village. Like Haddon, the buildings were arranged around two courts, with the outer court entered through a gatehouse, past a block of offices with servants' quarters above. In the inner court, the chief tower, which stands 72 feet high, contained a series of prestigious lodging rooms, each fitted with fireplaces and garderobes, the top room being the best. The north range contained the state reception rooms, a large hall whose windows were fitted with stained glass and were originally full length before the insertion of a floor level, a great chamber rising above a service floor and a basement, and a detached kitchen block. The skyline was pierced with chimneys rather than battlements, for this manor house

was not built with defence in mind. It probably had a garden, like Cromwell's Nottingham Castle, and was conceived as a ceremonial building like the tall, brick Tattersall Castle that he had begun in Lincolnshire in 1434. This was a man who was displaying his wealth on the largest, almost royal scale. When it was finished, the building was 416 feet long and over 256 feet wide. We know from the accounts that all the craftsmen were Englishmen who worked under the direction of the chief masons, John Entrepas and Richard North.

Cromwell's formal connections with the gentry of Derbyshire were limited. Upon his death in 1456 he left South Wingfield to the second Earl of Shrewsbury. The Talbot family resided there from time to time and Mary, Queen of Scots spent part of her imprisonment there under the guardianship of the sixth earl. It was badly damaged in the Civil War and became a farm in the nineteenth century as it gradually fell into decay. John Talbot, who was created Earl of Shrewsbury 1442, married Maud Neville, the heiress of the Furnival barony that was based at Sheffield Castle, whose Derbyshire possessions included Eyam, Stoney Middleton, Bamford, Bradwell and Brassington. Successive generations added to these estates, so that by the later sixteenth century the Talbots were great Derbyshire landowners.

Fragments survive of three medieval Derbyshire gentry houses that were built at a much more modest level. The medieval square tower of Fenny Bentley Old Hall belonged to the Bentleys until they became extinct in 1432. It has lost its parapet, but is still three storeys high. Perhaps it formed the gateway to the rectangular manor enclosure? A large funnel-shaped fishpond, with a dam and sluice can be seen nearby. At Mackworth Castle the only survival is the front wall of the gatehouse, which was erected between 1495 and 1500 with a four-centred arch forming the entrance and battlements and gargoyles adorning the upper storey. A large house platform north of the gateway marks the seat of the Mackworths, stewards to the Touchets of Markeaton, until they moved

Mackworth Castle. The only surviving portion of the 'castle' or manor house that the Mackworth family erected on the site of their old family home in the closing years of the fifteenth century is the front wall of the gatehouse, surmounted by battlements and gargoyles. Maxwell Craven and Michael Stanley suggest that the rebuilding got no further than the gatehouse and that when John Mackworth died in 1489, his young son had no opportunity to finish the project.

Timber-framed halls or manor houses are rare in south Derbyshire; Hartshorne Upper Hall is one of the best. Erected by John Benskin about 1629, probably on the site of the old manor house, it has been restored but retains much of its original structure and appearance. It stands on a substantial stone plinth. The ground storey features close studding, but the jettied storey above has herringbone patterns, rare in this part of the county.

to Rutland in the sixteenth century. Near Breadsall parish church the Old Hall combines stonework with timber-framing in a small square hall with a fitted bench of medieval date arranged around two of its sides.

The few surviving late-medieval post-and-truss buildings in the county tend to be the better-quality manor houses of the minor gentry. At South Sitch, Idridgehay, a fine timber-framed house with decorated close studding was altered in 1621 by George and Millicent Mellor. Unusually for a Derbyshire house of this status it has a thatched roof. Earlier generations of the Mellors had lived in an L-shaped house with a hall open to the rafters and a timber-framed firehood. Hartshorne Upper Hall is a timber-framed manor house of

two storeys, which may once have been much larger. It was built by John Benskin, yeoman, who had acquired the freehold by 1635. The studs that rise from a solid stone base are set close together and are decorated with diagonal patterns that are unusual in Derbyshire. The jettied upper floor was rebuilt or re-faced with brick in the seventeenth century. At Sinfin, Arleston House is a sixteenth-century, two-storeyed farmhouse whose square-panelled timber frame rises from a stone floor. The moat to the north of the house surrounded the former residence of the Bothe family. And at Church Broughton the purlins, braces and struts of the roof and walls of the Old Hall have been dated by dendrochronology to 1466.

In north Derbyshire the most interesting medieval manor house is Holmesfield Hall, the successor to the Norman motte-and-bailey castle and the later moated site. It was built during the time of William, Lord Lovell, who had married the heiress of the Deincourt estate, and it has been dendro-dated to 1452–54. Stanley Jones's survey of the building before it was converted into a modern residence showed that a carved canopy marks the spot where the lord sat on formal occasions at the east end of a two-bay hall, next to the private rooms that included an upstairs solar. A carved boss on the king-post roof suggests that the main room was open to the rafters in the usual medieval style and enough wattle-and-daub survives in the roof trusses to prove the nature of the original infilling. Three bays of lodgings extending southwards at the eastern end of the hall have a dendrochronology date of c.1454–58. The whole building became a barn and cattle shelter when it was replaced at the west end by a seventeenth-century hall, which stands partly on the foundations of the service end of the medieval manor house.

Holmesfield Hall. The timber-framed hall that was erected in the 1450s was the successor to the nearby Norman motte and the medieval moated site as the manorial centre for the absentee lords of Holmesfield. The sturdy timber posts of this extension to the hall have been dated by dendro-chronology to 1454–58. They were exposed to external view until the hall was converted into a modern dwelling in the 1990s. The building had been clad with stone and used as a barn after a new hall had been built in the early seventeenth century.

PHOTOGRAPH: AUTHOR

In the neighbouring parish of Norton a Georgian hall has completely replaced its medieval predecessor, but we have a lease from 1400, when Thomas de Chaworth, the lord of the manor, granted the site to William Shemyld, but reserved to himself the right of 'breaking down old houses and of carrying them away and selling them'. Even a substantial timber-framed building could be dismantled and then pegged together again on a new site.

Profit and conflict

During the fifteenth and well into the sixteenth century uncertain profits and the higher wages that labourers were able to negotiate at a time of low population levels persuaded many landlords that it was no longer worth their while to manage their demesne lands to grow cereals for the market. In many parts of Derbyshire rents were low and much land stood vacant. In the south of the county the brief revivals in the 1410s and 1420s and again between the 1450s and 1470s were not sustained and the market for land stagnated until about 1540. But the pastoral economy of the northern uplands and occasional pockets of good pasture further south fared better. The rearing of livestock was a rewarding pursuit except in the slump of the third quarter of the fifteenth century. The men who continued to graze cattle and sheep on their own pastures and who took the chance to lease part of the Duchy of Lancaster's vast estates did well at a time when many others struggled to make a good living.

Ian Blanchard has shown that as prices for livestock products continued to rise in the fifteenth and early sixteenth centuries the Duchy was able to raise the rents for its moorland farms, such as the Hartington sheep ranches and the Edale cattle booths. The owners of Derbyshire's lowland manors did not breed their own oxen, preferring instead to replace their working animals from the upland stock farms. These specialised farms had good-quality, sheltered grazing in the river valleys and summer grazing rights on the moors above. Cows and ewes provided milk and cheese for the market, but at that time falling population levels meant that it was unprofitable to rear livestock for beef or mutton.

The Vernons benefited most from the exploitation of the Peak District pastures from the late fourteenth century onwards. In addition to their own extensive pastures, they leased the grazing rights in the Campana ward of the Forest of the Peak and a cattle farm in Edale. Their highest recorded numbers of animals were 1,071 sheep in 1423–24 and 222 head of cattle, including 50 oxen, in 1428–29. Large flocks of sheep were no longer profitable by the mid-fifteenth century, but favourable conditions returned in the 1470s. This renewed buoyancy enabled Henry Vernon to buy most of Kirk Langley and to build up an extensive estate in north-west Derbyshire, including the manors of Bakewell, Baslow, Bubnell, Cold Eaton and Hazlebadge, other properties in and around Ashover, Bakewell, Baslow, Birchill, Bowden and Hassop, and land in the south of the county at Derby, Netherseal and Trusley. As well as

Edale from Rushup Edge. The first part of Edale's name is taken from the Anglo-Saxon word *eg*, an island, perhaps an island of greenery amongst the barren mountains. In the Middle Ages the valley was used to rear young cattle at vaccaries before they were fattened on lusher pastures elsewhere. Several of the Edale farm names end in *-booth*, a Viking word for a cattle-rearing farm.

PHOTOGRAPH: AUTHOR

drawing a substantial income from his estate, Henry enjoyed the patronage of Henry VII and became a courtier of national standing.

The Foljambes, too, reinforced their position as a leading gentry family in north Derbyshire by profiting from livestock farming and buying up land as it came on to the market. In the last two decades of the fifteenth century Henry Foljambe consolidated his inheritance around Walton, Chesterfield and Newbold and bought new estates in the Peak District and down the Derwent valley from Darley Dale to Derby. He also profited from the various offices that he held: deputy steward of Chesterfield, steward of the Chaworths' north Derbyshire estate, receiver of rents and bailiff for Beauchief Abbey, and bailiff of Scarsdale wapentake.

By the early sixteenth century the numbers of cattle and sheep in the Forest of the Peak had become so large that the deer could not find adequate grazing.

Meadow Place Grange. This farmhouse in the White Peak, west of the deserted village of Conksbury and south of Lathkill Dale, stands on the site of a medieval grange that belonged to Leicester Abbey. The name of the site was originally Meadow Plot or Plek (an alternative name for a plot), but it may have come from the abbey, founded in 1143 as St Mary of the Meadows. In the Tudor period there was a bitter dispute here over grazing rights and firewood, typical of many arguments at a time when the pastures of the White Peak were increasing in value.

PHOTOGRAPH: AUTHOR

An enquiry in 1516 recorded 960–980 cattle, 4,000 sheep and 320 horses there and found that 360 deer were in so poor a condition that they were unlikely to survive the winter. The commissioners recommended the removal of the sheep, but the problem was not solved until the number of deer was reduced later in the century as the fashion for hunting declined. The problem of overstocking also caused bitter disputes about grazing rights on the common pastures in many Peak District townships. The court rolls of the manor of Over Haddon, for instance, recited the tenants' complaints that the abbot of Leicester had deprived them of their common rights in Lathkill Dale. The abbot retorted that Chanon Dale was part of his manor of Meadow Place and both sides produced elderly witnesses to support their claims. An angry controversy continued over two or three decades, with the tenants ignoring orders of the Council in 1529 by breaking hedges and putting their own beasts on the disputed land. Similar arguments created tension between lords and peasants in the manors of Castleton, Hartington and Wirksworth.

Numerous objections to the exploitation of common land by ruthless landlords, and sometimes its enclosure for private pastures, were made in the late fifteenth and early sixteenth centuries. The tenants of Brassington complained that Ralph Eyre, who leased a pasture from Dale Abbey, grazed not only his own cattle and sheep on the commons but other livestock for which he received yearly rents and that he had driven away and impounded their cattle. The tenants of the manor of Matlock complained about Philip Leche's enclosure of 40 acres of common and the tenants of Elton were upset that William Old and others had put 1,000 sheep on their commons. At Ashbourne the tenants destroyed the dikes and gates used by Humphrey Lowe to enclose part of the common pastures and at Alderwasley rioters pulled down hedges newly made by Anthony Lowe on disputed pastures. The gentry families that

grew rich in these years pursued their own selfish advantage unscrupulously, but they sometimes met fierce resistance.

These quarrels were not only between ruthless rich men and ordinary farmers, but between feuding gentry families, such as the Vernons and the Blounts. Assaults, abductions and murders were often gentry crimes. Lawless bands had terrorised parts of Derbyshire back in the reign of Edward II. The Coterel gang, including Roger Savage, the heir of John Savage of Stainsby, and John and William Bradburne, the sons of Roger Bradburne of Hough, and many others were protected by Lichfield canons, notably Robert Bernard, the vicar of Bakewell, and by gentry such as Sir Robert Tuchet of Markeaton, his brother Edmund, the rector of Mackworth, and Robert Foljambe, the bailiff of High Peak. None of the gang was ever convicted for theft, extortion or murder. A feud between the Stathams of Morley and Duchy officials erupted into violence on 18 June 1381, at the time of the rising known, inappropriately, as the Peasants' Revolt, when a band of rebels led by the Stathams burned the

All Saints church, Mackworth. This fine church, near Derby, stands alone in the fields to the east of the village that it serves. Mackworth lies in an area of deserted and shrunken settlements, so it seems likely that the village was once larger. Much of the architecture dates from the early fourteenth century, but the church was rebuilt in the Perpendicular Gothic style in the later Middle Ages. As the church tower has no external door and holes in the stonework show that the door to the nave could be barred by timbers, it has been surmised that it could have been designed for defence.

PHOTOGRAPH: CARNEGIE

Augustinian priory at Breadsall, assaulted the prior and canons, and went on to seize Horston Castle; they were all pardoned for their crimes. Most notoriously of all, a long-running feud between the Pierrepoints and the Foljambes came to a head on 1 January 1434 during a service at Chesterfield parish church when Henry Longford and William Bradshaw were murdered and Sir Henry Pierrepoint was wounded by Thomas Foljambe and others.

Lead

The other way for a man of means to become richer was to invest in the lead trade, both as an owner or lessee of mining dues and as a smelter, or 'brenner'. The trade was subject to boom and slump but in successful times substantial profits could be added to those made from rearing sheep and cattle. Between 1360 and 1420 many lead mines, such as those in Lathkill Dale and around Hartington, were worked out as far as the water table, but in the 1420s a new vein north of the river Wye, known as the Cheprake, was opened, and mining began at Great and Little Longstone, Rowland, Hassop and Calver. From about 1460 output increased rapidly as new mines were opened at Nestor Rake, near Matlock, and on the Ravenstor, Yokecliff and Gang Rakes, near Wirksworth, and about 1506 production restarted in the parish of Hartington. Between 1460 and 1530 the output of Derbyshire lead mines sometimes rose to an annual 3,800 loads of ore, the equivalent to 380 fothers of smelted lead.

By 1400 the Duchy's mineral dues were leased to entrepreneurs, many of whom were landowners of gentry or yeoman status, who had the necessary capital to buy ore from the miners and pay the wages of their smelters. One prominent High Peak lead merchant and brenner was Thurstan de la Bower, a yeoman of Tideswell, who had smelting hearths or boles on the escarpment above Baslow and property in Tideswell, Little Longstone, Monsal and Tunstead. By the late fifteenth century brenners were the dominant figures in the industry and were employing wage labourers to mine the lead ore. The Vernons are the best documented of the several gentry families who were involved in smelting. They owned mines themselves or in partnership with other gentry smelters. In 1497, for example, Roger Vernon and Henry Foljambe took a 20-year lease of the Duchy of Lancaster's lead mines in Wirksworth wapentake and Robert Eyre took a similar lease of the High Peak mines. They also bought large quantities of ore directly from the miners and obtained further supplies by owning or leasing the collection of tithes and the rights of lot and cope. The lot duty amounted to one-thirteenth of a miner's production, while cope was levied upon the purchaser in every sale of ore, at the rate of 4d. (later 6d.) a load. The lessee of the Duchy's lot and cope was also entitled to a third part of a newly discovered lead rake, known as the 'lord's meer'. After the 1530s the lessee of the Duchy's lot and cope took on the important office of barmaster, with responsibility for calling the barmote courts that regulated the industry.

The recovery of the lead industry between 1480 and 1540 was swift. Within Wirksworth wapentake production increased six-fold during those 60 years. Most of the workforce were free miners, whose customary rights to mine lead wherever they found it extended across the Duchy of Lancaster's Peak estates, known as the King's Field. They worked in gangs of two or three and employed a labourer to carry ore up the shaft and to clean it at the surface. Their freedom was largely illusory, for most miners owed money to the wealthy smelters and lead merchants. After the miners had moved on, poor scavengers known as 'cavers' dug over the miners' rubbish tips searching for scraps of ore. Most mines were small and in the Middle Ages they were worked as opencast quarries which followed the line of the lead rakes along the surface of the land. By the 1540s about 400 lead miners were at work in Derbyshire. Most of them were part-time farmers who stopped mining at lambing time and at harvest and when their mines were flooded in the winter months. Free miners were usually copyholders with common rights on the pastures and some prospered in a modest way as the heads of well-established yeomen families. The taxation returns known as the lay subsidies of 1524–25 and 1543 show that although a tiny group of minor gentry who owned their own land and acted as lead smelters and merchants were found in Wirksworth and Matlock, Peak District villages rarely contained a gentry house.

The recovery of the Derbyshire lead industry spluttered to an end in the middle years of the sixteenth century through lack of improved technology.

Tideslow Rake. The spoil heaps of one of the High Peak's major lead rakes stretch in a straight line towards the Neolithic burial mound at Tideslow, named after Tidi, an Anglian leader who was buried here many centuries later and after whom Tideswell is also named. Lead was found close to the surface here and so was probably mined from the Middle Ages onwards. Many rakes have been re-worked for fluorspar in modern times.

PHOTOGRAPH: SHEILA EDWARDS

Smelting was restricted to the spring months when the strong prevailing winds from the south-west stoked the flames of the bonfires in the ridge-top boles until the lead began to melt. By the end of the Middle Ages only Wirksworth wapentake was able to supply ore of sufficient quality for a process that was dependent on the unreliable patterns of the weather. A second limitation was that although the White Peak had great resources of high-quality ore, most of it lay below the water table. The lead industry could expand no further until successful drainage technology was installed.

Other industries

The Derbyshire iron industry remained on a small scale before the charcoal-fuel era of Elizabethan times. Late medieval references to the mining and smelting of ironstone are scrappy and usually come from the large estates, such as Bolsover (1366–67) and Morley Park (1480–81), or from the monastic granges. No medieval iron smelting site has yet been excavated in Derbyshire, but a charge that Thomas Leake, the bailiff of Scarsdale, had diverted water

Derbyshire has some of the best alabaster tomb effigies in the country, including those at Norbury, Morley, Bakewell, Ashbourne, and this one, at Youlgreave, depicting Thomas Cockayne, who died in 1488.

from the royal mill at Newbold to power his forges shows that water-powered forges were in use by 1500. The great era of the industry was yet to come, however.

Sufficient iron was made for the scythemakers who have been noted from the late fourteenth century onwards in and around Derby and Chesterfield, the first known one being John Meysham of Derby (1378). Scythes were made in Norton parish from at least 1459, when John Parker of Little Norton was described as a scythesmith. During the early sixteenth century a few scythe-smiths were recorded in the neighbouring villages of Barlow, Brimington, Dronfield and Eckington, with another cluster on the coal-measure sandstones east of the river Derwent at Belper, Horsley, Kilburn, Makeney and Swanwick. The first known Derbyshire scythe-mill was recorded on the Ecclesbourne in 1466, three more were erected there in the next few years, and another was built soon afterwards on Derby corporation's new weir on the Derwent. The first recorded scythe mill in north Derbyshire was situated on the river Rother at Holbrook, near Staveley, in 1489, but the river Sheaf, which formed Norton's north-western border, soon became the river where most of the north Derbyshire scythe-grinders went to grind their blades.

Medieval potteries were in production at Derby, Burley Hill, Chesterfield, Ticknall and the monastic houses of Dale and Repton. In the thirteenth and fourteenth centuries four coal-fired pottery kilns at Burley Hill, north of Allestree Park and just south of Burley Lane, produced glazed and unglazed jugs and pitchers, cooking pots and dishes. Pottery was also made in Pothouse Lane, Chesterfield from at least the fifteenth century and at Ticknall by the early sixteenth century. At Dale Abbey encaustic paving tiles for covering the

floor of the choir and nave were manufactured in a kiln near the gatehouse. Over 60 different patterns have been identified there, including grotesque designs, tilting knights on horseback and the coats of arms of local families, such as Cantilupe, Deincourt, Ferrers, Grey, Morley and Zouche.

Alabaster, a form of gypsum, was quarried at Chellaston and used by skilled carvers for making high-class tombs in England and France. For example, in 1367 some best-quality alabaster was sent to Windsor for the Garter Chapel and in 1414 a French mason visited Chellaston to purchase alabaster for the abbey of Fécamp in Normandy. In 1419 Thomas Prentys and Robert Sutton of Chellaston were commissioned to make the tomb of Ralph Greene and his wife at Lowick (Northamptonshire) by the following Easter at a cost of £40. A fifteenth-century tomb in All Saints, Aston-upon-Trent, only two miles from the site of the Chellaston quarry, has three standing angels bearing shields, a pattern used by the same Chellaston firm. Such tombs were originally richly painted and gilded. Another school of skilled craftsmen, some of whose altar-pieces, images of saints and effigies were exported to the Continent, worked at Nottingham from the fourteenth century to the Reformation and a workshop at Burton-on-Trent produced the early sixteenth-century work of Henry Harper and William Moorecock in the parish churches at Ashover, Chesterfield and Cubley. The Fitzherbert effigies at Norbury are among the finest alabaster monuments in Derbyshire.

The Baslow court rolls contain several references to the millstone trade. In 1383, for instance, Adam del Hull was brought before the court for not having an annual licence to carry millstones over the moor. Two years later, the rolls record that 'John de Criche and Adam Lymebrenner ... took up the quarry for stone and millstones of Lady Juliana Vernon at Baslow ... [at] 100s. per annum', and that 24 pairs of millstones were currently standing in the quarry. In 1479 a man was paid 14 shillings to carry a pair of millstones from Nicholas Eyre's quarry in Hathersage township to Whiston Mill, 16 miles away. The Eyres also had a quarry at Yarncliff in their manor of Padley within the parish of Hathersage. Some small cash books that were possibly written by Ralph Eyre of Offerton, include accounts of millstone making at Yarncliff in 1466. The Eyres employed hewers on a piece-rate basis during the summer months to make millstones to the satisfaction of an overseer, and their chapmen took the stones to customers as far as Loughborough, some 45 miles away. Wages were paid in advance to the eight hewers, including the aptly named Jankyn Stonhewer, in order to guarantee a contract for pairs of finished millstones of 15 or 16 hands diameter; a hand is a precise measurement of four inches.

Meanwhile, the manufacture of woollen cloth had spread from the towns into the countryside, but it was on a small scale in Derbyshire when compared with the thriving trade in the West Riding of Yorkshire. Between 1355 and 1380, for example, some of the inhabitants of Alport, Baslow, Nether Haddon, Rowsley and Stanton were employed as part-time clothiers. Like most rural workers, they combined their craft with farming a smallholding. Mills for fulling cloth

Yarncliff Wood millstone. This abandoned millstone in Yarncliff Wood, Padley Gorge, was never completed, presumably because it was flawed. It is not possible to date such stones, but it is known that in 1466 Ralph Eyre's workmen, including Jankyn Stonhewer, were making millstones here. One side of this stone was completed and the hole inserted, but it was never turned over so that the hewer could work on the underside. Eyre employed eight hewers at Yarncliff and their products were sold as far away as Loughborough.
PHOTOGRAPH: AUTHOR

after the weaving process was completed spread into the countryside and caused disputes with corn millers over water rights. We find, for instance, that on 3 May 1354 John of Edensor was accused in the Baslow manor court of diverting a watercourse owned by the lord of the manor into his own fulling mill; he was ordered to fill it up.

Communications

Riverside settlements, such as Ashford or Cromford ('the ford at the bend'), were often founded at key fording or ferrying points. In the later Middle Ages stepping stones and the stone foundations of fords were regularly replaced by bridges. Thus the 'Mitham ford' of 1285 had become the 'ford of Mithombrigge' by 1343 and the Grundleford of 1248 had become Grindleford Bridge by the sixteenth century. Medieval bridges needed to be sturdy enough to withstand the force of flood water and wide enough to take the wains that were loaded

Cromford Bridge. Cromford – 'the ford at the bend' – was an ancient crossing point on the road over the river Derwent from Wirksworth to Chesterfield. The bridge can be dated from the style of its high Gothic arches to about 1500. It was widened in the eighteenth century, with rounded arches on the upstream side, to twice its original width. Such sturdy bridges were paid for out of county rates and so their maintenance is recorded in quarter sessions records. The presence of several county bridges, spaced a mile or two apart across the Derwent, attests to the volume of traffic along these routes in the late Middle Ages.

LOWER
A medieval bridge of this size often had a chantry chapel attached, where a prayer could be offered for a safe journey and a contribution made towards the upkeep of the bridge. These chapels were dissolved in 1547 and Cromford's survives only as a ruin on the western bank of the river.

PHOTOGRAPHS: AUTHOR; CARNEGIE

with lead or millstones. In 1386 Will of Hucklow was fined 6*s.* 8*d.* at the Baslow manorial court because he 'carried millstones over Basselow Bridge contrary to the order made'.

Surviving examples of medieval bridges are difficult to date with confidence, for they have been frequently repaired and altered and have been widened to twice their width in later times. Sometimes, as at Darley or Matlock, it is only by looking at the ribs of their pointed arches that evidence of their medieval origin can be found. Bakewell bridge may be as early as 1300, judging by the style of its five low arches over the Wye, but those across the Derwent are later. The late fifteenth-century bridge at Cromford is intact on the southern side, but it was clearly widened to twice its original width in the eighteenth century and given rounded arches on the upstream side. Bridges that were wide enough to take wains and carts spanned the Derwent at regular intervals of between one and two miles. Clearly, they would not have been constructed had the traffic in heavy goods not been substantial. The

1531 Statute of Bridges gave justices of the peace the power to levy a county rate towards the upkeep of these major bridges, but the smaller, wooden bridges were maintained by manor courts and private individuals until civil parishes accepted responsibility for them in Elizabethan times.

Salt was one of the most important commodities that was carried over these bridges and across the moors to the medieval market towns of Derbyshire, Nottinghamshire and Yorkshire, for it was used to preserve food as well as to provide flavour. The people of the midland counties got their salt from the natural brine springs of the Cheshire wiches (the salt works at Northwich, Middlewich and Nantwich). The distinctive set of names which were attached to the routes from the wiches, such as Salterway, Salter Hill or Salter Ford, show that the carriage of salt was the most important trade along them. Amongst the best-known names, Salters Lane descends to Matlock Bridge, Saltergate leads into the heart of Chesterfield, Saltergate Lane is signposted near Bamford Station, and beyond Woodhead Saltersbrook divided Derbyshire from Yorkshire and Cheshire.

Farms and farmhouses

Throughout the late Middle Ages the typical Derbyshire farmer kept a few head of cattle and a small flock of sheep and grew cereals in the townfields. He held his land by copyhold tenure, in other words his proof of ownership was a copy of an entry in the manor court rolls, and he was able to pass his property on to his eldest son upon payment of an entry fine. The level of rent was fixed by custom. Many farms continued in the same family for generations. If families moved, they usually stayed in the same neighbourhood, or 'country', bounded by the nearest market towns. People who were used to the way of life of the southern lowlands rarely ventured into the Peak District or the varied countryside of north-east Derbyshire.

Even in the White Peak, villages were surrounded by their open fields, which were clearly demarcated from the common pastures beyond by a deep ditch. These communal fields were divided into long, slightly curving strips in the usual manner of medieval England and in many places the old plough patterns are preserved on the ground by ridge-and-furrow. Scattered references in deeds are our main source of documentary evidence. From the second half of the fourteenth century, they include '1 rood of land in the field of Eyam' (1351) and the 'town and fields of Tatynton and Presteclyff' (1379), and in the Dark Peak the 'town and fields of Hope' (1387) and the 'town and fields of Thornhill' (1391). Fifteenth-century deeds mention land 'within the towns fields and meadows of Eyam, Riley, Foolow, Hucklow, Bakewell, Youlgreave and Castleton' (1400), 'a messuage and 3 acres 3 roods of land scattered in the fields of Tideswell' (1403), 'one messuage and 32 acres in Wormhill of which 18 acres and the messuage lie in Mylnfeld and 14 acres in Herdwykwall' (1410), the 'town and fields of Bradwall, Burgh, and Schatton' (1441), and 'four acres of land in the town fields of Tunstead, of which one acre lies upon The Tunsteed called Brene aker ... one acre lies upon The Coppielawe called Thamlynflat aker ... five roods likewise ... half an acre called Longhalfaker ... and one Butte in Wyndill' (1456).

Medieval peasants were not just concerned with meeting their own needs; they were always prepared to sell any surplus at the local market. The Black Death had provided survivors with opportunities to farm more land or to earn higher wages, so they could afford a better diet and improved accommodation. The typical buildings of a late-medieval farm in the midland counties comprised the farmhouse, kitchen, bakehouse and barn. Houses and barns were usually 10 to 15 metres in length, but only one-room deep. Their quality varied considerably according to the means of the owner and the availability of local building materials. The excavated dwelling houses and barns from the final stage of the deserted village of Barton Blount had been framed with upright timbers resting on pad-stones. Elsewhere in the lowlands, walls were sometimes constructed of clay lump if sufficient timber was hard to find or too expensive to buy. Most villages contained a variety of buildings that ranged from the sturdy houses of the yeomen down to the insubstantial cottages of the poorest labourers.

Few of Derbyshire's medieval timber-framed houses survive and most of what can be seen from the outside is in the south of the county. However, the best example of a yeoman's house is found at Norton Lees, formerly just inside Derbyshire's northern border but now within Sheffield, where it serves as Bishops' House Museum. It was erected as a timber-framed open hall about 1500 and was given a cross-wing about 50 years later. The whole building was

Bishops' House, Norton Lees. Now within Sheffield, where it is an attractive folk museum, this late medieval timber-framed house once stood just inside Derbyshire. It was the home of the Blythe family, yeomen farmers and organisers of the local scythe trade. The main body of the house (*right*) was erected about 1500; the wing in the centre of the picture was built fifty years later. Both used the king-post style of the more substantial houses of the district.

PHOTOGRAPH: L. NUTTALL

framed in the better-quality, king-post style of north Derbyshire and the West Riding by the Blythe family, who were yeomen farmers and organisers of the local scythe trade.

At a more humble level, a considerable number of cruck-framed houses, cottages and barns, most of them hidden from view, can be found in certain parts of Derbyshire, though most are post-medieval in date. Only two cruck buildings have been dated by dendrochronology to the late Middle Ages; blades at Aston End in Coal Aston were felled within 15 or 20 years of 1409 and those at the Thatched Cottage, Stanley, were ready for use in the spring of 1446. They are our best evidence for the style of accommodation and outbuildings of ordinary farming families. A survey in 1967 found 52 surviving cruck buildings and noted about another 30 with fragmentary remains or which had been demolished in recent memory. Most of Derbyshire's cruck-frames were erected on the well-wooded, coal-measure sandstones, with the greatest concentration stretching northwards from the west of Chesterfield to Barlow, Dronfield and the Yorkshire border (and beyond). Only a few cruck-framed buildings remain standing in the Peak District or the southern lowlands, though five were identified between Derby and Melbourne, for in these districts such inferior-quality timber-framed houses, cottages and barns were replaced by stone or brick buildings in the eighteenth and nineteenth centuries.

Although it has been much restored, this timber-framed building in Derby is basically the one that was erected in the sixteenth century. It has been licensed as an inn since 1580. Derby had numerous inns and alehouses, for not only was it the county town and a market centre, it was a convenient stopping place on northern highways heading for London.

PHOTOGRAPH: CARNEGIE

Cruck-framed house, Melbourne. The sturdy but simple cruck frame was used in modest-sized houses, cottages and barns in the fifteenth, sixteenth and seventeenth centuries. Most Derbyshire crucks are found towards the Yorkshire border, but a few scattered examples can be seen in the southern lowlands. As was usual, this Melbourne example was originally open to the roof. An upper floor was inserted later and the wattle-and-daub infilling replaced with brick.

PHOTOGRAPH: AUTHOR

Surnames

During the thirteenth and fourteenth centuries Derbyshire's peasant farmers and labourers followed the fashion of their social superiors by adopting hereditary surnames. Many of these distinctive names, particularly those that were derived from the scattered farmsteads and hamlets of the Peak District,

Bagshaw acquired its name from this bag-shaped hollow in the hills near Chapel-en-le-Frith. The owners or tenants of many of the isolated farms in the northern part of the Peak District took their surnames from their homes. At the time of the hearth tax returns of 1670 the surname Bagshaw was still concentrated in the High Peak, but since then has become widespread. Despite this, its greatest concentration remains within a few miles of its place of origin.

PHOTOGRAPH: AUTHOR

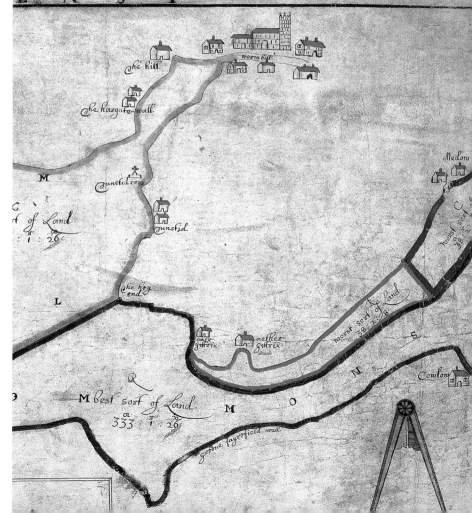

This map of Wormhill township in 1675 shows the two 'Gittrix' farmsteads that became Great Rocks Farm. The place-name means 'the great valley', outlined in red and blue on the map. It is the source of the local surname Greatorex. The old church at Wormhill can be seen (*top*), which may be compared with the rebuilt church shown on page 425.

THE NATIONAL ARCHIVES, MPC 1/85(2).

remain concentrated in Derbyshire and its neighbouring counties. Our chief source of evidence is the poll tax return of 1381 that survives for many of the townships of the High Peak, but some names were recorded much earlier. In the Derbyshire eyre of 1281, for instance, a Matthew Drabble was charged with selling wine without paying tax; Drabble was probably an Old English personal name. Other rare surnames in this category include Outram, which originated in Holmesfield, and Jeffcock, a pet form of Geoffrey, which was recorded in the manor court rolls of Eckington in the late fourteenth century. Surnames that arose from nicknames include Wildgoose, which was recorded at Foston and Somersal in 1281, and Innocent, which appears in the poll tax returns for Tideswell a hundred years later. The rarity and continued local concentration of these names suggest that they each have a single family origin.

Occupational names usually had multiple origins, but that of Boler was restricted to the smelters of lead on Derbyshire's windy Bole Hills. A Ralph le Bolere was recorded at Eyam in 1300, and amongst the taxpayers in 1381 were Robert and Ralph Boler of Castleton, John Boler, senior and junior, of Darley, Nicholas Boler of Ashford, another Nicholas Boler of Tideswell and a William Boler of Wormhill.

Derbyshire's most distinctive surnames are those that were derived from small places in the hills. In 1381, for instance, the taxpayers of Bowden township (now Chapel-en-le-Frith) included two Bagshaws, a Bradshaw, a Kinder, a Needham, an Ollerenshaw and a Rowarth, all of whose names came from farmsteads within the township or from close by. Other Bagshaws had already moved from their hamlet to Castleton, Eyam and Youlgreave and they eventually became prolific in north Derbyshire. The Heathcotes, who had taken their name from the Garendon Abbey sheep farm high above Hartington, were by now living in Buxton and Tideswell; in the fifteenth century one branch moved to Chesterfield, where they became prosperous traders and councillors. By 1381 the Padleys were living in Bakewell, Eyam, Tideswell and Wormhill, as well as at their ancient residence in the parish of Hathersage. Greatorex is a less obvious example that was derived from Great Rocks Farm, Wormhill, a place-name that was recorded in 1251 as Greaterackes, meaning the great valley; in 1381 Henry de Gretrokes paid poll tax at Youlgreave.

Some Derbyshire surnames, notably Alsop, spread far and wide, but they were the exception. Surname distributions show that most people did not venture beyond the 'country' with which they were familiar, though they moved frequently within it. Other north Derbyshire settlements that have produced local surnames include Darwent, Froggatt and Ronksley and numerous names that have been corrupted over the centuries or which reflect local pronunciations. So, Bonser is derived from Bonsall, Bowser from Bolsover, Answer and Ensor from Edensor, Hounsfield from Holmesfield, Newbound from Newbold and Tisdall from Tideswell.

Parish churches

As the great age of church rebuilding in Derbyshire was the fourteenth century, many projects had been completed before the Perpendicular Gothic style came into fashion in the late Middle Ages. Derbyshire was slow to recover from the prolonged recession after the Black Death and had little surplus wealth to build anew. The county's famous architect, Henry Yeaveley, moved from the place where his surname was derived to seek his fortune in London. In Derbyshire, the Perpendicular style was used mostly for modest improvements, such as a

This magnificent church tower – the finest in Derbyshire – is all that remains of the medieval church of All Saints, Derby. It dates from the second and third decades of the sixteenth century and was designed in a highly decorative version of the Perpendicular Gothic style. It is still the first building to catch the eye on Derby's skyline.

PHOTOGRAPH: CARNEGIE

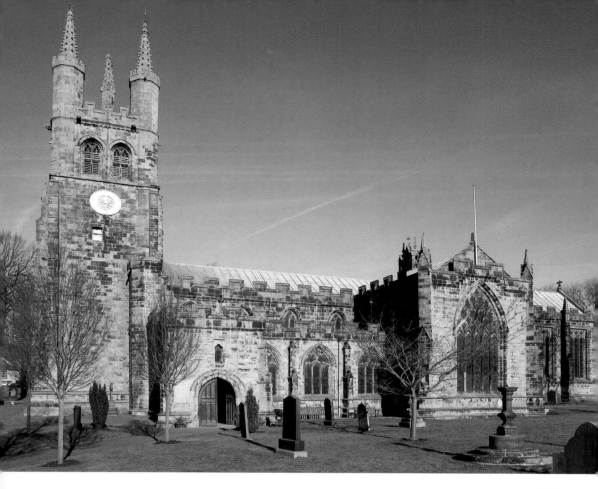

Known popularly as 'The Cathedral of the Peak', St John the Baptist's church, Tideswell, dates from a long period of rebuilding in the fourteenth century. The wealthy Staffords, Foljambes and Bowers were major benefactors, but all the parishioners would have contributed to making the church by far the finest in this remote part of the Peak District.

PHOTOGRAPH: CARNEGIE

heightened tower, battlements on the skyline, windows with straight mullions, or a new porch, such as the fine, two-storeyed example at Hope. The most ambitious scheme was the construction of the new west tower at All Saints, Derby, which was completed in 1532. The tower still dominates the city's skyline, rising to ornamental battlements and pinnacles and with rich decoration in each of its three stages.

The rebuilding of Tideswell church continued after the calamity of the Black Death. The flowing tracery of the east window matches the Decorated work of the transepts, but the large windows that fill most of the north and south walls are straight-headed in the new style. When the body of the church was finished, a tower was raised at the west end, not over a crossing as at Ashbourne, Bakewell, Chesterfield and Wirksworth. It is entirely in the Perpendicular style, with broad, dramatic pinnacles and a huge tower arch, yet the stonework does not look much later than the rest of the church. It must be the earliest example of the new-style tower in Derbyshire.

The rebuilding of Tideswell church in the Decorated and Perpendicular Gothic styles over many decades in the fourteenth century was financed from the income derived from the rising demand for lead from the Tideslow rake and other local mines. The parish was the home of wealthy individuals, notably Sir Nicholas de Stafford, John Foljambe and Thurstan de la Bower, who were the leading benefactors, but all the parishioners would have been expected to contribute according to their means. Sir Nicholas, a descendant of a Norman family that had held land in south Derbyshire since the Conquest, was lord of the manor of Tideswell by 1372. A brass in memory of John Foljambe, who

Foljambe wall-monument, All Saints church, Bakewell. This alabaster memorial to Sir Godfrey Foljambe and his wife was carved in 1385, an unusually early date for a type of wall-monument that became popular in the sixteenth century. Pevsner describes it as 'internationally remarkable'. Sir Godfrey was the chief steward of the Duchy of Lancaster and a prominent member of John of Gaunt's circle. He founded the chantry of the Holy Cross in Bakewell church in 1344 and was interred there in 1377. From 1360 he had been the lessee of Bakewell manor.

PHOTOGRAPH: CARNEGIE

Effigy of Sir Thomas de Wensley, All Saints church, Bakewell. Sir Thomas held lands in Bakewell, Darley, Wensley and Winster and in the late fifteenth century he was constable and bailiff of the Duchy of Lancaster's estates in the High Peak. He is shown here in the Newark, or 'new work', of Bakewell church wearing the Lancastrian collar formed by the repeated letter S and a helmet embossed with 'IHC Nazaren' (Jesus of Nazareth). He died from wounds received at the battle of Shrewsbury in 1405.

PHOTOGRAPH: CARNEGIE

RIGHT
Monument of George and Grace Manners, All Saints church, Bakewell. Sir George Manners of Haddon Hall, lord of Bakewell, died in 1623 but his wife Grace (Pierrepoint) lived until 1649. She was the Lady Manners who in 1636 founded the school in Bakewell that still bears her name. This large monument against the north wall of the Newark in Bakewell church depicts the couple and their nine children. Verses from the Bible are inscribed on the arches above the kneeling children. Their first son died at birth, so the second son, John, inherited the Haddon and Bakewell estates. In 1641 John also succeeded his cousin as eighth Earl of Rutland and the owner of extensive estates in Leicestershire and Lincolnshire, centred on Belvoir Castle, which then became the family's chief residence.

PHOTOGRAPH: CARNEGIE

died in 1383, records that he made many gifts towards the fabric of the church. His family were long established in Tideswell as foresters and landowners with properties in several neighbouring villages. In 1364 John Foljambe and Thomas de la Bower, the lead smelter, were prominent amongst the founders of the Guild of St Mary, whose chantry chapel is now the Lady Chapel. In 1392 this guild was re-founded by Sir Nicholas de Stafford, James Foljambe (the grandson of John) and others, with an endowment of 200 acres to support two priests. The ordinances refer to 'the brethren and sisters' of the guild, which seems to have been modelled on the one dedicated to the Holy Cross that had been founded in Bakewell church by Sir Godfrey Foljambe and Anne, his wife, in 1345. Foljambe had risen in the service of John of Gaunt and in 1361 had obtained a lease of the manor of Bakewell. At various times, he was constable of the High Peak, steward of the honour of Tutbury, and chief steward of the Duchy of Lancaster. He died in 1376 and after the death of his wife a wall monument was commissioned to commemorate them in Bakewell church. Carved in alabaster to a very high standard, it is the only surviving

Wall painting, St Michael and St Mary's church, Melbourne. The interiors of medieval churches were ablaze with colour, but most of this vivacity was deliberately destroyed at the Reformation. Derbyshire has few surviving examples of medieval wall paintings. This portrait of a horned devil with outstretched wings above gossiping women with smaller devils on their backs adorns the north-west tower pier. Judging by the costumes, it dates from the fourteenth century.

PHOTOGRAPH: CARNEGIE

medieval example of a type of memorial that became popular much later. Pevsner regarded it as 'an internationally remarkable monument'.

The larger and more prosperous rural parishes also had guilds that endowed chantry chapels in the church. At Dronfield a chantry dedicated to St Mary was founded in 1392 by Ralph Barker of Dore and others, to support two priests to help serve the outer parts of this extensive parish. Early in the sixteenth century it was converted into a guild by further endowments from local people and after the Reformation the building opposite the church became the inn that is now known as the Green Dragon. Similar chapels were founded by guilds at Baslow and Eckington and by private individuals elsewhere. As gifts to monasteries fell in favour in the later Middle Ages, endowing a chantry chapel became the new fashion. The best documented are the two chapels at Crich that were founded by Sir William de Wakebridge, a successful royal administrator, judicial officer and knight of the shire, who possessed a small estate there. After the Black

Death had killed most of his close relations, he endowed the chantry of Sts Nicholas and Catherine on the north side of the church and the chantry of St Mary in the south aisle. The late fourteenth-century effigy of a bearded man in a long frock, in the north aisle, is presumably that of Sir William, who died in 1370. Such chapels were stripped of their altars and ornaments and their properties confiscated when Edward IV dissolved all chantries in 1547.

All Saints, Derby, was exceptional in being the county's only remaining collegiate foundation, staffed by a sub-dean, six prebends and six vicars,

Portrait of Sir William Cavendish, first Earl of Devonshire (1551–1626), 1576, artist unknown. The Earl was the eldest son of Sir William Cavendish and Bess of Hardwick.

J. Earl of Devonſhire

1576.

Æ. SVÆ. 25

chaplains and stipendaries. Chesterfield parish church had a staff of 13, including the vicar, curate, gild priests and chantrists, while the number of staff serving the parish churches of Ashbourne, Bakewell and Wirksworth varied between seven and eight. Most Derbyshire churches, however, had only one or two priests in the years leading up to the Reformation.

The few schools that were recorded in Derbyshire in the Middle Ages were probably taught by chantry priests and accommodated within the parish churches. The ancient grammar school at Derby may have been attached to the collegiate church of All Saints but by the mid-twelfth century it was the responsibility of the new Darley Abbey; after the dissolution of the abbey, it was refounded in 1554. Chesterfield had a grammar school by 1323–37, which was dependent on the parish church. Dronfield had a school by 1496–1501, another was planned at Melbourne in 1514, and Bishop Robert Pursglove sponsored one in his native town of Tideswell in the early sixteenth century.

Dissolution of the monasteries

In the late 1530s Henry VIII closed all the 650 monasteries in England and Wales. The monastic life that had flourished in Derbyshire for more than four centuries came to an end between 1537 and 1539. Then, in 1547–48 Edward VI followed his father's example and dissolved all the chantry and guild chapels and the hospitals. The sites of these religious establishments were plundered so effectively that little now remains to be seen. The usual practice of Sir William Cavendish, the auditor of the Court of Augmentations that was set up to administer the monastic properties and revenues confiscated by the crown throughout the land, was to bring in masons and carpenters to pull the roofs off the monastic churches and other buildings so as to destroy any possibility of their reuse. This wealthy courtier's introduction to Derbyshire was when he accompanied Dr Thomas Legh to oversee the dissolution of Darley and Dale abbeys in 1538. He did very well, financially, out of the dissolution of the monasteries.

The few monastic houses that were established in Derbyshire were the typical size of those provided for Augustinian and Premonstratensian canons. On the eve of the dissolution of the monasteries the county had just over 80 regular clergy and a substantial number of lay brothers and paid servants in its abbeys and priories, as well as lodgers such as retired abbots or priors and those who had purchased a 'corrody' to end their days there and be buried within the precincts. Henry VIII's commissioners searched for scandal to justify their brutal take-over but failed to find it. Derbyshire's monasteries continued in their seemly way to the end.

The Augustinian abbey at Darley was Derbyshire's largest monastic institution. Its annual income was assessed in the *Valor Ecclesiasticus* (1535) at £258. At the Dissolution on 22 October 1538 the 15 canons were pensioned off and the 56 servants received gratuities, or redundancy payments as they would

Dale Abbey. Little remains above ground level of this Premonstratensian abbey in south-east Derbyshire, but the great arch of the east window of the chancel gives an impression of the former size and glory of the abbey church. It is over seventeen feet high and enough masonry survives to show that the glass was arranged within geometrical tracery. It therefore dates from the late thirteenth century. In the foreground are the foundations of the rest of the church, which have been exposed by excavation.

PHOTOGRAPH: AUTHOR

be called today. Gilt and silver articles and 160 fothers of lead were reserved to the Crown and the rest of the property was sold at a bargain price to Sir Henry Sacheverell of Morley. Dale Abbey's annual income of £144 supported 17 Premonstratensian canons, four of whom were usually absent, serving the parish churches of Heanor, Ilkeston, Kirk Hallam and Stanton. Upon the dissolution on 24 October 1538 most of the goods and stock were sold to Francis Pole of Radbourne. The south range was gradually demolished over the next century, as it was stripped of its building stone, lead, glass, pavement tiles, timber and roofing materials, but the west range was still habitable in the early eighteenth century. The best surviving late-medieval stained glass in Derbyshire was taken from the cloister and installed in the windows of Morley church. The Premonstratensian Beauchief Abbey was valued at £126 and was dissolved on 4 February 1537, 'without giving any trouble or opposition'. The abbey and what became known as the Liberty of Beauchief were bought

The images in the windows at St Matthew's church, Morley, form the best collection of medieval glass in Derbyshire. The glass was installed here after the dissolution of Dale Abbey, where it had been commissioned to glaze the new cloister in 1482. It was repaired and added to in 1847. One window (*above*) depicts the legend of St Robert of Knaresborough and the story of the Invention of the Holy Cross. It depicts the martyrdom of St Cyriacus by the emperor Justinian (represented by the triple crown), a story taken from the Golden Legend of Jacobus de Voragine. Other panels in the south aisle depict the donors in late fifteenth-century dress, represented conventionally (*left*); the four evangelists and their attributes (*facing page, left*); and an abbot (signified by crozier and tonsure) with an archbishop (with cross staff and mitre) (*facing page, right*). St Matthew's church stands apart from the village but close to the former manor house and its outbuildings.

PHOTOGRAPHS: CARNEGIE

by Sir Nicholas Strelley, lord of Ecclesall, on the opposite side of the Sheaf valley, while the rest of the estate was split up and sold to local landowners. The Augustinian Repton Priory had an annual income of £118 and the canons had sufficient funds to pay a large fine, or bribe, to postpone their dissolution until 25 October 1538. Legh and Cavendish found the house 'greatly spoiled and many things purloined away, part of which they recovered'. They sold the estate to a steward of Thomas Cromwell, Thomas Thacker of Heage, who immediately took up residence in the prior's lodgings. Finally, the Dominican friary in Derby surrendered on 3 January 1539. Twenty-six friars had lived there in 1324, but their number had dropped to six. By 1562 the property was owned by William Bainbrigge, the bailiff of the corporation on three occasions, who built a timber-framed, gabled mansion on the site.

Those who benefited locally from the dissolution of the monasteries were mostly well-established gentry families who had ready cash available from the profits of lead smelting. Sir Francis Leake of Sutton purchased manors and former granges at Alfreton (Beauchief), Duckmanton (Welbeck), Dunston and Holme (Lenton), Harewood Grange (Beauchief), Scarcliffe (Darley and Newstead) and Tibshelf (Brewood) and two-thirds of the tithes of lead in the parishes of Bakewell, Hope and Tideswell (Lenton). His cousin John Leake of Hasland bought the manor of Oakerthorpe (Darley). Thomas Babington of Dethick, the lessee of Wigwell Grange, near Wirksworth, bought various Darley Abbey properties, including Wigwell, and the Breadsall Priory estate, which he re-sold at a profit four years later. His uncle, Rowland Babington of Normanton bought former monastic property at Coton, Mouldridge Grange, Normanton and Roystone Grange. Sir Henry Sacheverell, was appointed steward of the site of Dale Abbey and purchased the rectory estates of Aston-on-Trent, Morley and Weston-upon-Trent from the abbey of St Werburgh, Chester. And as we have seen, Francis Pole of Radbourne bought the goods, stock and estate of Dale Abbey, including the granges at Boyah, Littlehay and Stanley. The head of a less well-established family of lead smelters who grasped the opportunities offered by the Dissolution was Ralph Gell of Hopton, who purchased the tithes of the parishes of Markeaton and Mackworth (Dale) and the rectories of Bakewell, Hope and Tideswell, including one-third of the lead tithes.

Courtiers also had a share of the spoils. The Earl of Shrewsbury bought King's Mead, Derby, the Peak District estates of Worksop Priory, the chantry lands of Crich and Monyash and the lands of the Guild of St Mary, Dronfield. Other beneficiaries included the Duke of Suffolk (Breadsall), the Duke of Northumberland (Calke) and Lord Mountjoy (Yeaveley and Barrow). Sir William Cavendish did not immediately buy former monastic lands in Derbyshire, but after his marriage to Bess of Hardwick and his move to Chatsworth in 1549 he was able to use his official position to exchange or purchase a considerable estate of former monastic property in his new county before his death in 1557. The family that were to become Derbyshire's greatest landowners arrived as the Middle Ages drew to a close.

All over England the population dropped dramatically during the horrors of the Black Death. Repeated visitations of the plague caused the decay of towns and the shrinkage and sometimes the desertion of villages and hamlets. In Derbyshire, the effects on the landscape are most noticeable in the south-western parts of the county, especially on the claylands. The descendants of the survivors improved their standard of living, but Derbyshire remained poor and rather remote. At the end of the Middle Ages it ranked a lowly 35th in a table of the wealth of England's 38 counties.

CHAPTER
SEVEN

The Elizabethan and early Stuart era

Population

In the late 1530s the English population began to grow again. It rose rapidly during the reign of Queen Elizabeth and by the time of the Civil War in the 1640s it had nearly doubled to about 5 million. It was almost back to the high level which it had reached about 1300, before the disaster of the Black Death. We have no firm figures, but the national ecclesiastical census returns of 1563 suggest that the population of Derbyshire was then about 50,000 and that by the time of the hearth tax returns of 1664–70 it had risen to more than 70,000, perhaps quite a bit more as we do not know how many people were exempt from the tax. As we shall see, the most spectacular increases occurred in the lead-mining townships of the White Peak, where poor men flocked to work in the new mines that were opened up when the trade began to flourish as never before and small villages and hamlets were transformed into some of the most populous places in the Derbyshire countryside.

The population of the whole of western Europe started to grow again at this time, though sudden outbreaks of disease frequently reversed the trend. The unusually high number of recorded burials in the Darley parish register between March 1557 and April 1558 may have been the result of the 'sweating sickness' (probably a virulent form of influenza) that swept England in the late 1550s, while the high number of deaths that were recorded in Derby in 1586, 1592–93, 1605, 1646 and 1665 were probably caused by repeated visitations of plague, which remained endemic in England between the Black Death and the mid-1660s. From 1558 to the mid-1580s the number of recorded baptisms in the parish of Chesterfield was always larger than those of burials, but then in October 1586 a cryptic note in the parish register states: 'Here began the great plague of Chesterfield'. In the previous 25 years burials in the parish had never exceeded 70 per annum and were usually much less, but about 300 people died between October 1586 and November 1587. The disease lay dormant in the winter months, but was virulent in the following summer, when 154 people

Saxton's Map of Derbyshire, 1577. Between 1574 and 1579 Christopher Saxton, the greatest mapmaker of the Elizabethan age, made the first set of county maps for England and Wales. Towns, villages, parks, rivers and hills are depicted.

DERBYSHIRE: A HISTORY

Sir Thomas Cockayne and his wife. Sir Thomas died in 1592 and he and his wife were commemorated by this large wall monument, constructed of alabaster, in the family's chapel in the north transept of St Oswald's church, Ashbourne, where his ancestors had been lords since at least the mid twelfth century. The memorial is in fashionable contemporary style, the life-sized figures kneeling opposite each other across a prayer desk. Their children are depicted below.

PHOTOGRAPH: CARNEGIE

died in June, July and August. Burials again exceeded baptisms in 1590–92 and 1597 and the pestilence reappeared in 1603 (mainly in Brimington) and in 1609. But if we take all the years between 1560 and 1603, the 3,174 baptisms in Chesterfield parish exceeded the 2,713 burials, with a mean average of 72 baptisms each year compared with 62 burials. Plague continued to strike randomly, but local population levels quickly recovered as young couples seized the economic opportunities provided by these visitations to marry earlier and so have more children.

The worsening climate has led some historians to refer to the period from about 1540 to 1700 as the Little Ice Age, but this is an exaggeration for it was punctuated by occasional warm summers and mild winters. There is, however, no doubt that some English winters in the early modern era were exceptionally harsh. The Youlgreave parish register recorded that on 16 January 1616:

began the greatest snow which ever fell uppon the earth, within man's memorye. It covered the earth fyve quarters deep uppon the playne. And for hepes or drifts of snow, they were very deep; so that passengers both horse & foot, passed over yates, hedges & walles. It fell at 10 severall tymes, & the last was the greatest, to the greate admiration & feare of all the land, for it came from the fowre parts of the world, so that all entryes were full, yea the South parte as well as these mountaynes. It continued by daily encreasing until the 12th day of March (without the sight of any earth, eyther uppon hilles or valleyes) uppon which daye (being the Lorde's Day) it began to decrease; and so by little & little consumed &

wasted away, till the eight & twentyeth day of May for then all the heapes or drifts of snow were consumed, except one uppon Kinder's Scout, which lay till Witson week & after.

This bad winter was followed by ten further falls of snow in April, some a foot deep, and then by a prolonged drought in the summer months.

Towns

At the beginning of Queen Elizabeth's reign in 1558, Derby was a small town by modern standards, with a population of only 2,000–2,500 people. Even so, it was twice the size of Chesterfield and Wirksworth, the only other Derbyshire towns with more than 1,000 inhabitants, and was soon to grow quickly. It served as the centre of county administration, as a thoroughfare town and as a busy regional market centre. According to William Camden's *Britannia* (1610 edition), its retail trade was 'to buy corn, and having turn'd it into Malt, to sell it again to the high-land countries; for the Town consists chiefly of this sort of Merchants'. In the same year, the borough depicted on John Speed's map was still confined within its medieval limits between the river Derwent and the Markeaton Brook, with the same, ancient pattern of streets and lanes and five parish churches. As yet, no suburbs had encroached on the surrounding fields. The only major new feature on Speed's map was the town's water supply, which was brought by a conduit from the Derwent to the north-east corner of the Market Place.

Within this ancient plan, however, many new buildings were erected during the sixteenth and seventeenth centuries. The county's gentry families, such as the Cavendishes, Babingtons, Leigh of Egginton, Pole of Radbourne, Sacheverell of Morley and Port of Etwall built town houses for occasional use and the wealthier Derby tradesmen celebrated their rise in fortune by adopting the new architectural styles. The town's sixteenth-century Guild Hall, which was built on the southern side of the Market Place, had a stone ground floor which served as the gaol and a timber-framed upper storey that was used as the corporation chamber and offices. The government of the borough, which since 1204 had been vested in two annually elected bailiffs, was replaced in 1637 by that of a mayor, ten aldermen, 14 brethren and 14 capital burgesses. Except for a brief period during the Civil War, this was how Derby was governed until the Municipal Corporations Act of 1835.

Derby lay on major highways from Lancashire and the West Riding of Yorkshire to London. It was probably connected to the capital by weekly carrying services long before John Taylor published his *Carriers' Cosmographie* in 1637. Taylor noted that carriers from Derby and other parts of Derbyshire lodged at an inn called the *Axe*, near Aldermanbury in the City of London, every Friday and that other Derby carries were to be found at the *Castle* in Wood Street every Thursday or Friday. One of these regular services may have been provided by John Armitage of Chesterfield, who in 1661 described himself in his will as 'London carrier'.

A William Senior map of c.1635 shows that Chesterfield, too, was still confined within its medieval limits. In 1563 the town's population was about 1,000–1,200, though that of the parish as a whole had reached about 2,700. The town's burgesses had resisted George, the sixth Earl of Shrewsbury's attempts to destroy their semi-independence and bring them firmly within his manor. In 1598, eight years after his death, they obtained a charter of incorporation. The income of the mayor and burgesses, however, was modest and the manorial and parochial officers retained large shares of responsibility for the town's affairs. Chesterfield remained the leading market and fair town for north-east Derbyshire and had many well-to-do tradesmen, such as brewers, butchers, tanners, shoemakers, glovers, saddlers, metalworkers and woodworkers, and shopkeepers including drapers, mercers, grocers, chandlers and ironmongers. When he died in 1588 Thomas Heathcote, a dyer, owned vats and leads, wool, flax, hemp, madder, copperas, galls and alum. In the same year, Thomas Denyson, a draper, had a stock of variously coloured friezes and cottons; he was owed money by four men from Kendal, three from Shrewsbury, two from Leeds and one from Rochdale, and part of his stock was a Rochdale frieze. Probate inventories of metalworkers include those of Henry Reynsha (1537) and Richard Johnson (1559), who each had a store of superior-quality Spanish iron imported from the Basque Country through Bawtry; Richard Stevenson (1561), who had two smithies and 'wares in the shope in the marketstide'; and Stephen Rogers (1590), who had rod iron, nails, locks and household and farm ironmongery in his smithy and warehouse.

One of the most successful Chesterfield families were the Heathcotes, who had established several branches in the town since their move across the Peak District in the fifteenth century. About 1500 Ralph Heathcote inherited through marriage the bell foundry that had been established there half a century earlier; his sons William and George built up a flourishing business. The probate inventory of George's son, Ralph (1577), shows that he was a tradesman of considerable substance, with bell moulds valued at £10 and a newly cast bell worth £7 11s. od. Ralph's eldest son Godfrey and his grandson Ralph continued to work the foundry until the middle of the seventeenth century. The distinctive marks of the Heathcotes are found on a number of bells in local churches. Other branches of the Heathcote family became prosperous lead merchants, as did the Clarkes, Milnses, Websters, Morewoods, Gladwins, Stoneses and Burtons, for Chesterfield was the obvious centre of trade, well sited near the smelting mills and on the routes to the inland port of Bawtry.

We know little about Elizabethan Wirksworth except that it recovered from its medieval decline as the lead trade prospered anew. It grew to about the same size as Chesterfield but remained a market town without any burgesses. It did, however, control the lead trade of Wirksworth wapentake through the Moot Hall, which was described in 1650 as a timber building 'containing three

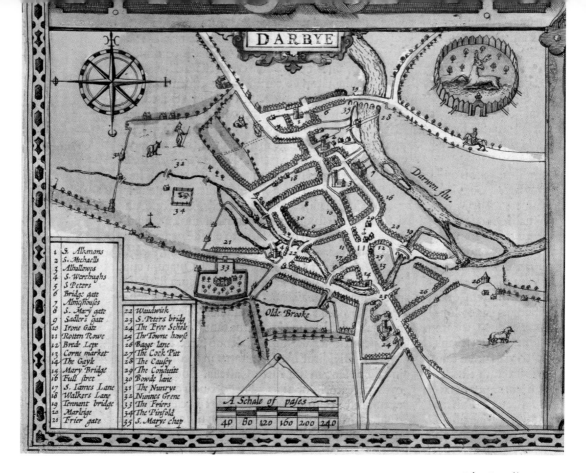

John Speed's Map
of Derby, 1610.
The county town
was by far the
largest settlement in
Derbyshire, yet it
contained fewer than
2,500 inhabitants,
and it had not yet
grown beyond its
medieval limits.
The river Derwent,
in particular,
remained a barrier to
expansion in the east.
The key highlights
the major buildings
and streets in the
borough.
BRITISH LIBRARY

bayes of building under which court room are built six butchers' stalls and two butchers' shops on the west side thereof'. This was replaced in 1814 by the present one-storeyed, stone building in Chapel Lane.

In 1563 Ashbourne and Bakewell had only about 600 inhabitants each and their burgesses were a distant memory. The two towns had not yet recovered their medieval prosperity. A map of 1547 (see page 180) shows Ashbourne as it had been laid out in Norman times, though with its market place partly infilled; the Cockayne family dominated the town from their large hall at the eastern end. When Ashbourne prospered again in the late sixteenth century, a fine grammar school was erected at the west end of the main street. At Bakewell in 1602 Sir John Manners, lord of the manor, founded a hospital by the south-east gate of the churchyard, with a town hall and court room above the lodgings, and a new Market Hall, with open arcades on the ground floor and an upper, enclosed storey, both now much altered. Derbyshire's other small medieval market towns, such as Bolsover, Chapel-en-le-Frith and Tideswell, had no more than about 500 inhabitants in 1563 and Alfreton had fewer than 400. They were hardly distinguishable from villages except on market days and at the annual fairs.

The Moot Hall was where the Barmote Courts for the King's Field in Wirksworth wapentake were held to regulate the lead trade and to settle disputes. This building in Chapel Lane was erected in 1814 to replace a previous one in the Market Place. A special dish for measuring lead ore is held in the hall. The court still meets twice a year, under a steward appointed by the Duchy of Lancaster, although very little lead is still mined.

PHOTOGRAPH: CARNEGIE

The gabled Bakewell almshouses by the south-east gate of the churchyard were built in 1709 in the garden of the former St John's Hospital, which had been founded by John Manners of Haddon Hall in 1602. His descendant, the first Duke of Rutland, reconstructed the hospital as a terrace of housing for six men and refurbished the adjacent town hall and butter market. This area remained the focal point of the town until the Square was laid out in front of the Rutland Arms in 1805.

PHOTOGRAPH: AUTHOR

Ashbourne Free
Grammar School.
The school was
founded for the
boys of the town
and neighbourhood
in 1585 by a group
of local gentlemen
led by Sir Thomas
Cockayne, but work
was not finished
until the first decade
of the seventeenth
century. The
Cockayne coat of
arms appears over
the entrance. This
substantial building
in Church Street
included accommo-
dation for the master
and his assistant, the
usher.

PHOTOGRAPH: CARNEGIE

The Cavendishes and Talbots

Derbyshire's transformation from a remote and largely unknown county with relatively few castles, monasteries or great manor houses (though with the magnificent exceptions of Haddon Hall and Wingfield Manor) into a place with some of the grandest country houses in England began with the single-minded ambition of a redoubtable local woman who is now known to everyone as Bess of Hardwick. She was born in a small manor house on the site of Hardwick Old Hall in 1527, one of four daughters and a son of a declining minor gentry family that had owned a few hundred acres at Hardwick for at least six generations and had taken their name from the place. She went to live as a gentlewoman's servant with Lady Zouche of Codnor Castle and at the age of 16 she married her cousin Robert Barley of Barlow Hall. When he died a few months after the marriage, she received the usual widow's third of his income, and then probably continued to serve in great households, like many young women of her status at that time. Perhaps she entered the service of the Greys of Bradgate (Leicestershire), for it was in their chapel in 1547 that she married Sir William Cavendish, the very rich government servant who had already been married twice and who had two surviving daughters. Cavendish had provided for himself very well in an age when government servants were expected to enrich themselves from their offices. He had profited from the dissolution of the monasteries and from 1546 his main source of wealth was from his post of Treasurer of the Chamber.

All Bess's eight children – three boys and three girls and two infants who died young – were born to Sir William. Clearly, he was infatuated with her, for Bess persuaded him to sell his former monastery lands in Hertfordshire and to move to the edge of some of the wildest moors in Derbyshire, not far from her ancestral home. He bought Chatsworth in 1549 and the 8,000 acres of the lordship of Ashford the following year. Then, in 1552 he exchanged his church lands with the Crown for the former monastic manors of Doveridge, Marston-on-Dove and Church Broughton (Tutbury Priory), Blackwell (Lenton Priory) and Meadow Place Grange and its rectory manor of Youlgreave (Leicester Abbey). He also bought the manors of Pentrich and Oakerthorpe (Darley Abbey) and Bradbourne (Dunstable Priory). In 1552 he and Bess began to build at Chatsworth on a site that was liable to flood and difficult to reach across the moors. A painting and a needlework view show a tall house arranged around a courtyard and set amongst formal gardens which stretched as far as the building that was later given the romantic name of 'Queen Mary's Bower'. On the skyline to the east, the striking Hunting Stand was erected in the 1580s. Chatsworth began the fashion for tall, compact houses in north Derbyshire and beyond. William Senior's map of 1617 shows how the moors came right up to the Stand, so that travellers from the Chesterfield direction got a sudden view of the great house and gardens in all their splendour below. At that time, the highway from Chesterfield to Bakewell passed near the south front of the house on its way to the bridge over the river Derwent by the corn mill and up through the village of Edensor; it was diverted around the edge of the estate in the eighteenth century when the grounds were landscaped.

The Stand, Chatsworth. High on the ridge overlooking Chatsworth House, The Stand is a notable landmark and a fine place from which to view the estate. It is the best surviving structure from the days when Sir William Cavendish and Bess designed Old Chatsworth. Its name implies that hunting parties began their pursuit of deer within the park from here, while others watched the progress of the chase from the numerous windows, but it was no doubt used for other social purposes. In 1662, for example, it was described as a 'neat rotundo or Summer house'. An account of 1601 noted, 'In the Stand, a bedsted, a mattriss, a fetherbed, too blankets, a bolster, a table'.

When Sir William Cavendish died in 1557, he left Bess a life interest in Chatsworth and a substantial portion of his other property. A remarkable group of aristocratic dynasties trace their origins back to William and Bess. The line from their eldest daughter, Frances and her husband Sir Henry Pierrepoint, became Dukes of Kingston; that from their second son, William, became Dukes of Devonshire; that from their youngest son, George, became Dukes of Newcastle; and that from a later female line became Dukes of Portland. Bess's greatest ambition remained unfulfilled, however. She encouraged the marriage of her daughter, Elizabeth, to Charles Stuart, the Earl of Lennox, whose only child, Arabella, was a rival claimant to the throne after the death of Elizabeth, but who came to a sad end in the Tower of London.

Bess's third husband, Sir William St Loe, came from an old-established family in Somerset. He was a favourite courtier of Queen Elizabeth, Captain of the Guard and Butler of the Royal Household. When he died in the winter of 1564–65, he ignored the claims of his previous family by leaving much of his property outright to Bess. On 9 February 1568, Bess married again, this time sensationally to George Talbot, sixth Earl of Shrewsbury, the richest and most powerful man in the Midlands and the North of England, who had built up a great estate and had invested profitably in lead and iron. A loyal supporter of Queen Elizabeth, he was appointed Lieutenant-General of Yorkshire, Derbyshire and Nottinghamshire, a member of the Privy Council, a recipient of the Order of the Garter, and Earl Marshal of England. His chief seat was Sheffield Manor Lodge, which he and Bess enlarged in splendid style, and his other properties included Pontefract and Tutbury Castles, Wingfield Manor, Worksop Manor (which he rebuilt as a fine up-to-date house), Rufford Abbey, and a house by the baths at Buxton. Two of his children by his first marriage to Lady Gertrude Manners, daughter of Thomas, the first Earl of Rutland, were married to Bess's children at the same ceremony: Gilbert Talbot, who became the seventh earl, married Mary Cavendish, the youngest daughter, and Grace Talbot married Henry Cavendish, the eldest son. Bess's ambitions for her descendants were thwarted, however, for Gilbert and Mary had three daughters but no sons, and Henry and Grace had no children.

Portraits in Hardwick Hall show Bess as a woman who was used to getting her own way and George as a gloomy and inflexible man who stood on his dignity. His high-handed treatment of the Chesterfield burgesses and his tenants in the Forest of the Peak was typical of a man who was used to being obeyed.

Queen Mary's Bower, Chatsworth. The name is fanciful, though the original structure does date from about the time when the Scottish queen was held captive at Chatsworth in the 1570s. It perhaps served as a banqueting house, a viewing platform, and even a fishing lodge. It was ruinous by 1773, and owes much of its present appearance to a considerable restoration in the 1820s.

PHOTOGRAPH: AUTHOR

MARIA REGINA

Bess of Hardwick. Born into a decaying Derbyshire gentry family, Bess prospered through her four marriages. Sir William Cavendish was her second husband and George, sixth Earl of Shrewsbury and the wealthiest aristocrat north of the Trent, was her fourth. This portrait at Hardwick Hall was once thought to be Mary, Queen of Scots, hence the MARIA REGINA inscription.

The marriage broke down completely in 1584, the year that George was finally released from the considerable burden of the custodianship of Mary, Queen of Scots, an unwelcome duty that he had endured since 1569. Mary's household numbered at least 50 and so George had been faced with considerable costs as well as problems of security and logistics. Mary and her court were moved around between Sheffield Manor Lodge, Chatsworth, Wingfield Manor and Tutbury Castle as the need to cleanse and re-provision these residences arose. In the summer of 1573 she made her first visit to Buxton, where George had just built a hostelry adjoining the baths and near St Anne's Well. Following the publication of Dr John Jones's treatise on the beneficial effects of the waters, Buxton once again began to attract visitors from far and wide; Lord Burghley came in 1575 and the Earl of Leicester made two visits in 1578 and 1584.

About 1583 Bess had bought the house and estate where she was born at Hardwick from her brother. After the estrangement from George and during the conflict over who owned Chatsworth, Bess began to build what is now known as the Old Hall on the site of her birthplace. She does not seem to have employed an architect, for despite its commanding position on a ridge the house appears irregular and unorganised. The top storeys of the two substantial wings that rise above low rooms on either side of the gabled hall contain lofty state rooms, lit by enormous windows, but the overall effect is unsatisfactory. When George died in 1590 Bess received a very large widow's jointure and recovered complete control of all her lands from before her last marriage. Now in her early 60s, she had become one of the richest people in England. She had the resources to employ Robert Smythson, one of the greatest architects of the time, to design and build a New Hall alongside the old one. But work on the Old Hall was not abandoned; indeed, it continued after the New Hall was ready in 1597. The Old Hall provided accommodation for both guests and servants and so enabled the New Hall to be built on a relatively small scale, grand though it appeared on approach.

Robert Smythson was responsible for many of the distinctive buildings that were erected in the East Midlands and Yorkshire in the late sixteenth and early seventeenth centuries. Before coming to Hardwick, his work in Nottinghamshire had included Wollaton Hall for Sir Francis Willoughby and Worksop Manor for George and Bess. Whether we regard the buildings that were commissioned by the Talbots and Cavendishes as the romantic piles of an inventive and exuberant age or as blatant displays of wealth by hard and unscrupulous people, we now see them as national treasures and a principal part of Derbyshire's heritage. Smythson designed the New Hall as a large rectangular block with six small square towers arranged symmetrically around it. Mark Girouard, who has done so much to enlighten us on the work of Smythson and his contemporaries, has memorably compared the views of the sides of the house with the impression of a sailing ship bearing down upon us in full speed. The Elizabethans went in for height and mass, for enormous windows in the Tudor Gothic style (for glass was expensive and therefore a status symbol, never mind the draughts), for geometrical patterns and for 'devices' such as the large initials ES (Elizabeth Shrewsbury) and her countess's coronet that stand out on the skyline amongst the Flemish strapwork, together with the Hardwick stags, Cavendish serpents and Talbot dogs that decorate the interior. The building stone was quarried on the hillside,

The two halls built by Bess of Hardwick. The now ruined Old Hall on the left was erected on the site of her birthplace after her separation from George, the sixth Earl of Shrewsbury. After his death, her inherited wealth allowed her to commission Robert Smythson to build the New Hall which has ensured that her name lingers in popular memory.

PHOTOGRAPH: MALCOLM DOLBY

and elsewhere on her extensive estates Bess had her own glass works and iron forges at Wingfield, alabaster quarries at Creswell and black marble quarries at Ashford, lead mines at Bonsall and Winster, and supplies of timber from numerous woods.

The main entrance into her new house passes through a classical loggia into the great hall, which stands two storeys high across the centre of the building in a very different arrangement from the previous medieval pattern. Bess spent most of her time in the first-floor rooms, but on special occasions she presided over the company in the state apartments on the top floor, whose importance was marked externally by the largest windows. The Long Gallery that Smythson designed along the entire east front was the finest in the kingdom. Elaborate ceremony was more important than warm food, which cooled as it was brought from the kitchen in a procession led by a trumpeter up the massive flights of stone stairs to the Great Chamber. There, Bess sat beneath a huge plaster frieze that represented the goddess Diana presiding over a boar hunt in the forest. Real trees were incorporated within the vividly coloured frieze and, over the fireplace, the motto attached to the royal coat of arms became 'Dieu est mon droit' as Bess inserted a letter s into the second word, so that it stood

This effigy of Bess of Hardwick takes pride of place in the south aisle of Derby Cathedral. John Smythson, the son of the architect of Hardwick Hall, designed the alabaster figure for Bess six years before her death in 1607. She is interred in the vault below the former Cavendish chapel. Bess is shown with her countess's coronet. We get a good impression of how alabaster monuments were once painted in bright colours.

The alabaster monument of George Talbot, sixth Earl of Shrewsbury, the estranged husband of Bess of Hardwick, in Sheffield parish church (now Cathedral). He is depicted as a knight in armour, with his feet on a talbot dog.

This alabaster cadaver tomb of the two eldest sons of Sir William Cavendish and Bess of Hardwick dominates the chapel on the south side of the Victorian church in the estate village of Edensor. The sculptor was probably Maximilian Colt, a Flemish immigrant who became the King's Master Carver. Sir Henry Cavendish, the elder son, died in 1616 with no legitimate heirs. Sir William, the second son, who became the first Earl of Devonshire, died in 1626. Two martial figures flank the monument, which is surmounted by a huge broken pediment, with the family coat of arms rising above. An angel blows a trumpet and holds an inscription tablet. Below are full-size representations of a suit of armour and a figure in noble robes. Under the black columns are representations of the two bodies. William is covered by a shroud. Henry is depicted as a skeleton on a straw mat (*below*). Later generations of the Cavendish family rejected such pompous absurdities and opted for simple graves at the top of the churchyard.

out as ES. Perhaps it was as well that Queen Elizabeth was too old to visit Hardwick. Perhaps, too, Bess hoped that a future Queen Arabella would sit in state here. Mark Girouard concludes: 'There is probably no other house in England which is so closely connected in popular imagination with one person. And she was a person to be reckoned with.'

At the same time as she was building at Hardwick, Bess was erecting yet another house at Oldcotes, which was finished by 1599. It has been demolished and no illustration survives, but a Smythson drawing of a building very much like Hardwick but on a smaller scale may have been the model. It was built for Bess's second son, William, and stood in the valley north-west of Heath, below Sutton Scarsdale. William was to inherit Hardwick and, after the death of his elder brother, Henry, in 1616 Chatsworth too. The brothers are commemorated by a grandiose Renaissance monument in the south chapel of Edensor church, designed by Maximilian Colt. Bess was buried with great pomp in All Saints church, Derby, in 1608, whereas her estranged husband, George, was interred many miles to the north in the parish church of Sheffield. They, too, have enormous alabaster monuments.

After the death of Gilbert Talbot, seventh Earl of Shrewsbury, in 1616 with no male heirs, the Cavendishes were undoubtedly the dominant family in Derbyshire and Nottinghamshire. William became Lord-Lieutenant of both counties and in 1618 was created the first Earl of Devonshire. (Although the Cavendishes had no land in Devon, the title was vacant and it was not possible to become Earl of Derbyshire because the title of Earl of Derby was used by the Stanleys of West Derby, Liverpool.) William continued the family policy of buying Derbyshire estates whenever they came on to the market. By the 1620s he owned nearly 100,000 acres, of which 43,916 acres were in Derbyshire, 25,923 acres in Yorkshire, and the rest scattered in nine different counties. Of course, much of this extensive estate, including nearly 20,000 acres in Hope Woodlands, was rough moorland grazing. The maps and surveys that William Senior was commissioned to make of William's scattered properties and those of his brother Charles, who was based at Welbeck and Bolsover, are now our principal source of information about the landscape history of Derbyshire in the first half of the seventeenth century.

Sir Charles Cavendish, the youngest of Bess's sons, was famed for his skill as a horseman and swordsman and for his bravery as a soldier in the Dutch wars. He was a good friend of his step brother, Gilbert Talbot, from whom he bought Welbeck Abbey and Bolsover Castle at very reasonable prices. He turned to Robert Smythson for ideas about how to convert the ruined motte-and-bailey at Bolsover into a fairy-tale castle for chivalric knights and ladies straight out of Spenser's *The Faerie Queen*. Great tournaments in armour and elaborate fancy dress were held in the courtyard and between 1612 and 1614 a 'Little Castle' was erected on the motte in imitation of a medieval keep. This was adorned with turrets at three corners and with a big staircase tower at the fourth, but a compromise between the austerity of the Middle Ages and the convenience demanded in the Jacobean era was made when square-headed windows (though much smaller than was usual) were preferred to narrow medieval slits. The illusion was preserved best on the garden front, which has hardly any windows. Inside, the basement of the Little Castle was divided between the kitchen, a large cellar and offices, whose roofs were supported by simple stone-vaults. The hall and the parlour on the ground floor had more elaborate rib-vaults and the walls were painted with scenes from the Labours of Hercules. The principal rooms that were placed on the first floor consisted of the Star Chamber, a withdrawing room or marble closet, the best bed chamber and two inner chambers decorated to represent the pagan and Christian versions of the after-life. Other chambers were placed on the top floor, but this was a place for occasional brief stops rather than a gentleman's seat. The floors throughout were constructed of gypsum plaster.

After the death of Sir Charles, his son, Sir William, finished the decoration as was intended. The paintings are modest in quality and allegorical and theatrical in style, but their recent, careful restoration has cast away much of the gloom and has opened our eyes to the original appearance of the Star Chamber. A mixture of Gothic and Renaissance sources were used, particularly in the unique set of eight hooded chimney pieces, whose Gothic shapes embrace classical details taken from Serlio's book of architecture. They were each designed in a highly individual manner by Robert Smythson's son, John, another gifted architect who went on to transform Bolsover Castle into a highly desirable residence.

In 1618–19 John Smythson was in London, drawing fashionable architectural features, such as the Dutch gables at 'My Ladye Cookes house' in Holborn, the windows opening on to balconies in the Low Countries style at Arundel House, and the rustication of the basement storey that Inigo Jones had designed for the Banqueting House in Whitehall. On his return, he inserted two external balconies into the Little Castle and added Holborn gables and classical details to the new stables at Welbeck. When Sir William Cavendish became Lord Lieutenant of Derbyshire in 1628, he needed a major house in the county to match his Nottinghamshire seat at Welbeck, so he asked John Smythson to design the Terrace Range at Bolsover along the line of the hill on the south side of the courtyard. In May 1633 Charles I and Queen Henrietta Maria were entertained at Welbeck on their way to Scotland with a production of a Ben Jonson masque. On their return on 1 July 1634, the king and queen were taken to Bolsover for one day's entertainment, including a new Jonson masque, 'Love's Welcome at Bolsover'. The surviving text shows that this started in the parlour chamber, where the Five Senses are depicted, and then moved outside for the 'dance of mechanics', including a surveyor, carver, mason, carpenter, etc, an allusion to the fact that the new range of building was not quite complete. The final part of the masque was performed in the garden by the central figure of a fountain Venus. This garden was enclosed by massive walls, which included some of the masonry of the medieval bailey.

Hardwick Hall. Bess wished to be remembered and the building of the New Hall at Hardwick late in her life has ensured that she is. No other house in England is so associated in popular perception with a particular individual. Designed by Robert Smythson, the leading architect of the age, the hall is crowned with Bess's initials, ES for Elizabeth Shrewsbury, and with her coronet.

Haddon Hall: Long Gallery. In the 1580s John Manners, who had inherited Haddon through his marriage to Dorothy Vernon, commissioned Robert Smythson to design this elegant extension to the medieval manor house overlooking his new gardens. Long galleries were a fashionable feature of the late Elizabethan age.

The 'Little Castle' at Bolsover (seen in the background) was designed by Robert Smythson for Sir Charles Cavendish, and erected between 1612 and 1614. It occupies a striking position on top of the escarpment, on the ruins of a Norman motte-and-bailey. Its style harks back to the Middle Ages, but it was given up-to-date windows, for this was a house to show off to visitors, including royalty. Charles I and his queen were entertained here in 1634 by Sir Charles's son, Sir William, the future Duke of Newcastle. By then, Sir William had commissioned Robert Smythson's son, John, to design a Terrace Range (to the right), which included fashionable features from London such as Dutch gables. Only the external walls of the range are still standing, but in recent years English Heritage have carried out a great deal of painstaking restoration work of the whole site.

Chimney-piece in the Pillar Parlour of the Little Castle. Eight hooded chimney-pieces, each of unique design, were improvised upon examples in Book IV of Sebastiano Serlio's *Books of Architecture*, which had been translated into English in 1611. The chimney-pieces were constructed of local magnesian limestone and inlaid with Derbyshire marble and alabaster from the Cavendish estate. This one in the Pillar Parlour has Doric coulmns and a strapwork crest, but the general form is Gothic rather than Classical.

The new range at Bolsover was gutted in the eighteenth century, but the ruined shell survives to the full height of the Holborn gables. A long gallery was provided but the state rooms were added later by John Smythson's son, Huntingdon, in the years leading up to the Civil War. Whether father or son designed the Riding School is uncertain, for its exact date is not known, but it was built for Sir William Cavendish (later, the first Duke of Newcastle), an expert rider whose treatise on horsemanship (1658) became a standard text for haute-école techniques in various parts of Europe, including the royal courts at Vienna and Madrid.

Meanwhile, Haddon Hall had been converted from a medieval fortified dwelling into a fine Elizabethan country house. Sir George Vernon had been styled the 'King of the Peak', but he was the last of a long line and when he

Bolsover Castle in 1698. The 'castle' that was built in the first half of the seventeenth century for Sir Charles Cavendish and his son, William, Duke of Newcastle, was erected on the site of a genuine Norman castle, constructed for William Peveril, but was intended not for defence, nor to intimidate the local population, but to express the ideals of chivalry and the displays of pageantry that were favoured at the courts of Elizabeth I and the early Stuarts. The great Elizabethan architect Robert Smythson designed the 'Keep' or 'Little Castle' for Sir Charles, and his son John Smythson enlarged the building into a country house for this branch of the Cavendishes, whose main seat was at Welbeck Abbey (Nottinghamshire). The view shown here was drawn by the Dutch artists Jan Kip and Leonard Knyff.

BRITANNIA ILLUSTRATA (1707)

died in 1565 his estate passed to John Manners, the husband of his second daughter, Dorothy. During the time of Sir John (who was knighted in 1603 and died in 1611), larger windows were inserted to give more light to the house, interiors were refurbished and a splendid Long Gallery and a matching garden front were added. The Haddon Hall accounts for September and October 1582 contain payments to Robert Smythson, who was then working at Wollaton, and the armorial glass in the Long Gallery has a 1589 date, though the rich panelling may have been added later. Trevor Brighton has shown that the Long Gallery was designed to overlook new pleasure gardens through its two canted bays and central square projection. The measurements of the gallery fit those of the garden, thus proving that they were designed as a unity. Balustrading, garden steps, the bowling terrace above and the limestone buttresses of the lower garden were added at the same time; a garden sundial bears the date 1591. These pleasure gardens were improved and given their present appearance in the second half of the seventeenth century, using stone from Stanton Moor, and a new bowling green was laid out at the end of the lime avenue in the park, to the north of the Hall.

Robert Smythson also designed tall houses for prominent servants of the Talbots and Cavendishes. The largest of these was Barlborough Hall, which according to dates on the porch and the great chamber fireplace was erected in 1583–84 for Francis Rodes, a lawyer in the Earl of Shrewsbury's circle, who in 1585 became a justice of the Court of Common Pleas. The house was built of brick, disguised later by stucco, with magnesian limestone dressings, and was arranged around a central courtyard. Two tall storeys rise above a high basement and four towers pierce the skyline; the chimneys that accompanied them were removed in 1875. Large amounts of glass fill the mullioned and transomed windows, especially those of the great chamber. A smaller version (without a long gallery) of the earl's Worksop Manor, Barlborough Hall was very like Smythson's Heath Old Hall, near Wakefield, which was demolished in 1961. The Rodes family also commissioned John Smythson to build a new house on the site of Barlborough Old Hall; they were created baronets in 1641 and continued at Barlborough until 1743.

A small, but strikingly tall house at North Lees, Hathersage, was designed by Robert Smythson for occasional use by William Jessop of Broom Hall, Sheffield, another high-ranking servant of the Earl of Shrewsbury. One of the plaster ceilings carries the date 1594 and displays the crest and motto of the Jessops and other mottoes, including that of Rodes. The house was perched high on a hill and built in the style of the hunting lodges at Sheffield Manor and Chatsworth, rising three or four storeys over a basement. Decorative merlons on the parapet hide the flat, leaded roof, from which extensive views could

Barlborough Hall. An aerial view, looking east, of the substantial Elizabethan hall built for Sir Francis Rhodes, a self-made man from Staveley Woodthorpe who became a judge in the Court of Common Pleas and a member of the circle of George Talbot, sixth Earl of Shrewsbury. It is dated 1583 on the porch and 1584 on a fireplace and was probably designed by Robert Smythson, best known for Hardwick Hall. It has the tall, compact plan, arranged around a small courtyard, and projecting bays extending upwards into the towers that Smythson used in other commissions in Derbyshire, Nottinghamshire and Yorkshire. It was very similar in plan and style to the demolished Heath Old Hall in the West Riding. Set in a large park, secluded from the village, the hall is now used as a school.

PHOTOGRAPH: MALCOLM DOLBY

be enjoyed. In the seventeenth century this fashion for tall houses was copied by Derbyshire gentry and yeomen families. Spectacular examples include The Hagge, Staveley, which Sir Peter Frecheville built in 1630, Anthony Woolley's Riber Manor House of 1633, and later farmhouses such as Broomhill Farm, Brackenfield, and Raven House, Ashover.

The gentry

Many of Derbyshire's leading medieval gentry families, such as the Greys of Codnor, Shirland and Sandiacre, the Babingtons of Dethick, the Chaworths of Alfreton, the Longfords of Longford and the Foljambes of Walton, died out in the male line between the late fifteenth and the seventeenth centuries. Prominent amongst the survivors were the Fitzherberts in their old manor houses at Norbury and Padley and at their new halls at Somersal Herbert and Tissington. Somersal Herbert Hall – Derbyshire's largest and most

Derbyshire's best timber-framed house, Somersal Herbert Hall is in the south-west corner of the county. It has a 1564 datestone in its entrance, but may contain earlier work. It was built for John and Ellen Fitzherbert at a time when timber-framed houses were still fashionable. The timbers are arranged in a variety of styles: close studding, herringbone, and decorative quatrefoils in the gables. Its asymmetrical appearance adds to its charm. The garden front was encased in brick in the eighteenth century.

PHOTOGRAPH: AUTHOR

delightful timber-framed house – was built in 1564 for John Fitzherbert. The entrance front, facing north-east, has two storeys and attics, reaching up to an irregular, gabled roof line, with rich decoration above the close studding of the lower parts. The windows are framed by wooden mullions, the larger ones also with transoms. Two later phases of building can be dated to 1712 (when the south-west front was entirely rebuilt in brick) and 1850 (long after this branch of the Fitzherberts had become extinct). Timber frames had gone out of fashion at this social level by 1609, when Tissington Hall was built for Francis Fitzherbert in coursed rubble carboniferous limestone with millstone grit dressings. This square, medium-sized house of five bays was adorned with mullioned and transomed windows, a two-storeyed central porch, a parapet instead of gables, numerous chimneys, and a walled garden to the front. Its original character is still apparent, despite later remodelling and additions by Francis's descendants.

A good example of a rising family in the Elizabethan period is provided by the Fanshawes, minor gentry from Fanshaw Gate, Holmesfield. Henry Faunchall's eldest son, John, who was bailiff of Holmesfield manor in 1543, received a grant of arms in 1571. The younger son, Henry, rose in the legal profession to become Queen's Remembrancer in the Court of Exchequer. Upon his death in 1568 he was succeeded in that post by his nephew Thomas, who in 1579 founded Dronfield Grammar School in fulfilment of Henry's bequest. Thomas's long tenure of office until his death in 1601 was very profitable and allowed him to buy a London town house and country estates in Hertfordshire

and Essex. Five more Fanshawes succeeded Thomas as Queen's Remembrancer, an office that was held by the family for about 150 years.

The most successful of the minor gentry families that retained their Derbyshire roots were the numerous branches of the Eyres, who made their fortune from the mining and smelting of lead and the grazing of large flocks of sheep. As early as 1505 Roger Eyre of Holme Hall, Newbold, and his brother John were smelting lead at Holmesfield. The leading member of the family in the late Elizabethan period was Rowland Eyre, whose manors of Hassop, Rowland and Calver were 'customary liberties' outside the 'King's field' and so were not subject to the royalties of lot and cope. He was fortunate too in that a major lead rake lay beneath Longstone Common. By the 1580s Eyre was also leasing the Queen's mines in the High Peak and was investing in the new smelting technology. In 1607–08 his two sons, Thomas and Gervase, had 'new mills' which were soon polluting the atmosphere in the Cordwell valley and attracting complaints at the Holmesfield manor court. The Eyres showed little regard for the wellbeing of others as they sought to enrich themselves. In the 1570s Rowland Eyre of Hassop enclosed his own lands and converted farms to pasture in Rowland. His father had a flock of no more than 160 sheep, but Rowland and his son, Thomas, kept over 1,000, which in summer time they grazed on Longstone Moor. Having established the family's fortunes before his death in 1626, Rowland Eyre built a new house at Hassop, some of whose features survived the rebuilding of the 1820s; on the edge of the estate another gabled hall is known as the Dower House.

As we shall see, most of the new minor gentry houses in north Derbyshire were built out of profits from the lead trade. A fine example is Cutthorpe Old Hall, which was built in 1625 alongside a low, timber-framed building

Highlow Hall was built high on the hills between Offerton Moor and Eyam Woodlands in the late sixteenth or early seventeenth century for a junior branch of the Eyre family. A drawing of about 1710 shows that the house once had north and south wings. The probate inventory of Thomas Eyre, appraised on 12 December 1633, names the principal ground-floor rooms as the hall, dining parlour and two parlours used as bedrooms. The service rooms consisted of a kitchen, buttery, dairy, brewhouse and larder. The bedrooms on the first floor were named as the great chamber, white chamber, and chamber over the buttery, and two other chambers were used for storage. The room above the porch was the servants' chamber.

A great barn, a cowhouse and a workhouse where farm equipment was stored stood across the farmyard, and two other barns were located in the fields. The inventory also listed 378 sheep, a corn mill and a lead smelting house.

for Alderman Ralph Clarke of Chesterfield, whose father had been the town's first mayor and a merchant who exported lead through Bawtry to Hull and London. The three-storeyed main range and porch tower provide a spectacular vernacular version of the north Derbyshire fashion for tall houses.

Enclosures

The Tudor and early Stuart period saw a great deal of the upland wastes and many of the open arable fields brought into private ownership, sometimes by agreement but often by high-handed action from the nobility and gentry, including the lessees of the manors of the Duchy of Lancaster. The purchasers of former monastic granges were particularly keen to press their rights, as they saw them, even if the memory of these was preserved only in old documents. Before the dissolution of the monasteries, peasant farmers had hotly disputed the right of the owner of a grange to pasture huge flocks of sheep on the common wastes. Now, the opposition took the form of litigation and rioting, especially when a lord or lessee tried to enclose a sheepwalk with fences or walls. In 1569 riots broke out at Mainstonefield, when Godfrey Bradshaw enclosed 48 acres of common land near Chinley that had belonged to a grange of Merevale Abbey. Further aggravation was caused when the lessees of the Duchy of Lancaster estates and the lords of other manors within the High Peak tried to raise the level of entry fines and rents to match or exceed inflation.

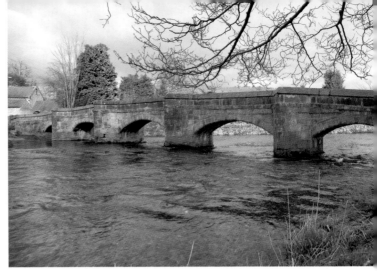

Built in 1626 for Bernard Wells, a prosperous lead merchant from Gloucestershire, Holme Hall near Bakewell was among those high-status Derbyshire houses which had battlements rather than gables, and a projecting central tower porch and bay windows. The building has recently been restored.

This sturdy little bridge across the Wye, built in 1664 to connect Holme Hall with the road from Bakewell to Buxton, is wide enough only for horses and pedestrians. Packhorse bridges as such do not have segmental arches, separated by cut-waters and recesses, nor are they quite so early, and this bridge is best regarded rather as a private bridge for the hall.

Dower House, Hassop. This seventeenth-century, gabled hall stands near the entrance to the grounds of Hassop Hall. The history is difficult to unravel, but both buildings seem to have been constructed for Rowland Eyre, who made a fortune out of sheep farming and lead smelting, or perhaps by one of his sons; we do not know when it gained the name Dower House. Three storeys high, with projecting wings and string courses, it was built of local limestone, with millstone grit dressings. The mullioned windows are small for such a large house of this period.

In the 1570s George Talbot and Bess enclosed parts of Ashford Moor against the wishes of the freeholders. In 1576 a complaint was made by 360 poor cottagers from the Tideswell area against George, arguing that his enclosures in the Forest of the Peak had deprived them of sufficient pasture for their cows, which for many were a vital source of sustenance. Three years later, tenants from the manors of Ashford, the Forest of the Peak and Glossop Dale went to London to air their grievances before the Privy Council. They protested about the unreasonable behaviour of George's bailiff, William Dickenson of Sheffield, and his servants, George Scargill and Nicholas Booth, who had raised their rents and enclosed and let out a large area of common waste. To George's chagrin, the Queen and the Privy Council decided in favour of the tenants. The mightiest man in Derbyshire had been successfully resisted.

Landowners and tenants became increasingly adversarial during the late Elizabethan period and conflicts over rights between settlements became more frequent. In 1652 the 94-year-old Adam Woolley of Bonsall recalled that fifty years previously his neighbours had felt they were 'streatned for Roome about their houses' and so put their cattle on Masson Moor in Matlock; they were prosecuted for trespass. The minor gentry and wealthier yeomen who were involved in the lead trade followed the example of the major landowners by enclosing on a smaller scale and the pressure on available land in the White Peak was increased when large numbers of squatters who came to work as labourers or cavers in the lead mines built cottages and took in a few acres of land. Most of these encroachments were eventually made legal when the lessees of the Duchy manors enforced the payment of rents. As the population rose in the last three decades of the sixteenth century agreements to restrict the number of animals that could graze the commons were made in manor courts. In some manors, the farmers consolidated their holdings by exchanging scattered strips and enclosing part or the whole of their common pastures. Most of Stanton common, for instance, had been enclosed by 1622, but the process was uneven from manor to manor. Returns to the justices of the peace in 1630–31 made it clear that most of the pasture in Appletree and Wirksworth wapentakes had long since been enclosed and that the former open fields in the High Peak had mostly been divided by mutual agreement.

Attempts to 'disafforest' Duffield Frith and the Forest of the Peak in order to ease the financial difficulties of the Crown caused fierce debate, hard bargaining and violent resistance. Duffield Frith was finally released from forest laws in 1633, but the battle over the Forest of the Peak was not resolved until the late seventeenth century. An extensive survey of Duffield Frith in 1560 had revealed that the 862 acres of managed woods varied in size from over 200 acres down to small plots of just two acres. Some oak woods produced both timber and underwood in the classic manner. Other woods were divided into 'hags' which were felled on a 10-year rotation for harvesting specific trees, such as alders for scaffolding and chestnut and oak for charcoal. Holly was grown as winter fodder for the deer and sheep and the tenants had the right to collect the undergrowth as firewood. In 1581 a commission reported that woodland management had been neglected and that the foresters had allowed outsiders to buy fuel wood and browse. Another survey in 1587 found no recent coppicing and a general neglect that was causing the woodland to deteriorate badly. The barren wood grounds of Hulland Ward had been depleted 'by cattle that took shelter and browse there in winter', and the tenants had taken so much timber for the repair of mills, weirs, pales and fences that nothing of value was left. The 509 copyholders, freeholders, ancient cottagers and householders responded by petitioning Queen Elizabeth to say that 'tyme out of mind' they had 'enjoyed common of pasture for any number of cattle in the waste of the Fryth; had taken crop and browse for these cattle as often as necessary in hard weather, snow or frost, from the feast day of St Martin up 'til the end of February'; and that they had 'houseboote, heyeboote, plowboote and hedgeboote plus reasonable firewood to burn for fuel'. Now, they were fearful that the woods would be leased, all ancient rights and customs would go, and that they would be charged for what had previously been free. Nevertheless, they were worried about the increasing number of commoners within the frith, which no longer functioned as it had, for all the deer were gone. It was Charles II's need for money that reopened the debate in 1625 and led to Duffield Frith's disafforestation eight years later.

Farming

A series of bad harvests in the last 15 years of the sixteenth century kept the fear of famine uppermost in people's minds. Improved farming practices provided enough food in all but the worst years of harvest failure, but demand from an ever-growing population brought inflation to add to the general woe. Farming systems became increasingly specialised as yeomen and husbandmen sought to offer products that paid best at the market place. The Trent and Dove valleys offered good grazing for dairy cattle. By the mid-seventeenth century improved and more complicated methods of floating water meadows by artificial channels to encourage early and lush growth had been introduced in Staffordshire townships such as Tutbury and no doubt on the Derbyshire banks of the rivers as well. William Senior's map of Marston-on-Dove in 1616 depicts 76 acres of meadows that were seemingly farmed in common by 14 tenants, including six who each held less than two acres. The open arable fields had been much reduced by piecemeal enclosure and, significantly, the survey of the lord's lands started with the dairy house. The meandering river was navigable for boats, which were anchored at the 14-acre island called the 'Boate steaner'.

Most of the townships in the south of the county were dependent almost entirely on agriculture. Senior's 1626 map of Church Broughton, in the heavy clays to the west of Derby, depicts four open fields, covering 357 acres, but many 'intakes' around their edges and numerous closes by the village. The meadows alongside the brook that winds its way through the township from west to east measured 77 acres. Beyond lay the 32 acres of the Bent and the 78 acres of the Heath, names that are still marked on the 'Explorer' edition of the Ordnance Survey map. At Church Langley in 1640, Senior drew a street village of a church and 21 houses, with three open fields covering 302 acres, many closes and a moor or common of 86 acres. But no open fields survived at Pentrich (1611) or at either Litchurch or Windley (1631). At Walton-upon-Trent the open fields were enclosed by agreement in 1652.

Mixed husbandry was the normal practice on the fertile soils that overlay the magnesian limestone in north-east Derbyshire. In three maps of Bolsover, drawn between 1630 and 1637, Senior showed the small, planned town, still confined within its medieval limits, the three open fields covering 355 acres in the north-east of the township, and the 361 acres of Bolsover Moor beyond. The north-western area included the 433 acres of 'Woodhouse grounds', with the hamlets of Over and Nether Woodhouse, and further north the 888 acres of 'The Common called Shuttlewoode' and the adjacent 396 acres of 'The lordes coppice'. Such large woods were unusual on the magnesian limestone. They have long since disappeared, partly under the former Markham Main Colliery, but a small settlement known as Shuttlewood and the names Woodside and Shuttlewood Common are still marked on Ordnance Survey maps.

The parish of Eckington was typical of much of the coal-measure sandstones in having remnants of open fields, but far more closes and extensive woods and commons. A survey of the manor in 1650 noted 614 acres of coppices or spring woods: Eckington Park (450), Hanging Lees (48), Lightwood (99) and Common Wood (17). An estimated 1,000 acres of common and waste grounds were divided between Eckington Marsh, Bramley Moor, Ridgeway Moor, Plumbley Wood, Base Green, Eckington Leys, Mosborough Moor, Little Moor, Spinkhill Moor and Emmett Carrs. The surveyor thought that they were 'for the most part very barren and yield little or no profitt to the present Lord of the Manor, the Tenants thereof having the Herbage for their Cattle'.

Further west, 80 probate inventories for Dore and Totley, drawn up between 1539 and 1644 show that farmers placed more value on their cattle and sheep than on their cereals. Oats were grown for both humans and animals and were often mixed with barley as spring-sown blend corn or 'dredge', but some wheat was sown before winter and often mixed with rye as hard corn or 'maslin'. Peas and hay were the only other crops recorded. Three out of every four farmers kept a flock of sheep, though no-one had many, and most kept a few dairy cows and stores that were reared to replenish the herd or for fattening on richer pastures elsewhere. Oxen were commonly used as draught animals, but as the seventeenth century progressed farmers increasingly turned to horses. In all, 70 farmers kept an average of seven head of cattle. Dore and Totley had no wealthy graziers to match those in neighbouring townships, such as Ralph Leeke of Hasland, esquire (died 1575), who had 53 head of cattle and 190 sheep, Robert Mower, yeoman of Barlow Woodseats (died 1620), who kept 30 head of cattle and a flock of 80 sheep or Thomas Burton of Cartledge (died 1645) who had nearly 300 sheep. The large number of inventories that have survived for the sixteenth- and seventeenth-century parish of Chesterfield confirm that in this district more emphasis was placed on livestock than cereals. It is noticeable that whereas cattle were differentiated by the appraisers as kine, bullocks, heifers, twinters, stirks, steers, oxen, young beats, etc., cereals were often valued collectively as corn.

This detail of Burdett's map of Derbyshire (1767) shows the extensive commons and coppice woods within Eckington parish.

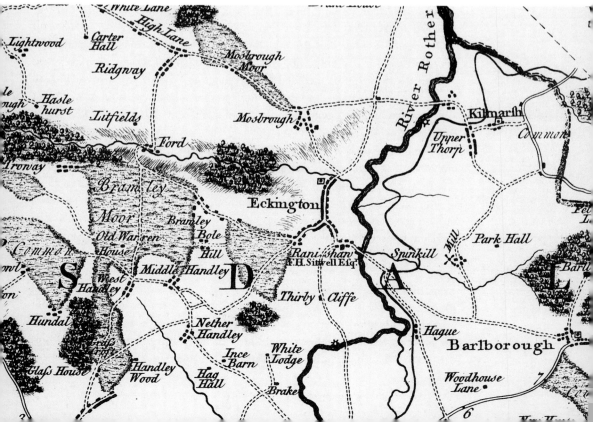

Turf gates, Crookstone Moor. The right of turbary – the common right to dig turf or peat for winter fuel on the moors of a township – was important before coal was supplied cheaply by trains and lorries. The right to dig peat was regulated through manor courts. In 1624, for instance, the Holmesfield manor court ordered that, 'No person, or persons, shall dig or make any Peate Pitts upon the moore, but, immediately after the getting of such peate, slytt the same whereby the water may issue forth'. Offenders were fined 3*s*. 4*d*. This group of holloways leading through the heather from Hope to Crookstone Moor were 'gates' formed by the horse-drawn carts and sledges of the peat cutters. The character of extensive stretches of moorland landscape in the Dark Peak has been changed by the large-scale removal of the layers of peat since the late Middle Ages. Crookstone Moor was one of the widest and deepest turbaries.

The extensive Cavendish estates in the Dark Peak township of Hope Woodlands were mapped by William Senior in 1627. The 22 farms were scattered in or above the Upper Derwent and Ashop valleys, mostly on the sites of medieval predecessors, but much of the 19,627 acres of this moorland township consisted of 'bad pasture' or 'out pasture'. Each isolated farmstead was surrounded by a small number of irregular-shaped, drystone-walled fields and an enclosed pasture known as a hey. On the moors above, sheepwalks and cattle outpastures were clearly defined by earthen banks and ditches, most of which can still be traced on the ground. Farmers also had specific common rights to dig peat for their fuel, to quarry stone for their buildings and walls, and to gather firewood from the woodlands in the valleys. Holloways leading up to the moors often peter out at the places where peat was dug, for in time large stretches of moorland were stripped of their peat cover.

In 1631 the corn of the High Peak was reported to be 'chiefly oats and oatmeal, little other grain growing'. Plenty of farmers earned enough from grazing livestock and from lead mining to import other cereals and malted barley from Derby market. In 1640 it was claimed that even in the better farming land on the southern edge of the Peak, 'the greatest parte of the inhabitants of the towne & township of Wirkesworth doe Buy a great parte of their Corne … and … Malt … from Derbie, Mansfield, Nottingham & other Remote places'. In times of dearth, of course, those who did not grow their own corn were the first to suffer.

Senior's map of Sheldon in 1617 marked 'The common feelde' to the north of the village, much encroached upon. It measured 156 acres and was divided between 22 tenants; a further six farmers and three cottagers had no land in this communal field. The west end of the street village funnelled out towards the

81-acre 'common pasture', which looped round the common field. To the north, the 172-acre Great Shacklow Wood descended the steep hillside to the river Wye in the same distinctive shape as today. From the other side of the village, Sheldon Moor (1,339 acres) stretched to the southern and eastern township boundary. A Bolehill was sited on the eastern edge of the moor and various lead rakes ran from east to west. Several miles due north, Senior's map of Grindlow (1631) depicted a small settlement of about ten houses, with numerous curving strips in the open fields at about 1,000 feet above sea level.

The typical holding in the White Peak – as in the rest of Derbyshire – was the small family farm. A survey of Crich, on an outlier of the carboniferous limestone in 1655 shows that 29 people held under 10 acres each, another 29 farmed between 10 and 30 acres, and a further seven held between 31 and 128 acres. Such farmers were dependent on their rights on the common and often on their wages in the lead mines or from crafts. The yeomen who farmed more than 30 acres of land were mostly copyholders or lessees of the lord's land, those with 10–30 acres were the poorer husbandmen, and below them were growing numbers of cottagers and people with no land at all. As the lead miners emphasised in a petition of 1616, many of their number were landless, having but 'a cowe or twoe apeece to give them milke'.

The lead industry

From the middle of the sixteenth century the Derbyshire lead industry recovered so well from its late medieval decline that it became the leading supplier in Europe. In the early 1540s Derbyshire's mines produced only 3,000 loads of ore a year, but by 1600 annual output had reached 34,000 loads and by the 1640s 120,000 loads. Smelters and merchants enjoyed massive profits and many small settlements within the White Peak were turned into industrial villages as 'poor country people' swelled the ranks of miners, cavers and hirelings from the early 1570s onwards. Andy Wood has calculated that between 1563 and 1670 the population of Eyam parish grew by 398 per cent, Carsington by 361 per cent, Stoney Middleton by 297 per cent, Matlock by 220 per cent, Youlgreave by 123 per cent and Ashford and Sheldon chapelries by 129 per cent. The rate of growth in non-mining townships was much less and the large and remote parish of Hartington, away from the lead fields, suffered net population loss. Old patterns of population densities had been changed out of recognition.

FREE MINERS AND CAVERS

Most mines were small and resembled opencast quarries. In the 1540s only about 400 men worked in the Derbyshire lead mines and most of those stayed on their farms during the lambing and harvesting seasons or when the mines were flooded in winter time. Just a small number worked through all or most of the year, either as free miners or wage-labourers. By 1581, however, the number of men who mined or sieved lead ore in the Peak District was estimated at about

2,000. Many of these workers were entirely dependent on mining or caving for a living. Christopher Schütz, who had arrived in England in 1566, invented a method of drawing iron wire (which was in demand for sieves, wool cards and knitting needles) and established a works at Hathersage. The new sieves, set in a tub of water, enabled the cavers to make more money by turning over the deserted workings of the High Peak than they did when their tools were merely picks and hammers.

On the eve of the Civil War some 90 per cent of the male working population of Wirksworth, Cromford and Middleton were involved in mining. Elsewhere, this proportion varied considerably from place to place. In Brassington and Carsington free miners still outnumbered the cavers and hirelings, and even in the smaller, poorer upland settlements of Wardlow and Sheldon free miners had not yet been undercut by those who worked for wages. In Castleton and Bradwell, Tideswell and Litton, and Eyam and its neighbouring villages free miners remained dominant, with the cavers and hirelings forming between one-quarter and one-third of the mining workforce, but in Great and Little Hucklow, where 59 per cent of the male villagers were involved in mining, almost half of them were hirelings and cavers.

David Kiernan has showed how Derbyshire's rise to pre-eminence in the lead industry was based on improved technology in mining and smelting. The ventilation of the deeper galleries was tackled by shafts and wind pumps that were operated by bellows, water was drained away by the use of horse gins and rag-and-chain pumps, and roofs were supported by oak props. All this capital investment was provided by the gentry smelters and lead merchants. For example, the Tearsall rake that was mined in Wensley from the 1630s was owned by a coalition of gentlemen; rag-and-chain pumps were installed to lift water and 644 loads of ore were raised to the surface between August and December 1634 by six-hour shifts of wage labourers working night and day. The best, but most expensive, way of draining the new, deep mines was to drive a sough into a hillside from a lower point in an adjacent valley, or from a deeper valley. The first sough in Derbyshire was that constructed by the Dutch entrepreneur Cornelius Vermuyden between 1629 and 1636 to drain the rich Dove Gang lead mines between Cromford and Wirksworth. It is possible to travel through the White Peak without being aware of these immense underground projects, but many soughs are still effective today, two or three centuries after they were constructed.

In 1653 Edward Manlove published, in verse form, an account of the customs and liberties of the lead mines within Wirksworth wapentake. Part of it reads:

> By custom old in Wirksworth Wapentake
> If any of this nation find a Rake,
> Or Sign, or leading to the same; may set
> In any Ground, and there Lead-oar may get:

They may make crosses, holes, and set their Stowes,
Sink Shafts, build Lodges, Cottages or Coes.
But Churches, houses, gardens, all are free
From this strange custom of the minery.

A cross and hole a good possession is,
But for three dayes: and then the custom's this,
To set down Stowes, timbered in all men's sight,
Then such possession stands for three weeks right …
For then such Stows none ought for to remove;
And the Barghmaster ought to make arrest,
Upon complaint, if mines be in contest,

Receiving Fourpence for his lawful Fee,
That the next Court the wrong redress'd may be …
The thirteenth dish of oar within their mine,
To th'lord for Lot they pay at measuring time;
Sixpence a Load for Cope the Lord demands,
And this is paid to the Barghmaster's hands …

And two great Courts of Barghmoot ought to be
In every year upon the minery,
To punish miners that transgress the Law,
To curb offenders, and to keep in awe
Such as be cavers, or do rob men's Coes,
Such as be pilferers, or do steal men's Stows …

For stealing oar twice from the minery,
The Thief that's taken fined twice shall be,
But the third time, that he commits such theft,
Shall have a knife stuck through his hand to th'Haft
Into the Stow, and there till death shall stand,
Or loose himself by cutting loose his hand.

Cobnor Wood, Barlow. An inquisition of 1324 mentions 'a wood called Cobbenouere', whose name means 'Cobba's *ofer*', a ridge with a flat top shaped like an upturned boat. By Elizabethan times it was being referred to as a springwood. In 1630 'Cobnor Spring' covered 109 acres, in exactly the same outline as today. The lead smelters used it to convert wood into white coal for their furnaces. A large group of white coal kilns can be found near the top of the wood. At the summit of the hill, the field known as 'Cobnor Top', which, in 1630, separated Cobnor Wood from 'The Coppice', also retains its ancient shape and appearance. This part of the Barlow landscape has probably not changed since medieval times.
PHOTOGRAPH: AUTHOR

As the number of wage labourers increased, the free miners became increasingly tenacious of what they saw as their ancient right to mine lead wherever they found it. They were strongest in the manors of Matlock and Wirksworth, including Cromford, Middleton and Bonsall, but in other manors the right of free mining was allowed only by the licence of the lord and was sometimes aggressively refused. At various times between 1561 and 1591 free miners in Wirksworth wapentake were driven away by armed attacks by the lords, servants and tenants of the manors of Alsop, Ballidon, Bradbourne, Cowley, Elton, Snitterton and Wensley and from the former granges at Aldwark, Griffe, Steeple and Willersley. The dispute was brought before the

Court of Exchequer and the Duchy of Lancaster in 1591–1593, when the free miners received the backing of the lessee of the rights of lot and cope, Gilbert, the seventh Earl of Shrewsbury, and emerged victorious.

The Manners family at Haddon Hall, by then Earls of Rutland, were consistently hostile to the free miners' claims. The most violent dispute of all was that in the middle years of the seventeenth century in the manors of Harthill and Nether Haddon. In a show of strength in May 1648 nearly 200 free miners came to Haddonfields to assert their right to dig ore, but they were resisted by the Earl's stewards, retainers and freehold tenants. The Earl initiated prosecutions for riot at the quarter sessions, assizes, the Court of King's Bench and the House of Lords, as a result of which 11 miners were imprisoned in Fleet Gaol. The dispute rumbled on and another riot broke out in 1658, but the Earl was triumphant.

SMELTERS AND MERCHANTS

A new method of smelting lead ore by the use of heated white coal brought to a high temperature by a water-powered bellows in a smelting mill alongside a fast-flowing stream was introduced from the Somerset Mendips into Derbyshire in 1552. It did not achieve much success until 1569, when William Humphrey, who had acquired a monopoly, built a mill at Beauchief on the county's northern border. The new method did not depend on the vagaries of the weather and was capable of smelting low-grade ore. Humphrey's success encouraged the local aristocrats and gentry to successfully challenge his monopoly and to build mills on their own estates, especially in the wooded valleys, where fuel could

Side Lane, Holmesfield. This deep holloway, which descends from Horseleygate into the Cordwell valley, was mentioned in a Holmesfield manor court roll in 1588, when two men were ordered to cut down timber that prevented the passage of carriages. These carriages were the loaded wains of the lead smelters in the valley bottom. Holloways were deepened much more by wheeled vehicles than by packhorses. Land-slip since the way was abandoned, until its re-use in modern times by occasional walkers and horse riders, has turned the U-shaped route into a V-shape. In the nineteenth century Samuel Smiles described such holloways as horse tracks in summer and rivulets in winter.

PHOTOGRAPH: AUTHOR

be obtained readily, between the river Derwent in the west and a line running south of Sheffield to Chesterfield in the east. By the 1580s the old bole hills had been abandoned. As production soared at the mills, the demand for ore encouraged the sinking of deeper mines and the cavers' re-working of the wastes of old rakes. David Kiernan concludes that between 1569 and 1584 'a small-scale localised industry wedded to a primitive smelting technology and producing small quantities of a high quality product mainly for the domestic market was transformed into a major overseas trade'.

George, the sixth Earl of Shrewsbury, was at the forefront of this revival and after his death in 1590 William and Charles Cavendish, the knightly families of Vernon, Foljambe and Sacheverell, and numerous gentry of lower rank became actively involved. Some of these were old smelting families who had adopted the new technology and had thus increased their fortunes. They included rising men, notably the Eyres of Hassop and the Gells of Hopton, and minor gentry and yeomen in Scarsdale wapentake, such as the Barleys of Barlow, Burtons of Cartledge, Linacres of Linacre, Mowers of Barlow Woodseats and Strelleys of Beauchief. The Burtons made their fortunes from lead smelting in one generation. Thomas Burton started off as an illiterate, small stock farmer at Cartledge, but two of his sons became sheriff of Derbyshire. The Mowers were small yeomen farmers in Holmesfield and Barlow, but Robert Mower became known as 'the great lead merchant' of Barlow Woodseats Hall.

Chesterfield's location near the smelting mills and on the way to the inland port of Bawtry enabled it to overtake Wirksworth as the commercial centre of the lead trade. Prosperous merchants who bought properties in the surrounding countryside included the Heathcotes (who bought the Cutthorpe Hall estate in 1614), the Milnses (who built up the Dunston estate) and the Taylors (who bought the Durant Hall estate from the Alsops). A few miles further north, the Morewoods of Norton parish, descendants of Hallamshire yeomen, had a son based in London to whom, in 1625, they shipped 1,874 fothers of lead, 292 firkins of red lead and 128 firkins of lead shot; this amounted to 61 per cent of the total Derbyshire trade in that year. Derby, too, served as an export point where the Bainbridges of Friar Gate traded in lead and Peak wool in the 1570s and 1580s and Edmund Sleigh became a large shipper of lead to London in the 1590s.

Other industries

The iron industry was of far less importance but was nevertheless undergoing its own technological revolution. In 1500 the Leakes were operating a water-powered ironworks near Newbold Mill on the outskirts of Chesterfield, but for most of the sixteenth century such sites appear to have been bloomeries. The first recorded charcoal blast furnace in Derbyshire was built about 1582 by Sir John Zouche of Codnor at Loscoe, together with a forge at Hartshay and a wiremill at Makeney. New furnaces were sited on streams that powered the bellows, close to the bell pits and charcoal woods. The seventh Earl of Shrewsbury's works were producing bar iron at Stretton (1593) and Barlow (1605–6) and a few years later at Toadhole Furnace, near Shirland, in association with a forge at Crich Chase. Philip Riden has shown that early in the seventeenth century a number of blast furnaces and forges were built by several gentry families in the Rother valley, including the Hunlokes at Wingerworth, the Leakes at North Wingfield, and the Frechevilles at Staveley, and a furnace that was built on the Earl of Kingston's estate at Whaley in 1617 was linked to a forge at Cuckney (Nottinghamshire). George Sitwell of Renishaw was the first of Derbyshire's professional ironmasters. He erected furnaces at Plumbley and Foxbrooke in his native parish and in 1656 constructed Derbyshire's earliest slitting mill for the conversion of bar iron into rod iron for local nailmakers. From the 1650s, in partnership with William Clayton of Whitwell, he leased the Frecheville furnace and forge at Staveley and the forge at Carburton (Nottinghamshire). He also leased a furnace at North Wingfield, which he worked with his forge at Pleasley His letterbook reveals him trading through Bawtry, Deptford and London and exporting saws to Barbados.

Much of the iron that was produced in north-east Derbyshire was used by the secondary metalworker-farmers in the parishes bordering upon Hallamshire. Norton had become the main place that supplied scythes to the farmers of northern England and lowland Scotland. Between 1559 and 1579 the Norton parish register named 11 scythesmiths, two scythe-strikers and a scythe-seller, some of whom were already forging considerable quantities of scythes and grinding them at wheels on the river Sheaf. When William Blythe of Norton Lees, yeoman, died in 1632 he owned 650 long scythes, 450 scythes of a second sort, 450 of a third sort and 350 Scottish scythes, but he is likely to have been a middleman and not just a producer. Meanwhile, some Attercliffe and Darnall families, led by the Staniforths, had migrated to the Moss valley in the parish of Eckington, where for several generations they combined farming with the making of sickles.

Coal continued to be mined on a limited scale for local markets in many parts of the exposed coalfield. Between 1550 and 1615 small coal mines, which were usually leased to partnerships, were recorded at Bolsover, Butterley, Chesterfield, Duffield Frith, Eckington, Heanor, Langley, Oakerthorpe, Ripley, Stanley, Swanwick, Tibshelf, Wingerworth, and in the south of the county at Gresley, Newhall and Swadlincote. Output increased steadily in the early seventeenth century, when at least 23 pits were each producing over 10,000 tons a year. A prominent figure in the trade was George Turner, who in 1620 became the sole owner of the coal and ironstone rights in Alfreton and Swanwick. His son John, 'a rich collier', purchased the Swanwick estate.

The deciduous woods of north Derbyshire were managed for both their timber and their underwood, which was used for multifarious purposes such as making poles, handles or pit props, but most were coppiced on a rotation basis for the principal purpose of providing charcoal for the ironmasters and white coal for the lead smelters. A list of the Derbyshire and Nottinghamshire woods of William Cavendish of Welbeck and Bolsover in 1642 noted 4,000 cartloads of timber, 600 cartloads of ash wood, 3,000

Renishaw Hall and gardens. Derbyshire's gentry owed much of their wealth to their investments in local industries and from royalties on the coal that was mined on their estates. In the middle years of the seventeenth century George Sitwell was the county's leading ironmaster. His house forms the core of the present building, which dates from the 1790s onwards. The gardens were re-designed in Italian style by Sir George Sitwell between 1886 and 1936. Here we see the classical temple in the Camelia Walk. The restoration of the gardens in recent years by Sir Reresby and Lady Sitwell has made them a popular visitor attraction.

PHOTOGRAPHS: RENISHAW HALL

White coal pit, Rose Wood, Barlow. Scores of Q-shaped depressions such as this can be found in the deciduous woods of north Derbyshire, east of the river Derwent and west of a line running south from Sheffield to Chesterfield. They are the sites where white coal was prepared as fuel for the lead smelters. White coal pits are characteristically bowl-shaped, about 12 to 15 feet in diameter and two to four feet deep, now often full of leaves. Most were built into a slope, with a gap on the downward side to provide a draught and to assist in drainage. Excavations have shown that a hearth was situated at the bottom of the pit. Leases of woods to lead smelters refer to white coal pits or kilns from the mid-sixteenth to the mid-eighteenth century, when lead was smelted in water-powered mills in the river valleys. In a lease of 1586, for example, Peter Barley of Barlow agreed to provide 'kyln dried wood commonly callid whyte cole'. Chopped and dried wood was converted into fuel that was less dark than charcoal, which generated too much heat for the lead ore hearths. Rose Wood took its name from a row of trees that marked the Barlow/Holmesfield boundary. The Mowers of Barlow Woodseats Hall coppiced this wood at regular intervals and converted much of the underwood into both charcoal and white coal.

PHOTOGRAPH: AUTHOR

cartloads of coppice wood, 2,000 cartloads of log wood, 40 loads of poles or 'grove timber' for the lead mines, 5,000 cartloads of cordwood or stackwood, 500 cartloads of charcoal and 1,000 horseloads of white coal. Leases such as that for Linacre woods granted to Thomas Burton of Cartledge in 1596 commonly refer to 'pittes and kylnes for white Coale and Charcoale', with 'sufficyent turffe braken and hillinge … for the necessarie Coalinge', and to the free passage of horses and carts.

The quarrying of millstones blossomed into an important Dark Peak industry during the Elizabethan era. The largest quarries were on the gritstone edges on the eastern side of the river Derwent, especially at Stanedge and Millstone Edge in the parish of Hathersage. A tithe dispute in 1590 shows that 13 hewers in the parish each made twelve pairs of stones a year, roughly one a fortnight. The hewers were part-time farmers, so their quarry work was not continuous.

Between them, they made over 300 millstones each year. These were taken to Bawtry for export to many parts of England. 'Peak' or 'Grey' millstones were used for grinding the inferior grains, whereas millers preferred stones from the Rhineland or the Paris basin when grinding wheat.

The carboniferous limestone of the White Peak was quarried and burnt to be spread on sour land or to be used as mortar in buildings. Fourteen limekilns were at work alongside the quarries at Dove Holes in 1650 and ten more at Bradwell town end, these 'being sett upp ordinarily and taken downe again by the people att their pleasure without any licence'. The spreading of lime was one of the agricultural improvements of the age. In 1652, for example, the freeholders of Carsington agreed on the temporary enclosure of the 62 acres of their lower, stinted pasture, which was to be ploughed and put to tillage for seven years and laid open after each harvest. Every man agreed to lay at least 60 horse loads of well-burned limestone per acre within the first four years and at the last ploughing to ridge up his lands and 'leave the same evenly harrowed whereby to be better grass in future'.

Vernacular architecture

The timber-framed tradition continued well into the seventeenth century, both in towns such as Ashbourne, where the evidence is often hidden behind later brick or fake timber façades, and in the countryside. Cruck frames continued in use for the houses and cottages of husbandmen and labourers or as barns and other outbuildings, particularly on the coal-measure sandstones of north-east Derbyshire, where eight examples have provided dendro-dates between the 1550s and the 1630s. Houses built in other timber-framed styles can be found in the same district or scattered throughout the southern lowlands, including the small towns of Melbourne and Repton, but Maxwell Craven and Michael Stanley's survey of Derbyshire country houses does not include many substantial timber-framed buildings. Rare exceptions are the

Wakelyn Old Hall, Hilton. The exuberance of the timber framing is an unexpected sight in south Derbyshire, where houses of this period and quality are rare. It was probably built by William Wakelyn early in Queen Elizabeth's reign. The cross wings are projected a little, with slightly jettied gables around a central hall, with an off-centre entry. The brickwork of the ground floor dates from the eighteenth century. It declined in status in the late nineteenth and early twentieth centuries but was restored in the 1950s.

PHOTOGRAPH: CARNEGIE

fancifully decorated, sixteenth-century Wakelyn Old Hall at Hilton, a house at South Sitch, Idridgehay, which was renewed by George Mellor in 1621, and Mickleover Old Hall, built by Robert Crotchett, an officer in the parliamentary army, in 1648. Elsewhere in Derbyshire, timber-framed buildings catch the eye because they are unusual.

The stone, gabled halls, lit by mullioned and transomed windows, that were built by minor gentlemen and rich yeomen are often labelled 'Elizabethan', but in Derbyshire most of them were not erected until well into the seventeenth century. An early example at Aston-in-Peak was built by Thomas Balguy in 1578, according to a datestone in an elaborate cartouche on the front of the house. Another from 1611 is Hartington Hall, an H-shaped and gabled, stone-built house that now serves as a youth hostel. It was built by Thomas Bateman, whose grandfather had acquired the estate at the dissolution of the monasteries. In the mid-1620s Isaac Smith re-styled Padley Hall, Ripley, with a symmetrical south front of local ashlar sandstone and a stone slate roof. The three equal gables and the two-storeyed porch were given large mullioned-and-transomed windows and string courses in the modern style. But behind this fine exterior the timber-framed house that the family had lived in since at least 1565 remained intact. As in the West Riding of Yorkshire, it is common to find remnants of earlier timber-framed houses inside these stone-built halls and farmhouses, particularly in the roofs, where old timbers have been cut down to size and re-fitted.

Snitterton Hall, too, was re-fashioned in the 1630s with an up-to-date south front in local ashlar gritstone, but much of the older house was preserved. The builder was Col. John Milward, the second son of John Milward of Thorpe and Broadlow Ash. The new front consisted of a two-storeyed central block under an embattled parapet and balancing cross-wings with three-storeyed gables rising to ball finials. String courses and mullioned windows were arranged symmetrically, but a clue to the existence of an older house behind this façade is provided by the off-set entrance which, despite its Ionic columns, looks as

Snitterton Hall. The existence of an older building is hinted at by the off-centre entry that led into the former open hall. Like many former gentry houses, the hall declined in status in later times and from the middle of the eighteenth century it was tenanted as a farm. The hall was restored to its former glory in the twentieth century.

if it once led into a medieval great hall that was open to the rafters. The use of rubble limestone for the side and rear walls, out of sight of the main front, also suggests the incorporation of an earlier building.

Youlgreave Old Hall Farm, however, was built entirely anew in 1630 for a member of the Barnsley family, with fashionable gables and mullioned windows. The ground-floor windows have transoms also. Local coursed limestone was used for the walls, but the quoins, lintels, window dressings and roof are of millstone grit. The main block is only one room deep, with the living room (the 'house') separated from the kitchen by an axial chimney stack and the entrance. The wing contains a parlour, which served both as the best bedroom and a withdrawing room, and a rear buttery and staircase. All these rooms had chambers over them; the storage chamber above the kitchen was reached by an external stair. The L-shaped plan is typical of many of the houses that were erected by yeomen or minor gentry in the north midlands during the first half of the seventeenth century, but the use of local building stones gives Old Hall Farm a distinctive character.

The Peacock, Rowsley. Originally known as Rowsley Hall, this substantial gabled building with projecting central porch was built in 1652 for John Stevenson, yeoman: perhaps his wealth came largely from the lead trade? Several Stevensons or Stephensons were lead smelters in Brampton and Dore in the Elizabethan and Stuart period. The hall later became part of the Haddon estate and was converted into an inn with the Manners family peacock as its sign.

The Hallowes, Dronfield. A large, gabled hall with stringcourses, mullioned windows, and projecting wings, built of local sandstone, The Hallowes was built in 1657 for Andrew Morewood, a member of a leading family of lead smelters and merchants whose surname came from an upland farm just north of the county boundary and who spread into the Norton/Dronfield district. In 1933 The Hallowes became the club house of the local golf club.

Other north Derbyshire halls from the mid-seventeenth century include Rowsley Hall, now The Peacock Hotel (built for John Stevenson, yeoman, in 1652), The Hallowes, near Dronfield (erected by Andrew Morewood, lead smelter, in 1657) and Offerton Hall, high on the moors above Hope and Hathersage (the home of Robert Glossop, yeoman, in 1658). Further down the social scale, many a yeoman's farmhouse was rebuilt in the seventeenth century, with mullioned windows and perhaps a gable in a parlour wing that gave a house an L-shaped plan. They were a great improvement on their predecessors and were far better furnished. Probate inventories tell a story of gradual improvement in the standards of accommodation from the late Elizabethan period onwards. The earliest Dore and Totley inventories, for example, show that most farmhouses were sparsely furnished, simple structures with only one or two rooms that reached up to the rafters. The cooking was done over the fire in the 'house', for the kitchens that were occasionally recorded from 1595 onwards were small unheated rooms that were used simply for preparing food.

Offerton Hall. Standing on the edge of the moors high above the Hope valley, this typical Derbyshire yeoman's hall was built for Robert and Mary Glossop in 1658. In 1670 'Widdow Glossopp' was taxed on six hearths here. The use of local millstone grit and heavy roofing slates ensured that the house fitted perfectly into the landscape. It has projecting, gabled wings and the standard window arrangements of the time.

PHOTOGRAPH: AUTHOR

Farmhouses became more spacious in the seventeenth century, when the better-off farmers began to insert ceilings to provide extra rooms above, though most were furnished with little more than the basic items of tables, chairs, stools, beds and chests for storage. Refinements were rare.

The poor

The cottages of the poorest section of society were so meanly built and furnished that they do not survive. We are left with the strong impression that they consisted of just one or two rooms, framed with cruck blades and open to the rafters. We need not mourn their passing. As the national population grew, the late Elizabethan government was forced to deal with the problem of poverty by making each parish responsible for its own paupers. Under Acts of 1597 and 1601 unpaid overseers of the poor were elected at Easter vestry meetings and empowered to raise local rates to provide for the 'deserving poor'; begging was forbidden and was punished by whipping. Overseers' accounts do not survive for the early decades of this new system, but Derby had two houses of correction for rogues, one for the county and one for the borough, and a house of correction was built on the banks of the Hipper at Chesterfield in 1615 to serve Scarsdale and High Peak.

The Elizabethan Acts empowered parishes to set the poor at work. In 1624, for example, Chesterfield corporation agreed with John Steere of Lincoln, jerseyman, 'who in consideration of certain quarterly payments and the

Sacheverell Almshouses, Morley. This row of six almshouses, each containing two rooms, was founded by Jacinth Sacheverell, esquire, in 1656, to provide for three elderly people from Morley and three from Smalley.

PHOTOGRAPH: CARNEGIE

provision of coals, agrees to teach certain poor people in Chesterfield to work by spinning of jersey, knitting of stockings or such other works as the parties to the agreement should think most commodious for the benefit and relief of the poor people of Chesterfield'.

Public payments from the rates were supplemented by private donations in the poor box or at the house door and by bequests in wills. Wealthy individuals helped by founding almshouses for the elderly destitute. In 1550 the almshouse known as Etwall Hospital was founded by Sir John Port, the son of a wealthy judge, for six poor persons. In 1584 Anthony Gell endowed an almshouse for six aged people at Wirksworth, which his brother and heir Thomas Gell of Hopton built facing the churchyard. In 1597 Bess of Hardwick founded almshouses close to All Saints church, Derby, that were completed two years later for eight men and four women. In 1631 Richard Crowshawe, a native of Derby

About 1584 Anthony Gell founded this hospital, or group of almshouses, for six poor men, at the eastern end of the churchyard in Wirksworth. The adjacent grammar school, which he had founded in 1576, was rebuilt in 1828 in neo-Gothic style (*below*). Gell's alabaster effigy is in the north chapel of the parish church.

PHOTOGRAPH: CARNEGIE

Wirksworth Grammar School. The school was founded on the edge of the churchyard in 1576 by Anthony Gell. The original building was replaced in 1828 by this unusual but attractive structure that was topped with the sort of battlements and pinnacles that adorn medieval churches in the Perpendicular Gothic style, and lit by symmetrical windows with small panes and emphatic drip moulds above. The builder was a local mason, William Maskrey.

PHOTOGRAPH: CARNEGIE

who had prospered as a London goldsmith, left most of his considerable estate for the benefit of the poor of All Saints parish. And at Ashbourne, Owfield's almshouses were built between 1614 and 1630, facing Church Street.

Communications

An Act of 1555 ordered each parish or township to elect an annual overseer of the highways, who was charged with raising local taxes. Every able-bodied householder had to work on the highways four days a year (raised to six in 1563) under the overseer's supervision or to pay someone else to do the job. This system worked in a rough-and-ready way, though much of the heavier haulage was confined to the summer months. As we have seen, Derbyshire was connected to London by weekly carrying services and to the towns of the neighbouring counties. Wheeled vehicles were in common use, even in the uplands. Wains, for instance, were recorded in 43 of the 215 Chesterfield inventories that were appraised between 1521 and 1603, though only three sturdier carts were mentioned.

A government enquiry in 1577 recorded 18 inns, five taverns and 726 alehouses in Derbyshire. Of these, seven inns, two taverns and 61 alehouses were found in the county town. Buxton and Sudbury had two inns each, Chesterfield and Ashbourne one each, and the other five were scattered in

the countryside at Brailsford, Clowne, Mercaston, Morton and Mugginton. The vintners in charge of the taverns were found in Derby (2), Ashbourne, Chesterfield and Eckington. The lowly alehouses were most numerous in north Derbyshire, with 231 in Scarsdale wapentake and 110 in High Peak, compared with Wirksworth 110, Morleyston & Litchurch 92, Appletree 61, and Repton & Gresley 61.

The accounts of the steward of Haddon Hall for 1549–51 and 1564–65 record in detail the provisions that he obtained for Sir George Vernon's household. His sources of supply included local markets and fairs, urban shops, local families, and hawkers. When he needed wines and groceries, he or his men went to Chesterfield, ten laborious miles beyond the East Moor, or they travelled 15 miles in the opposite direction to Ashbourne. On his visits to Chesterfield the steward bought rye, veal, mustard, sugar, prunes, raisins, a gallon of claret wine, malt, hops, drinking cups, and 'all kinds of seafish'. Chesterfield had direct links with the inland port of Bawtry, but few places in the country were more landlocked than Ashbourne, where the steward was nevertheless able to purchase wines, vinegar, spices, raisins, prunes, pepper, sugar, cloves, mace and beef for Christmas pies. Exotic groceries from distant lands must have been available to anyone who could afford them, otherwise they would have been delivered directly to the great houses, as were the oysters, mussels, eels, pike, white herring and other fish that were consumed at Haddon. Derbyshire was not as cut off as might be supposed before the age of turnpike roads, canals and railways.

Yet most people did not move far from their place of birth, unless they were attracted by the chance of making their fortune in London. Though the parish boundary was no obstacle, movement was generally restricted to the district or 'country' that was bounded by the nearest market towns. In 1615 the 80 year-old John Land of Brassington testified that while he 'hath knowen the mannor of Wirkesworth threescore yeares … [he] doth not know the mannor of Ashburne, because he hath had little to do there'; Ashbourne is only six miles from Brassington. Giving evidence in 1640, some Wirksworth men referred to Derby, lying only 12 miles away, as a 'remote place'. Even the Peak District does not seem to have had a unity in people's minds, for it was divided into its lead fields. Only the travellers who entered or left the Peak District formed a clear idea of its identity, yet to us it appears to have been one of the most distinct 'countries' in the whole of Tudor and Stuart England.

Protestants and Catholics

During the brief reign of Edward VI (1547–53) the Protestant Reformation destroyed many of the altars, images, fittings and ornaments of Derbyshire's medieval churches, leaving them with a bare appearance. Then, after the five years of Mary's reign, during which England returned to the Catholic faith, the Protestant form of religion was enforced under Elizabeth. The wording of the wills of the second half of the sixteenth century omitted standard Catholic references to the Virgin Mary and the holy company in heaven in favour of Protestant formulae taken from books of advice on how to draw up a will. Most Derbyshire clergymen seem to have taken the Oath of Supremacy recognising the monarch as the head of the Church of England, though they did not rush to do so. Robert Pursglove, a native of Tideswell who had been prior of Guisborough, suffragan bishop of Hull and holder of other ecclesiastical benefices, declined to take the oath and retired to Tideswell.

Some Derbyshire gentry families were determined to remain Catholic, though perhaps with an outward show of conformity. The most unwavering of these was Sir Thomas Fitzherbert, lord of Norbury and husband of the daughter and heiress of Sir Arthur Eyre of Padley. For 30 years Fitzherbert was fined repeatedly until he had forfeited two-thirds of his family property. His brothers and sisters, along with members of their families, also suffered as recusants. The situation was exacerbated by the presence in Derbyshire of Mary, Queen of Scots, a Catholic who would have succeeded to the throne had Elizabeth died. Tension rose in 1586, when Anthony Babington, the young squire of Dethick, led a failed plot to murder Elizabeth. No-one in Derbyshire joined the rebellion and he was put to death in a gruesome manner; Mary was executed the following year.

In 1588, the year of the Spanish Armada, the Protestant hierarchy were nervous about possible Catholic support for the invasion. On 28 July George Talbot, sixth Earl of Shrewsbury, wrote to John Manners requesting him 'to cause a general watch to be kept day and night … near Chapel-en-le-Frith, Glossop Dale, and the Woodlands, and to apprehend all vagrants or rogues'. The persecution of seminary and Jesuit priests in Derbyshire had already begun and on 12 July George Talbot and his armed retainers had made a surprise visit to Padley Manor, where he found not only Sir Thomas Fitzherbert, his son Anthony, and three daughters, but the two Catholic priests, Nicholas Garlick and Robert Ludlam. All the men were consigned to Derby gaol. Nicholas Garlick had been born in Glossop parish and had been the master of the school that Pursglove had endowed, before training for the priesthood at the English College in Rheims. He was deported from England in 1583 but had returned, thus risking the death penalty. Robert Ludlam had been born at Radbourne and had been ordained priest at Rheims in 1581. They were joined in Derby gaol by Richard Simpson, another foreign-trained priest, who had been arrested in the Peak District towards the end of 1587. On 24 July 1588 all three were hanged,

The medieval manor house at Padley, in a remote part of the parish of Hathersage, passed through marriage from the Eyres to the Fitzherberts of Norbury, a leading Derbyshire Catholic family. In the summer of 1588, at the height of fears about a Spanish invasion, the Earl of Shrewsbury lead a party of armed men to Padley, where they found the Fitzherbert family and two Catholic priests. The priests were arrested and then hanged, drawn and quartered at Derby. In 1933 this south range of the medieval hall was converted into a Catholic chapel in memory of the martyrs. The original chapel was above the main entrance and the ground-floor offices.

PHOTOGRAPH: AUTHOR

Above the arch leading into the tower at St Lawrence's church, Eyam (formerly dedicated to St Helen), is the medieval image of a skeleton, perhaps part of a scene depicting the Dance of Death. During the reign of Queen Elizabeth I a new scheme displayed the emblems of the twelve tribes of Israel, two of which are seen here in mutilated form. This series was modified and repainted, either in Elizabeth's reign or in the early seventeenth century; then in 1645, when the Puritans were in control, all the images were replaced by the Creed and the Lords' Prayer within elaborate frames. Subsequently, all this work was hidden under a coat of plaster until part of it was re-discovered in 1868, when the galleries were removed. In 1963 the Elizabethan scheme was restored.

drawn and quartered, together with a condemned murderess whom they had converted the night before. Long after Armada year, many of the inhabitants of the High Peak parishes of Hathersage and Tideswell, led by their gentry families, remained faithful to the Catholic cause.

Protestantism was often the driving force behind the foundation or rebuilding of grammar schools during the sixteenth and early seventeenth centuries: at Derby (1554), Repton (1557), Tideswell (1560), Duffield (1565), Hartshorne (c.1575), Dronfield (1579), Wirksworth (1584), Ashbourne (1585), Staveley (1586), Risley (1593) and Chesterfield (1598). Schools that were founded in the seventeenth century include Hayfield (1604), Fernilee (1629), Ashford (1631), Bakewell (1636), Shirland (1637), Buxton (1647), Matlock (1647), Norton (1654) and Spondon (1657).

Although some of the early lecturers at Chesterfield church were Puritans, Derbyshire was infertile ground for those who wished to speed the changes initiated by the Reformation. On the whole, the county's parish priests were not well educated, nor were they well paid. A parliamentary commission in 1650 reported that only 13 of the 112 benefices in Derbyshire were worth more than £90 a year; at the other end of the scale 66 were worth less than £50 and six less than £10; and most of the curates of parochial chapelries earned less than

Repton School was founded in 1557 as a grammar school by Sir John Port of Etwall on the site of the dissolved Augustinian priory. During the sixteenth and seventeenth centuries former priory buildings such as these were converted and much rebuilt. In the nineteenth century Repton became a well-known public school for boys. It is now co-educational.

PHOTOGRAPH: CARNEGIE

Hopton Hall ridge-and-furrow. The house that the Gells built from the seventeenth century onwards has an uninterrupted view across a park to the south. As with many of Derbyshire's country houses, this is because of the removal of tenants' houses and the abandonment of the old, communal methods of farming.
The ridge-and-furrow patterns of the former open fields of Hopton can still be seen in the foreground.

PHOTOGRAPH: AUTHOR

£10. Only 41 per cent of the Derbyshire clergy earned the minimum stipend that was recommended by the House of Commons and many served more than one parish in order to make ends meet. George Fox, the Leicestershire-born founder of the Society of Friends, was an itinerant preacher in Derbyshire between 1647 and 1650. The Quakers, as they soon became known, gained converts in eastern parts of Derbyshire between Chesterfield and Derby and in various lead mining communities in the Low Peak. Otherwise, Derbyshire (unlike Yorkshire and Nottinghamshire) offers little evidence for religious dissent before the Civil War.

Civil War

Though William Cavendish, Earl of Newcastle, had been put in charge of royalist forces in the North at the start of the Civil War in the summer of 1642, the gentry of Derbyshire were at first overwhelmingly neutral. Few of them rallied to the Crown when Charles I raised his standard at Nottingham. The turning point came early in December 1642, when Sir John Gell, the head of a new gentry family at Hopton Hall, garrisoned Derby with at least 700 men on behalf of Parliament. He gained the enthusiastic support of the Derby burgesses, enforced his will by stern discipline, and remained Governor of Derby until he was deprived of his office because of many complaints, once the king surrendered in 1646. His troops earned an unsavoury reputation for plundering the homes of royalist supporters, such as the Stanhopes of Bretby and the Sacheverells of Morley. These were years of misery for many, when houses and churches were vandalised, horses, food and bedding were confiscated, troops were billeted upon householders without payment, rents and bills were unpaid, trade was disrupted, and heavy taxes were levied.

The nobility supported the royalist cause, though the Lord-Lieutenant, the Earl of Rutland, was a lukewarm parliamentarian. Trevor Brighton has calculated that two-thirds of the Derbyshire gentry were royalist in varying degrees, though families such as the Eyres, Leakes, Pegges and Revells were divided amongst themselves. Most of the merchants and lawyers supported Parliament, as did the great majority of the lead miners. Derbyshire saw numerous skirmishes and sudden attacks on halls and manor houses, but the major battles of the Civil War were fought beyond the county's borders. Two of the major casualties at the end of hostilities were Wingfield Manor, part of whose curtain walls was blown up by gunpowder, and Eastwood Hall, Ashover, both of which had been fortified by royalists during the war. The leading royalist families had their estates sequestered. In most cases, these were returned upon payment of a heavy fine, but a few men, notably the Earl of Newcastle at Bolsover, the Earl of Chesterfield at Bretby, Sir Andrew Kniveton of Bradley and Rowland Eyre of Hassop, forfeited their possessions until the restoration of Charles II in 1660. A much more serious consequence was the loss of life. Brian Stone has estimated that some 1,500 soldiers from Derbyshire were killed in action.

The period between the Reformation and the Civil War saw the emergence of the Cavendish family as the dominant landowners in Derbyshire, with magnificent houses at Chatsworth, Hardwick and Bolsover and huge estates in the northern half of the county. It was a time when towns began to grow again and the countryside slowly took on a new appearance with the enclosure of many of the old open fields and commons. In High Peak and Scarsdale wapentakes the mining and smelting of lead enabled some families to amass new wealth, much of which went into rebuilding their houses, but it also produced populous villages full of poor workers. In the White Peak, in particular, the contrast between the rich and the poor was marked more sharply that it had been in the late Middle Ages.

From the Restoration to the Industrial Revolution, 1660—1760

CHAPTER EIGHT

Population

Derbyshire was still thinly populated when Charles II was restored to the throne in 1660. When the hearth tax was first levied in 1662 Derbyshire was ranked 30th of the English counties in terms of the total number of hearths that were assessed. Nevertheless, its population was growing and by 1700 had reached about 114,000, nearly half of whom lived in the north Derbyshire wapentakes of High Peak and Scarsdale, where lead mining and industrial crafts offered employment alongside work on a farm or for those with no land. The large numbers of seventeenth-century halls that survive in the villages and countryside in the northern half of Derbyshire demonstrate the rising wealth of enterprising men in contrast to the high numbers of poor people who were exempted from paying the hearth tax in lead-mining villages such as Eyam, Great and Little Hucklow, Sheldon, Stoney Middleton and Tideswell in the High Peak, at Aldwark, Brassington, Carsington, Cromford, Hopton and Middleton in the Low Peak, and at Clowne, Coal Aston, Dronfield, Hasland and Killamarsh in Scarsdale. Most of the purely agricultural villages in the wapentakes of Appletree and Repton & Gresley, in the south of the county, had smaller populations.

Plague erupted for the last time in 1665—66 before disappearing as suddenly and mysteriously as it had arrived in 1348—39. When it appeared in Derby in 1665, the better-off moved quickly away and the farmers and traders avoided the market place. Instead, a 'Headless Cross', consisting of four steps and a stone cover, was erected as a trading point a little way out of town at the top of Nuns Green. Those offering goods for sale stood at a distance chewing tobacco in an attempt to ward off infection, while buyers put their money in a vessel filled with vinegar.

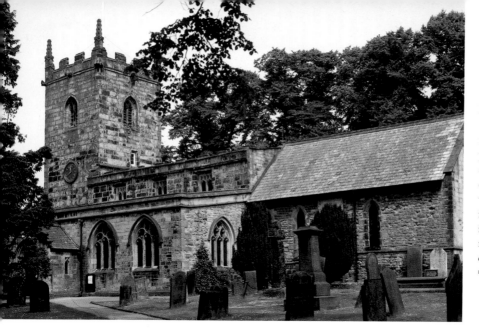

St Lawrence's church, Eyam. When plague broke out in Eyam in 1665, services in the medieval parish church were abandoned for fear of infection. They were held instead in an open space in Cucklet Delf, a former quarry south of the village street.

PHOTOGRAPH: AUTHOR

Derbyshire's most famous sundial is placed over the priest's door on the south wall of the chancel of St Lawrence's church at Eyam. It was made in 1775 by a local mason, William Shore, and was designed by a Mr Duffin. A Latin inscription urges the reader to cultivate an enquiring mind; another comments that life passes like the shadow on the dial. This shadow indicates local time, and noon time at various named places around the world. It also indicates the month and the sign of the zodiac. The two churchwardens in 1775 are named as William Lee and Thomas Froggat.

PHOTOGRAPH: CARNEGIE

Plague arrived at Eyam at the end of summer in 1665 at a cottage close to the churchyard, where George Viccars, a travelling tailor, had asked Mary Hadfield for lodging while he sold clothes in the village. On the morning of 2 September he woke with a malignant fever, screaming with pain and vomiting blood. The Revd William Mompesson, who had seen the signs of plague before, immediately recognised the angry haemorrhagic spots on the tailor's chest. He took the funeral service on 7 September. This account of the arrival of plague is typical of stories told in other parts of England, where an epidemic began with the arrival of a stranger or with the return of a resident from a plague-infested place. On 17 September Mary's three-year-old son, Edward succumbed to the disease, followed by near neighbours of the Hadfields, then Mary's elder son, Jonathan, died. From the meticulous record of plague deaths in the parish register and from Sue Scott and Christopher Duncan's studies here and elsewhere, it is clear that for the first ten days the victim was not infectious, then for the next three weeks or so, during which no outward signs of the disease were displayed, the infection could be spread unwittingly. When the unmistakable signs finally appeared, most victims died five agonising days later. The entire process was drawn out over 38 days between infection and death, a delay that explains why the plague was such an effective killer. It is now known that this 'pestilence' was not bubonic plague transmitted by fleas carried on the backs of black rats, which is what we believed for most of the twentieth century, but a different, unidentified disease caused by a virus that was spread directly from one person to another by droplet infection. Amazingly, Mary Hadfield survived. So did Elizabeth Hancocke, who buried her husband and six

Mompesson's Well, Eyam. This well on the northern parish boundary of Eyam, high above the village, is said to have been used as an exchange point during the visitation of the plague. According to the story that was handed down by the villagers over the generations, essential items brought by outsiders were left for collection and the people of Eyam paid for them with coins deposited in the well so as to reduce the risk of infection. The well was named after the Revd William Mompesson, who led the villagers' battle for survival. It is now difficult to separate the undoubted horrors of a dreadful visitation of the plague, as recorded in the parish register, from the romantic tales that were published by William Wood in 1842.

PHOTOGRAPH: AUTHOR

children, and the gravedigger, Marshall Howe, who contracted the disease but recovered. Presumably, they had inherited a genetic resistance from previous outbreaks, perhaps as far back as the Black Death of 1349.

Under the leadership of the Revd William Mompesson and the Nonconformist minister, the Revd Thomas Stanley, the infection was contained within the community by the decision of the villagers to stay within their parish boundaries when the disease took hold. Some of the wealthier families, such as the Bradshaws, moved away early, but most villagers had little or no choice. Contemporary hearth tax returns show that most of Eyam's householders had just one hearth and that many were too poor to pay the tax. Even if they had somewhere to go, they would have faced hostility. The constable of Sheffield ordered the erection of a sentry box at the southern edge of the town, specifically to keep watch for anyone coming from Eyam.

The number of plague victims fell during the winter months but rose rapidly in the spring and summer of 1666. No fewer than 78 died in the month of August. In all, 260 of the 1,200 or so parishioners died during the 14 months of the epidemic before the disease disappeared as winter drew near. One of the last victims was Catherine Mompesson, the rector's wife, whose tombstone stands in the churchyard near the ancient Mercian cross. Graham Ullathorne has calculated that people with 61 different family names were affected by the Eyam plague, but that none of the core surnames with a long history in the parish was wiped out. The epidemic at Eyam was the last outbreak in England of a viral disease that had been endemic for over three centuries.

Towns

In 1662 Derby was the 40th largest town in England judging by the 1,479 hearths in its houses. Derbyshire's other market towns were modest in size. Chesterfield had a total of 685 hearths, Wirksworth 382, Ashbourne 358 and Bakewell 224, but some of these figures include houses in the surrounding countryside. The populations of the smaller towns were not much bigger than those of some rural townships: the scattered settlements of the parish of Eckington, for example, contained 214 hearths.

The War Office Returns of 1686, which recorded the country's available guest beds and spare stabling facilities, show that Derby had an exceptionally high number of 841 guest beds and 547 spaces in its stables; just over a third of the available guest beds in the whole of Derbyshire were to be found in the county town. Derby was important not only as the county capital and a thriving regional market centre but as a great thoroughfare town on the highway from London to Manchester and to the heart of the West Riding. Ashbourne, which came second in the list, was the natural stopping point beyond Derby, where travellers could refresh themselves before tackling the weary journey across the Peak District to Manchester or into Staffordshire. It had long been a natural market centre where the great Midland Plain met the White Peak. Chesterfield was the natural centre for north-east Derbyshire and Wirksworth and Bakewell had almost as many stables as Ashbourne, but significantly fewer guest beds as they were not on major through routes. Between them, Derbyshire's five leading towns had just over half of Derbyshire's guest beds and 40 per cent of its stables. The next group of towns – Buxton, Tideswell, Alfreton, Crich and Chapel-en-le-Frith – stood out amongst the smaller market centres.

Derby's outstanding building was the Shire Hall, which had been built in 1659–60 in St Mary's Gate. In 1693 the borough had 694 houses, 120 alehouses and 70 malthouses, which supplied places far and wide. On her visit to Derby five years later Celia Fiennes noted that the houses were 'built all of brick or for the most part'. She admired All Saints church and its Devonshire monuments, and Sorocold's waterworks and the shops, though she complained that 'this is a dear place for strangers'. She also noted that great quantities of gloves were made there. George Sorocold, who had settled in Derby in 1684, was one of England's most talented mechanical engineers. In 1692 he designed a waterwheel which could be adjusted to the changing level of the river Derwent. This pumped water from just south of St Mary's bridge chapel to a cistern in St Michael's churchyard, from where a complicated system of about four miles of pipes bored out of elm led to a stone conduit in the Market Place and to private customers in nearby houses. The system remained in use until 1841 and was so successful that Sorocold was invited to install water supply systems in other towns, including Leeds, Norwich, Portsmouth, Bristol and Sheffield, and to construct Liverpool Dock. The machinery that he designed and built for Thomas Cotchett's first silk-throwing mill (1702) and for Sir

Thomas Lombe's later mill (1718–20) established his reputation as the leading mechanical engineer of his time.

Derby was about to become a fine Georgian town. In the second decade of the eighteenth century William Woolley of Marston-on-Dove wrote that Derby was 'a very large, populous, rich and well-frequented borough town' with 'many very good houses, especially on all parts of the outside of the town, mostly of brick'. He estimated the population at about 4,000 and thought that few inland towns in the kingdom were its equal and that it contained many persons of good quality with a great number of coaches. Friday and Wednesday markets and six annual fairs a year were held in the handsome market place. He described the principal trade as:

> that of malting, with which they supply a great part of Cheshire, Staffordshire and Lancashire, by which many good estates have been raised. As also the bakers' trade, which from this town supplies most of the Peak country with bread made of hard corn, they having not much but oats amongst themselves. The town is also very famous for very good ale, which the brewers send to London and other parts, to good advantage. It is also a thoroughfare or rather, storehouse for lead; to which place it is brought on horses from Wirksworth and other smelting mills; and from Derby carried in carts and wagons to Wilne Ferry, five miles distant: where it is embarked in barges and carried down Trent to

'a very large, populous, rich and well-frequented borough town … [with] many very good houses, especially on all parts of the outside of the town, mostly of brick.'

WILLIAM WOOLLEY ON DERBY

BELOW RIGHT
Silk winding
machine, Derby
Silk Mill Museum.
Derby led the way
in the mechanised
silk trade from the
1720s. Women and
children worked in
the spinning mills,
while the men
worked at home at
their looms. By 1789
Derby had 12 silk
spinning mills, which
together employed
1,200 people, but
the trade declined
in the Victorian
period. Other silk
mills were erected
between 1732 and
1760 at Stockport,
Macclesfield,
Congleton, Leek and
Sheffield.
PHOTOGRAPH BY CARNEGIE,
WITH PERMISSION OF DERBY
MUSEUMS AND ART GALLERY

Gainsborough and Hull to be shipped for London and other parts, and parts beyond the seas.

He added that a considerable number of framework knitters worked in Derby and its neighbourhood and that the town had 'a very large district of excellent good arable, pasture and meadow lands belonging to it, all round'.

About the same time, Daniel Defoe described Derby as 'a fine, beautiful and pleasant town; it has more families of gentlemen in it than is usual in towns so remote, and therefore here is a great deal of good and some gay company.' In his view it was 'a town of gentry, rather than trade … yet it is populous, well built, has five parishes, a large market-place, a fine town-house, and very

handsome streets'. He thought that some of the Derbyshire gentry preferred to reside here rather than on their estates in the inhospitable Peak. He too praised Sorocold's water works and the silk mill.

The Derby silk mill was the wonder of its age and the prototype for Richard Arkwright's cotton mills at Cromford later in the century. The first mill was built in 1702 on the banks of the river Derwent by Thomas Cotchett, but the mill that achieved national fame was its successor that was erected on the same site between 1718 and 1722, when John and Thomas Lombe introduced Italian technology to throw silk on machines driven by water power. George Sorocold was the engineer in charge of both projects. At the same time, in 1720, an Act of Parliament was obtained to make the river Derwent navigable between Derby and the river Trent; an old idea had at long last come to fruition.

In 1697 Celia Fiennes entered Chesterfield from the north, past the coal pits and quarries, and found the town was 'all built of stone'. She thought that Chesterfield 'looks well, the Streets good the Market very large; it was Saturday which is their market day and there was a great Market like some little faire, a great deale of corne and all sorts of ware and fowles ... in this town is the best ale in the kingdom generally esteemed.' Two or three decades later, Defoe described Chesterfield as 'a handsome populous town, well built and well inhabited'. Neither of them commented on the church spire, which presumably was not then crooked.

Defoe found that Wirksworth too was 'a large well-frequented market town ... well supplied, and the provisions extraordinary good; not forgetting the

'A large well-frequented market town ... well supplied, and the provisions extraordinary good; not forgetting the ale.'

DEFOE ON WIRKSWORTH

ale.' He was told that people travelled 12 or 15 miles to the town on market day. At a court held on 15 May 1693 at the Three Swans, Wirksworth, the local constable presented a return listing three innkeepers, 37 alehouse keepers, six grocers, four ironmongers, two apothecaries, six blacksmiths, two bakers, two chandlers, nine tailors, three weavers, five swailers, six butchers, two millers, two shearmen, two dyers, a pedlar, three 'softmunglers', five 'applemunglers', and two feltmakers. The great growth of the lead trade had made Wirksworth populous. In 1673 Richard Blome had observed that Wirksworth had 'the greatest Lead-market in England', and in 1712–15 Woolley claimed that the town was 'rich by reason of its mines as trade, and well inhabited and has many good houses in it' and that the Tuesday market was 'very considerable, as great as most fairs – it being the only lead market in this county, as also for oatmeal and bread, which last is brought from Derby, whose bakers have found it a beneficial trade thither'. From Wirksworth, lead was taken by road to Derby and Wilne Ferry or across the moors and on to Bawtry. One of the wealthiest Wirksworth lead merchants was Francis Bunting, whose personal estate in 1695 was valued at £16,423. He had shipped 876 fothers of lead via Hull in 1672 and 917 fothers in 1680.

Celia Fiennes thought that Ashbourne was 'a pretty neate market town' and Woolley's opinion was that it was 'now an extraordinary good market town and much improved in buildings, which makes it well inhabited by gentry as well as good traders. Its fairs are many and famous for horses etc.' Bakewell was another 'pretty neate market town' when Celia Fiennes visited it. A generation earlier, in the autumn of 1662, Edward Browne had found that, 'Their houses are most of them built without mortar, stones heaped upon stones make a substantial wall and by their own weight keep strong and fast. They cover their houses with a slate from local hills. The buildings are low and seem natural rather than artificial.' When the Manners family withdrew from nearby Haddon Hall, Bakewell became a rural backwater, characterised more by small farms and alehouses than town houses. On market day, pigs were sold at the foot of North Church Street, horses near the town bridge, sheep and cows in front of the White Horse Inn (now the site of the Rutland Arms) and corn, butter, cheese, eggs and poultry were offered for sale within and around the Market Hall in Bridge Street.

The social pull of the larger towns was dependent on facilities such as assembly rooms and horse racing. The racecourse on Whittington Moor, Chesterfield, staged a three-day event from 1727, Bakewell races started the following year, those at Ashbourne and Wirksworth in 1732 and those on Sinfin Moor, Derby in 1733. The smaller towns were more workaday. A census of Melbourne and its hamlet of King's Newton taken in 1695 named 20 farmers or landowners, 44 labourers and 54 men who were employed in 29 different trades or crafts. But even the smaller towns were improving in appearance. Woolley thought that Duffield, for instance, had 'several very good houses and inhabitants'.

In the late seventeenth century a new type of town grew up when the fashion for visiting spas in the hope of improved health spread from the Low Countries and Germany. People had been taking the waters at Buxton since Roman times and in the 1670s the third Earl of Devonshire (whose family had purchased the manor of Buxton in 1663) had remodelled the Old Hall and baths after a fire; further improvements to the baths were made in 1695–96, but Celia Fiennes was not impressed on a visit soon afterwards. In 1710 the second Duke commissioned John Barker of Rowsley to remodel the baths and in the 1720s the south façade of the present hotel was built. The well-to-do stayed there, but most visitors to the spa found accommodation in the inns and lodging-houses in Higher Buxton, adjoining the Market Place, such as the White Hart, the Eagle and Child or the King's Head. Defoe reported that 'The Duke of Devonshire is lord of the village, and consequently of the bath itself; and his grace has built a large handsome house at the bath, where there is convenient lodging, and very good provisions.' Buxton's great days as a spa town still lay well ahead.

LEFT
Now in Derby Silk Mill Museum, this loom was originally worked in the Hanging Bridge Mills on the river Dove at Ashbourne, owned by Bowner-Bond Narrow Fabrics Ltd. Bond's began making tape at Alrewas in 1795 and moved to Ashbourne in 1866. Wirksworth was another centre of the tape and narrow fabrics trade.
PHOTOGRAPH BY CARNEGIE, WITH PERMISSION OF DERBY MUSEUMS AND ART GALLERY

The Elizabethan Old Hall in Buxton, in which Mary, Queen of Scots had stayed in 1573, during her captivity under the supervision of George Talbot, sixth Earl of Shrewsbury, was replaced by the present hotel in 1670, with later additions in the classical style. Part of the Crescent, designed by John Carr and built during the 1780s, is seen in the background.
PHOTOGRAPH: CARNEGIE

The warm springs at Matlock Bath had long been known before a public bath was opened about 1698. Woolley remarked on the 'tolerable conveniences of lodging' and provided an early description of 'a most delicate landscape ... very steep, high cliffs over against one of which, in a very romantic situation, runs into Derwent several silver springs'. But Defoe's reaction was grumpy: 'This bath would be much more frequented than it is, if two things did not hinder; namely, a base, stony, mountainous road to it, and no good accommodation when you are there ... the bath is milk or rather blood warm, very pleasant to go into, and very sanative, especially for rheumatick pains, bruises, etc.' Soon after his visit, two Nottingham men, Smith and Pennell, bought the lease, blasted the approach road through the Scarthin rocks at Cromford and improved the amenities. The New Bath was soon opened near the old one and by the middle of the eighteenth century visitors were penning enthusiastic reports on the beauties of the place and the excellence of the facilities.

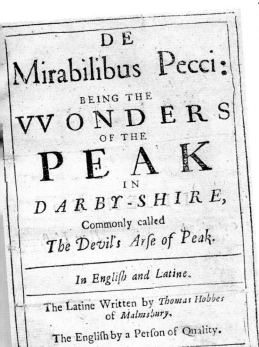

Increasing numbers of visitors came in search of the Wonders of the Peak. William Camden, the great Elizabethan antiquarian, had been the first to write about them, but the full list of seven – Chatsworth House and the natural wonders of Eldon Hole, Peak Cavern, St Anne's Well at Buxton, Poole's Cavern, Mam Tor and the ebbing and flowing well at Tideswell – was established by Thomas Hobbes's *De Mirabilibus Peci* (c.1636) and Charles Cotton's *Wonders of the Peak* (1682). Daniel Defoe refused to be impressed, except with Eldon Hole and Chatsworth, but the search for wonders helped to turn the Peak District into an early tourist attraction.

Religion and politcs

The Derbyshire returns to the Compton ecclesiastical census of England in 1676 are incomplete,

'Matlock Bath from Lovers Lane' by Thomas Smith, 1743. The commercial exploitation of Matlock's warm springs began in 1698 with a small bath below Masson Hill. In 1727 two Nottingham men, Smith and Pennell, greatly improved the Old Bath by providing private rooms and a large assembly room, and by improving the route from Matlock Bridge, including the blasting a way through Scarthin rocks. A second hotel, the New Bath, was soon opened. Visitors in 1755 found 'agreeable landscapes, fine woods, pleasant walks, high rocks, steep hills, and romantic views; which, together with the constant rolling of the Darwent Streams, render it a perfect Paradise'. Thomas Smith, the artist, was a celebrated landscape painter who was known as 'Smith of Derby'. His eight views of scenes in Derbyshire and Staffordshire around 1743 were influential in promoting the idea that precipices and cascades in the countryside were sublime.

but they nevertheless numbered 51,077 communicants over the age of 14, of whom 97 per cent conformed to the Church of England, 928 (1.8 per cent) were Protestant Dissenters, otherwise known as Nonconformists, and 596 (1 per cent) were Catholics. The late seventeenth century and most of the eighteenth was a quiet period for the Anglican church, when little attempt was made to evangelise and few new buildings were erected. The grand exception was All Saints church (now Derby Cathedral), whose nave and chancel were entirely rebuilt in 1723–25 by Francis and William Smith of Warwick to the designs of James Gibbs, and whose superb wrought-iron chancel screen was created by the local smith, Robert Bakewell. Two other Georgian churches of note are St Mary, Mapleton, a small building with a west tower crowned by an octagonal dome and lantern, and St Martin, Stoney Middleton, which has an unusual octagonal nave and lantern, erected in 1759. The best surviving interior is that at Beauchief, where about 1662 Samuel Pegge converted the space under the tower into a chapel that still has its box pews, communion table and three-decker pulpit, untouched by Victorian refurnishing. Also of note is William Woolley's report in 1712–15 that Ashbourne church had 'lately got a pair of organs, being I think the only church in the county that has them'.

Derbyshire's Catholics were mostly concentrated in a few rural parishes where the leading gentry remained faithful to the old form of religion and kept a succession of Jesuit priests; at Norbury (Fitzherberts), West Hallam (Powtrells) and Hathersage and Hassop (Eyres). In the more tolerant times after the 'Glorious Revolution' of 1688, a new Catholic chapel was built at North Lees, Hathersage, the medieval chapel at Newbold was restored and private chapels at Hassop and Wingerworth were opened to the tenants of the Eyres and Hunlokes, respectively. The Derbyshire 'papist returns' of 1705–06 show that Catholicism was still overwhelmingly rural and concentrated in a few parishes: Ashbourne, Barlborough, Dronfield, Eckington, Hathersage, Norbury, Tideswell, West Hallam and Wingerworth. Most Derbyshire parishes had no Catholics.

Protestant Dissenters were spread thinly in 1676, with only two parishes having significant numbers: 19 per cent at Shirland (mostly Quakers) and 16 per cent at Brailsford. Derbyshire did not have the Dissenting strongholds of counties such as the West Riding of Yorkshire. However, within a year of the 1689 Toleration Act, 252 Nonconformist preachers were licensed at the quarter sessions. The most famous of these was William Bagshawe of Ford, the celebrated 'Apostle of the Peak', the eldest surviving son of William Bagshawe, a wealthy lead trader of Great Hucklow, Litton and Ford Hall. Bagshawe's ministry since his refusal to conform in 1662 had covered much of the north-western part of the Peak District and he had founded Presbyterian congregations at Ashford, Bradwell, Charlesworth, Chelmorton, Great Hucklow, Malcoff, Stoney Middleton and elsewhere. He was succeeded at Malcoff by James Clegg, a young preacher and doctor from Lancashire, under whose ministry

St Martin's church, Stoney Middleton. The tower is of the late medieval Perpendicular Gothic style, familiar in many parts of Derbyshire, but the design of the rest of the church is unique. It dates from 1759, when the Revd John Simpson of Stoke Hall was minister, and it was built by a local mason, William Booth. The new church is octagonal and rises to a lantern storey lit by semicircular windows, The lower windows are circular. Sir Nikolaus Pevsner's judgement was, '... a rarity, if not a visually very satisfying one'.
PHOTOGRAPH: AUTHOR

'Matlock Church' by Joseph Farington, R.A., 1817. Farington was a leading illustrator of county histories, who made several visits to the Peak District between 1776 and 1817. St Giles's church retains its Perpendicular tower but was otherwise rebuilt in Victorian times.

Chinley Chapel was built in 1711. In the years of toleration, Elder Yard Chapel, Chesterfield, was opened in 1694 for the Presbyterians (from 1818 Unitarians) at the expense of Cornelius Clarke of Norton, and about four years later Derby got a handsome Presbyterian chapel in Friar Gate (which was demolished in 1974). Meanwhile, Quaker monthly meetings were held for Scarsdale at Chesterfield, for High Peak at Slack Hall, near Chapel-en-le-Frith, the home of the Lingards, for Wirksworth and Appletree at Monyash, and for south Derbyshire at Breach (Caldwell). The most active and celebrated Friend in this period was John Gratton of Bakewell. The Quakers thrived in the years of persecution, but they became respectable after the Toleration Act, lost their zeal and declined in numbers towards the mid-eighteenth century.

The first stirrings of Methodism in Derbyshire occurred when John Wesley preached at Ashbourne and Hayfield in 1755. The Methodists had early links with the Moravians, the followers of Count Zinzendorf in Germany, whose views were based on those of the fifteenth-century martyr, Jan Hus. In 1740 the Revd John Toltschig formed a small Moravian society at Ockbrook, where a congregation was formally founded in

LEFT
This wall monument in the north aisle of Derby Cathedral commemorates Richard Crowshawe of London, esquire, who died in 1671. A local man who became Master of the London Goldsmiths' Company, he was buried in London but was commemorated in Derby because he had 'done much good to this towne and this his native countrye' through his generous charity.

PHOTOGRAPH: CARNEGIE

The modern nave of All Saints, Derby, was designed by James Gibbs and built by William and Francis Smith of Warwick. Gibbs wrote that, 'The plainness of the Building makes it less expensive and renders it more suitable to the old steeple' (which was preserved). The nave is deliberately low, with just one storey of windows. The Tuscan columns which divide the nave from its aisles were placed on tall pedestals to allow for box pews. The present colour scheme dates from 1972. The wrought-iron screen between the nave and the chancel was designed by Gibbs and made by Robert Bakewell, Derby's famous blacksmith. The central parts are original and the rest has been faithfully restored.

The mayor's pew at Derby is adorned with decorated ironwork, also by Robert Bakewell. It incorporates a painted represen-tation of the city badge (a stag enclosed by park palings).

Chinley Chapel. James Clegg, Nonconformist minister and medical practitioner, noted in his diary: 'Our new place was finished in the year 1711 and at first multitudes flocked to it and I hope some good was done.' Chinley Chapel served the scattered farms and hamlets of the High Peak around Chapel-en-le-Frith. A flourishing Dissenting congregation had been established in these parts during the late seventeenth century by William Bagshawe, known as the Apostle of the Peak. The chapel is the finest early Nonconformist building in Derbyshire and its original interior fittings remain complete.

PHOTOGRAPH: CARNEGIE

1750 under the leadership of the Revd John Ockershausen and a chapel was consecrated two years later. In 1757 work began on the building of separate houses for single brethren and sisters, followed by buildings for married couples and separate schools for boys and girls, who were taught by the two pastors. This unusual, brick-built settlement, comparable with that at Fulneck in the West Riding, survives on the edge of the village. The original brethren worked as farmers, shoemakers and framework knitters and the sisters were employed in needlework and embroidery. The burial ground behind the chapel records names on flat slate tablets.

Religion and politics intertwined in the 'Glorious Revolution' of 1688, when the Catholic king, James II, was replaced by the Protestant Dutchman, William of Orange, and his wife, Mary, James's daughter. The revolution was plotted in Derbyshire in the summer of 1688 by three local grandees: William Cavendish, fourth Earl of Devonshire, Sir Thomas Osborne, Earl of Danby, and his Yorkshire neighbour John D'Arcy, the grandson of the first Earl of Holderness. They met on Whittington Moor at a convenient point between Chatsworth, Kiveton and Aston Hall, but rain forced them to shelter in the Cock and Pynot at the junction of the Dronfield and Eckington roads in Whittington, now the Revolution House museum. They planned that, when William of Orange landed, Osborne's men would seize York and Cavendish would take control of Nottingham and Derby. These places were indeed secured but the prevailing wind caused William to divert to Torbay. No battle was fought in England (though the victory at the Battle of the Boyne is still celebrated by the Protestant Orangemen of Ulster), but the triumph of Protestantism and parliamentary democracy became known as the 'Glorious Revolution' and the plotters were rewarded handsomely with new titles. In Derbyshire, Cavendish was supported by John Manners of Haddon and Robert Leake, the third Earl

Moravian chapel, Ockbrook. The chapel that was consecrated in 1752 by Bishop Peter Boehler was the centrepiece of the Moravian settlement on the edge of the village of Ockbrook in south Derbyshire. It still has a thriving congregation.

A house for the minister was built behind the chapel in the same year. The members of the settlement led a communal life and tried to be self-sufficient, but were ultimately forced to take jobs outside. Many of the houses in the settlement are still occupied by Moravians, but the school that was built in 1822 closed in 1915 and the present school on the same site is independent.

PHOTOGRAPHS: CARNEGIE

of Scarsdale, and by Philip, second Earl of Chesterfield at Bretby, William Sacheverell of Morley and John Coke of Melbourne.

When Queen Anne died in 1714 and the throne was offered to the Protestant ruler of Hanover, George I, the Jacobite rebellion in favour of the Catholic James Stuart received little active support in Derbyshire. Nor did the 1745 rebellion led by James's son, 'Bonnie Prince Charlie', but Derby became famous as the place where the Highlanders turned back, realising that their cause was lost. On 4 December Charles and his army of about 7,500 men arrived from Ashbourne and billeted themselves on the local population. They caused little damage but much alarm and on the morning of 6 December began their retreat, which ended in defeat a few months later at the Battle of Culloden.

Great houses

Two years before the 'Glorious Revolution', William Cavendish, the fourth Earl of Devonshire, had been banished from James II's court for a violent attack on a Colonel Culpepper and had spent his time by rebuilding his house at Chatsworth. He said later that it had not been his intention to rebuild the old house entirely; by refashioning just one wing at a time, the Elizabethan courtyard plan was therefore preserved. His architect was William Talman of the King's Works, who was actively involved with the rebuilding of the royal palace at Hampton Court. Later, Talman also designed Kiveton Hall (demolished 1811) for Cavendish's fellow-conspirator, the Earl of Danby, by then Duke of Leeds. At Chatsworth, Talman designed the south wing, which was constructed between 1686 and 1689, and the east wing of 1689–91, both in the newly fashionable English Baroque style. The Hampton Court team also worked on the interior: Laguerre and Verrio on the paintings, Cibber on the

Revolution House, Old Whittington. In 1688 Thomas Osborne (Earl of Danby), William Cavendish (Earl of Devonshire), and John D'Arcy (son of the Earl of Holderness) met on Whittington Moor, half-way between Chatsworth and the south Yorkshire seats at Kiveton Park and Aston to plot the events that would lead to the deposing of James II in favour of William of Orange. The three men are said to have sought shelter from the rain in an alehouse known as the Cock and Pynot (a magpie). The building, reduced in size and much restored, was opened as a museum in 1938. D'Arcy died in 1688, but the other two conspirators were duly rewarded with dukedoms.

PHOTOGRAPH: AUTHOR

The brief visit of Bonnie Prince Charlie to Derby in 1745 had little effect on the county's history, yet this equestrian statue now has pride of place in the Cathedral Green redevelopment scheme. The silk mill is in the background.

PHOTOGRAPH: CARNEGIE

Chatsworth. The south front of the house stands out in the weak winter sunshine. To the right is the contemporary cascade, one of the few remnants of the formal gardens that were swept away in the eighteenth century. On this side of the Derwent sheep graze in the former open arable fields of Edensor, which became part of 'Capability' Brown's landscaped park. On the skyline, the Elizabethan hunting stand rises above the sixth Duke's woods and his long extension to his ancestral home.

PHOTOGRAPH: CARNEGIE

sculpture and Tijou on the ironwork. The woodwork, however, was carved by a gifted local craftsman, Samuel Watson. The state apartments were arranged on the top floor of the east wing, where the long gallery had been.

A bird's eye view of Chatsworth in 1699 by the Dutch artists Knyff and Kip shows the contrast between the two new wings and the remaining Elizabethan work. The house was set amidst fashionable formal gardens, designed in the French and Dutch style by the royal gardeners, George London and Henry Wise. These gardens were altered in 1702–03 by the construction of a canal pond that was fed by water flowing from the moors down a cascade designed by Grillet (a pupil of Le Notre of Versailles fame) and through the Cascade House designed by Thomas Archer, who had replaced Talman as the estate's chief architect. The west front of the house was built in 1700–03, then the north front of 1705–07 had to be connected to Talman's work by a bow-shaped wall to conceal the fact that the house was not a perfect rectangle because of its piecemeal construction. The Duke of Devonshire now had one of the finest and most up-to-date houses in the land.

It is no longer obvious that during the seventeenth century the Cavendishes had an aristocratic rival in the south of the county. Sir John Stanhope of Elvaston and Cubley (died 1611) was descended from a north-eastern family which had moved to Nottinghamshire. His eldest son, Sir Philip, was created Baron Stanhope of Shelford in 1616 and Earl of Chesterfield in 1628. From him were descended the later Earls of Chesterfield of Bretby and the Earls

Bird's-eye view of Chatsworth, 1699. The Dutch artists Kip and Knyff drew this view in 1699 and published it in their *Britannia Illustra* in 1707. The old Elizabethan west and north fronts of the house had not yet been rebuilt in the fashionable Baroque style favoured by the new south and east fronts. The formal gardens in Dutch and French style had just been laid out but the canal pond had not yet been dug. The Stand or hunting tower was still set amongst rough moorland. The old highway from Chesterfield to Bakewell descended the slope from the Stand and then turned along the southern wall of the gardens to the bridge over the river Derwent by the old corn mill. In the eighteenth century both these buildings were demolished and the road was diverted.

BRITANNIA ILLUSTRATA (1707)

Stanhope of Chevening (Kent) and from his second wife came the Earls of Harrington of Elvaston. The first and second Earls of Chesterfield built a magnificent country house at Bretby, which became their principal seat after Shelford was destroyed in the Civil War. Knyff and Kip's bird's-eye view of Bretby in *Britannia Illustrata* (1707) shows a large Jacobean house arranged around three sides of a courtyard that had been rebuilt from the 1670s onwards in the French style of Louis XIV's court. Large, formal gardens were laid out in parterres, terraces and long rows of trees at the same time and later waterworks were installed by Grillet. It is our misfortune that the fifth earl demolished this splendid building and replaced it in 1813 with an undistinguished house in a castellated Gothick style. The gardens are now covered with modern hospital buildings and the earldom is extinct.

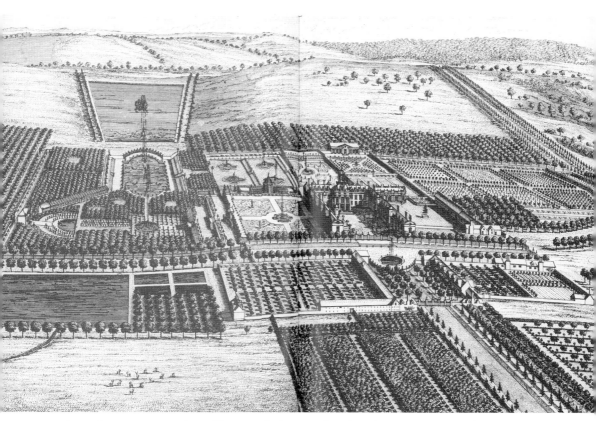

Bretby Park in 1699. Kip and Knyff's view of a house and gardens that were once one of Derbyshire's chief glories, owned by the Right Honourable Phillip Stanhope, Earl of Chesterfield. The large Jacobean house had been rebuilt in the 1670s in the French style, to the designs of Louis Le Vau. The gardens, parterres and water features including lakes, canal and fountain were constructed in the French manner in the 1680s under the direction of Monsieur Grillet, the designer of the cascade at Chatsworth. The house was demolished between 1777 and 1781 and in 1813 work began on the new house designed (at least in part) by Sir Jeffry Wyatville. In 1926 a children's TB hospital was opened at Bretby and much of the park was sold as farmland.

BRITANNIA ILLUSTRATA (1707)

On the south-western border of Derbyshire, George Vernon, the future High Sheriff and MP for Derby, began to build Sudbury Hall in 1659. His original design conformed to the old Elizabethan or Jacobean style with a central, two-storeyed porch and slightly projecting wings at the front, a long gallery and the use of diaper patterns marked by dark bricks. But in the 1670s the provincial craftsmen were replaced by London carvers, plasterers and painters, the mullioned windows were given round arches, surmounted by an oval, and the house was finished with a hipped roof, topped by a cupola. It was completed a decade or so before work began on Chatsworth.

South Derbyshire acquired other stately homes in the first half of the eighteenth century. The hall at Kedleston that Francis Smith designed for the Curzon family in 1701 is known only from a painting, for it was replaced by the present great house in the 1760s. Calke Abbey was built on the site of an Augustinian priory in 1701–04 for Sir John Harpur, to replace his house at Swarkestone, and Melbourne Hall was built on the site of the medieval bishop's residence. It contains some early seventeenth-century work, but was re-styled in the first decade of the eighteenth century and again in the 1720s and 1740s. Of particular interest are the gardens that were designed in the 1690s by London and Wise, before the house was remodelled. Thomas Coke, the owner of Melbourne and Vice-Chamberlain to Queen Anne, chose a plan for the gardens 'to suit with Versailles'. The focal point is Robert Bakewell's intricately carved, wrought-iron arbour of 1706–11.

Further north, Francis Smith designed (the demolished) Wingerworth Hall in 1726–29 for Sir Thomas Hunloke and a new house at Locko Park in 1737 for Robert Ferne (which was much enlarged in the nineteenth century). His finest house was undoubtedly Sutton Scarsdale, which was begun in 1724 for Nicholas Leake, the fourth and last Earl of Scarsdale. Now a ruined shell on a hillside overlooking the M1, on the opposite side of the valley to Bolsover Castle and Hardwick Hall, it was once Derbyshire's grandest country house

Melbourne Hall arbour. Robert Bakewell (1682–1752), the son of a blacksmith, Sampson Bakewell of Uttoxeter, and his wife, Mary, the daughter of a Derby blacksmith, was a craftsman of national standing. He was trained in the London workshop of Jean Tijou (who was known for his work at Hampton Court and Chatsworth) and was living in Derby when he was commissioned to design this arbour by Thomas Coke of Melbourne, as a focal point of the gardens which had been laid out by George London and Henry Wise, the royal gardeners who had recently worked at Chatsworth. The wrought-iron, domed arbour, which was completed in 1711, is a beautiful composition with intricately carved scrollwork patterns, oak branches and laurel leaves.

since Chatsworth and was set in formal gardens and a landscaped park. Several of the rooms that were decorated with superb plasterwork are now on display in the Philadelphia Museum in the United States of America.

Halls and vernacular architecture

In the late seventeenth and early eighteenth centuries the minor gentry of the Peak District continued to favour gabled halls built of local stone and lit by mullioned windows. John, the grandson of William Wright of Great Longstone, built Eyam Hall in 1676 (according to a date on a rainwaterhead), Wormhill Hall was begun in 1697 by Adam Bagshawe, and Slack Hall, near Chapel-en-le-Frith, was built by Thomas Slacke as late as 1727. Further east, the coal-measure sandstone district, stretching right up to the Yorkshire border, has an impressive collection of gabled halls, many of them built from the profits of lead smelting.

A large number of yeomen farmhouses were also erected in this period. The village of Higham, for instance, has five that can be dated between 1668 and 1699 and the Moss valley contains several, some of which were partly financed from the trade in scythes and sickles.

Changing fashions in vernacular architecture are evident on a walk through the central streets of Dronfield. The earliest structures contain remnants of timber-framed buildings. An L-shaped building, set back from the High Street, which had been downgraded to a barn until its modern conversion, has a fifteenth-century king-post roof; a recently restored building at the south-eastern edge of the churchyard has timber posts that have been dated by dendrochronology to 1527; and on the opposite side of Church Street the sagging roof line and the ridge pole that protrudes from a row of shops provide clues that this building is framed with four bays of crucks. The handful of buildings that retain sixteenth- and seventeenth-century features, such as gables or mullioned windows, include the original grammar school, Rookery Cottage, Vale House, the former Rock Inn and the Green Dragon Inn, which was remodelled in the nineteenth century on the site of the medieval Guild of St Mary the Virgin. Old photographs show two other large inns in a mid- or late seventeenth-century style in the central streets that have now been

demolished. But the finest houses date from a prosperous era at the turn of the century, when Dronfield was a flourishing small market town. At the top of High Street the present Library was formerly the Manor House that Ralph Burton, a wealthy member of an old lead smelting family, erected in the 1690s in the new symmetrical style, with a hipped roof that no longer has its chimney stacks, and cross windows that have been replaced on the front with sash windows. Across the street, a contemporary building known as The Hall, the home of John Rotherham, lead smelter and millstone quarry owner, also has the cross windows with a central mullion that were typical of the time and a symmetrical appearance instead of gables. Yet beyond the valley, Chiverton House and Rose Hill, two imposing, neighbouring residences, combine some old features such as gables and string courses with fashionable cross windows and new-style symmetry. Datestones suggest that they were both updated in the second decade of the eighteenth century by lead smelters. Back in the central streets, the greatest break with tradition came when a house for the usher of the grammar school was built in brick by public subscription in 1731, followed by the Old Vicarage next door. As in other places where stone was the common building material, the usher's house was so unusual that it got the name of Red House.

The Hall, Dronfield, which John Rotherham built around 1700, lies next to the remains of a high-quality, timber-framed hall of the early fifteenth century, which seems to have been the old manor house. Rotherham was a prosperous lead smelter; his tall, symmetrical, double-pile house retains its original cross windows. It was the most up-to-date building in Dronfield when it was erected. Parapets adorn the top storey on both sides of the house. The original structure of the rooms is preserved. Sturdy, re-used timbers were used in the cellars and the attic storey, where some were arranged as upper crucks.

PHOTOGRAPH: AUTHOR

By the second quarter of the eighteenth century the minor Derbyshire gentry were building well-proportioned houses with sash windows. In the north of the county opportunities to rebuild depended on the varying fortunes of the lead industry, so the legacy from the Georgian age is less evident than from the previous era. In south Derbyshire, where no stone was available, halls and farmhouses were built of brick, though with stone quoins and lintels. Repton Grange was built about 1725–35 for Joseph Holbrook, a former Alderman of the City of London, five bays wide and three storeys high under a pitched roof. Craven and Stanley suggest that Francis Smith of Warwick designed Ravenstone Hall, which was built in 1726 for Roger Cave of Eydon. In 1739 William Smith, the son of Francis, designed Radburne Hall for German Pole and in 1741 Catton

Chiverton House, Dronfield, another of the large houses that were built by lead smelters. The house may actually be earlier than the 1712 datestone, which might merely commemorate a change of ownership. The two turrets at each end of the front were slightly later additions.

PHOTOGRAPH: AUTHOR

Great Longstone Hall. Set back from the road at the western end of the village, this house must have made quite an impact when it was completed in 1747 for, unusually in the Peak District at that time, it was built of brick, though with stone quoins and parapet. It was built for John Wright, the descendant of a long line of Longstone's most prominent family.

Sycamore Farm, Hopton. In the middle years of the eighteenth century brick was introduced into the White Peak as a prestigious, new building material: this undated farmhouse to the east of Hopton has a brick front and a central bow with Venetian windows.

On the opposite side of the road from Sycamore Farm is this guide stoop. Unusually, this stoop bears the date 1705, perhaps the initiative of Philip Gell, MP of Hopton Hall. The ways to Ashbourne, Bakewell and Wirksworth are marked on the other three sides.

Hall for Christopher Horton. Other well-proportioned brick houses from this time include Mapleton Manor, which was built about 1735 for Thomas Rivett of Derby, MP, and Twyford Hall, the home of the Bristowe family. The finest brick-faced Georgian house in a stone area is Great Longstone Hall, which was built for John Wright in 1747. In the same year, brick was also used at Parwich Hall and about that time at Sycamore Farm, Hopton.

Communications

Seventeenth- and eighteenth-century travellers thought that the hills of north Derbyshire were the among the wildest and most difficult to cross in the

whole of England. When Daniel Defoe rode from Chesterfield to Bakewell he came to

> a vast extended moor or waste, which, for fifteen or sixteen miles together due north, presents you with neither hedge, house or tree, but a waste and houling wilderness, over which when strangers travel, they are obliged to take guides, or it would be next to impossible not to lose their way.

Celia Fiennes too had been apprehensive about 'the steepness and hazard of the Wayes – if you take a wrong Way there is no passing – you are forced to have Guides as in all parts of Darbyshire.' Even local people feared the moors in bad weather. When the Revd James Clegg of Chinley Chapel arrived safely in Crich on 5 February 1735, he wrote that 'a kind providence directed me safely over the East more'. His diary has many references to accidents when he was returning home in the dark. Yet despite these undoubted dangers and difficulties, diaries such as Clegg's record a great deal of movement within a neighbourhood or 'country' bounded by the nearest market towns and some of the wildest moors are criss-crossed with tracks that have been worn hollow by packhorses and wheeled vehicles taking industrial goods to market places or inland ports and returning with corn and malt. Most journeys were made in the summer months, but the carriers, salters, jaggers and badgers were familiar with the moors in all the changing seasons.

In 1709 the Derbyshire JPs ordered parish and township overseers of the highways to erect 'For the better convenience of Travelling, where two or more cross Highways meet … a Stone or Post with an inscription theron in large Letters, containing the Name of the next Market Town to which each of the said joyning Highways leads.' Many moorland stoops survive with the date 1709 carved upon them, though some are later and seven are inscribed 1737 to conform with another order. Together with the guide stoops of the West Riding, they form by far the largest collection in England and are invaluable

Bridge across the Bar Brook, Big Moor. This simple bridge, consisting of two huge slabs resting on firm foundations, was used by jaggers bringing horses ladened with lead ore from mines in the White Peak towards the smelting mills in the river valleys to the east. It has the date 1742 inscribed upon it. 'H1777' was carved when the inhabitants of Holmesfield perambulated their boundaries in that year.

PHOTOGRAPH: SHEILA EDWARDS

Bridge at Slippery Stones. Since 1959 this bridge has spanned the upper course of the Derwent, but until 1942 it was sited four miles downstream at the village of Derwent, which was about to be submerged under a reservoir. Although it was only wide enough to take horses, the bridge was paid for out of county rates. Quarter sessions records show that it was erected at Derwent in 1683–84 by the county mason, Simon Holt.

Packhorse bridge, Burbage Brook. Packhorse bridges date from about 1650 to 1750, the era before turnpike roads were created to cater for wheeled vehicles. They were built by private individuals or at parish expense under the supervision of the overseer of the highways. This undated example was the joint responsibility of the inhabitants of Dore and Hathersage, for it spanned their boundary stream close to Carl Wark. It is a sturdy bridge but without parapets.

testimony to the attempts that were made to improve the ancient highways in the decades before the construction of turnpike roads. The trouble and expense of erecting them could not have been justified if these moorland routes had not been well used. In lowland parts of Derbyshire stoops were unnecessary because villages and hamlets were thick on the ground and a traveller could always ask his way.

Many of the causeys that were laid down across wet and difficult terrain also date from this time. Most of them consist of thick slabs of millstone grit or other sandstones of various shapes and sizes arranged in a single or, occasionally, a double line. They were intended primarily as horse paths leading to market places and parish churches. Some were paid for by private individuals but the majority were constructed under the parish repair system supervised by the overseer of the highways. Another improvement came with the replacement of wooden packhorse bridges with new ones constructed of stone. Surviving examples date from the late seventeenth to the mid-eighteenth

Peak District guide stoops. In 1709 the Derbyshire JPs ordered the overseers of the highways of each township and parish that, 'For the better convenience of Travelling, where two or more cross Highways meet in your said Liberty you are required forthwith … to erect or fix … in the most convenient place, where such ways join, a Stone or Post with an inscription theron in large Letters, containeing the Name of the next Market Town to which each of the said joyning Highways leads.' Surviving stoops are an invaluable aid in tracing old packhorse routes. Their spellings are often phonetic.

LEFT TO RIGHT

The road to Bakewell over Beeley Moor. Travellers including Celia Fiennes and Daniel Defoe came this way from Chesterfield with the help of guides.

The road across Beeley Moor, not to Offerton (a hamlet ten miles in the opposite direction), but to Alfreton (often pronounced Offerton locally). The style of the pointing hand is similar to that on the previous stoop, suggesting that the same mason carved it.

An unusually long inscription on a stoop in Longshaw Park, marking the way to Hathersage and so to Chapel-en-le-Frith. The other sides mark Chesterfield, Sheffield and Tideswell.

PHOTOGRAPHS: AUTHOR

A re-discovered stoop on Beeley Moor, which was buried by the Home Guard during the Second World War in case enemy parachutists landed nearby. These sides mark the ways to Bakewell and Wirksworth.

PHOTOGRAPH: AUTHOR

century or just beyond. They include the smaller county bridges authorised by JPs meeting at quarter sessions, such as that now standing at Slippery Stones but originally built in 1683 for the village of Derwent further downstream. The packhorse bridges that survive were on routes that were never made into turnpike roads and which were sited high up minor river valleys or in remote parts of the moors. The simplest were constructed on huge slabs resting on firm foundations. When a road was turnpiked, the first objective was to widen the bridges to take wheeled traffic.

Villages as well as towns were served not only by travelling hawkers, pedlars, petty chapmen and badgers, but by shopkeepers. Surviving Derbyshire trade tokens dated between 1649 and 1672 were issued by 106 men from 33 different places, including 17 villages. The War Office returns of 1686 show that no fewer than 257 places in Derbyshire had at least one guest bed on offer and that 250 places had at least one spare stall in a stable. About two out of every five of the county's guest beds and about half the extra stabling facilities were situated in villages and hamlets. Some of these were important crossing points on the Trent, such as Shardlow, Swarkestone and Weston, and others were recognised stopping points at junctions, such as Hilton, where the road from Uttoxeter to Derby was met by the highway from Nottingham.

In the early eighteenth century, William Woolley noted that at Wilne a ford took the London road across the Trent when the river was low:

> but besides, there is a great ferry boat for horses and carriages. At this ferry is a custom house for lead, cheese, salt, pitch, tar etc, which are carried from thence in great barges of 20 tons burden that row, sail and tow to Gainsborough and there shipped for London and other parts.

Wilne Ferry lay half a mile south of Great Wilne, a settlement that had

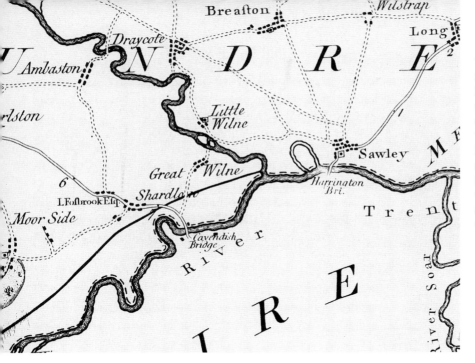

This detail of Burdett's map of Derbyshire (1791 edition) shows the crossings of the river Trent by Cavendish Bridge at Shardlow and Harrington Bridge at Sawley, which replaced the old Wilne Ferry.

replaced the deserted medieval village of Church Wilne on the other side of the river Derwent. In the mid-seventeenth century the ferry settlement was developed as a busy inland port by Leonard Fosbrooke, who leased the franchise of the ferry from the Cokes of Melbourne. It lost its leading position in 1738, when the road between Derby and Loughborough, now the A6, was one of the first to be turnpiked and the road was re-routed through the village of Shardlow; between 1758 and 1761 the Cavendish Bridge was built downstream from the ferry to the design of James Paine and largely at the expense of the fourth Duke of Devonshire. An Act of 1699 allowed Sir William Paget to make the upper Trent navigable between Wilne Ferry and Burton-on-Trent, a stretch that was then leased to George Hayne, a Wirksworth merchant who divided the river monopoly with the Fosbrookes of Shardlow Hall. Shardlow's great days as a canal port still lay well in the future. Meanwhile, in 1720 the river Derwent had been made navigable as far as the Trent, one of the nation's busiest rivers.

The first turnpike road in Derbyshire was that which was authorised in 1724 to improve the highway from Buxton to Manchester. In 1738 the two branches of the southern section of this important highway, linking Derbyshire with London, were also turnpiked. One branch came from Hurdlow, Ashbourne and Brailsford to Derby and Wilne Ferry, the other from Newhaven via Pikehall, Brassington, Hognaston, Mugginton, Kedleston and Markeaton to Derby. The link between Hurdlow and Buxton following the line of the Roman road was turnpiked in 1749. Meanwhile, in 1739 the route across the moors from Bakewell to Chesterfield was turnpiked to facilitate the carriage of lead to the

'... the steepness and hazard of the Wayes — if you take a wrong Way there is no passing — you are forced to have Guides as in all parts of Darbyshire.'

CELIA FIENNES

Described in 1802 as 'lately built by the Duke of Devonshire', Newhaven House Hotel stood about half way along the turnpike road from Ashbourne to Buxton, at the junction with roads from Cromford and Youlgreave.

PHOTOGRAPH: AUTHOR

The George Hotel, Tideswell. This eighteenth-century coaching inn was a welcome stopping point for travellers on the turnpike road from Sheffield to Buxton, who had crossed the moors to Grindleford Bridge and climbed up the steep Sir William Hill before following the ridge to Great Hucklow, where Tideswell church came into view. The road was turnpiked in 1758.

PHOTOGRAPH: AUTHOR

inland port of Bawtry. In the late 1750s and early 1760s 'turnpike mania' took hold in Derbyshire. In 1756 the route from the industrial West Riding via Sheffield and Chesterfield to Derby was turnpiked, with a branch from Duffield to Wirksworth; three years later the highway from Newhaven to Alfreton and Bakewell was improved and in 1760 so was the route from Matlock and Darley Dale to Chesterfield. In north Derbyshire Sheffield was connected to Manchester by the turnpiking in 1758 of an ancient moorland route through Hathersage and the Winnats Pass to Sparrowpit Gate and Chapel-en-le-Frith or by a branch leading across Grindleford Bridge, up Sir William Hill to Tideswell and Buxton. All these early turnpike roads were designed to improve existing highways. New routes were not created until the very late eighteenth and early nineteenth centuries.

This steep climb through a gap in the limestone hills beyond Castleton was known as *le Wyndeyates* as far back as 1330. It is an appropriate name, for it means 'the pass through which the wind sweeps'. This ancient route was guarded by a succession of forts – at Mam Tor, *Navio*, and Peveril Castle – long before the route was turnpiked in 1758 in order to link Sheffield with Manchester. An easier approach up the flanks of Mam Tor was created in 1802, but when landslip forced the closure of this route in 1979 the old way up Winnats Pass became busy again.

PHOTOGRAPH: CARNEGIE

LOWER

Tolls were collected at this crossing of the river Derwent from medieval times, for example on millstones. When a new bridge was built in the eighteenth century this small shelter was erected for the toll keeper. Modern traffic crosses the river further downstream, just beyond the village.

PHOTOGRAPH: CARNEGIE

The lead trade

When travellers reached the White Peak they knew they had entered a special 'country', marked by the rough appearance and incomprehensible dialect of the inhabitants and the spoil heaps of the lead mines. By the middle of the seventeenth century most of the remaining woods had been 'putt downe and destroyed' for fuel in the smelting mills or for timbering in the pits. The mills polluted the river valleys, while the rubbish on the surface of the lead rakes that had been discarded by the miners was constantly turned over by cavers in the hope of finding something of value. As Andy Wood has concluded, in terms of its economy, social structure, material culture and physical appearance, the limestone part of the Peak District had become an extensive industrial region a century or more before the beginning of the classic period of the Industrial Revolution.

In 1660 the Derbyshire lead mining industry was on the verge of rapid change as the traditional free miners became dominated by large-scale capital enterprises. The hearth tax returns of 1664 and 1670 show that many lead mining villages consisted almost entirely of houses with just one or two hearths, many of which were tenanted by families who were exempt from the tax on the grounds of their poverty. Wirksworth, Matlock, Bakewell, Ashford and Youlgreave were more socially differentiated than the upland mining villages, yet even the townships in the valleys included high proportions of single-hearth and exempted households. The poorest communities included Sheldon, where only two of the 53 householders had two or more hearths, and Wardlow, where 38 of the 39 householders were either exempt from payment or possessed just a single hearth. Further north, in Castleton 98 of the 106 householders had either one hearth or were exempt and in Bradwell 80 of the 85 householders were in the same category. Great and Little Hucklow had the highest exemption rates in Derbyshire, with 84 and 74 per cent, respectively. At Eyam, 63 per cent of the householders were exempt and 53 of the 59 who were taxed there paid on just one hearth. In townships such as these, the lead mining industry had become either the prime or the only source of income for the majority of the householders.

As mines got deeper, flooding problems became acute and substantial investment in drainage soughs by lead mining companies was needed. Fortunately, the mining area was intersected by deep river valleys, so soughs discharged water from working levels into the rivers Derwent or Wye. The first was Vermuyden's 1,000 feet Longhead Sough, which was driven between 1629 and 1636 to drain the Dovegang Mines at Wirksworth. Cromford Sough (whose outflow was later used by Arkwright to help power his cotton mills) was begun about 1673. More than 30 soughs had been constructed by 1700 and by the late eighteenth century some were over a mile long.

After the final ejection of free miners from his manor of Nether Haddon in 1658, the Earl of Rutland invested large sums of money in drainage equipment for his new mines at Haddonfields. But aristocratic families rarely invested in mining operations outside their own estates. Instead, they were content to collect tolls and tithes. The lesser gentry, however, became increasingly involved in the lead industry. By 1660 about 70 per cent of the gentry families of north and west Derbyshire had some financial interest in mining and large numbers of farmers, craftsmen and even some free miners held shares in large mines or became partners in drainage operations. During the eighteenth century gentry families took control of all aspects of the lead industry: mining, smelting, transport and marketing. Few investors came from beyond the Peak District.

William Woolley has provided us with a detailed description of the mining and smelting of lead in Derbyshire in the 1720s:

> In discovering of mines they make use of digging a little and if they find it promises earth, as the miners call it, then they bore and if thereby they find encouragement, they let down their stows or marks of possession, which are little pieces of wood made in the shape of a windle or curb of a well or mine. The ore, when it is well dressed from the rubbish that grows thereon and washed, is fluxed and a furnace made of cylinder fashion, into which is put … some white coal, as they call it, which is small white wood made dry and hard with fire and charked and blown up with a huge pair of bellows which are turned in the nature of a mill. And when the metal is melted it runs out of a little hole at the bottom into the hearth (which is hollow and has a little channel in it for the clear metal to run, [leaving] the ashes behind on the hearth), so runs into a large stone trough out of which it is loaded into the mould for pigs or half-pigs of lead, which is placed ready at hand in one of a pair of scales, the other having the weight of the mould and of the pig of lead as it ought to be. And as they put in the melted metal they continue to scum – which scumming ashes and rubbish that comes out of the furnace, when they have a good quantity, they melt it over again and make a coarser sort of lead called slags. But you must note that the morning-made lead is the best and softest, for when the furnace is hot by long use, the metal is harder and more brittle. There is a corrosive sulphur in the ore, which flies up into the smelting – which occasions a disease called the 'belland', known by difficulty of breathing, loss of appetite, yellowness of complexion, a dry cough and hoarseness, attended with swelling limbs and joints which are rendered useless; which is taken by working in the lead mines or the smell of the fumes of the ore in smelting. This distemper falls upon the horses and cows that eat grass or drink water at the mill.

In his *Tour Through the Whole Island of Great Britain*, published not long after Woolley was writing, Daniel Defoe crossed Brassington Moor in the Peak District and arrived at:

> the mouth of the shaft or pit by which they go down into a lead mine; and as we were standing still to look at one of them, admiring how small they were, and scarce believing a poor man that shew'd it us, when he told us, that they went down those narrow pits or holes to so great a depth in the earth … we were agreeably surprized with seeing a hand, and then an arm, and quickly after a head, thrust up out of the very groove we were looking at.

They were shown how the miner thrust himself upwards by placing his elbows and feet 'upon pieces of wood fixt cross the angles of the groove like a ladder'.

The man was a most uncouth spectacle; he was cloathed all in leather, had a cap of the same without brims, some tools in a little basket which he drew up with him, not one of the names of which we could understand but by the help of an interpreter. Nor indeed could we understand any of the man's discourse so as to make out a whole sentence; and yet the man was pretty free of his tongue too.

For his person, he was as lean as a skeleton, pale as a dead corps, his hair and beard a deep black, his flesh lank, and, as we thought, something of the colour of the lead itself ... Besides his basket of tools, he brought up with him about three quarters of a hundred weight of oar ... We asked him how deep the mine lay which he came out of. He answered us in terms we did not understand; but our interpreter ... told us it signified that he was at work 60 fathoms deep, but that they were five men in his party, who were, two of them, eleven fathoms, and the other three, fifteen fathoms deeper.

Aerial view of Bonsall Moor, showing the pock marks and lines of old lead rakes. These are earlier than the drystone walls that were erected in the late eighteenth century when the commons and wastes were enclosed.

The miners referred to these crude ladders as 'stemples'. The other method of entry was through levels tunnelled into the hillside.

Aerial photographs of Bonsall Moor show that the common practice of the miners was to sink shallow shafts close together. When drainage and ventilation methods improved, deeper and longer levels were sunk but, as in coal mining, the extraction of lead ore remained a heavy pick-and-shovel job. The usual tool was a pick with a pointed end that was inserted into small cracks and a blunt end shaped like a hammer head for heavy striking. After a crack had been widened, wedges were driven in and large pieces of rock were broken off by repeated hammering. Another technique involved the lighting of a fire against the rock face. When the rock became extremely hot, water was douched on it so that the face fragmented. Another common method was to bore a hole into the face, fill it with quicklime and stop it with a wooden bung. When water was poured through a hole in the bung, an intense chemical reaction with the quicklime split the rock. Gunpowder was not used in Derbyshire lead mines before the late seventeenth century.

When mines were worked at deeper levels, ventilation problems increased. The soughs that were driven through shale released deadly firedamp and other gases. A primitive solution was to lower red hot coals in baskets to create minor explosions, but the common method was to work bellows by hand or water wheel to blast fresh air through metal or wooden pipes encased in clay. Water wheels were also used to pump out the water, following the example of the Earl of Rutland who used five at Haddonfields in 1680. In the eighteenth century large sums of money were spent on installing Newcomen steam or 'fire engines' for this purpose, especially in the rich mines of the London Lead Company around Winster and Elton. The first one was installed by 1717 in Yatestoop Mine, Winster, where on 28 September 1730 James Clegg noted in his diary that he 'saw 3 curious Engines at work there which by the force of fire heating water to vapour a prodigious weight of water raisd from a very great depth, and a vast quantity of Lead orr laid dry'. By then, the annual

Lead crushing circle, Odin Mine. The Odin mine on the slopes of Mam Tor was mentioned in 1280, making it the oldest named lead mine in Derbyshire. A rich seam of lead was struck in 1706. Twenty years later, twelve men mined the ore, fifteen boys drew or pumped water, and seventeen women dressed the ore on the surface. The circular stone seen here was linked to a horse that went round and round the paved circle, crushing the ore that was placed beneath it.

PHOTOGRAPH: AUTHOR

output of the Yatestoop mine equalled the total output of the whole Derbyshire lead field in 1580.

Even in the new, deep mines, ponies continued to pull the ore on sledges and later in tubs along rails; in a few places such as the Speedwell mine at Castleton boats were used. The ore was raised to the surface up shallow shafts by hand winches or up deeper and wider shafts by a horse gin. At some old mines traces of a 'gin circle' can still be seen at the pithead, where a horse walked round and round to work a winding drum. There, women and boys, wielding hammers, reduced the ore to pea size and separated it from waste rock and unwanted minerals by sieving it in a vat of water. The largest pieces of ore were then taken to the ore house to be raked across a stream of water in an inclined, elongated trough. They were then crushed by a rotating stone worked by a horse in a circle, such as the one that can still be seen at the former Odin Mine near Mam Tor, and washed, before being carried by packhorses, led by jaggers, to the smelting mills. These were often built several miles away from the mines, for hearths blown by bellows needed both water-power and fuel known as 'white coal' from the coppice woods to the east of the river Derwent. Water-powered smelting mils were used from about 1570 until they were replaced by coal-fired reverberatory furnaces known as cupolas, which could use lower grades of ore on any suitable site. The first cupola in Derbyshire was erected in Ashover in 1735. It was a very different type of furnace, for the ore was not in direct contact with the fuel. Instead, a draught was induced by a long flue and chimney to draw the flames from the burning coal over the ore. Pigs of smelted lead were taken from the mills and furnaces in two-wheeled wains to the nearest river ports, such as Bawtry, and later to the canal heads. At Bawtry, cargoes of lead weighing about ten tons were taken down the river Idle to Stockwith on the river Trent, where they were transferred to larger vessels which sailed to Hull or directly to London.

Leadmill House, Hazleford. The house occupies the site of a lead smelting mill where the Highlow Brook flows into the river Derwent, south of Hathersage. The mill was built about 1600 by Robert Eyre of Highlow Hall and when Robert's son, Thomas, died in 1633, his inventory listed lead, bellows and tools at the smelting house. The mill was worked until at least 1676. The weir across the brook fed a culverted goit to the mill. No traces of the former mill can now be seen.

PHOTOGRAPH: AUTHOR

Other industries

From the Restoration to the middle years of the eighteenth century the Derbyshire charcoal iron industry produced much the same annual output as before. Some new furnaces replaced old ones but the total number remained constant. Derbyshire and Nottinghamshire accounted for about one-tenth of national production. The leading figure in the trade was George Sitwell of Renishaw, whose interests in the Staveley and Foxbrooke furnaces, the Staveley and Carburton forges and the Renishaw slitting mill were taken over in the 1690s by a partnership led by the Foleys of Herefordshire, then in the early eighteenth century by the Spencers of Cannon Hall, Cawthorne, the leading ironmasters in South Yorkshire, and their partners. Much of the iron that was produced was used by rural metalworkers, such as the makers of nails, scythes and sickles. The hearth tax returns of 1670–72 show them concentrated in the parishes of Eckington and Norton, on the borders of Hallamshire. Norton parish was the North of England's major supplier of scythes and the Troway quarter of Eckington parish was the leading centre of sickle production. The local metalworkers combined their trade with farming and used the water-powered sites in the Sheaf and Moss valleys to grind their products. In the second quarter of the eighteenth century, water-powered rolling and slitting mills were introduced into south Derbyshire, especially after the lower Derwent was made navigable. Woolley recorded a rolling and slitting mill at Makeney, William Evans built rolling and slitting mills at Derby in 1734, a rolling mill was constructed at Wilne in the 1730s and a slitting mill at Borrowash in the 1760s.

Thirty-five mines were producing coal in Scarsdale wapentake in 1662. Alfreton and Swanwick were the leading centres and John Turner, the son of John, the 'rich collier', was wealthy enough to build Swanwick Hall in

Industry in the Moss valley. Eight or nine grinding wheels, powered by the Moss Beck, were once at work in the Troway quarter of Eckington parish near the north Derbyshire border. From Elizabethan times onwards, the Moss valley specialised in the production of sickles and the leading families — the Staniforths, Cowleys, Turners, Booths and Huttons — prospered as yeomen-craftsmen who sold their products far and wide. Little remains to be seen of this former rural industry, except for some dams and a few converted buildings, such as the warehouse at Birley Hay (*below*), which has been re-roofed in Welsh slate but otherwise retains its former character. In 1702 John Savage of Birley Hay bequeathed to his eldest son John 'all stithies, bellows, tools, instruments and utensils belonging to the trade of sicklesmith' and 'my mark which I sett upon my sickles'.

PHOTOGRAPHS: AUTHOR

1672–73. Another leading coal merchant was Godfrey Haselhurst of Carter Lane, Alfreton, 'a great dealer in Coles', who was said to be worth £10,000 in 1687. By the late seventeenth century, the Derbyshire coalfield was of sufficient importance to be noted by national commentators, such as John Houghton, who in 1692 wrote that 'the chiefest Cole-mines' in the county were at Smalley, Heanor and Denby, 'through which abundance in summer are carried as far as Northamptonshire, from whence is brought back barley'. Twenty years later, Woolley noted that coal was mined at Denby, Mapperley, Stanley and

LEFT

Holloway, Offerton Edge. Holloways can rarely be dated precisely, but a letter written by Thomas Eyre of Thorpe in the parish of Hathersage shows that this one was constructed in the summer of 1722 'so as the milne stones might pass'. It descends the moorland slope towards Hathersage from a small quarry that was worked for a few years in the 1720s. Holloways such as this were commonly made so that millstones could be carried on a smooth surface by horse-drawn sledges as far as the highways.

RIGHT

Millstone Holloway, Longshaw. This pronounced holloway leads from Millstone Edge, the most important millstone quarry in the Peak District towards the close of the seventeenth century. It heads in the general direction of the highways that led to Bawtry, the inland port. The 'Milne Stone gate' where Ralph Burton of Dronfield died after falling off his horse in 1714 seems to have been the continuation of this route.

PHOTOGRAPHS: AUTHOR; SHEILA EDWARDS

elsewhere in the Erewash valley and that Heanor was 'a good large town ... On the east side is pretty good land, but on the other side is barren but in the same is a very great quantity of large, good and durable coal.' He also observed that, further south, Newhall was 'of note for a considerable coal delph with which it supplies a great part of the country, though they are none of the best sort of coal'. Like the rural metalworkers, the coal miners were part-time farmers. Landlocked Derbyshire could not compete with the Northumberland and Durham coalfield, which had immediate access to the sea and was highly developed by this time.

Coal was the fuel used by the potters of Ticknall, who flourished in the late seventeenth century before North Staffordshire dominated the trade. Janet Spavold and Sue Brown have shown that the village had 17 potteries by 1689 and its slipware products were sold over much of the Midlands. Unsophisticated kick wheels driven by the potter or his apprentice were in general use, though treadle mechanisms had been introduced recently. Probate inventories record the boards on which wares were placed to dry, together with the spades, shovels, mattocks and hackers for digging and chopping the clay and tools for grinding lead for the glaze. Most of the Ticknall potters combined their craft with farming a smallholding. Inventories and other records also provide glimpses of the specialist pot hawkers and their families who packed pots with straw into wicker baskets or panniers and sold them at markets and fairs and by travelling the countryside knocking on doors. In 1670, for example, William King left an old horse and 15 shillings worth of Ticknall pots.

National commentators also knew that the Peak District was the leading producer of millstones. In 1673 Richard Blome observed that Derbyshire had 'great quarries, out of which Mill-stones are got, also Grindstones, and Scyth-stones, which imploy many hands in working up, and are dispersed over great part of the Nation' via Bawtry. In 1692 John Houghton remarked on the 'rich Quarries of Mill-stones' that 'served most part of the Kingdom, and they are worth 8, 9 or 10 Pounds the Pair, and Grindstones of all sorts, from 5 or 6 Foot Diameter and under, and Scythe-stones in abundance, which serve all parts of the Kingdom'. Further south, William Woolley noted the gritstone quarries at Little Eaton, Breadsall and Duffield Bank, the alabaster quarries at Ambaston and the lime trade at Crich.

Meanwhile, the East Midlands hosiery trade was growing in both the towns and the surrounding countryside. The Revd William Lee had invented the stocking frame at Calverton (Nottinghamshire) back in the 1580s, but it was slow to take hold in his native district. At the time of the Restoration, however, about 650 framework knitters were at work in farmsteads and cottages in Nottinghamshire, Leicestershire and Derbyshire, south of Alfreton. By the early eighteenth century framework knitting had become one of England's most spectacular growth industries. Some masters had a considerable interest in farming as well as trade; in 1748, for example, Thomas Pyinger of Loscoe was a small employer with six frames in his shop, worth £40 5s. od., and farm stock valued at nearly £67. The earliest knitters commonly had a single frame and a smallholding but during the eighteenth century men with little or no land became the characteristic figures in the trade. Framework knitting provided employment for the growing population and supplied much of the capital, the techniques and the labour force for the revolution which Derbyshire helped to pioneer in the textile industry in the second half of the eighteenth century.

Farming and enclosure

On the alluvial and clay soils of the southern lowlands, farms were generally of small or medium size. At Cubley in 1677, for instance, 30 tenants held 2,032 acres among them and 19 cottagers held a further 46 acres. In Woolley's day the land there was mostly enclosed pasture. He described Spondon as having 'very good land of all sorts, especially meadowing, which lies on the banks of the river Derwent. The town is pleasantly and healthfully situated on a hill, with fine cornfields around it.' Chaddesden had 'a large district of good field land and excellent meadows reaching down to the Derwent side. It has likewise some woodland and common towards Morley.' Breadsall too had 'good fields about it and meadows reaching down to Derwent' and Foremark had 'very good meadows' on the banks of the Trent, but its upland was 'very sandy and partakes of a great range of commons adjoining'.

Woolley also had instructive comments on those villages which had shrunk since the Middle Ages, sometimes to the point of desertion. Kedleston was a small village with 'pretty good land'; Hoon consisted of 'four or five houses or large farms'; Barton Blount of 'three or four scattering houses and a forge on the brook that runs through the fields'; and Sinfin was 'a small hamlet lying at the west end of a wet moor of a large extent that takes its denomination from it, but all the towns round has right of common there. It has been a considerable town but now but two or three houses.' Alkmonton and Sapperton were small hamlets and Eaton-upon-Dove 'a small village', while Hungry Bentley consisted of 'some scattering houses in Barton parish'. Upper and Nether Thurvaston were 'two small hamlets consisting of several large farms. It is good, middling, enclosed land'; Edlaston was 'a small church town … middling, enclosed land'; and Osmaston: 'a small church town … pretty good, middling land', mostly enclosed in a low and watery situation, with 'the benefit of good commons'.

The conversion of arable strips into temporary grass leys and of large open fields into more complex systems enabled many townships in this lowland part of Derbyshire to remain unenclosed. Examples of agreements to enclose open fields include West Hallam (about 1713) and the piecemeal enclosures at Weston-upon-Trent from 1660 onwards, so that by 1755 'what was arable before is now converted into pasture land'. Dung, lime and marl, often mixed together, were the common manures and the natural grasses of the region were preferred to new crops such as clover. The average number of beef and dairy cattle recorded in farmers' inventories in the lowlands was 16 per farm. Dairy products made the grazing grounds alongside the Trent and the Dove famous. The trade expanded rapidly in the late seventeenth century in order to meet a far greater demand than before, London cheesemongers established a factory at Uttoxeter and cheese chambers became a feature of lowland farmhouses. By the eighteenth century nearly all the farmers south of Alfreton made various quantities of cheese. Meanwhile, oxen were gradually replaced by horses as draught animals and Ashbourne and Derby horse fairs acquired wide reputations. Most lowland farmers also kept a few pigs and half the flocks of sheep numbered over 50.

In the north-eastern corner of the county, farmers on the magnesian limestone pursued mixed husbandry, where the cultivation of cereals was as important as the dairy or the rearing of livestock. An average of 11 head of cattle per farm, a flock of sheep and a few pigs were kept and wheat, barley, oats and peas were grown. Clover was introduced at Barlborough by 1724 and was common in the district by the 1740s. Here, too, some open fields were enclosed before the mid-eighteenth century. At Scarcliffe and Palterton 550 acres of open field and 420 acres of waste were enclosed by act of parliament in 1726 and at Elmton the open fields and Markland common were enclosed by Sir John Rodes in 1732–35.

The farms on the coal-measure sandstones were generally small ones of between ten and 30 acres or even less, secure tenures were normally held by leases for terms of years and many tenants combined farming with a craft. The cottages, such as the 31 that were recorded on the wastes of Eckington in 1650, were often occupied merely by the payment of rent twice a year, at Ladyday and Michaelmas. This eastern part of Derbyshire was characterised not only by villages and market towns but by hamlets and dispersed farmsteads. Hill meadows and pasture closes were collectively far more extensive than the open arable fields that had once surrounded each settlement. The open fields were gradually encroached upon or divided by agreement until few remained to be enclosed by act of parliament. Where they survived, as at Wadshelf, many of the strips were converted to grass. On the other hand, many townships retained their large commons until the age of parliamentary enclosure; in 1692 for example the commons of Tibshelf covered 363 acres. Thirty years later, Titus Wheatcroft approved of Ashover's 'four rich and spacious commons well furnished with all sorts of moor game, besides foxes, hares, and the like', and its 'ten fair woods, and several very good springs of water for fish to breed'. The farmers of this district placed equal emphasis on livestock and cereals. The number of cattle averaged 13 a farm and tanning was an old and important industry in and around Chesterfield. Wheat and oats were the chief crops and many farmers also grew barley and peas. The importance of cereals is attested by the 54 corn mills that were operating in Scarsdale wapentake in 1652. New crops such as clover and turnips were mentioned only occasionally. Improvement usually took the form of liming and Titus Wheatcroft claimed that Ashover was 'especially noted for limestone and lime kilns, which furnisheth all the country round about us with lime for land and building'.

Writing about Wirksworth wapentake, William Woolley observed:

It is but a barren country feeding or rather I may say, breeding great numbers of sheep and by reason of the coldness of the climate, get but little corn grain except oats, which are seldom ripe until September or October, so that generally speaking it is but indifferent country to live in, being barren of wood and other fuel. Their fences or partitions of land are most made of a rough grit or limestone without mortar.

Woolley concluded that 'if it were not for the profit of those noble mines' most of the wapentake would be 'barren of inhabitants'.

The influx of men searching for work as cavers on the lead rakes was such that by 1649 30 cottages had been erected upon the wastes of Wirksworth. Numerous cottagers were recorded in the manors of Castleton and High Peak in 1650 and, two years later, 76 cottages were listed in a survey of the

Youlgreave area, namely 20 at Bradford, 28 at Caldwell End, 11 on Winster waste, 10 others in Winster tithing and 7 on the waste of Stanton tithing. Squatters eventually paid entry fines and annual rents for leases and so were welcomed by the landowners. The farmers of the Peak District held their land by tenures that were favourable compared with other parts of the county. On the Duchy of Lancaster estates, land in the manors of Castleton and High Peak was mostly freehold and in Wirksworth manor copyholders had the right to sublet land for lives or years by copy of court roll, to make fines certain at one year's ancient chief rent and to pass on their estates to their descendants. Common rights were a vital asset; the copyholders of Wirksworth manor claimed by prescription not only common of pasture for all manner of cattle, but liberty to get turves, peats, clods, limestone, clay, marl, sand, gravel, slate, stone, heather, fern, furze and gorse, and to fell or cut hollies or underwoods that grew on the wastes.

The open fields of the Peak District were by now of minor importance and many soon disappeared. Those at Beeley were enclosed in the middle of the seventeenth century; in 1674 ten farmers agreed to enclose lands which were dispersed in the open fields, meadows and pastures of Tissington; and in 1667 it was claimed that the tithes of Brassington had been greatly reduced in value 'as the town (as all other thereabouts) is enclosed, yet formerly maintained tillage … Now by mowing the ground they get more profit with less labour and charge, by reason the poorer sort, who are numerous, employ their labour in lead grounds in lordships 4 or 5 miles around.' This conversion of arable land to meadow also meant that fewer sheep were kept; 'Brassington has 73 oxgangs of land whereof 35 have not one sheep belonging to them. All the fields of Brassington have been enclosed about 50 years, except part of a field enclosed 30 years ago.'

Chelmorton's former open fields. High on the limestone plateau, the farmers of Chelmorton grew corn in their open arable fields in the level and relatively fertile area by the village. As in the neighbouring townships, these fields were enclosed by the agreement of the farmers long before the period of parliamentary enclosure. The field walls preserve some of the old strip boundaries, extending from the farmhouses and their crofts in the village street. The Town Ditch, which separated the arable fields from the common pastures, can still be followed along the southern edge, while continuous field walls mark the other boundaries, particularly on the hillsides to the north and the east.

PHOTOGRAPH: AUTHOR

Long Lee, Rowarth. Dated 1663 on its projecting porch, this house stands on a knoll overlooking Rowarth on the edge of the Pennines to the north of New Mills. It was built for John Hyde, whose ancestors had lived at Long Lee since at least the early fifteenth century. The building consists of the 'house' (*left*), which was entered through the porch, and a kitchen and a parlour in the wing to the right; all three rooms had chambers above. The substantial farm outbuildings include one now known as the Chapel, which has a 1679 datestone. John Hyde died in 1703; his tombstone is in one of the farm buildings.

Peak District inventories normally listed cereals simply as 'corn', most of which was oats. Farmers in both the Dark and White Peak kept an average 16 head of cattle and often flocks of more than 100 sheep. George Hambledon of Ballidon, husbandman (1668) had 200 sheep and 90 lambs; John Goodale of Tissington, yeoman (1692) had 184 sheep, 40 ewes and 40 lambs; Joshua Barnsley of Aldwark Grange (1748) had 400 sheep and 85 lambs; and John Kinder of Hill House, Glossop, yeoman (1748) had 147 sheep worth £33, yarn and wool priced at £30, and woollen cloth valued at £39. A wool fair was held annually at Chapel-en-le-Frith and the manufacture of woollen cloth was a rural textile industry that was well established in north-west Derbyshire and adjoining parts of Cheshire. John Radcliffe of New Mills (1694), for instance, was a yeoman who had two pairs of looms and a dyeing lead. Several yeomen farmsteads in this district were rebuilt in stone in the late seventeenth or early eighteenth centuries. The most impressive is Long Lee at Rowarth, built for John Hyde in 1663. Just before his death in 1698, Edward Bower, a yeoman, clothier and woollen draper of Torr Top in Whittle, built a new house alongside his old one. His second son, Thomas, owned a fulling mill, paper mill and tannery, but the finishing and sale of woollen cloth remained the family's main source of income.

The extensive commons and wastes were graded into the best, middle and worst sorts. Castleton manor had 732 acres of the best grade, 150 acres of the middle grade, and so much of the worst kind that the size could not be estimated nor the bounds defined at all accurately. In 1688 Bradwell had 1,352 acres of commons of all grades and in 1741 those at Litton covered about 3,000 acres. Great tracts of the wildest moors, which received up to 60 inches of rainfall per annum, were suitable only for rough grazing by sheep. The best pastures were reserved for cattle.

Many of these commons and wastes were enclosed during the second half of the seventeenth century. For example, in 1659 Rowland Eyre of Hassop and other owners of rights to graze cattle on the common pasture of Priestcliffe Lees, Taddington, agreed to divide and enclose. Selfish enclosure by the Bagshawes at Litton and then on parts of the commons of Abney and Great Hucklow in 1665 met with fierce resistance, but numerous examples of enclosure by agreement may be cited from other parts of the Peak District. By 1665 nearly half of the 900 acres of land at Fairfield, near Buxton, had been divided up and in 1673 the pastures at Beeley were enclosed by agreement. Common grazing grounds that had been limited to so many animals per farm, depending on the size of the holding, were divided at Kniveton (1697), Tissington (1726), Doveridge (1731) and Alsop-en-le-Dale (1758), while a unanimous agreement to enclose 153 acres of pasture at Eyam in 1702 made the freeholders 'very well pleased contented and satisfied.'

The greatest enclosures took place on the extensive Duchy of Lancaster estates within the Forest of the Peak. In 1673 the Duchy started the legal procedure for the enclosure of much of the manors of High Peak and Castleton, despite the opposition of the poorer inhabitants. The commons were divided between the freeholders and the Duchy, whose officers leased their share to farmers of large sheep flocks. The commons of Hope and other parts of the High Peak were divided in 1675, an agreement to divide the Castleton commons was reached by 1691, and the division of common pastures near Chapel-en-le-Frith was completed in 1714, when the freeholders were allowed to enjoy their 973-acre portion.

As thousands of acres of land in the High Peak came on the market, new farms were created and tracks and roads were constructed. Fieldwork by Derek Brumhead and Ron Weston has revealed that a considerable amount of physical evidence for these divisions survives in the landscape around Chapel-en-le-Frith and New Mills, in the 9,402 acres of the section of the Forest that was known as Bowden Middlecale. In 1640 an agreement had been made between the Duchy of Lancaster and over 80 freeholders, portions had been allotted and the red deer had been rounded up and destroyed, but everything came to a stop when the Civil War broke out. A parliamentary survey of 1650 found that within Bowden Middlecale were 69 'certain small cottages and little parcels of ground called intacks encroached upon the waste ground', and that 22 of them had no lease. The process of enclosure was resumed at the end of 1674, when the crown's portion was granted on a long-term lease to Thomas Eyre of Rowtor Hall, near Winster. Amongst his creations was the 127-acre Piece Farm, standing high at 800 feet on Ollersett Moor, which in 1715 he granted on a 999-year lease to John Downes of Hall Walls in Thornsett Hamlet. Many other lots were sold in smaller pieces. Meanwhile, in 1711 the freeholders and tenants obtained a final decree concerning their half, but they were in no hurry to enclose; indeed, apart from the Thornsett commons in 1774, acts of parliament authorising enclosure of commons and wastes were not obtained until well into the nineteenth century. The maps that were made in 1640 record the boundaries of hamlets and the divisions between the two parts exactly

'"He has never once been out of sight of the smoke of his own chimney" was a common High-Peak proverb; and all proverbs have their foundation in nature and truth.'

CHARLES WHETSTONE, 1807

DERBYSHIRE: A HISTORY

as they are marked by walls today. For example, the boundary between the hamlets of Ollersett and Beard follows a roughly made wall that rises over the moorland to the parish boundary at Chinley Wall. It separates the king's part in Ollersett from the tenants' part in Beard; a ditch appears intermittently on the Beard side.

The poor

The poor continued to be looked after by a mixture of public relief and private charity. Many a Derbyshire church has a charity board listing donations of land whose rents were to be spent on providing the poor with food and other necessities and some villages have almshouses founded by a wealthy and pious local benefactor. For instance, Etwall hospital was rebuilt in 1681 and the Pole almshouses in Barlborough were opened in 1752. As the national population rose, the poor became an increasing charge on parish rates. In 1683 the better-off inhabitants of Crich claimed that they were 'overcharged with poore' and in 1711 the freeholders of Bradwell declared that their village was 'so overcharged with the multitude of the poore that are therin that the inhabitants ... thereof are not able to relieve them, but they are forced in great numbers to wander about from towne to towne to ask for relief'. Surviving accounts show that, on the whole, those who were considered deserving were treated well. In late seventeenth-century Ripley, for example, we find payments to Alice Morley for five weeks when she was sick and for someone to attend her, Katherine Radford was given a shilling when a heavy snow fell, Ann Sellars was paid to look after William Bacon when he had broken some bones, Alice Eaton was provided with flax to spin and a poor woman in child labour was washed, given food and drink and a shift. But overseers were quick to bring others whom they did not believe were legally settled in their parish before the meetings of the quarter sessions in an attempt to make other parishes pay for them. Disputes over settlement certificates took up much of the JPs' time.

Parishes were also increasingly concerned to put the poor to work, even if their schemes rarely turned out to be profitable. In Wirksworth, for example, the poor were set to 'manufactures' and in the High Peak to building the walls which enclosed the commons. Some adopted the power authorised in 1723 to erect a workhouse. One was built on Dale Moor in 1738 for a group of neighbouring parishes, Taddington acquired a workhouse in 1753, and another was opened in 1767 at Ashover for a large group of parishes.

The JPs also ordered the building of houses of correction for offenders in various parts of the county. One which was recorded at Ashbourne in 1660 was replaced by a new building in 1722; that which served the High Peak was opened at Tideswell in 1711; and that at Wirksworth was re-founded in 1727. The Derby house of correction for county offenders (which stood in Walker Lane) was amalgamated in 1756 with the county gaol. All were done away with after the passing of the Poor Law Amendment Act of 1834.

Latin House, Risley. This small village in south-east Derbyshire has a remarkable collection of schools provided by the wealthy owners of the hall and park on the opposite side of the road. In 1593 Katharine Willoughby founded a school next to the church that her husband had just erected. In 1706 her descendant, Elizabeth Grey, paid for one of the finest Queen Anne houses in the county in order to accommodate the schoolmaster, his usher, and pupils. Blue and red bricks form a chequerboard pattern on the ground floor, whereas the upper floor is entirely red. The elaborate pediment of the door, the window frames and quoins are in stone. Tall, brick chimneys rise from the hipped roof. In her will of 1720 Elizabeth Grey also endowed a Latin school and a girls' school, then in 1758 an English school was opened for boys. A house for the English master was built in 1771 and the house shown here became the house of the Latin master and his boarders, acquiring the name Latin House. Other Derbyshire schools founded in the late seventeenth century include West Hallam (1662), Fairfield (1662), Whittington (1674), Brampton (1679), Ashover (1684), Norbury (1687), Longford (1688), and Chapel-en-le-Frith (1696).

PHOTOGRAPH: AUTHOR

In the middle years of the eighteenth century it was not yet obvious that Derbyshire was soon going to play an important role in launching the Industrial Revolution. The manufacture of hosiery was still a hand-craft industry, the production of iron was stable and the mining of coal remained relatively small scale. Derbyshire's most important industry was the mining and smelting of lead. Within the next hundred years all this changed; the lead trade collapsed while the other industries boomed, the county's population soared to new heights and large new settlements transformed the eastern half of the county.

An industrial revolution, 1760 to 1840

In 1801 the first British census recorded 161,567 people in Derbyshire. At that time, far fewer people lived within the whole of the county than within present-day Derby. Despite the recent industrial changes, Derbyshire was still overwhelmingly rural and most people stayed within the neighbourhood or 'country' with which they were familiar. The Peak District was a world apart form the agricultural villages in the southern lowlands and on the magnesian limestone belt in the east. In 1807 Charles Whetstone, a Methodist preacher, observed (with some exaggeration) that:

> Perhaps no part of England retained so much of ancient customs as were to be found amongst the inhabitants of the *Peak* in *Derbyshire*: Their dialect, prejudices, and superstitions (all gross and of very long standing) were in great degree peculiar to themselves. Their blind and childish partiality in favour of nativity, and their total ignorance of the rest of the world, extinguished in their minds almost every spark of curiosity or enterprise after objects remote. If an individual made a journey of 80 or 100 miles ... it was sure to be talked of by his neighbours as well as himself, as a great event, for a long time afterwards – '*He has never once been out of sight of the smoke of his own chimney*' was a common High-Peak proverb; and all proverbs have their foundation in nature and truth.

In the second half of the eighteenth and the first half of the nineteenth centuries British couples started to marry earlier and have more children; at the same time, death rates began to fall. The national population grew to unprecedented levels. By 1841 the number of people living in Derbyshire had risen to 272,202.

Towns

With 10,832 inhabitants in 1801, the borough of Derby was the 36th largest town in England and by far the biggest in Derbyshire. In the next 40 years its population trebled to 32,741. Long before these changes, Burdett's map of 1763–67 had shown that, although some expansion had begun along the London road in the south, Derby was still largely confined within its medieval limits and was surrounded by fields and orchards. By 1831 Samuel Lewis could note that:

The town is large and well built; for, notwithstanding the want of regularity in their appearance, many of the more modern houses are

The Derbyshire entries in the sixth edition of William Owen, *Book of Fairs* (1770).

ALFRETON: Fri. mkt. July 30 fair for horses and horned cattle.

ASHBOURNE: Sat. mkt. Feb 13 fair for horses of all sorts and horned cattle; April 3. May 21 and July 5 fairs for the same, and wool; Aug 16 fair for horses and horned cattle; Oct. 20, Nov. 29 fairs for black, heavy and other horses and horned cattle.

ASHOVER: April 25 and Oct. 15 fairs for cattle and sheep.

BAKEWELL: Mon. mkt. Easter Monday, Whitsun Monday and Aug. 13 fairs for cattle and horses; Mon. after Oct. 10 the same, Mon. after Nov. 22 for cattle and horses.

BELPER: Sat. mkt. May 12 and last day of Oct. fairs for cattle and sheep.

BOLSOVER: Fri. mkt.

CUBLEY: 30 Nov. fair for fat hogs.

CHAPEL EN LE FRITH: Thurs. mkt. Thurs before old Candlemas, Feb. 13, March 29, Thurs. before Easter, April 30, Holy Thursday, three weeks after Holy Thurs. fairs for cattle; July 7 fair for wool; Thurs. before Bartholomew day, Aug. 24 fairs for cheese and sheep; Thurs after Sept. 29, Thurs. before Nov. 11 fairs for cattle.

CHESTERFIELD: Sat. mkt. Jan. 25, Feb. 28, April 3, May 4, July 4 fairs for cattle, horses and pedlars; Sept. 25 fairs for cheese, onions and pedlars; Nov. 25 fair for cattle, sheep and pedlars.

CRICH: Old Lady-day, old Michaelmas-day fairs.

DERBY: Fri. mkt. Jan 25, Wed. in Lent Assize-week, fairs for cheese; Fri. in Easter week fair for horned or black cattle; Fri. after May-day, Fri. in Whitsun week, July 25 fairs for horned cattle; Sept. 27, 28, 29 fair for cheese; Fri. before Michaelmas meeting by custom for horned cattle.

DARLEY FLASH: May 13, Oct. 27 fairs for sheep and cattle.

DRONFIELD: Thurs. mkt. Jan. 10, April 14, July 15 fairs for sheep and cattle; Sept. 1 fair for cheese.

DUFFIELD: March 1 fair for cattle.

HIGHAM: Fri. mkt. First Wed. after New-year's day fair.

HOPE: May 1, Sept. 29 fairs for cattle.

MATLOCK: Feb. 25, May 9, July 16, Oct. 24 fairs for horned cattle and sheep.

NEWHAVEN: Oct. 30 fair for sheep, cattle and horses.

PLEASLEY: May 6, Oct. 26 fairs for sheep, cattle and horses.

RIPLEY: Wed. in Easter week, Oct. 23 fairs for horses and horned cattle.

SAWLEY: Nov. 12 fair for foals only.

TIDESWELL: Wed. mkt. May 3 fair for cattle, First Wed in Sept., Oct. 18, fairs for sheep and cattle.

WIRKSWORTH: Tues. mkt. Shrove Tues., May 1, Sept. 3 fairs for horned cattle.

'Derby from the Meadows', 1846. Henry Burn's view looks up the river Derwent towards the tower of All Saints church. In front of the church is the Derwent Foundry and, to the right, the terraced Derwent Row. In the centre is Cox Brothers' lead works in the Morledge, framed between William Strutt's fireproof, six-storey calico mill of 1792 and the Guildhall, remodelled after a disastrous fire in 1841. A long wooden bridge and towpath marks the weir where the Derby Canal crosses the river. Ten factory chimneys can be seen, but haymaking and grazing continue in The Holmes and other riverside meadows.

spacious and handsome; it is lighted with gas; the streets are regularly paved, and considerable improvement has recently taken place ... Until of late years, silk was the principal article of manufacture; but to that has been added those of cotton and porcelain, which are carried on to a great extent ... there are now nine silk-mills, worked either by water or steam. The weaving of silk was also introduced here in 1827. The porcelain manufacture was established in 1793, and has been brought to great perfection; it gives employment to about two hundred persons.

The population of Chesterfield rose more modestly from 4,267 in 1801 to 6,212 in 1841, but most of the important industrial developments took place beyond the boundary of the borough, in the outlying parts of the parish, particularly in the township of Brampton. The population of the whole parish rose from 7,330 to 11,231 during the same period. In 1828 Richard Phillips thought that Chesterfield was 'dull' and 'worn out'. Three years later, Samuel Lewis wrote:

the houses are of brick, roofed with stone; the streets are indifferently paved, but well lighted with gas, by an act of parliament obtained in 1825,

Wirksworth from the east. The ancient minster church remains the focal point of the market town.

and are plentifully supplied with water conveyed by pipes from Holm, two miles west of the town. There are a subscription library and a theatre: assemblies are held monthly in a suite of rooms at the Castle Inn; and races take place in the autumn ... Several of the inhabitants are employed in tambour work, and the manufacture of bobbin net-lace, gloves, and hosiery: there are also a silk-mill and a cotton-mill.

'Their dialect, prejudices, and superstitions (all gross and of very long standing) were in great degree peculiar to themselves.'

A thriving lead trade in the early nineteenth century enabled Wirksworth's population to grow from 2,978 in 1801 to 4,122 in 1842, before it fell and then stagnated. The town acquired some substantial stone-built Georgian houses, but in 1831 it was still not lit or paved in a regular manner. The population of Ashbourne (without the suburb of Compton) was 2,006 in 1801 and after reaching 2,246 in 1831 it fell slightly in the next decade to 2,158. Ashbourne was an important staging-post on the long-distance route between London and Manchester and a popular place for tourists visiting the Peak District, but it had little industry to support a rising population. It had become an attractive, brick-built town, with fine houses, inns and shops fronting the streets and the market place and artisan houses hidden from view in numerous yards. Its middle-class inhabitants enjoyed assemblies and a theatre and Lewis thought that:

The entrance from London is highly picturesque, commanding a fine view of the vale on the left, and of Ashbourne Hall, the seat of Sir William

m on Stone by S. Rayner.

ASHBOURN
W. ENTRANCE, SHEWING THE GRAMMAR SCHOOL.

Published by Dawson & Hobson A...

Ashbourne in the 1830s. Samuel Rayner's lithograph, published in 1839, shows a carrier's waggon arriving through the western end of the town, past the Elizabethan grammar school on the left and Dr John Taylor's tall mansion on the right.

BY COURTESY OF DR TREVOR BRIGHTON

Boothby, Bart., on the right; the vicinity abounds with pleasing and richly varied scenery ... the principal support of the town is derived from its markets and numerous fairs. The market is on Saturday.

In the late eighteenth century Bakewell began to change from a sleepy market town to an attractive Georgian centre, though its growth was modest. In 1778 Richard Arkwright built a cotton mill at Lumford and houses for his workers, including the terraces of New Street and Arkwright Square. Around the town a number of fine houses were built for well-to-do professionals, notably Castle Hill House, which the attorney, Alexander Brossley erected in 1785 in grounds that extended from the bridge over the Wye up to the skyline at Ball Cross. Then, at the start of the new century, the Duke of Rutland improved the centre of the town by removing the shops and houses that cluttered Bridge Street in order to enlarge the market place (today's Square) in front of the new Rutland Arms, which opened in 1805. This fine coaching inn was equipped with stables for tourists and other travellers. In one week in June 1818 no fewer than 655 coach passengers passed through the town. In an attempt to rival Matlock Bath and Buxton, the Bath House was leased to White Watson, who extended it and laid out a botanical garden with two summer-houses with tufa walls and thatched roofs lined with mineral specimens and fossils; today these gardens have herbaceous borders and beds of annuals. In 1826 the livestock market was removed from the central streets and was soon 'extremely well supplied with store and fat cattle and sheep'. Two years later the bridge was widened to take two-way traffic. In 1801 Bakewell's population was 1,412; by 1841 it had risen modestly to 1,976.

The spa towns were beginning to flourish, though their great days were yet to come. At Buxton the fifth Duke of Devonshire, enriched by the profits of his Ecton copper mines, commissioned John Carr, the famous York architect, to design major improvements. A marble-lined Well House was completed in 1783 for St Anne's Well, the baths were remodelled and several inns were rebuilt or improved. In the 1780s a grand Crescent was reared near the Old Hall and baths, the road to Manchester was diverted and the grounds sloping down to St Anne's Well were landscaped. The Crescent was divided between the Duke's town house in the centre, St Anne's hotel to the west and the Great Hotel to the east. Shops, a lending library and other accommodation were provided on the ground floor, while the Assembly Rooms within the Great Hotel contained card and coffee rooms and a splendid ballroom. Carr also designed an enormous square stable block for 120 horses and their coachmen and grooms on a site well north of the river Wye, with a covered ride for use by visitors in bad weather. Yet in 1790 John Byng thought 'Buxton is a most uncomfortable, dreary place'; perhaps he caught it on one of its many wet days? Further improvements were made in the early nineteenth century, including more work on the baths, the building of The Square in 1806–07, new houses on Hall Bank and a new St John's church (1811). Real growth began in 1848.

RIGHT
Buxton market cross in front of the Town Hall. Although the cross looks older Buxton did not acquire its market charter until 1813. The old market hall was replaced by the Town Hall in 1889.
PHOTOGRAPH: CARNEGIE

The construction of turnpike roads in the late 1750s and 1760s encouraged visitors to try the facilities at Buxton and Matlock Bath. In 1789 Pilkington wrote: 'The water at Matlock, like that at Buxton, has gradually risen to the degree of reputation, which it now possesses ... the bath houses, in conjunction with the private lodgings in their neighbourhood, will accommodate about 150 persons.' By then, The Temple, the *Old Bath* and the *New* and other hotels provided accommodation for some 500 visitors. The pleasure grounds that were named The Heights of Abraham after General Wolfe's victory at Quebec in 1759 were opened about 1800 and visitors were united in their praise of the beauties of the rocky landscape rising from the river Derwent. George Lipscomb of Birmingham, for instance, wrote in his *Description of Matlock Bath*:

The Crescent, Buxton. In the 1780s the fifth Duke of Devonshire tried to make Buxton into a spa town that would rival Bath. He began by commissioning John Carr to design The Crescent on the hillside, close to the original St Anne's Well. The central part was intended as the Duke's occasional lodging, but it soon became The Centre Hotel, with St Anne's Hotel (*left*) and the Great Hotel (*right*) occupying the wings, together with shops, a lending library and other accommodation on the ground floor. The Assembly Rooms formed part of the Great Hotel. In 1795 Carr also designed an enormous square stable block for 120 horses and their coachmen and grooms behind The Crescent. In 1859 this was converted into the Devonshire Royal Hospital, then in 1881–82 the courtyard was covered with a huge dome, 156 feet in diameter, which at that time was the largest in the world. To the left of the photograph is St John the Baptist's church, which stood in an isolated position at the edge of the town when it was built in 1811. Top right is the Palace Hotel, designed in the style of a French château in 1864 by Henry Currey; it soon became Buxton's leading hotel. The fashionable housing beyond the hospital dates from the late 1860s.

'Valley in Derbyshire'. From the 1740s onwards Thomas Smith of Derby was one of the first artists to paint or to draw dramatic landscapes in the dales of the White Peak. His works continued to be engraved in the later years of the eighteenth century, when the taste for picturesque views was at its height and tourists were venturing into remote parts of the Peak District.

It has gaiety without dissipation, activity without noise, and facility of communication with other parts of the country undisturbed by the bustle of a public road. It is tranquil without dullness, elegant without pomp, and splendid without extravagance. In it the man of fashion may at all times find amusement, the man of rank may meet with society by which he will not be disgraced, and the philosopher a source of infinite gratification; while they who travel in search of health will here find a silver clue that leads to her abode.

It was industry, however, that provided the key to rapid growth. As we shall see, by 1801 Strutt's mills were such a major employer that Belper had become the second largest town in Derbyshire, with a population of 4,500. Forty years later, it had risen to 9,885.

Country houses

The fourth Duke of Devonshire made no changes to the house that the first Duke had built at Chatsworth, but he altered its surroundings radically. Formal gardens were already going out of fashion in the 1720s and 1730s when the third Duke commissioned William Kent to redesign the grounds on the south-eastern side of the house, but when the fourth Duke inherited in 1755 the views on the other sides were obscured by outbuildings, parterres and kitchen gardens and the old deer park still stretched up the hillside from the river to the moors. Part of the straggling village of Edensor could be seen across the river. Work on the new landscape began in 1758 with the destruction of the rabbit warren north of the house and gathered momentum the following year when the Duke's copper mines at Ecton promised huge profits. Lancelot 'Capability' Brown was employed to devise a scheme that would remove the remaining formal gardens and terraces and to create a 'natural' park where the open fields of Edensor had been; their huge extent is revealed in the present landscape by the survival of ridge-and-furrow patterns. The creation of new turnpike roads across the Peak District at this time may have prompted the decision to close old routes, such as that which descended from The Stand along the southern edge of the formal gardens to the corn mill and bridge and up through Edensor to Ball Cross and Bakewell. Instead, travellers from Chesterfield to Bakewell had to skirt the estate through Baslow or Beeley. The old bridge and mill were demolished, the small part of the village of Edensor that could be seen from the house was removed, and James Paine designed Beeley Bridge to take the main highway through the park. Paine also designed a new private bridge across the Derwent, a corn mill in a striking classical design which served additionally as an eye-catcher near the southern edge of the park, and a solitary brick building, which served originally as an inn for those who were not important enough to be accommodated at the house. Meanwhile, the course of the river was altered, vast amounts of earth were moved, thousands of trees were planted or re-planted, and much of the land was drained by soughs and put to pasture in order to create a fashionable parkland setting for the house. As Chatsworth was now approached from the north-west, the old stables and offices were replaced by the enormous stable block that Paine designed on the hillside to the north of the house. By 1773 the park covered 2,327 acres; 50 years later, it was much enlarged towards Baslow after an exchange of land with the Duke of Rutland.

In 1811, the 21-year-old sixth, 'Bachelor', Duke became one of the richest men in England when he inherited an estate of nearly 200,000 acres in England and Wales. He decided that the house was not big enough for entertaining guests and for storing and displaying his growing collection of books and art. In the 1820s Sir Jeffry Wyatville, who had secured his reputation at Windsor Castle, designed a wing on the north side of the house that began with a library and ended in a belvedere and a theatre. When the great dining room in the new wing was finished in 1832, the sixth duke wrote, 'It answers perfectly, never feeling overlarge … It is like dining in a great trunk and you expect the lid to open.' The room beyond was used as a sculpture gallery, which displayed the numerous gifts bestowed by Tsar Nicholas when the Duke visited Russia as the British Ambassador, at his own expense. The Duke's wealth and interest in

'It has gaiety without dissipation, activity without noise, and facility of communication with other parts of the country undisturbed by the bustle of a public road. It is tranquil without dullness, elegant without pomp, and splendid without extravagance.'

MATLOCK BATH

Haddon Hall garden front. Samuel Rayner's lithograph shows Haddon Hall in 1836 when the house was standing empty. The Dukes of Rutland rebuilt their main seat at Belvoir Castle and so Haddon was never modernised. Rayner was one of the first artists to appreciate the romance of the site.

collecting art is demonstrated by the Oak Room, whose panelling and carved heads from a German monastery were bought at a London auction on impulse. As we shall see, a little later the sixth Duke and his head gardener, Joseph Paxton, turned their attention to the landscape on the hillside leading up to the moor and to remodelling the village of Edensor.

In the south of the county, the Curzons of Kedleston emerged as a Tory rival to the Whigs at Chatsworth. The house that Francis Smith had designed in 1701 lasted only half a century, for in 1759 the new heir, Nathaniel, first Baron Scarsdale, appointed Matthew Brettingham, who had recently worked on Holkham Hall (Norfolk), to design a house in the Palladian style. Curzon also turned to James Paine, then soon afterwards he met the ambitious young Scottish architect, Robert Adam, whom he asked to design a landscaped park and its buildings. Adam made such an impression that by about April 1760 he was put in charge of the new house. He kept all the main features of the

Palladian design proposed by Brettingham and Paine for the north front, but added a more dramatic central portico. However, he produced an entirely new design for the south front, which reflected the enthusiasm for Roman architecture that was shared by both the architect and the patron. The central feature was based on the Arch of Constantine and the dome of the Pantheon. It enabled the Hall and Rotunda to be lit from above, so that, instead of windows, their walls had medallions and niches with sculptures, like an ancient Greek or Roman temple. The state rooms on each side are also sumptuously furnished and decorated. Kedleston Hall took 30 years to finish and was immediately regarded as one of Adam's finest works and as one of the grandest buildings in England.

The Palladian and neo-Classical styles that were used in other country houses in a more modest manner include Foremark Hall, which David Hiorns (who had taken over William Smith's practice) built in 1759–61 for Sir Robert Burdett, and the demolished Doveridge Hall, which Edward Stevens designed in 1769 for Sir Henry Cavendish. In 1757 the Revd John Simpson commissioned William Booth of Stoney Middleton to design Stoke Hall in the style of James Paine, and about 20 years later Ashford Hall was built for John Barker, agent to the Duke of Rutland, probably to the design of Joseph Pickford.

Kedleston Hall, south front: South Derbyshire's rival to Chatsworth. In 1760 Nathaniel Curzon, first Baron Scarsdale, placed Robert Adam in charge of the grand country house that he was building and the extensive landscaped park around it. Adam's contributions were inspired by the architecture of Ancient Rome. The dome of the rotunda appears on the skyline.
PHOTOGRAPH: AUTHOR

Stoke Hall. Built with finely ashlared stone from the local quarry (which is still a source of good building stone), Stoke Hall is dated 1757 on rainwater heads. The owner of this solid Palladian house on the banks of the river Derwent below Froggatt Edge was the Revd John Simpson, who perhaps consulted James Paine (then working at Chatsworth) but chose William Booth of Stoney Middleton as his builder.
PHOTOGRAPH: AUTHOR

Hammerton Hall, Litton. In the second half of the eighteenth century ordinary Derbyshire farmhouses began to acquire a sense of proportion and style. Hammerton Hall, dated 1768, has a pediment and an arched window above its central door. But mullioned windows long remained in use.
PHOTOGRAPH: AUTHOR

Farming and enclosure

The dominance of livestock farming in most parts of Derbyshire in this period is obvious from the detailed reports of Thomas Brown and John Farey. In general, Derbyshire farmers concentrated on dairying and stock breeding and most farms were small or medium-sized. The production of cheese in the south and west of the county was still mainly a farmhouse activity, though by 1789 nearly 2,000 tons per annum were exported; by 1841 this figure had risen to 8,000 tons. The best cheeses were bought by factors for the London and continental markets and were usually sent by road to Wilne Ferry or to wharves at Willington, Shardlow or Derby, where they went by boat down the Trent to Gainsborough or Hull. Other cheeses were sold in Midland markets and specialised cheese fairs.

The cattle that were kept in Derbyshire in the late eighteenth century ranged from traditional breeds to the new Longhorns bred by Robert Bakewell in Leicestershire. Some of Bakewell's New Leicester sheep were introduced into the south of the county, but white-faced Woodlands were the main type in the Dark Peak and grey-faced Forest sheep were popular in the east. Derbyshire was also renowned for its breed of black cart horses that were sold at horse fairs up and down the country. The growing of cereals was largely restricted to the lighter soils of the gravel terraces and to the sandstone and magnesian limestone districts in the east. In the mid-1830s the estimated land use in Derbyshire was 166,426 acres of arable, 408,587 of grass and 46,649 of wood; in many of the Peak District townships more than 80 per cent of tithable land was under grass. Two changes that were noted by the assistant tithe commissioners were that wheat was now as important as oats, and at Melbourne, after the open fields and commons were enclosed in 1791, market gardens were formed on loamy and sandy soils to supply the nearby county towns of Nottingham, Derby and Leicester.

In the second volume of his *General View of the Agriculture of Derbyshire* (1813), John Farey wrote that most Derbyshire woods:

> appear to be very ancient, and few, if any of them, have been planted within a Century past, and yet large Trees are very rare in them, as might be expected, by those who observe and consider how destructive such are to Underwood (especially where pruning has been neglected), which by its frequent and considerable return, in most situations, is found more profitable than Oaks, or any other Trees, suffered to stand in such Woods longer than 50 or 60 years at most, owing to the very inadequate prices given for large Timber ...
>
> Almost throughout Derbyshire, the principal appropriation of the Underwood is to Puncheons, or Supports for the Coal-Pits, and for which purpose the Underwood requires to stand from 21 to 28 Years old, or about 25 Years on the average; the Stemples and Fails used in Lead-Mines, and the Ladder-shafts, Soughs, Gates, etc. leading thereto occasioned also a very considerable demand for stout Underwood Poles, until within a few years past, when the Mines have so much declined: the smaller Poles find a vend for making Fleaks or Hurdles, for Broom-sticks and Hedge-stakes, and other similar uses, and nearly all the remaining Underwood and Lop of the Wood Trees, are cut into Cord-wood, and converted to Charcoal near the spot.

The Derbyshire woods were commonly divided into 24 or 25 nearly equal parts so that they could be felled on rotation, but the drop in demand for charcoal and white coal from the ironmasters and lead smelters meant that the income from springwoods was now considerably less than from arable or pasture. One specialised trade that continued to thrive was the making of sickle handles from smaller birch and alder poles in Eckington parish.

During the second half of the eighteenth century and the first half of the nineteenth parliamentary enclosure made huge changes to much of the Derbyshire landscape. The remaining open-field systems were swept away and the commons and wastes were divided into square or rectangular fields by hawthorn hedges or drystone walls. Those landowners who possessed the majority of the land were able to override opposition through obtaining a private act of parliament for their parish or township. Derbyshire's first parliamentary enclosure act was passed in 1726 for the division of the commons and wastes in the parish of Scarcliffe and Palterton, but it was not until the 1760s that the movement got under way. It gathered momentum during the French Wars of 1793–1815 and 147 acts were passed by 1865. Some acts covered only a few hundred acres of remaining open fields and commons, but in the Peak District thousands of acres of moorland were enclosed. This was how the White Peak, in particular, acquired its modern appearance.

'Almost throughout Derbyshire, the principal appropriation of the Underwood is to Puncheons, or Supports for the Coal-Pits.'

As farmers were awarded allotments according to the size and value of their previous common rights, large landowners did well out of enclosure. The new roads across the former commons and wastes can be recognised by their straightness and their standard widths of up to 40 feet; they were the first roads to be planned since Roman times. In the southern lowlands, the new, tall Georgian farmhouses that were built in the fields beyond the villages were usually double-depth in style and so very different from the older farmhouses of the villages, though there too new farmhouses were soon erected. Their pleasant, symmetrical appearance was enhanced by the use of hand-made bricks of various textures and colours. In north Derbyshire the new farmhouses on the moorland edges were built of stones that were cleared from the new fields or dug from shallow delphs nearby. As cereal prices were high during the wars, some of the former wastes were converted temporarily into arable land and drained by ridges and furrows whose straight, narrow patterns, confined by the new field boundaries, distinguish them from the older ridge-and-furrow of the former open fields. Local labourers were employed to build the walls of the new enclosures that stretched for miles over the moors. The former moorland in the White Peak was successfully converted into pastures and hill meadows. In places such as Bonsall and Winster small barns dotted the landscape of the new fields, as in the Yorkshire Dales, and dew ponds, puddled with clay (and in modern times, concrete) were dug to retain rainwater for the livestock.

The wildest moors in the Dark Peak were converted by great landowners into compact estates for shooting grouse. The Duke of Rutland, for instance, acquired vast acreages of unproductive moorland upon the enclosure of his north Derbyshire manors of Barlow, Baslow, Brampton, Holmesfield, Dore, Totley and Hathersage. At Longshaw about 1830, he built an enormous

Abney Moor. In the era of parliamentary enclosure in the late eighteenth and early nineteenth centuries large stretches of moorland edges were brought into cultivation for the first time. Rectangular fields with tall, straight walls were created in the years immediately after the confirmation of an enclosure award. Crops were grown at first, but most of these fields soon became pastures.

PHOTOGRAPH: AUTHOR

Enclosure award road, White Peak. A green road laid out to a standard width according to a parliamentary enclosure award was a common sight in the Peak District in the early nineteenth century. Most are now covered with tarmac, but this example to the east of Monk's Dale, leading towards Wheston, retains its original character. It served both as a through road and to provide access to the new fields which had been created alongside it.

PHOTOGRAPH: AUTHOR

Many new fields, such as these seen on Brampton Moor (foreground), were brought into cultivation after enclosure, their rectangular shapes transferred from the surveyor's drawing board to the landscape. The largest landowners acquired vast acres of moorland, which they adapted for grouse shooting. Brampton Moor was enclosed between 1815 and 1827. The butts on the moor (just visible in the background) were erected a generation or so later.

PHOTOGRAPH: AUTHOR

Hurkling Stone, Big Moor. Natural features of the landscape were used as boundary markers by the various townships on the edges of the moors. Hurkling is a dialect word meaning crouching, an apt description of this boulder when seen on the skyline from below. It is inscribed by the letters MB (manor of Baslow) and H (Holmesfield), but the boundary was disputed and some of the letters have been chiselled out. The now dilapidated wall that approaches the stone was erected in the early nineteenth century when these moors were enclosed by various private Acts of Parliament.

PHOTOGRAPH: AUTHOR

Field barn between Bonsall and Winster. After enclosure of the commons and wastes farmers found it convenient to build small, two-storeyed barns in the distant new fields that had been awarded to them. Hay was stored above, and forked down to the livestock sheltering below. These barns are a distinctive feature of the White Peak and of parts of the Yorkshire Dales. Well over 100 of them survive in Bonsall parish.

PHOTOGRAPH: AUTHOR

shooting lodge in mock-Jacobean style with accommodation for his guests and even a chapel. The turnpike road was diverted and a nearby inn, known as Fox House after an earlier farming tenant, was built nearby for those who were not entertained at the lodge. Drives on to the moors were constructed and gamekeepers' lodges, two of which survive in lonely positions on the moors, were erected in similar mock-Jacobean style. The keepers shot foxes, crows and raptors and encouraged the rearing of young grouse, but Derbyshire's grouse moors were not yet managed intensely and shooting butts were not introduced until the mid-nineteenth century.

LEFT
Duke's Drive,
Longshaw. Upon
the parliamentary
enclosure of the
moors of Baslow,
Barlow, Holmesfield,
Totley and
Hathersage in the
early nineteenth
century the Duke
of Rutland amassed
a large estate for
shooting grouse.
In the late 1820s
he built Longshaw
Lodge to house his
hunting and shooting
parties. Here we see
the drive that was
made to take the
Duke and his guests
from the lodge on to
the moors.

PHOTOGRAPH: AUTHOR

The textile industry

HOSIERY

Derbyshire's leadership in transforming the manufacture of cotton into England's major industry came from a long-established background in framework knitting and the production of silk. As we have seen, Richard Arkwright modelled his mills at Cromford on the Lombe brothers' silk mill at Derby. A big step forward had been taken in 1759 when his future partner, Jedediah Strutt, then a Blackwell wheelwright and farmer, patented the 'Derby rib' machine for the manufacture of ribbed and therefore better-shaped stockings. Modifications soon enabled the mechanical production of gloves, shirts, drawers and caps and the production of wider fabric or several articles simultaneously. Framework knitting became the chief source of employment for the landless poor of south Derbyshire. Melbourne, for example, had no knitters in 1695, but by 1789 it had 80 frames in its cottages. The occupation became so common that it is was noted simply as FWK in parish registers.

Jedediah Strutt and his brother-in-law William Woolat moved to Derby, where they spun raw silk from London at their silk mill. By the time Strutt's patent expired in 1773 he had made a great deal of money; in 1785 he erected a second silk mill at Morledge. Master hosiers such as the Strutts owned large numbers of frames, which were rented by cottagers in towns and villages. On Monday mornings, the knitters fetched their raw materials from warehouses in Derby, Belper and other towns and on the following Saturday afternoon returned with their finished goods. Otherwise, they were supplied by 'bagmen'. In 1789 James Pilkington estimated that the Derby hosiers owned 1,156 frames, but that only 170 knitters lived in the borough. The frames were often placed in work rooms, some of which were in attics, lit by elongated windows beneath the eaves. In the 1780s frame rents were about ninepence a week and earnings averaged 10–14 shillings, but in the early nineteenth century earnings began to drop and as labour relations soured, strikes for higher wages broke out in 1814 and 1821.

The so-called Pentrich revolution of 1817 was a protest by a group of impoverished workers form Pentrich, South Wingfield and neighbouring villages who were duped by a government informer, William Oliver, into joining what they believed would be a large revolutionary force from the north of England. Thomas Bacon, a 64-year-old framework knitter who had read the works of Thomas Paine and had probably been involved in the Luddite destruction of machines, organised political meetings over several months at the White Horse Inn, Pentrich. On the night of 9 June about 50 men met at Hunt's Barn, South Wingfield, and set off for Nottingham, where they fled when they were faced by armed soldiers. Three of the leaders were hanged for high treason before a large crowd that gathered in front of the County Gaol in Derby and 14 other men were transported to Australia for life.

By the 1830s the average earnings of knitters amounted to nine shillings a week after deductions. As the population grew the number of frames continued to rise. Felkin's report of 1844 estimated that 43,900 of the nation's 48,500 frames were worked in Nottinghamshire, Derbyshire and Leicestershire. By then, the master hosiers had been replaced by hosiery firms, with large putting-out warehouses, such as those of Ward, Brettle & Ward of Belper, established in 1803. Steam-powered hosiery machines were introduced from the middle of the nineteenth century, but hand-operated frames long continued in use. Meanwhile, the number of silk mills continued to grow. By 1840 the borough of Derby had 17 spinning or weaving mills, Glossop had five or six, Chesterfield had one in Beetwell Street, and beyond the county boundaries Leek, Macclesfield, Sheffield and Stockport became important centres.

WANTED:
'*good Calico weavers ... if they have large families, may be accommodated with houses and have employment for their children.*'
ADVERTISEMENT, 1794

COTTON

Hand-spun cotton yarn was used in the hosiery trade from the 1730s. In 1764 James Hargreaves invented his spinning jenny, a multiple-spinning frame which enabled one person to spin several threads simultaneously. Four years later, the violent reaction to his machine forced Hargreaves to leave Lancashire for Nottingham, which had become the centre of the cotton hosiery industry, just as Derby was the leading place for the silk industry. A number of mills in north-west Derbyshire soon used the jenny.

Richard Arkwright followed Hargreaves to Nottingham. The water frame or roller-spinning machine that he invented in 1769 enabled the continuous spinning of cotton on machines that could be operated by unskilled workers. Ichabod Wright and Samuel Need (by then a partner of Jedediah Strutt) provided the finance to build the first cotton mill in Nottingham, but they soon found that they needed a much greater and relatively cheap source of power. In 1771 Arkwright decided to move to Cromford, where water-power was provided, though not always efficiently, by the Bonsall Brook and a drainage sough from a lead mine, close to where they flowed into the river Derwent. Much of his time was taken up with experiments and progress was slow. In 1775 Arkwright was granted a second patent which mechanised the preparatory processes of opening and cleaning the cotton, carding, and the making of slivers and rovers for the spinning machines. His greatest achievement, however, was to place these machines in water-powered mills, with a 'packaged' system of production that was soon copied in many parts of northern England and lowland Scotland. These new cotton mills produced cheap clothing and

Portrait of Jedediah Strutt (1726–97) by Joseph Wright. This serious-minded Unitarian, caught here in introspective mood, was the inventor of the Derby rib machine in 1759, a partner of Richard Arkwright at Cromford, and founder of the cotton spinning mills at Belper and Milford. He and his sons were paternalist employers who transformed Belper into a thriving town and whose benevolence included the gift of the Arboretum as a public park in Derby.

household textiles for the mass of the population and so greatly improved standards of personal hygiene and domestic comfort.

A big step forward came in 1776–77, when Peter Nightingale, a wealthy lead merchant and neighbouring landowner, provided not only the finance for a second mill, but a house for Arkwright overlooking the mill entrance and cottages for his workers. The mill site continued to grow and by 1789 Arkwright was employing 800 operatives. Despite disastrous fires, they continued to spin cotton until 1846. Cromford was a rather remote place and as only a few farmers and lead miners lived there before the mills were built Arkwright had to attract the women and youngsters that he needed for his workforce by offering suitable accommodation and by providing work for the men. A newspaper advertisement of 19 September 1781 looked for:

Forging and Filing Smiths, Joiners and Carpenters, Framework-Knitters and Weavers, with large Families. Likewise Children of all Ages; above seven years old, may have constant Employment. Boys and young Men may have Trades taught them, which will enable them to maintain a Family in short Time. Two or three young Men who can write a good Hand, are also wanted. By personal Application at the COTTON-MILLS, Particulars may be known.

Arkwright built houses that were superior to most working-class accommodation on offer at the time. On the top floors of the rows of cottages that he erected from 1776 in North Street and along the roads to Wirksworth and Bonsall men wove his yarn into calico while their wives and children worked long hours in his mills down in the valley. Other men worked in the loom shop or as framework knitters in spaces provided at the mill. His partners created similar industrial communities lower down the Derwent valley, the like of which had never been seen before. Jedediah Strutt employed men as farmworkers or carriers and built workshops for nailmakers and framework knitters, whose wives and children worked in his mills at Belper and Milford, while Peter Nightingale, who built his own mill at Lea in 1784, advertised for 'good Calico weavers' who, 'if they have large families, may be accommodated with houses and have employment for their children'. Arkwright took a paternal interest in the development of his new community at Cromford. In 1778 he built the Greyhound Inn by the market square and he created customs for his workforce, such as an annual festival of candle lighting when workmen and children, led by a band, paraded from the mills around the village and on their return received ale, buns, nuts and fruit. He founded friendly societies and clubs, notably a cow club, and in 1785 a new Sunday School, which immediately attracted 200 children. In 1797 his son opened Cromford church, which had been planned as a private chapel for Willersley Castle, the splendid house that Sir Richard had built on the other side of the river to his mills, but which was not completed until after his death. Unlike the Strutts, the Arkwrights were not Dissenters, and

The world's first successful water-powered cotton spinning mill was built by Richard Arkwright on a long, curving site near the banks of the river Derwent at Cromford. The complex of mills, warehouses and workshops seen here was built between 1771 and 1790. At the far end of the yard, on the right, is the first mill, extended in the 1780s but reduced by two storeys in a disastrous fire in 1929. It was powered by an overshot wheel with water brought by an aqueduct. The five-storeyed building to the left of the first mill was built between 1785 and 1790 as an extra mill and warehouse. The three-storeyed building on the other side of the principal entrance to the site was erected about the same time as a warehouse and counting house. The nearer buildings on the left provided space for workshops and machinery, including perhaps knitting frames. The first mill (*lower photograph*), now only three storeys high, is seen here from the outside.

the various Methodist chapels which were erected in Cromford in the nineteenth century were all built on land that lay outside the Arkwright estate.

The mill operatives employed by Arkwright and Strutt were mostly children, who were generally taken on between the ages of ten and 12 and kept until they left to learn a trade as a weaver or stockinger or perhaps as a nailmaker. They usually worked a 12-hour day, including breaks for breakfast and tea, with one hour off for dinner between each six-hour stint. This had been the practice at the first Derby silk mill. A big change, however, was the introduction of night work. A strict code of discipline was imposed, and wages were normally based on piecework.

Arkwright built further mills at Bakewell (1778), Wirksworth (1780), Cressbrook (1783) and Masson (1783), between Cromford and Matlock Bath. Masson was the largest of his mills, a six-storey brick building of considerable architectural pretension with Venetian windows and a central cupola. It was

Arkwright's Lower Mill (1776), which stood beyond the millpond, was demolished after a fire in 1890. The four-storeyed annexe building to the rear was built between 1787 and 1790 and is now used to display the history of the mills. The restricted nature of the site is evident from the annexe's proximity to the limestone ridge between the mills and the river Derwent. Water power came not from the river but from the Bonsall Brook and an old lead-mine drainage sough.

PHOTOGRAPH: CARNEGIE

Arkwright had to attract his labour force by offering decent housing with long back gardens. Pigsties such as this were a common feature at the bottom of the gardens.

PHOTOGRAPH: CARNEGIE

Constructed in 1785 by Richard Arkwright as a dam and sluice to control the flow of the lead mine sough and to force it towards the pond behind the *Greyhound*, this structure soon acquired the nickname of the Bear Pit. The sough water was diverted each Sunday, when the mills were not in use, so that the pond would have an adequate supply of water at the beginning of the working week.

PHOTOGRAPH: CARNEGIE

sited on the river Derwent and powered by a single water wheel. Arkwright's ambitious programme of mill building was motivated largely by his desire to make as much money as he could before his patents expired in 1783 and 1785. He also earned large royalties by licensing other mills. He was involved with mills in Lancashire and at the time of his death in 1792 he was about to expand in Scotland.

When Samuel Need died in 1781 his executors sold his share of the partnership to Strutt and Arkwright, who then agreed amicably to dissolve their association. Strutt had continued to spin silk at Derby and had begun to build cotton mills on his own account at Belper. The first, in 1776, was rebuilt as the South Mill in 1812; the second, in 1786, was rebuilt with an iron frame as the North Mill after a fire in 1804; the third, in 1795–96, was named the West Mill and was built to William Strutt's earliest fire-proof designs. By 1789 Strutt employed 600 operatives at the Belper site; by 1833 the number had risen to 2,000. In 1780 he had also built a mill downstream at Milford, together with bleaching and dyeing mills, and in 1792–93 his son William added a fireproof warehouse. The Milford site also included a foundry in which much of the ironwork for buildings (including the cast-iron windows of workers' houses) and water wheels was made. Most of the Milford complex of buildings has been demolished.

In contrast to some mills in north-west Derbyshire, including Arkwright's Cressbrook Mill, the Strutts did not make much use of the parish apprenticeship system. They relied instead on attracting families by offering houses

Willersley Castle. From 1782 Richard Arkwright had lived in Rock House, overlooking his mills, but in 1786 (the year he was knighted) he started to build a new and imposing residence to become known as Willersley Castle. This was sited on rising ground overlooking the river Derwent, but from where neither the Cromford nor Masson Mill could be seen. The architect was William Thomas of London, who combined a classical design with romantic battlements and turrets. The Hon. John Byng dismissed it as 'an effort of inconvenient ill taste'. The building was finished in 1790, but while it was being furnished the following year the interior was gutted by fire. Arkwright died before his 'castle' was completed. Willersley remained in the family's possession until 1936.

PHOTOGRAPH: CARNEGIE

Richard Arkwright built the two rows of 27 houses in North Street in 1776 to house his workers and their families. The street was the first systematically planned industrial housing in Derbyshire. The accommodation was of high quality by the standards of its time and superior to much later industrial housing. Each house is three storeys high but only one bay wide and one bay deep, with a single-storey kitchen at the back. The living room was on the ground floor, the bedroom on the first floor, and the attic served as a weaver's workshop, hence the row of lights. Each house had a long garden and pigsties at the rear. North Street set a pattern for further industrial housing in Cromford, although later houses did not reach this standard of construction.

North Mill, Belper. In 1804 William Strutt rebuilt the
North Mill in brick above the two stone storeys that
had survived a disastrous fire in the previous year.
Strutt was a pioneer in designing fireproof mills. His
new building was iron-framed throughout, clad with
plaster, and provided with brick and tile floors. The
attic storey was formerly used as a schoolroom. In
1831 Samuel Lewis wrote that at Belper, 'There are
five mills for the spinning of cotton, all belonging
to Messrs Strutt, who make their own machinery on
the spot ... Here is one of the largest establishments
in the kingdom for silk and cotton hose, in which
upwards of four thousand persons are employed,
principally residing in the surrounding villages.'

PHOTOGRAPH: CARNEGIE

ABOVE LEFT

Former nail-making workshop, Joseph Street, Belper. This is a rare survival from the many that Strutt built to
provide employment for the men whose wives and children worked in his mills. Small nailshops with a single
hearth such as this were less common than rows of shops where five or six men worked under one roof. In 1831
Samuel Lewis observed that, 'The nails made [in Belper], especially those for the shoeing of horses, are much in
demand, from the superiority of the rod iron made at Alderwasley, four miles distant, arising from the peculiar
quality of the coal in the neighbourhood.'

PHOTOGRAPH: CARNEGIE

LEFT

'Richard Arkwright's Cotton Mill', by William Day, c.1789. Day's watercolour is one of the earliest views of
the first mill that Richard Arkwright built at Cromford in 1771. The course of the drainage sough from the lead
mines is seen on the right, bringing water to help power the mill over a cast-iron aqueduct (now demolished).
The Hon. John Bing, an early visitor, deplored the loss of rural tranquility: 'I saw the workers issue forth at 7
o'clock, a wonderful crowd of young people ... a new set then goes in for the night, for the mills never leave off
working ... These cotton mills, seven stories high, and fill'd with inhabitants, remind me of a first rate man of
war; and when they are lighted up, on a dark night, look most luminously beautiful ...'

PHOTOGRAPH BY CARNEGIE, WITH PERMISSION OF DERBY MUSEUMS AND ART GALLERY

The first mill at Cressbrook (originally known as Grassbrook) was a building of four storeys built in 1783 for Richard Arkwright. It burned down in November 1785, and was rebuilt in 1787 on the same foundations by Richard Arkwright II. Supplies of raw cotton came by cart from the canal at Chapel-en-le-Frith. Between 1814 and 1816 Francis Philips, a Manchester merchant and cotton spinner, built a large new mill that was powered by the river Wye rather than the Cressbrook. This handsome 12-bay structure was erected in some style with a four-bay pedimented centre and a lantern on the hipped roof. Cast-iron columns were used to prevent the spread of fire. In 1823 a third mill was built here. William Newton, the manager from 1810 to 1830, employed about 300 parish apprentices from workhouses in London and other cities. In 1817 an apprentice house was built to the rear of the mill, with a later 'Gothic' addition. Other apprentices were accommodated in eight two-roomed cottages. Newton and his wife treated the apprentices kindly, but the hours of work were long. Cressbrook Mill closed in 1965 and, after many years of neglect, it was restored and converted into apartments.

PHOTOGRAPH: AUTHOR

that were superior to those occupied by most working-class people. The first at Belper were Long Row and the Clusters, built during the 1790s. In time, a new community was formed near the mills at the north end of the town, away from the original settlement of nailmakers around the market place. In 1789 Belper had 433 houses, by 1801 it had 873 and by 1821 the number had risen to 1,239. Terraced cottages were also built at Milford in 1793–94 on the side of Hopping Hill overlooking the river Derwent. The Strutts were Nonconformists who erected Wesleyan and Baptist chapels and Lancasterian schools, as well as farms to provide fresh produce.

Further down the Derwent valley, the Evans family of Derby iron founders were linked with the Strutts through marriage. In 1783 Thomas Evans and his

The East Mill of 1912 at Belper towers over Strutt's original North Mill (*right*). In the foreground can be seen the elaborate sluice gates which still control the flow of the river Derwent past the former cotton mills.

PHOTOGRAPH: CARNEGIE

Long Row, Belper. Between 1792 and his death in 1797 Jedediah Strutt built this substantial row of houses for his employees and their families. Thirty-five of the original 77 houses were built with local sandstone three storeys high. They are of comparable quality to those of Strutt's former partner, Richard Arkwright, at Cromford.
PHOTOGRAPH: CARNEGIE

In 1783 the Evans family founded a major cotton-spinning enterprise in what was already an industrial hamlet on the banks of the river Derwent to the north of Derby. The mill was rebuilt in 1789 after the first building had been destroyed by fire. The family continued to extend the mill in different phases up to 1821 and to provide housing for their workers in an unplanned, piecemeal way over 50 years or so. The surviving complex formed an essential part of the successful bid for World Heritage Status for the Derwent valley Mills in 2001. The Darley Abbey mills are amongst the most complete early cotton factories and the workers' settlement has survived almost intact, though with many small improvements in modern times. Further housing for workers was provided in neighbouring Allestree.
PHOTOGRAPH: CARNEGIE

Bamford Mill. Although it was recorded in Domesday Book, Bamford ('the ford marked by a tree') remained a hamlet until the late eighteenth century. About 1780, following Arkwright's success at Cromford, Christopher Kirk converted his corn mill into one of the many cotton spinning mills that were being erected in remote parts of the Derbyshire countryside. This mill was destroyed by fire in 1791 but it was rebuilt by Samuel Moore, a mill owner of Ancoats, Manchester, and developed by his son, William Cameron Moore, and his descendants, who lived at Bamford Hall. A weir across the river Derwent diverted water to a wheel that was the sole source of power until a beam engine was installed in the 1850s. By 1860 Bamford had over 850 inhabitants and a new church, and the mill employed 230 men, women and children. Since its closure in 1965 the mill has been converted into apartments.

PHOTOGRAPH: AUTHOR

A cotton spinning mill, modelled on those at Cromford, was built at Litton in 1782 by Elias Needham and Thomas Firth. This was the mill that became notorious for the harsh treatment of its apprentices, as revealed in a sensational manner in *The Memoir of Robert Blincoe*, a London orphan who lived and worked here from 1803 to 1814. The new mill, seen here, was built in 1874.

PHOTOGRAPH: AUTHOR

Ruins of Oldknow's Mill, Mellor. Samuel Oldknow's cotton spinning mill on the river Goyt on the boundary of the township of Mellor, was one of the largest to be worked on the Arkwright system. It was built between 1790 and 1793 and at the height of production in 1804 it employed about 550 people (the great majority of whom were women and children) and operated 10,080 spindles. The central building was six storeys high, 210 feet long and 42 feet wide, with three-storeyed extensions at each side, making the total length about 400 feet. The mill was destroyed by fire in 1892 and in the late 1930s the remaining ruins were largely demolished. The site of the mill now forms part of the fancifully named Roman Lakes Leisure Park.

PHOTOGRAPH: CARNEGIE

sons, William and Walter, converted a flint-grinding mill at Darley Abbey into a cotton-spinning mill. After a disastrous fire in 1788, he rebuilt it immediately. He also built houses such as Lavender Row for his workers, followed eventually by a church and a school. By 1830 his mill employed over 500 workers.

In 1789 Pilkington recorded 22 cotton-spinning mills in Derbyshire, including those at Litton, Cressbrook, Bamford, Calver, Tansley, Lumsdale, Lea, Pleasley and Wilne. The mill at Litton, which was built in 1782 by Elias Needham and his cousin Thomas Firth, gained national notoriety upon the publication of *The Memoir of Robert Blincoe*, a London orphan who was apprenticed under Needham between 1803 and 1814. Although Blincoe's story was printed as a sensational piece of propaganda a long time after the events they claimed to describe, there is little doubt that he and his fellow apprentices were poorly fed, brutally treated and forced to work more than the statutory 12 hours a day. When Needham went bankrupt in 1815, at least 80 apprentices had to be supported on parish relief; ten of them died in the next three years. The various Factory Acts from 1819 and 1833 onwards dealt with the worst abuses and shortened the hours of work of both women and children in the mills. After 1833 no-one under 18 was allowed to work more than 12 hours a day or 69 hours a week and factory inspectors were appointed to enforce the law.

On the other side of the White Peak, cotton mills were constructed in the Arkwright style in the north-west corner of the county, in and around the extensive parish of Glossop. Samuel Oldknow built an impressive six-storeyed mill at Mellor in 1790–91 and others followed at Glossop, Hayfield and New Mills in the early years of the nineteenth century. In 1831 Samuel Lewis reported 'about fifty cotton-mills, five extensive establishments for calico-printing, two clothing-mills, a manufactory for cloth, and another for brown paper'. The population of the sprawling industrial settlements in the huge parish of Glossop grew from 8,883 in 1801 to 22,898 in 1841. At Dinting, Edmund Potter built a calico mill in 1825 and others were soon erected along the valley of the river Sett. At New Mills, the Goyt and the Sett provided ample supplies of flowing water, so by 1846 eight cotton-spinning mills, four calico printing mills, four candlewick mills and two dyeing mills had been established, together with engraving, printing and bleaching businesses. Lewis commented on Hadfield that, 'About thirty years since this district was almost entirely an agricultural one, and but thinly inhabited; but now there are many flourishing cotton factories (some of them on a large scale), which afford employment to nearly the whole of the population.'

The factory-based cotton industry that Arkwright and the Strutts created led the way in the Industrial Revolution, but the centre of the industry soon moved from Derbyshire to Lancashire, which had easier access to supplies of raw cotton and, when steam power took over, plentiful supplies of coal. By 1901 no less than 85 per cent of the workforce in the cotton mills in England and Wales lived in Lancashire. Many of the Derbyshire mills had long since been converted to other uses or stood derelict. Richard Arkwright II sold his cotton mills (except for Cromford and Masson) and invested his capital in land in various parts of England and in government stocks. In 1824 he bought the Sutton Scarsdale estate, where he was succeeded by his second son Robert; Peter, the third son, inherited Willersley Castle and continued to spin cotton; and the other three sons lived on landed estates in Leicestershire, Herefordshire and Staffordshire. Jedediah Strutt had three sons to succeed him in 1797; George continued to manage the mills at Belper, while William (the expert in the design of fire-proof buildings) and Joseph managed the business in Derby. The Strutts continued to run the family firm at Belper until 1897, when it was sold to the English Sewing Corporation.

Lead

The amount of Derbyshire lead that was mined and smelted in the middle years
of the eighteenth century was never surpassed. The boom years of the 1750s
and 1760s were soon followed by another prosperous period from the late 1780s
until 1796, but four years of depression followed. During the nineteenth century
the number of mine workings declined dramatically in face of competition and
costly technological difficulties once the old veins had been worked out. In 1809
Derbyshire had 292 lead mines and 18 cupolas, but the quality of the ore was
generally inferior to that mined previously. The county's lead industry faced
prolonged periods of depression in 1816–18 and 1824–33, when Matlock was
typical in that 'The lead mines were formerly worked to a great extent in the
parish, but at present there are only a few in operation.' Trade recovered for a
time, but during the second half of the nineteenth century most of Derbyshire's
lead mines became exhausted.

Some mines were very profitable in the boom years, notably Dovegang
(Wirksworth), Gregory (Ashover), Odin (Castleton), Blythe (Alport), Portway
(Winster and Elton) and the various mines at Eyam, but many of the small
mines hardly broke even. During the prosperous years of the eighteenth century,
extensions of several old veins, such as those on Hucklow Edge and at the Odin
mine, were worked at considerable profit once new soughs had been driven to
drain them. These astonishing feats of engineering extended for several miles
underground and released millions of gallons of water. Between 1742 and 1764
the 2¼ mile Yatestoop Sough at Birchover was constructed to drain the mines in

The Odin Lead
Mine. Lead was
mined here in the
Middle Ages, but the
deep underground
veins were not
exploited until the
early eighteenth
century, when
effective drainage
methods were
introduced. Here
we see the end of
a drainage channel
hacked out of the
limestone rock below
Mam Tor.

PHOTOGRAPH: AUTHOR

Meersbrook Sough. In 1772 work began on an ambitious scheme to drain the lead mines under Wirksworth into the river Derwent south of Cromford. Francis Hurt of Alderwasley, lead smelter and industrial entrepreneur, was the leading shareholder. The arch under which the water emerges on the bank above the river is inscribed 'FH 1772'. More than 200 soughs were engineered in the lead fields of the White Peak, mostly in the seventeenth and eighteenth centuries. Millions of gallons of water still flow through this arch daily, to the benefit of the Severn Trent Water Authority.

PHOTOGRAPH: AUTHOR

the Winster area. In 1772 work began on the Meersbrook Sough, which passes under the town of Wirksworth, and with its variant branches has a length of some five miles; the entire scheme was not completed until 1846 and 17 million gallons of water still flow through it every day. One of the most famous was the Hillcarr Sough, which was designed to drain the mines on Alport Moor into the river Derwent and was driven for about four miles at about 700 feet below the surface; work began in 1766 and within two years it had paid for itself as the water table was lowered by 65–70 feet. The ventilation problem in the mine was solved in 1778–79 by sinking an air shaft from Stanton Moor. More than 200 soughs have now been identified in the Derbyshire lead field by members of the Peak District Mines Historical Society.

Smelting was transformed gradually by the introduction of reverbatory furnaces or cupolas, which were fuelled by coal that was kept separate from the ore. The first in Derbyshire was built in 1735 by the London Lead Company at Bower's Mill, Kelstedge, near Ashover. But it was not until the late 1780s that cupolas had generally replaced water-powered smelting mills. The remains

This view of a lead smelting works at Stoney Middleton was drawn by Sir Francis Chantrey and engraved by W.B. and George Cooke in 1818 for inclusion in Ebenezer Rhodes, *Peak Scenery, or Excursions into Derbyshire*. John Barker erected the Storrs Cupola in Middleton Dale about 1777 and the Duke of Devonshire had another nearby. Stoney Middleton was also a major limestone quarrying and lime-burning centre.

Drawn by F.L. Chantrey A.R.A.   Engraved by W.B. Cooke.

of a cupola at Stone Edge with its square-built chimney, dating from c.1770, form the best-preserved smelting site from this period. The largest works was Cow Hay smelting mills at Lea, where Peter Nightingale built a cupola in the 1740s. His son Peter combined lead smelting with a cotton-spinning mill that he built at Lea in 1784. After his death in 1803 the smelting works were taken over by William Shore, the husband of his niece.

Although the Gregory mine near Ashover had a steam 'whimsey' or winding engine by 1796, it was well into the nineteenth century before most of the larger mining companies replaced their horse gins by steam winding engines. By 1777 at least 20 atmospheric steam engines were installed in Derbyshire, 13 at lead mines and the rest in coal mines. The best-known local builders of all types of steam engine were Francis Thompson of Ashover and his son Joseph. In 1777 Francis built an engine at Norbriggs Colliery, Staveley, and in 1782 a 64½-inch bore pumping engine 510 feet below the surface at the Yatestoop lead mine. The 57 inch-bore engine that he erected in 1791 at Oakerthorpe Colliery is now in the Science Museum.

By about 1770 free miners were of little importance and many of the cavers who scavenged the old rakes were women. Most of the smaller mines in and around Wirksworth and Castleton stopped working by 1800 once they had reached the water table. The lead mining villages began to lose population and the families that remained saw their incomes drop. In 1796 the Duke of Rutland's agent wrote that at Foolow 'the poor people in this neighbourhood never suffr'd as they do now'. In Ashover the poor rate doubled between 1790 and 1808 and doubled again between 1808 and 1815. By 1820 the money spent on the poor of that parish was seven times that of 1790. Some families moved to the coalfields, others to the textile mills of Lancashire and Cheshire.

Yet others managed to continue in the old way. In 1834 the Poor Law commissioners reported that nearly all the miners in the long and straggling village of Middleton-by-Wirksworth owned their cottages and had a few acres of grazing land attached. The village of Winster, near the deep mines of the large companies, contained some sturdy middle-class houses in a reasonably ordered appearance in contrast to the usual straggling arrangement of small groups of terraced cottages in other villages. Bradwell was much more typical in its haphazard growth, with cottages of all shapes and sizes on every available piece of land in the valley bottom or perched alongside the tracks climbing up to the mines. Bonsall, too, was free from the control of a squire and so grew in a piecemeal, unorganised way. Many of its houses were small farms with a few acres on which cattle could graze, while some of the cottagers were involved in domestic work for the cotton mills further down the valley. The coexistence of industry and agriculture, whether in combination or not, was still normal in the Peak District during the reign of Victoria. In the Hope valley, for instance, settlement consisted of nucleated villages of farmers, miners and craftsmen, industrial hamlets of textile workers near the mills by the rivers, and isolated farmsteads dotted about the hillsides.

This map of the 'Mines & Veins in Crich & Wake Bridge Liberties' was made on 22 June 1784 to distinguish the various lead mines, rakes and drainage soughs of the different owners. Crich (together with Ashover) stands well to the east of the major Derbyshire lead field, on detached layers of carboniferous limestone.

Iron

Coke had been used as a fuel from the mid-seventeenth century in such businesses as drying malt in Derby, but experiments by Derbyshire iron smelters were not successful until the second half of the eighteenth century. This heralded the huge changes that transformed the eastern half of Derbyshire and adjacent parts of Nottinghamshire. By 1784 all the pig-iron that was made in the East Midlands – amounting to 10 per cent of national production – was smelted with coke. Some of the sites of the old charcoal-fuelled ironworks were converted to other industrial uses, such as a rolling mill at Wilne or cotton mills at Borrowash and Pleasley, but others were closed down. By 1806 coke-fired furnaces at Brampton, Butterley, Duckmanton, Hasland, Morley Park, Renishaw, Riddings, Staveley, Stonegravels and Wingerworth had a combined

Winster Market Hall. Winster was a prosperous place in the late seventeenth and eighteenth centuries because of the large-scale lead mining enterprises in the vicinity. The Main Street has the look of a small town rather than a village, and indeed Winster had a Saturday market, established by 1690. The market hall dates from about that time, judging by the cross windows in the upper storey. The stone arches below were once open in the usual fashion to provide a sheltered space for trade on market days. The brick upper storey was rebuilt in 1904 and the building presented to the National Trust two years later.

annual output of 10,329 tons of pig-iron and Derbyshire was England's fourth largest producer. J.B. Nielsen's invention of the hot-blast smelting process raised output and reduced fuel consumption and by 1848 Derbyshire furnaces were making about 95,000 tons of pig-iron a year.

The Hurts had been landowners in the Ashbourne area since the fifteenth century and had prospered from smelting lead, but Francis, who had inherited the Alderwasley estate through his mother, was the first member of the family to invest in the iron industry. In 1764 he built a blast furnace and forge by the Derwent, using water power to blow the bellows. The following year he leased an ironstone mine on Heage Common and in 1767 he bought the manor of Heage, including the Morley Park estate which contained coal and ironstone. There in 1780–82 he erected a new steam-blown, coke-fired blast furnace, which supplied the forge and rolling mill at Alderwasley. Francis left his ironworks at Morley Park and Alderwasley to his elder son Francis, the last gentry ironmaster in the county. In 1811 the iron business was leased to John and Charles Mold, who refurbished the old furnace at Morley Park in 1818 and added a second furnace seven years later.

Unlike the Hurts, most landowners were content to lease their properties to ironmasters. In the 1750s Walter Mather had taken over the Wingerworth, Hartshorne and Kirkby furnaces and the Makeney forge and had built a rolling mill at Borrowash. In 1783 he took a lease from the Duke of Devonshire of the Staveley ironworks, which he rebuilt with a coke-fired furnace, a steam engine and a forge. Meanwhile, in 1781 Joseph Butler of Killamarsh (the son of a York land agent) and his partner George Matthews (a Shropshire ironmaster) had obtained a lease of the Hunlokes' ironworks at Wingerworth. There, in 1788, they built a plateway that ran for about a mile between their ironstone mines and their new steam-blown, coke-fired furnace and foundry. Coke was also carried along the plateway from Lings to Ankerbold and then by road to Wingerworth. In 1787 Butler took over a foundry at Stonegravels near the Chesterfield Canal and in 1800 he bought an ironworks at Killamarsh, where he soon erected a forge and rolling mill. He obtained the limestone that was needed for flux from a quarry that he owned at Ashover. Somehow he also found time to breed horses and farm by the latest methods. The severity of the post-Napoleonic depression forced him to close his Wingerworth furnace, the colliery at Lings and some other enterprises.

In 1775 John Smith, the son of a Sheffield Master Cutler, had founded the Griffin Works at New Brampton on the western edge of Chesterfield. By the 1790s his sons, led by Ebenezer, had built a new ironworks nearby, opened a number of collieries and ironstone pits, and founded a new ironworks at Duckmanton called the Adelphi Works. In 1806 the Smiths made 1,700 tons of pig-iron at the Griffin Works and 900 tons at Adelphi, the combined total making the firm the largest ironmaking business in Derbyshire at that time. The Griffin Works cast the cylinders of Boulton & Watt steam engines and those of Francis Thompson of Ashover and made cannon and cannon balls for the war against Napoleon. The firm also made heating stoves, cooking ranges and grates. They were hit badly by the post-war depression; the Griffin Works closed in the early 1830s, but production continued at the Adelphi works until 1845.

Further south, the minerals of the 3,000-acre estate of the Earls Stanhope in

A view looking south after the opening of the Midland Railway's Erewash Valley line (*left*) in 1861–62. The North Midland Railway from Derby to Leeds is seen to the right. An early signal box stands in the foreground. The ironworks and collieries of the Clay Cross Company are seen in the background.

the parishes of Stanton-by-Dale and Dale Abbey, close to the newly constructed Erewash Canal, began to be exploited in 1791 by the founding of the Dale Abbey Ironworks and the sinking of ironstone pits and collieries. Early attempts to build a business ended in bankruptcy, but in 1845 Benjamin and Josiah Smith of the Adelphi Ironworks took over the lease and within a year they had built two new blast furnaces alongside the Nutbrook Canal. Soon, another furnace, a foundry, workshops, fitters' rooms and new cottages for employees were built alongside a branch line of the Midland Railway. Ironstone was brought from pits on Dale Moor and limestone by canal from Hopton quarry. By 1848 the Stanton works was producing 200 tons of pig-iron a week, an output that was bettered only by the 210 tons of the Butterley Company's Codnor Park ironworks. A slump in the demand for iron bankrupted the Smiths in 1849, but creditors keep the works going and in 1878 it was incorporated as the Stanton Ironworks Co. Ltd.

A mile to the north of the Codnor Park ironworks stood another major enterprise, the Riddings Ironworks which Thomas Saxelby and two associates had founded in the last decade of the eighteenth century. By 1806, under the skilled technical management of the metallurgist David Mushet, the Riddings blast furnace was producing 1,450 tons of pig-iron a year, the third highest output of any Derbyshire ironworks. In 1808 James Oakes of Derby bought two-thirds of the shares and ten years later he bought out the remaining partner.

The increased production of iron in east Derbyshire boosted the secondary metal trades, particularly the manufacture of scythes and sickles in the parishes of Norton and Eckington on the borders of Hallamshire. When William Cobbett visited Mosborough in 1830 he observed that a prodigious quantity of scythes and sickles were exported to the Unites States of America. A year later, Samuel Lewis reported that the market for these agricultural hand tools also extended as far as Russia and Poland. Meanwhile, the Belper nailmaking industry flourished until it was faced with the competition of machine-made nails. Bagshaw's 1846 *Directory* noted that 400 people there were making common nails and a further 250 were making horse nails, but that 'the trade has long been in a declining condition here, and is now suffering severely from the competition of machinery in other parts of the kingdom'.

Coal mining

The coalfield on either side of the Derbyshire/Nottinghamshire border was exploited on an increasingly large scale during the nineteenth century until it became one of the greatest in England. Deep pits were also sunk in the South Derbyshire coalfield near the boundary with Leicestershire and drift mines produced smaller quantities of coal from shallow pits near Buxton and New Mills; Farey counted 21 small collieries between Simmondley in the north and Thatch Marsh in the south. He also observed that in the deep pits in east

The statue of
George Stephenson
which stands outside
Chesterfield station.

Tapton House,
Chesterfield. Set on
a hilltop to the east
of Chesterfield and
still surrounded by
its 94-acre park,
this Georgian brick
house stands close
to the earthworks of
a Norman ringwork
castle. The house
was begun by Isaac
Wilkinson in 1782
and extended by him
in 1794. In 1837 it
was let to George
Stephenson, the
celebrated railway
engineer, who lived
here until his death
in 1848, when he was
succeeded by his son
Robert, and later by
the colliery owner
Charles Markham.
It became a school
in 1931, when the
grounds were made
into a public park.
It now houses
innovation and
conference centres.

Derbyshire the 'longwall' system, worked by gangs that were hired and led by 'butties', was in use and that steam engines had been installed to pump water or to work winding engines.

The Derbyshire coalmining industry expanded out of recognition once the railways opened up the market to London and other distant places. In 1836 Parliament approved the North Midland Railway Company's line from Derby to Leeds under their chief engineer, George Stephenson. When a a tunnel was made at Clay Cross, Stephenson saw that the coal seams which were exposed could be a rich source of coke fuel for locomotives, so in 1837 he and his son Robert, with George Hudson and Joshua Walmsley, bought the estate to mine coal and build coke ovens, blast furnaces and an iron foundry (for ironstone had been found between Stretton and Clay Cross). They then began to work limestone quarries at Crich, which were connected by a tramway to Ambergate, where 20 kilns were in operation by 1841. The company's early profits were invested in the building of cottages and amenities for their workers at Clay Cross.

The Children's Employment Commission that was set up in 1842 to investigate the work that children did in the mines reported that in Derbyshire no women or girls were employed, but more than 16 per cent of underground workers were boys below the age of 13. The commissioners interviewed some of the young workers, such as Abraham Wiseall, aged 14, who said that he had worked in Mr Hunter's pits at New Ripley for the last five years. At first, he earned a shilling a day, but for the last six months his wages had risen to 1s. 6d. He went down the pit at various times between 6 and 9 o'clock, had half-an-hour allowed for his dinner, and finished his shift by 6 pm. He ate water porridge and bread for his breakfast before he went to work and caught a mouthful of bread and cheese when he could, about 10 o'clock. His dinner, which was sent to him, consisted of bread, meat and potatoes and he had tea and dry bread when he got home. He was always too tired to play when he did a whole day's work. For the past year or so he had been attending the 'Ranters' Sunday School at the Primitive Methodist Chapel, Heage, but he was still in easy lessons and could not spell any words. About a year ago, he got his foot trapped between a pit prop and the coal on the corve that he was dragging and could not work for a month. His grandmother told the commissioner that he had lived with her ever since he was born and that he used to come home very tired and weak with being overworked. She had three sons working in the pits, aged between 32 and 18, and was convinced that, if parents could afford it, children ought not to work until they were nine years old, and not more than 12 hours a day, including one hour for dinner.

John Wilson, a 70-year-old miner from nearby Swanwick, said that he had worked in the pits since he was seven. At first, he drove the horse that worked the winding gin and earned 4d. a day. When he went down the pit at the age of ten, he earned about a shilling a day. He had been through the different occupations of a collier until 'last Christmas twelvemonths', but he was now asthmatic and rheumatic and had pains all over him. He thought that his rheumatism was caused by working in the wet and by the 'black damp' that made them all asthmatic by the age of 50. He had been pretty free from accidents, though he had been bruised and his arms and ankle put out now and then. He thought that a boy ought not to work in a pit until he was 12 years old, because he could not stand the fatigue; it was like working a horse too young. Twelve hours was enough for man, child, or horse to work; out of this they ought to have an hour for dinner and time should be allowed for other meals.

The 1842 Mines Act prohibited the employment of women and children under ten underground and appointed inspectors to see that the law was enforced.

THE BUTTERLEY COMPANY

The most successful industrial partnership in east Derbyshire in the late eighteenth- or early nineteenth-century was that which became the Butterley Company, the largest coal and iron business in the East Midlands. When the

Leawood Pumping Station. In 1849 Graham & Co., the Milton Ironworks, Elsecar (South Yorkshire) installed a steam engine to pump water from the river Derwent into the Cromford Canal, for in dry summers it was difficult to maintain water levels. The engine could pump almost four tons of water per stroke at the rate of seven strokes per minute. The flight of fourteen locks that took the Cromford Canal into the Erewash Canal at Langley Mill Basin meant that a lock full of water had to be replaced every time that a boat passed through.

Erewash Canal was extended in 1794, Francis Beresford of Ashbourne, the solicitor acting for the promoters, and Benjamin Outram of Alfreton, the assistant surveyor, spotted the mineral resources and bought the 200-acre Butterley Hall estate. Trading as Benjamin Outram & Co., they soon acquired a limestone quarry at Crich and erected lime kilns nearby. Then, William Jessop, the chief surveyor of the canal, and John Wright, a banker, joined the partnership and in 1791 the first blast furnace was built. Pig-iron, castings and coal were exported down the Cromford Canal, which passed through the ironworks, and from 1796 directly to Manchester along the Grand Trunk Canal; products sent by canal to Gainsborough and sea took six weeks to reach London. Between 1796 and Outram's death in 1805 annual iron production rose from 936 tons to 1,766 tons. Jessop's younger son William then took over the management of the partnership, whose name was changed in 1807 to the Butterley Company. Three years later, the company founded a new, integrated ironworks at Codnor Park.

When coal and iron industries recovered from the post-Napoleonic war depression in the 1820s, the company began to sink more collieries and to connect them by tramways to wharves on the Cromford Canal. The Codnor Park works was extended, so that by 1830 the Butterley Company employed about 1,500 people and accounted for more than a third of the total pig-iron production in Derbyshire. By 1848 annual output of pig-iron had risen to nearly 21,000 tons. The Butterley ironworks specialised in castings and engineering work, while Codnor Park concentrated on wrought iron and forgings.

Butterley Company Miners, 1874. These eleven miners were sacked by the Butterley Company, perhaps for trying to form a trade union in the year that the first trade unionists were elected to the House of Commons. Top left is Samuel Shooter, who was recorded in the 1871 census as a coal miner but in 1881 he was earning his living at Codnor Park as a pedlar. Both his son and brother-in-law were killed in mining accidents. The other men on the back row were G. Brown, S. Cox, G. Taylor, T. Vickers and J. Statham. In the front were J. Seal, W. Purdy, T. Wheeldon, J. Wright and T. Purdy. The photograph notes that the men were never charged, but the alleged offence is not recorded.

Soon after the Cromford Canal was opened in 1794, this warehouse was erected by Nathaniel Wheatcroft, who became the leading carrier. It is known locally as 'the gothic warehouse' because of its embattled parapet at the far end. The lean-to was added in 1814.

The warehouse was restored by the Arkwright Society and is now used for meetings and for educational purposes.

PHOTOGRAPH: CARNEGIE

The Butterley Company made an enormous range of iron goods: cast-iron rails and waggon wheels for tramways and railways, lock mechanisms for the Caledonian Canal, winding gear and cast-iron bridges for the Cromford & High Peak Railway, ironwork for numerous other bridges including Vauxhall Bridge, London, and Miller's Dale viaduct, a variety of steam engines and locomotives and, most famously, ironwork for the roof of St Pancras station, London, with a free span of 200 feet, covering four acres and weighing 6,894 tons. The period of the company's greatest prosperity began in 1830 when Francis Wright took over his father's two-thirds share ownership, married Selina Fitzherbert of Tissington and built the neo-Jacobean Osmaston manor, near Ashbourne (which was demolished in 1965).

The company accepted responsibility for housing most of its workforce. A small community of 20 cottages between 1797 and 1813, just north of the Cromford Canal, was given the name of Golden Valley. A row of six cottages were built at Greenwich, near Ripley in 1804; 25 dwellings were erected at Codnor Park by 1809; the new village of Ironville, sited between the Cromford Canal and the river Erewash, was founded in 1811 and grew gradually over the next 30–40 years; a row of ten cottages at Hammersmith was started in 1819; and a terrace of 47 cottages at Portland Row, Kirkby-in-Ashfield was erected in 1823. The company's cottages were usually two-up, two-down, with a privy and coalhouse in the back yard and a large garden. Day schools were provided by the company at Butterley, Codnor Park, Ironville, Riddings and Ripley and a Mechanics' Institute at Ironville, while Francis Wright personally met the cost of building Ironville church in 1852 when a new ecclesiastical parish was created.

Communications

ROADS

The early turnpike roads that were promoted by great landowners, business men and attorneys aimed not to replace old highways but to maintain and improve them. They climbed up steep hills and descended directly into the valleys. The ancient moorland route across the Strines, for example, was marked as a bridleway on Jeffreys's map of Yorkshire (1767–72), but during the 1770s it was made into a turnpike road and provided with bridges wide enough to take coaches and carts across a succession of deep valleys. It still bears the name Mortimer's Road, after the lord of Bamford who promoted the scheme to link industrial parts of north Derbyshire and the West Riding. It proved a costly mistake and was eventually abandoned.

The road from Sheffield to Chesterfield and Derby, which was turnpiked in 1756, proved much more successful. At first, it followed the old route, climbing from Heeley Bridge up Derbyshire Lane past Norton church and along Dyche Lane to Coal Aston, before descending Green Lane into Dronfield. From Unstone the traveller took the narrow lane that winds its way up to Old Whittington. Routes such as this, which were difficult for wheeled vehicles, were eventually abandoned in favour of easier ones. In 1795 the turnpike trustees decided to open the present Chesterfield Road to Meadowhead and Dronfield and to bypass Old Whittington with a new, direct route to Chesterfield across Whittington Moor. An increasing number of diversions were made to existing highways at this time. Some roads were lengthened to get a better gradient and others were terraced into hillsides or constructed in deep valleys on the banks of the rivers. In 1811, for example, the Winnats Pass was replaced by a road that wound its way up the slopes of Mam Tor and continued in a straight line below Rushup Edge to Chapel-en-le-Frith. The most ambitious of the new moorland routes was the Snake Pass, opened in 1821 and so called because half

Mortimer's Road, Ladybower. In 1771 Hans Winthrop Mortimer, Lord of Bamford, was instrumental in obtaining an Act of Parliament to make the ancient route over the Strines to Penistone into a turnpike road, so as to connect the industrial districts of north Derbyshire and the West Riding. The route was marked simply as 'Bridle Way' on a contemporary map before it was improved and bridges were constructed to take wheeled vehicles. This section, heading north of the *Ladybower Inn* towards Moscar, retains its old character, for it was by-passed later. The route is still known as Mortimer Road on its descent into Penistone. The venture was not a commercial success and the road ceased to be turnpiked in 1813.

PHOTOGRAPH: AUTHOR

Toll Bar Cottage, Grindleford Bridge. This toll house was built in 1758 to collect tolls on the new turnpike road from Sheffield to Tideswell and Buxton, via Sir William Hill. In the following year, the road from Grindleford Bridge to Calver and Bakewell was turnpiked, then in 1771 Mortimer's Road started here on its way to Hathersage, Bamford and Penistone.

Toll house by Slack Hall. This one-storeyed toll house was built to collect tolls on the new branch of the turnpike road from Sheffield via the Hope valley to Sparrow Pit Gate and so on to Manchester. This branch was created in 1812 up Mam Tor, along Rushup Edge, and down to Chapel-en-le-Frith. The toll house stands at a minor crossroads leading to local farms.

way between Ashopton and Glossop the Duke of Devonshire built an inn, which was distinguished by the sign of the Cavendish snake. It crossed some of the wildest scenery in Derbyshire, skirting the northern side of Kinderscout and climbing over Bleaklow. Meanwhile, in the southern lowlands, bridge trusts replaced ferries with bridges across the Trent and the Derwent. In 1790 the first Hartington Bridge put the ferry at Sawley 150 yards upstream out of business; later, a bridge crossed the Trent at Willington and a new St Mary's Bridge at Derby brought traffic across the Derwent.

The lack of adequate technology and of experienced road builders meant that the early turnpike trustees had to be content with old methods of repair applied more thoroughly and regularly than before. Turnpike trusts spent a great deal of money on levelling and draining and on laying stones, grit, chert, limestone gravel and hard slag from furnaces to maintain an adequate surface at least 20 feet wide. In 1817 John Farey reported that, with few exceptions, the Derbyshire turnpike roads were good and that the secondary roads, which were still maintained by the parish repair system, were fast improving. Those turnpike roads and lanes which crossed commons and wastes were widened and straightened by enclosure commissioners and new ones laid out. In such districts the modern road system owes little to turnpike trusts but a great deal to the parliamentary enclosure commissioners and surveyors.

Late eighteenth-century directories reveal a network of coaching and carrying services along the new turnpike roads, linking the market towns and

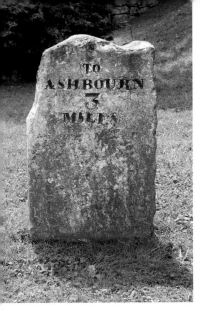

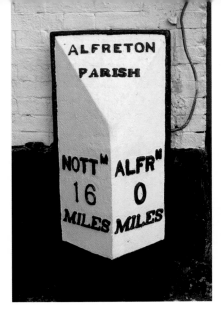

Turnpike milestones. Numerous milestones can still be seen alongside the roads that were turnpiked in the eighteenth and early nineteenth centuries. They were made in a variety of styles, first with stone and then with cast iron.

TOP LEFT

A stone milepost at Kniveton on the Ashbourne–Wirksworth road which was turnpiked in 1759. The stone is probably from that date.

TOP CENTRE

This milestone has an unusual method of informing travellers along the Sheffield to Chesterfield and Derby turnpike road that they have arrived at Alfreton.

TOP RIGHT

This mile post at Castleton on the Sheffield to Sparrow Pit Gate turnpike road of 1758 must be a later addition or replacement as it is made of cast iron.

LEFT

A cast-iron milestone on the 1793 turnpike road from Wirksworth to Duffield and so on to Derby and London.

PHOTOGRAPHS: AUTHOR

the capital city. End-on connections enabled goods and passengers to reach any part of the kingdom. In 1773 the *Derby Mercury* advertised the fact that Bromwell Powell's waggon came weekly from Bewdley on the river Severn, through the Black Country to Lichfield, Burton and Derby, where it met John Anderton's Sheffield waggon, which in turn connected with northern carriers going as far as Kendal. T. & M. Pickford and Co. conveyed or forwarded goods to all parts of the kingdom. This famous firm of national carriers was in business in the Goyt valley in the mid-eighteenth century, when James Pickford was 'the London and Manchester waggoner'. By 1803 the firm provided a service to London six days a week, each journey taking 4½ days. Pickford's successfully adapted their business by providing links with canals and railways. Some turnpike roads declined in importance when the railways came, but for a century or more they had been instrumental in providing quicker and more convenient communications. In their time, the 41 turnpike trusts in Derbyshire improved and maintained 591 miles of road.

CANALS

The most famous engineer in the early days of canals was a Derbyshire man. James Brindley was the son of a farm labourer from Tunstead in the parish of Wormhill; as a boy he was apprenticed to a Cheshire millwright. In 1759–61 Brindley constructed Britain's first major canal for the Duke of Bridgewater at Worsley, near Manchester, and then designed the Manchester-Liverpool Canal. His first involvement in his native county came in 1769, when he was asked to survey the route of a proposed canal from Chesterfield to Stockwith on the river Trent, by-passing the old river port at Bawtry. The promoters included the Duke of Devonshire, the Duke of Newcastle, the coal owners of north-east Derbyshire and the London Lead Company (who had a smelting mill at Ashover). An Act was obtained in 1771 and the work was completed in 1777, five years after Brindley's death. Its most spectacular feature was the 2,850-yard long Norwood tunnel. Several branches, for example that to the Adelphi Ironworks at Duckmanton, were added later. The new canal stimulated large-scale industrial development in the Derbyshire coalfield; within two years of the opening, a couple of coke-fired furnaces had been built on the outskirts of Chesterfield. In 1789 the merchandise transported along the canal included 3,862 tons of lead, 42,379 tons of coal, 7,569 tons of stone, 4,366 tons of corn, 3,955 tons of lime and 1,544 tons of iron.

Brindley had also taken charge of the Trent & Mersey Canal (or the 'Grand Trunk'), which linked Liverpool, Bristol and Hull. Work began in 1766 and was completed in 1777, a month before the opening of the Chesterfield Canal.

It was an immediate financial success. Shardlow quickly developed into a prosperous port under the leadership of the fourth generation of the Fosbrooke family. Merchandise was moved from narrow canal boats into the Shardlow warehouses, then taken by barges down the Trent. Two of the warehouses stored iron products, two were for salt, and a number of general warehouses had storage space for cheese. The agents of several bulk-trading firms were stationed there and stabling was provided for over 100 horses whose job was to tow the canal boats. Shardlow's population rose from about 300 in 1789 to 1,306 in 1841, but then it declined with the coming of the railways.

In 1777 an Act was obtained for the Erewash Canal, which wound its way around the Derbyshire/Nottinghamshire border for 11¾ miles between Langley Mill and the Trent below Sawley, where it connected with the new Soar Navigation into Leicestershire. Work began in May 1778 and the canal was officially opened in December 1799. When new collieries, with tramways to the wharves, and a coke-fired blast furnace at Stanton were opened nearby, the commercial success of the canal was assured. By 1792 70,000 tons of coal per annum were transported along it and by 1829 the yearly figure had risen to 170,229 tons. A peaceful rural valley was transformed into an ugly industrial landscape. Between 1793 and 1796 Outram also constructed the Nutbrook Canal, which stretched 4½ miles from the Erewash Canal through 13 locks to the coal pits at Shipley and West Hallam and the Dale Furnace which had been built in 1792.

Derby had been linked to the Trent by the Derwent Navigation since 1721 but this connection, dependent as it was on the seasonal variations of the river level, could not cope with industrial growth. In 1793 Benjamin Outram was appointed the surveyor of a canal from Swarkestone to Derby and on to Sandiacre on the Erewash Canal, with a branch to Little Eaton and a four-mile tramway to Denby; all three sections were completed in 1796. Here. too, coal was the most important traffic.

Marina, Newtown, New Mills. The Victoria Mill in the background was the largest and latest of a group of nineteenth-century, steam-powered cotton mills that were erected on the banks of the Peak Forest Canal, creating a 'new town'. It has the date 1860 on its chimney. The coal that was used in these mills came by the canal, and later by the railway that runs parallel to it. Boat trips can now be taken from the marina.

PHOTOGRAPH: AUTHOR

Between 1789 and 1794 William Jessop and Benjamin Outram constructed the Cromford Canal, an extension of the Erewash Canal from Langley Mill, with a spur to Pinxton. The canal went via Codnor Park, through a tunnel to Butterley, and on to Ambergate and Cromford, a journey of 14½ miles. It prospered immediately, for coal and mineral owners built tramways to connect their collieries, ironstone mines and limestone quarries to the wharves. Freight on the canal increased from 150,391 tons in 1803–04 to 289,217 tons by 1830–31; two-thirds of each figure was accounted for by coal. This success came about despite the technical problems that arose. The Butterley tunnel was not wide enough to take narrow boats from the Erewash Canal and a serious shortage of water occurred in 1844, when two-thirds of the supply from Cromford Sough ceased when the lead mines began working at a lower level. In 1849 a steam engine had to be installed at Leawood to pump water up from the Derwent.

In 1802 Peter Nightingale opened a cut from the Cromford Canal to his lead smelting plant at Lea Bridge, with the intention of it being the start of a new canal that would connect with the Peak Forest Canal (the first section of which had been finished by 1799), so as to provide a direct route between the Midlands and Manchester. Limekilns were constructed at the large canal basin at the Peak Forest Canal's southern terminus at Bugsworth, with tramway links to the quarries. But the project was too expensive, so instead the Cromford & High Peak Railway was constructed between 1825 and 1831 from a wharf on the Cromford Canal near Lea Bridge to a wharf on the Peak Forest Canal at Whaley Bridge.

In 1811 John Farey reported that, 'Vast quantities of Coals are annually sent out of the Counties of Derby and Nottingham southwards, by means of the Cromford, Derby, Erewash, Grantham, Leicester, Melton Mowbray, Nottingham, Nutbrook, and Trent canals.' The canals were hugely important in the development of the Derbyshire coalfields.

EARLY RAILWAYS

Horse-drawn tramways were used in the Derbyshire coalfield during the late eighteenth century to connect ironstone mines with blast furnaces and coal mines with canal wharves. The Cromford & High Peak was Derbyshire's first 'long-distance' railway. Josias Jessop, the son of William, was the engineer responsible for the construction of a route that included nine steep inclines along the 33 miles across some of the wildest terrain in the White Peak. At first, waggons were pulled by horses on the level stretches and hauled up the inclines by steam engines, then in 1841 a steam locomotive, the *Peak*, was bought from Robert Stephenson at Newcastle. A passenger service which was introduced in 1855 ran until 1877.

As with the canals, the transport of coal was the main stimulus for railway development in Derbyshire. The Midland Counties Railway between Leicester, Derby and Nottingham, engineered by George and Robert Stephenson, opened in 1839 and in the following year a line from Long Eaton to Rugby connected with the London & Birmingham Railway. By 1845 George Stephenson & Co. were using this line to send coal from Clay Cross to London. Meanwhile, the 72-mile North Midland line, through Ambergate, Chesterfield and Masbrough (Rotherham), was completed in 1840. The technical problems were solved by a series of ingenious solutions. In Belper the railway line had to be sunk in a

Middleton Top engine house. The only survivor of nine engine houses on the former Cromford and High Peak Railway, this one near Middleton-by-Wirksworth was erected in 1829 at the top of the 1:8 incline from the Cromford Canal. Its Butterley beam engine was connected to cables that hauled waggons up the incline until the closure of the railway in 1963. The route now serves as the High Peak Trail for cyclists and walkers.

PHOTOGRAPH: CARNEGIE

mile-long cutting crossed by ten bridges; at Ambergate the Toadmoor tunnel had to be cut through a mass of slithering shale; and at Bull Bridge George Stephenson had to engineer a tunnel beneath the Cromford Canal within yards of a bridge over the river Amber.

Derby was a natural focus for the major railways that passed through the Midlands. The Great Central Railway Station, later called the Derby Tri-Junct., was designed by Francis Thompson and built in 1839–41 at Castlefields, together with engine sheds for locomotive maintenance and sheds for carriage and waggon storage. The Midland Hotel was opened in 1840 and houses for railway employees were built nearby. Derby's great age as a a railway centre had begun.

Quarrying

LIMESTONE

Many limestone quarries were opened in the eighteenth century and numerous small limekilns were built to supply burnt limestone for farmers to spread on their acidic soils. A simple type known as a flare kiln, in which the charge was burned and then raked out, became common on farms. At the larger quarries, it was economical to use a large draw kiln, in which lime was charged, burned and discharged continually. Kilns were also built by the river and canal wharves in the Midland coalfields, for lime was the common back-carriage on boats that had sailed downstream ladened with coal. Large quantities of limestone were sent to ironworks for use as a flux in the smelting process. The Butterley Company had a quarry at Crich (now the nation's best working tram museum),

Stoney Middleton.
Sir Francis
Chantrey's engraving
of Stoney Middleton
in Ebenezer Rhodes,
Peak Scenery (1824),
looking up the 1759
turnpike road from
Chesterfield to Peak
Forest. The villagers
were mostly engaged
in the lead and lime
trades.

from where limestone was taken by tramway to kilns at Ambergate or along the Cromford Canal to the ironworks. The Cromford & High Peak Railway, which was completed in 1831, linked this canal by a series of steep inclines to the Peak Forest Canal and so to the extensive lime works at Harpur Hill and Dove Holes, near Buxton, where huge heaps of lime ash blighted the landscape. In 1813 Farey observed:

> On the south-west of Buxton, a considerable number of Persons, and some of them I fear not of the virtuous characters, have been permitted to burrow into and excavate themselves Huts, in the heaps of Lime-ashes or refuse of the numerous Lime-kilns there, in subterranean abodes … It is said that 200 persons or more inhabit these Huts.

Railways were cheap and efficient for transporting bulky industrial products such as limestone and lime. Branch lines led into quarries and to enormous limekilns. One of the earliest of the large limestone quarries along this railway was Middle Peak Quarry at Middleton-by-Wirksworth. Other large quarries were opened at Topley Pike, Eldon Hill and elsewhere near Dove Holes, from where a tramway transported limestone and lime to the canal basin at Bugsworth and so into Lancashire and the West Riding. Stoney Middleton became another major centre of lime-burning in the Peak District and, as we have seen, George Stephenson built 20 lime kilns at Ambergate alongside the Cromford Canal.

In the south of the county, Sir Henry Crewe's Ticknall limestone quarries and limekilns (which numbered at least 40 in the early nineteenth century) were linked by tramway to the Ashby-de-la-Zouch Canal.

ORNAMENTAL STONE

In 1752 Henry Watson of Bakewell, the son of Samuel Watson, the renowned carver at Chatsworth, built a water-powered mill beside the Wye on the outskirts of Ashford to drive machinery that he had patented the previous year to cut, saw and polish the local black marble for church furnishings, chimney pieces and tables and to turn columns and vases on lathes. He was soon also turning fluorspar, especially the purple-veined 'Blue John' from Castleton, which had been in demand for ornamental objects since the late eighteenth century. His business was continued by his nephew, White Watson, and the production of polished ornaments spread to Buxton, Castleton, Matlock and Derby, using also 'rosewood marble' from Nettlers Dale, 'mottled grey marble' from Monyash and 'Duke's red marble'. A light grey stone from the Hopton Wood limestone quarries which contained crinoid fossils known as 'Derbyshire screws' took a high polish and was much sought after for chimney pieces. Meanwhile, gypsum remained in demand, both for sculpture and for plaster. In 1789 Pilkington reported that the best gypsum came from Elvaston, but that the pits there had closed, and that 800 tons of gypsum were quarried annually at Chellaston, of which 500 tons were sent to the Stoke potters.

MILLSTONES

Millstone quarries were owned or rented by local gentry families who employed an overseer and who paid the hewers by piece-work. The hewer's first task was to choose a likely piece of rock to fashion into a millstone. In 1795 Erasmus Darwin wrote that:

It is usual in separating large millstones from the silicious rocks in some

parts of Derbyshire, to bore horizontal holes under them in a circle, and fill these with pegs made from dry wood which gradually swell by the moisture of the earth, and, in a day or two, lift up the millstone without breaking it.

Grooves and holes drilled into the quarry face at Millstone Edge on the boundary of Hathersage parish show, however, that in the later days of the trade

Reeve Edge millstone quarry. Abandoned millstones lie amidst the debris on the escarpment opposite the Burbage Brook from Carl Wark. These stones are of the later type that were used for pulping wood for paper, grinding paint, etc., but this quarry had been used for hewing millstones in earlier centuries. A reference to 'four paire milnestones now being at Reevedge' is dated 1647.

PHOTOGRAPH: AUTHOR

gunpowder was used to blast the rock from the face of a quarry. Large piles of debris litter the floors of derelict quarries. Unfinished or broken millstones that lie scattered amongst the bracken near Stanage and Padley Gorge include some that have been roughly finished on one side, then turned over and propped up so that work could start on the other. A hewer's tools included a pick, a heavy hammer or mall, a hammer called a kevel that was used for breaking stones and rough hewing, a reamer for drilling, a 'plug and feather' which had a combination of conical and flat wedges, and a punch, wedge, pitcher, hammer and adze. Smithies for sharpening and repairing these tools were built in sheltered spots in the quarries.

Moving a finished millstone without damaging it was a tricky job. Three men could lift and trundle one along from the quarry to the holloways that were dug to provide a reasonably smooth surface for the horse-drawn sledges that carried them to the wheeled vehicles, by which they were taken to Bawtry or other river ports in the summer months, when the roads were reasonably firm and dry, by part-time farmers in the traditional slack spell between the hay and corn harvests. In the late 1820s Stephen Glover reported that Derbyshire's 15 millstone quarries employed only about 100 hewers. In 1833, however, White's *Sheffield Directory* noted that Hathersage was still 'celebrated for excellent millstones'.

'Old Crown China Works' by William Mosley (1890). William Duesbury had built a national reputation for his 'Crown Derby' wares in the late eighteenth century. In 1848 some of the workforce moved to this site in King Street and revived the company as 'The Old Crown Derby China factory'.

1811 John Farey counted 22 potteries in Derbyshire. The expansion of the coal industry in eastern parts of the county had exposed many new beds of stoneware clays which were suitable for salt-glazing that produced a characteristic light to dark brown glossy finish for jugs, bowls, stewpots, teapots, coffee pots, mugs, bottles, spirit flasks, footwarmers for travellers and a variety of ornamental wares such as tobacco containers, ink pots and cordial flasks. Several such potteries flourished in the nineteenth century on the outskirts of Chesterfield: in Brampton and on Whittington Moor, notably Pearson & Co., founded in 1810. The Denby pottery that was founded in 1809 was taken over by Joseph Bourne in 1812 and long remained a family business that gradually took over most of its local rivals, including those at Codnor Park, Shipley and Langley Mill.

Creamware of a high standard was made at Cockpit Hill, Derby, from 1751 to 1779 under the leadership of John Heath. In 1756 Heath entered a partnership with Andrew Planché (of Huguenot extraction) and William Duesbury (an enameler from the Potteries) to manufacture porcelain. Duesbury was soon put in sole charge and the business prospered. His wares were aimed at the wealthy middle classes who wanted fine decorative art to display in cabinets or on the dining table; some products were modelled on Meissen and Sevres designs. In 1770 Heath and Duesbury took the lease of the famous Chelsea china factory in London and then they bought out the Bow china works. Duesbury ran the Derby, Chelsea and Bow factories together until the lease of the Chelsea works expired in 1784, when he transferred the plant and stock to Derby. In 1773 George III had granted Duesbury's company the privilege of marking its products 'Crown' Derby. In 1786 Duesbury was succeeded by his son William, who attracted a group of highly talented artists to model and decorate Derby china. After his death in 1796 the quality of Crown Derby declined. The works closed in 1848, but a group of former employees moved to King Street and continued business as the Old Crown Derby China Factory.

The poor

The Elizabethan Poor Law system, which gave civil parishes responsibility for maintaining the poor, survived until the passing of the Poor Law Amendment Act in 1834. In the second half of the eighteenth century some parishes built poorhouses to accommodate paupers and to put them to work. One was erected at Tissington in 1753 and another at Ashover in 1767, when 42 parishes combined resources. The Parish Poor House which was erected on the edge of the common at Banktop, Winster, in 1768 survives as a modern dwelling, high above the village. By 1776 Derbyshire had about 30 workhouses of this kind. Expenditure on the poor rose quickly in the late eighteenth and early nineteenth centuries as the national population grew in size and England was at war with France. By 1795 workhouses had been opened in each of four Derby parishes and at Chesterfield and Wirksworth. Sir F. M. Eden's enquiry in 1797 revealed that the Derby workhouses accommodated 152 paupers and that another 185 people were provided with 'out-relief'. The Chesterfield workhouse had 28 inmates, a further 25 received out-relief, ten had occasional relief and six had their rents paid. Wirksworth had 24 people within its workhouse and 92 on out-relief. Eden reported that, at Wirksworth, the weekly diet consisted of:

> Breakfast – Sunday, Wednesday, Friday – Bread and broth; rest of the week – Milk pottage. Dinner – Sunday, Wednesday, Friday – Bread, broth, butcher's meat, potatoes, etc; Monday – Baked puddings and treacle sauce; Tuesday, Thursday, Saturday – Bread and milk. Supper – Milk pottage and bread every day. On meat days the proportion is at 20 lbs meat for 30 persons … The Poor in the Workhouse have oat bread, but no beer or cheese, except at Christmas.

He went on to say that:

> A sort of gruel called water pottage, consisting of a small proportion of oatmeal, and a small onion boiled with water, was eaten with bread twice and sometimes thrice a day by many people in the neighbourhood. It was much used during the late hard season.

'The Poor in the Workhouse have oat bread, but no beer or cheese, except at Christmas.'

The poor law commissioners categorised villages as either open or closed to the poor, though a large number were not quite one or the other. Those that were closed included the numerous estate villages and those which were dominated by a few large farmers who were determined to keep out anyone who might become a burden on the poor rates. Farm labourers often had to walk from their open villages to work on a daily basis in the closed ones. Most of the south Derbyshire villages in the clay vales and by the major rivers remained purely agricultural. There, the farm labourers received lower wages than those which were paid in industrial parishes, so the problem of poverty was more acute. Self-help in the form of friendly societies provided some protection in hard times; in 1803 Derbyshire had 267 societies, with a membership of 21,505 men and 580 women.

In 1834 the Poor Law Amendment Act introduced a radically new structure that spread the payment of poor rates evenly. Groups of parishes were formed into Poor Law Unions that were managed by a committee of Guardians who were elected by the ratepayers. These unions were often the districts that were served by a market town and they sometimes extended over the county boundary. The main purpose of the 1834 Act was to cut the spiralling costs of relieving the poor by insisting that relief would be granted only to those who were prepared to leave their homes to live in the workhouse that each union was ordered to build and staff. These workhouses provided basic necessities but offered few comforts in a dull routine that included long spells of work.

Derbyshire was divided into nine poor law unions. The Chesterfield Union was first off the mark when a new workhouse for 300 inmates was opened in 1837. The Derby workhouse in Osmaston Road, which was opened in 1839, was sold to the Derby Crown Porcelain Company when a new workhouse was built in 1877 in Uttoxeter Road. The Belper Union covered 34 parishes, extending from Dethick, Lea and Holloway in the north to Mackworth in the south. Its new workhouse, designed by Giles Scott, was opened in 1840 for 300–400 inmates; later it became the Babington Hospital. The Ashbourne

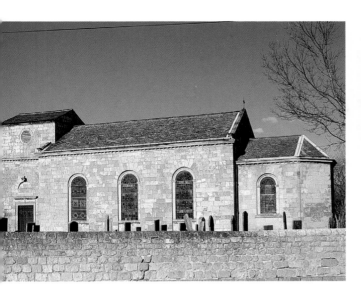

St Peter's church, Elmton. The medieval parish church was taken down and replaced by a new building in 1773. The west tower was never finished to its intended height, spoiling the composition. The arched windows are found only on this southern side. The apse is an early example of a feature that became fashionable again after disappearing in late Norman times.

All Saints church, Hassop. The west end of this Roman Catholic chapel was designed in the Classic Revival style by Joseph Ireland for the Eyres of Hassop Hall in 1816–18. The Eyres had remained Catholic since the Reformation, throughout a long period of persecution. Their chapel stands just beyond the entrance to the grounds of their hall.

LEFT
The Bakewell Union Workhouse was opened in 1841 at Newholme on the northern edge of the town. It was designed by the Sheffield architect, Thomas Johnson, in the style of a Jacobean manor house to accommodate up to 250 inmates. It closed in 1930 and, like many another workhouse, it became a hospital.

Union contained 61 townships within a ten-mile radius of the town, including 17 that lay in Staffordshire; the old Brassington workhouse was used until a new union workhouse was built in Ashbourne in 1848 for 160 inmates. The records of the Derby workhouse portray a strict regime with a rigorous daily routine, plain food and a basic education for the young, some of whom ran away as soon as they were able.

Religion

For most of the eighteenth century the Established Church made little effort to reach out to the growing numbers of industrial workers, but from the 1790s an evangelical emphasis on preaching began to spread and many churches were adapted to take large congregations. By 1824 four out of every five Derbyshire churches had galleries around their naves. The Lichfield Diocesan Church Extension Society, founded in 1835 by the evangelical Bishop Henry Ryder, was active in encouraging parishes to provide more accommodation. In the next 12 years an extra 17,323 seats were installed in 20 new churches and 41

enlarged old ones. In north Derbyshire, however, the Church of England was handicapped by its medieval legacy of large parishes. In such places, religious dissent flourished.

From 1791 Catholics were allowed to worship in places that they had registered at the quarter sessions. By 1836 chapels had been built at the old strongholds of Derby, Glossop, Hathersage, Hassop, Spinkhill, Tideswell, West Hallam and Wingerworth. Meanwhile, the older Nonconformist sects had become respectable and their members were often influential members of society. Some lost their zeal in so doing. By 1829 the Derbyshire Quakers had only nine meeting houses and 154 members. But the Congregationalists and Baptists responded to the evangelical movement and attracted more members. In 1791 William Hutton wrote that Derby was 'strongly tinctured with religious fervour'. After the Municipal Corporations Act of 1835 allowed Nonconformists to participate in local government, Joseph Strutt, a Unitarian and third son of Jedediah, became the borough's first Dissenting mayor.

During the 1760s John Wesley followed up his earlier visits to Ashbourne and Hayfield by preaching at Matlock Bath, Derby, Crich and 'a little village near Eyam' and later at Chesterfield, Chapel-en-le-Frith and Belper, but the growth of Methodism was slow before the nineteenth century. Then it grew so strongly that it challenged the Established Church. In 1829 Derbyshire had 201 Wesleyan chapels with 12,229 members and 62 Primitive Methodist chapels

Halter Devil Chapel. Attached to a brick farmhouse in the parish of Mugginton, near Hulland Ward, is a small, stone-built chapel that was built in 1723 and enlarged in 1890. A legendary tale tells us that a drunken farmer, Francis Brown, swore that he would ride into Derby that night even if he had to halter the Devil. In the dark he seems to have mistaken a cow for his horse, for he found it had horns. Brown fainted when the horned Devil disappeared in a flash of lightning. Upon his recovery, he forsook drink and built the chapel.

with 2,591 members. Primitive Methodism was born in Staffordshire in 1812, so the neighbouring agricultural parishes of south and south-west Derbyshire were easily accessible for travelling preachers.

The writers and artists of the Romantic movement of the late eighteenth and early nineteenth centuries looked on the Peak District with fresh eyes that no longer saw deformity and desolation but a landscape that was sublime and inspiring. War with France curtailed the Grand Tour on the Continent, so young aristocrats turned instead to the upland regions of Britain, of which the Peak District was the most accessible. Painters, notably Paul Sandby, J. M. W. Turner and J. P de Loutherbourg, were the first in the field, then in 1824 Edward Rhodes published *Peak Scenery, or the Derbyshire Tourist*, with illustrations by his friend, Sir Francis Chantrey (a native of Jordanthorpe in the parish of Norton). Turnpike roads made the Peak District more accessible and visitors arrived in increasing numbers to view Dovedale or to proceed up the Derwent and Wye valleys to Matlock Bath and Buxton and the Hope valley to Castleton, where Samuel Lewis informed them that the whole district 'abounds with greater natural curiosities than almost any other portion of the empire'. The Peak District had become a tourist attraction.

'Bridge over the
Nottingham Road
and Canal in Derby'
George R. Vawser
(Jr) *c*.1958.

PHOTOGRAPH BY CARNEGIE,
WITH PERMISSION OF DERBY
MUSEUMS AND ART GALLERY

Victorian and Edwardian times

Population

During the reign of Queen Victoria the population of Derbyshire more than doubled from 272,202 in 1841 to 621,636 in 1901. Most of this unprecedented rise occurred in the coalfield and the hosiery district in the eastern part of the county and on the outskirts of Derby. Chesterfield shared in this rapid expansion, but the ancient market centres on the edges of the Peak District at Ashbourne, Bakewell and Wirksworth were left behind; nor did Belper manage to keep up with the new industrial towns near the border with Nottinghamshire. Heanor's population rose from 3,058 in 1841 to 12,418 in 1901, Ripley's from 2,515 to 9,239, and Ilkeston's from 5,326 to 25,384.

In 1870, when Ripley was still a chapelry of Pentrich parish, *The Imperial Gazetteer of England and Wales* reported that the town stood at the terminus of the railway from Derby and Little Eaton, near the Cromford Canal, that it was well built, and that it carried on 'extensive trade in connection with neighbouring collieries, the Butterley iron-works, and an establishment for silk and cotton manufacture'. Heanor was a former small market town in the Erewash valley, served by a canal and railway, whose increase of population 'arose from the operations of a building society, and from the extension of coal mining and iron manufacture ... Hosiery and silk blonde lace are extensively manufactured.' Ilkeston, a small market town since 1251 and the proud possessor of a new town hall, stood on a hill near the canal and the terminus of a short branch of the Erewash valley railway. The parish church competed with five dissenting chapels and one for the Roman Catholics. The manufacture of hosiery and lace was 'extensively carried on'. The inhabitants of other parishes on the east side of the county were accommodated not just in the ancient settlements but in new rows of terraced houses in the countryside, near the coal mines and ironworks. The population of the parish of Alfreton rose from 7,577 in 1841 to 17,505 in 1901, that of Staveley from 2,688 to 11,420, of Eckington from 4,401 to 12,895 and of Killamarsh from 906 to 3,644.

This shift in population densities towards the east and south-east of the county was made more emphatic by the declining numbers of people who lived in the agricultural villages in the southern lowlands and in the lead mining districts of the White Peak. In these places, the highest number of inhabitants before young couples left in search of better and more reliable wages further east were usually recorded in the census of 1841. The following figures, comparing population totals in the 1841 and 1901 census returns are typical of the lowland villages: Atlow 156 – 112, Bradley 271 – 220, Brailsford 756 – 673, Breadsall 620 – 515, Church Broughton 652 – 522, Cubley 425 – 270, Doveridge 816 – 715. In this lowland district, the old market town of Repton (1,943 – 1,807) and Ticknall (1,271 – 630) also shrank and the canal port at Shardlow (1,306 – 948) suffered from competition from the railways. The population figures from the White Peak also reveal long-term decline, though with local variations depending on when the seams of lead became exhausted. Castleton's population dropped from a peak of 996 in 1831 to 547 in 1901. Other places continued to grow until 1861, then shrank towards the end of the century: Tideswell 2,057 – 1,910, Youlgreave 1,230 – 1,077 and Eyam 1,172 – 1,082. The population of most of the lead mining villages peaked in 1841, like the agricultural villages in the south, then fell remorselessly: typical figures are Abney 102 – 48, Brushfield 46 – 19, Calver 621 – 379, Flagg 239 – 178, Grindleford 110 – 32, Great Hucklow 242 –113, Little Hucklow 218 – 118, Middleton-by-Wirksworth 1,031 – 984, Monyash 435 – 349, Peak Forest 575 – 476, Rowland 99 – 53 and Winster 1,005 – 792.

Meanwhile, what had once been a remote part of Derbyshire, cut off by moorland from the rest of the county, now formed a flourishing textile district on the fringes of Cheshire and Lancashire. The population of the ancient parish of Glossop, which stretched as far south as the burgeoning settlement of New Mills, had already risen sharply from 8,883 in 1801 to 22,898 in 1841; by the end of the century it had reached 36,985. With the decline of the cotton industry in the mid-Derwent valley, this district became even more separate from the rest of Derbyshire. It looked outwards to Manchester and Stockport, not to Derby.

Towns

England's Victorian and Edwardian towns remained market centres, but they took on new roles as the places where workhouses and hospitals were built, railway stations, police stations, banks and post offices were opened, and shops ranging from small family businesses to department stores offered an increasing range of goods and services. But rapid growth also brought enormous social problems that were difficult to resolve. National legislation forced changes in local government. Under the Public Health Act (1848) local boards of health were elected to oversee sewerage and sanitation, then in 1872 they became urban sanitary authorities with additional responsibility for new housing. Local government reorganisation culminated on 1 April 1889 with the creation of the Derbyshire County Council and the county borough of Derby and in 1894 with the establishment of urban and rural district councils and rural parish councils.

The 1835 Municipal Corporations Act replaced the old administration of Derby with a corporation headed by an annually elected mayor, 12 aldermen and 36 councillors and served by a staff headed by a town clerk. Travellers saw a prosperous place where the leading county gentry had town houses and social life revolved around the assembly rooms. A visitor in 1841 spoke of general improvement and signalled out for praise the royal hotel, a new post-office and the bank in the corn market. A new town hall designed by Henry Duesbury was built the following year and from 1850 the Exeter Bridge gave direct access to the Market Place. Generous gifts to the borough from the Strutt family included an 11-acre arboretum, while Sir Michael Bass, the borough's long-serving Liberal MP, provided a recreation ground, two swimming baths, a free library, a museum and an art gallery.

But Derby also had its enclosed courts and slum dwellings, high death rates, an inadequate water supply and severe problems with sewerage, street cleaning and lighting. Overlapping responsibilities between various authorities hindered improvement, though some slums were cleared from the 1840s onwards and the streets were cobbled and gradually lit, first by gas, then from 1893 by electric lamps. The Markeaton Brook was culverted to prevent flooding and the seeping of sewerage, Iron Gate and St Peter's Street were widened and Rotten Row and the Shambles were removed from the Market Place. The infirmary was extended twice before it was rebuilt in 1891–94 as the Derbyshire Royal Infirmary.

A map of the borough of Derby that was drawn for the Board of Health in 1852 shows that the suburbs had not spread far beyond the ancient limits of the town. Few houses had been built further out than the Duffield Road/Kedleston Road junction to the north, Friar Gate in the west, the river Derwent in the east, and London Road bridge and the old workhouse on Osmaston Road in the south, though work had begun on the south-western suburbs of the Uttoxeter Old and New Roads. Enormous changes were soon to come, however. Derby had always been the county's major thoroughfare town; now its expansion was largely associated with its role as the provincial headquarters of the Midland Railway Company and the new manufacturing industries that the railways brought. The largest railway works in Europe were built in Litchurch, just beyond the town boundary to the south, and a new community was housed nearby. Many workers came from afar. The 1851 census revealed that 43 per cent of Derby's inhabitants aged 20 and over were born beyond Derbyshire. In 1877 the boundaries of the borough were extended to incorporate 'railway Derby', whose growth largely explains why the population of the borough more than doubled from 32,741 in 1841 to 69,266 in 1901. Edwardian Derby was one of the largest railway centres in England and the place throbbed with commercial activities of many kinds.

Relief sculptures now adorn the end of Exeter Bridge in Derby. These commemorate the lives of two Derby worthies: the philosopher Herbert Spencer (d. 1903) who was born in Exeter Row in 1820; and the historian William Hutton (d. 1815), born in Pull Street in 1723.
PHOTOGRAPHS: CARNEGIE

Chesterfield remained Derbyshire's second largest town, for it too attracted further heavy industry in the wake of the railways. The population of the borough (the old central township) rose from 6,212 in 1841 to 14,668 in 1901, that of the parish from 11,231 to 39,955. The old market town was surrounded with but not transformed by industrial activities and the shape of the Market Place remained that laid out in the twelfth century. The large Market Hall, which had been built in 1857 by the Chesterfield Market Company, was purchased by the corporation in 1872. The Liberal and Nonconformist majority on the corporation found that, as in other expanding towns, their most urgent problem was public health.

Derbyshire's other ancient market towns lost their former ascendancy during the reign of Victoria. Wirksworth's population peaked at 4,122 in 1841, fell slowly to 3,603 in 1871, then recovered mildly to 3,807 in 1901. In 1870 the *Imperial Gazetteer* noted the malting businesses, the manufacture of silk, gingham, and tape, and the neighbouring lead mines. A weekly newspaper

Derby in 1852. Even in early Victorian times, the pattern of the central streets of the borough was still medieval and the suburbs had not spread far. But now the Market Place could be approached directly from across the river Derwent, and the Markeaton Brook, which had defined the town to the south, was culverted. This map was drawn for the Board of Health, formed four years earlier.

was published and the town had the usual range of public buildings. Bakewell's population rose steadily from 1,976 in 1841 to 2,777 in 1901, but it did not keep up with its rivals, Buxton and Matlock. Yet the Victorian period saw much activity there, including a major restoration of the parish church in the 1840s and 50s and the improvement of the town centre with a new town hall and post office in the 1890s.

Ashbourne's population (excluding Compton) dropped from its peak of 2,246 in 1831 to 2,083 in 1871 and 1,795 in 1901. The railway had not compensated for the loss of stage-coach traffic and so the town preserved its Georgian character. Adrian Henstock's local history group have identified many of the buildings that still front the main street and market place as retail

Chesterfield's Victorian market hall of 1857 was built towards the western end of the huge, rectangular market place that was laid out in the twelfth century, at what was then the edge of the town. Steps lead up to a water pump in front of the picture and numerous stalls preserve Chesterfield's ancient character as a market town.

PHOTOGRAPH: CARNEGIE

Godfrey Sykes's view of Buxton Market Place in 1849, showing the market cross, stalls and shops, some of which were demolished under an improvement scheme of 1873.

Eagle Parade, Buxton. In 1890 the Chatsworth Estate, in co-operation with the local authority, commissioned a local architect, George Edwin Garlick, to improve the Market Place by redesigning the Eagle Hotel and adjacent shops in a curving row that took the name of Eagle Parade. Buxton was taking on the appearance of a fine late-Victorian town.

shops, pubs and other commercial properties whose owners lived at the top or to the rear of the premises. The artisans and labourers were housed in small, terraced brick cottages or in crowded yards that were rarely seen by travellers who passed through the town. These yards, which were reached either by a narrow alley or through a tunnel entrance, took their name from the owner or the occupant of the property that fronted the street. Ashbourne had about 25 yards, with accommodation for some 750 people, or nearly a quarter of the town's inhabitants. An analysis of the birthplaces of all the heads of households recorded in the 1851 census showed that 57 per cent were born outside Ashbourne. Most came from within ten miles, but a sizeable group had moved over 20 miles. The birthplaces of children in those 64 families which

Buxton Opera House. Opened in 1903, this delightful building was designed by Frank Matcham, the best known theatre architect of his day, who was commissioned by the Buxton Gardens Company. The Dejong Company of London designed the lavish interior. The tower on the right of this photograph is that of Buxton parish church, St John the Baptist's.

PHOTOGRAPH: CARNEGIE

had children under the age of 12 showed that many young families had moved frequently before arriving in the town.

Buxton and Matlock Bath outgrew these old market centres and developed into popular spa towns as the railways brought thousands of visitors. Buxton's population grew from 1,569 in 1841 to 2,531 in 1871 and to 6,480 by the end of the century. Mike Langham has explained how its present Victorian appearance took shape, starting with the Royal Hotel in Spring Gardens, which was built in 1849–52 for Andrew Brittlebank, a Winster solicitor and important Buxton landowner. The Devonshire estate was keen to develop the town and to sell land for building. Sir Joseph Paxton designed Buxton Park overlooking the town on the north-west, including some substantial houses, but Henry Currey was the architect who was responsible for much of the new developments. In 1852–53 the natural and hot baths were rebuilt, between 1853 and 1864 The Quadrant was laid out and by 1859 Buxton had about 425 houses and 20 roads or streets, a 50 per cent growth in the last ten years. The seventh Duke of Devonshire, who inherited the title in 1858, ordered his agents to start a policy of self-sufficiency, whereby the locally elected Board would play a leading role in investment in the town. In the next 20 years Buxton grew more rapidly that an any other time in its history. The number of inhabitants increased by 146 per cent and houses by 125 per cent, while the number of streets doubled to 42. From 1863 two stations built next to each other provided links with Manchester,

Buxton Pavilion. The pavilion and the extensive gardens that were laid out in front were opened by the seventh Duke of Devonshire in August 1871 and were an immediate success. This iron and glass structure was designed by Edward Milner, who had been Joseph Paxton's assistant in the erection of the Crystal Palace. A large concert hall was added four years later.

Derby and beyond and the number of staying visitors rose considerably. The provision of rented rooms in lodging-houses and apartments more than doubled as the town grew faster than its northern rival, Harrogate, and its neighbouring watering place, Matlock.

The Board and the Duke's agents controlled the layout of streets, drainage and sewerage and the types of property that were built. The best residential area of the town – Broad Walk, Devonshire Park, Buxton Park and Burlington Road – was reserved for villa residences. The Buxton Improvements Company was formed in 1869 to participate in joint ventures with the Devonshire Estate, including the new Pavilion Gardens in 1871, a large Concert Hall in 1876 and the conversion of Carr's great stables as a charity hospital for 300 poor people in 1879–82; the large, open circular area at its centre was covered by a gigantic dome, then the largest of its kind in the world. Buxton continued to grow at a slower pace until it reached its apogee as a health resort and fashionable residential town by 1905, when its hotels, hydros, apartments and lodging-houses catered for more than 4,000 visitors a week in the high season and some hotels, particularly the hydros, were open all the year round. The new confidence was marked by the opening of the Pump Room in the Crescent in 1894 and the Opera House in 1903. The largest source of employment in the town was that of servant in private houses, hotels and lodging-houses; professionals, shopkeepers, craftsmen and builders too benefited from the Buxton's growing reputation; but parts of the town had a more workaday character, for they were home to lime burners and coal miners who worked in the neighbouring countryside.

The population of the parish of Matlock, comprising the separate settlements of Matlock Bridge, Matlock Green, Matlock Bath and Matlock Bank, increased from 3,782 in 1841 to 7,798 in 1901. The opening of the Manchester to Derby railway in stages from 1849 provided access from London and the northern towns and on bank holidays Matlock Bath was crowded with visitors from the neighbouring counties. Matlock Bank was a quiet hamlet before Ralph Davies

The hydropathic establishment that John Smedley began in the mid-1850s lasted a hundred years until Derbyshire County Council bought it to convert into their headquarters. The original building stands on the other side of the street, behind these later extensions. By the time that the castellated building (*left*) was opened in 1867, Smedley was treating 2,000 patients a year. The huge building in a French-Italian style (*centre and right*) that was opened in 1885 became a fashionable attraction right through to the Second World War. The hydro had a private church, which was demolished in 1958–59. This steep hillside east of Matlock Bridge acquired a distinctive character with nine more smaller hydros, catering for the lower end of the market.

PHOTOGRAPH: CARNEGIE

of Darley Dale built its first hydropathic establishment there in 1851. This ancient treatment of illness by alternating applications of hot and cold water had recently been introduced into England and when John Smedley, the owner of Lea Mill spinning works, visited the hydro at Ben Rhydding, near Ilkley, he not only recovered his health but underwent a spiritual conversion. He eventually built six chapels based on his own religious and temperance ideas. An autocratic though philanthropic employer, he bought Davies's hydro in 1853 and, acting as his own architect, engineer and internal designer, he turned it into an enormous building with an unattractive exterior but with comfortable and ornamental rooms. The grand scale of the present building dates from the 1880s, when electricity was installed. When a new block, connected by a double-decker bridge, was opened in 1901 on the north side of Smedley Street, 330 people sat down to dinner. Matlock Bank soon attracted nine smaller hydros and the usual range of shops, public buildings and houses that made it a new, distinctive part of The Matlocks, as the various settlements in the parish had come to be called.

In 1860 Smedley published *Practical Hydropathy*, a mixture of evangelical piety and practical therapeutics. He ran his hydro on strict lines, forbidding dancing, wine, tobacco, snuff or card-playing and fining patients if they talked about their illnesses. An anonymous description of 1863 outlined the daily routine:

Early in the morning, before the mists are yet lifted from the valley, [the patient] begins his day. A cup of tea and a morsel of bread and butter are allowed him, after which he descends to the bathroom, there to be wrapped in the embrace of a wet sheet. Having recruited his energies with breakfast, about 11 a.m, he again attends to what he facetiously styles his aquarium, and is now probably treated to a pack, swathed like a mummy in many bandages, with a hot pad to his aching side, and much pungent mustard biting his legs and feet; or the soothing spinal applications, all done with a view to restoration of nature's power by mild application. Midday brings dinner, with its incomparable puddings and stewed fruits worthy of rapturous mention. Then comes a period of rest, during which all exercise is forbidden, whether of body or mind. Afterwards follows a third slight bath, or in some cases none, and with that the day's labours are over, and the remaining hours are devoted to amusement. Every newcomer is startled by the apparitions which cross his path at early morn – the gentlemen unkempt and unshorn, their shoulders wrapped in ruddy blankets – the ladies huddled up in dressing gowns, with hoods pulled over their unrestrained tresses, devoid of the attractions of science, innocent of crinoline, very different from the fairy-like beings who won his heart yesterday afternoon on the croquet-ground or last night in the drawing room. But perhaps the strangest scene to the unaccustomed eye is that which the public rooms present after dinner. Then, for 20 minutes, the custom is to recline at full length on the sofas, each one hugging a yielding cushion or a tender bolster.

Four years later, Smedley's hydro treated 2,000 patients per annum. Out of his profits, he was able to build a mock castle to live in at Riber, on the skyline to the south.

A few miles down the Derby Road, the population of Belper reached a peak at 10,082 in 1851, dropped to 8,527 by 1871 as the fortunes of the cotton industry fell during the American Civil War, and rose again to 10,934 by 1901. In the far north-west of the county, the cotton mills of Glossopdale continued to thrive in the early years of Victoria's reign and survived the hardships of the early 1860s, when sufficient supplies of raw cotton could not be obtained from America, but then began a long decline in the late Victorian and Edwardian era. Throughout the nineteenth century the majority of local people earned their living amidst the clatter of the machines in the huge mills that dominated the town. The Duke of Norfolk's agent developed the settlement known as New Glossop or Howardtown (after the family name of the duke), where he built the Town Hall (1837), the Market Hall (1844) and the railway station (1847). Glossop was made a municipal borough in 1866 and four years later, the *Imperial Gazetteer* reported that:

> The town is of modern growth; owes its rise mainly to a great extension of the cotton manufacture; ranks now in the county, as a seat of trade, next to Derby; has a post office under Manchester, a railway station with a telegraph, a banking-office, four chief inns, a town-hall and market house, a parish church, several dissenting chapels, a Roman Catholic chapel, a workhouse, a British school, national schools, an endowed school.

'The town is of modern growth; owes its rise mainly to a great extension of the cotton manufacture; ranks now in the county, as a seat of trade, next to Derby ...'

GLOSSOP, 1870

Riber Castle was built by John Smedley, industrialist and owner of the hydro on Matlock Bank, between 1862 and 1868, in mock-medieval style. He lived there until his death in 1874

Torrs Bridge, New Mills. This high-level bridge on Union Road was built across the river Goyt in the natural gorge known as The Torrs in 1884 to connect the industrial settlements of New Mills and Newtown, which had grown rapidly in the nineteenth century. New Mills takes its name from a manorial corn mill on the river Sett, near the present Woodside Garage. In 1391 this mill was referred to as the Beard corn mill because it stood within the boundary of the hamlet of that name, but after it was rebuilt about 1496 it became known as the New Mill. The small settlement that grew around it during the following century also took this name. During the Industrial Revolution, with the opening of textile mills in the Goyt and Sett valleys, the settlement grew out of all recognition and became known by its present name of New Mills. This was adopted as the official name of the parish in 1844.

PHOTOGRAPH: CARNEGIE

At New Mills on the border with Cheshire, steam power was introduced from the 1840s. In 1884 the opening of the spectacular Union Road bridge across Torrs Gorge, financed by the local Board, symbolised the confidence of the industrialists of this district in the late-Victorian era.

Railways

The River Trent, long the main communications artery for the Midland Plain, declined in importance when the railways superseded waterborne transport. Derby was the natural focal point for the main line railways that passed through the East Midlands and which opened up the Derbyshire–Nottinghamshire coalfield. In 1839 the North Midland Railway constructed a locomotive engineering works opposite Derby station and in 1851 began to build locomotives there. A railway carriage and waggon building works was added in 1873 and the entire industrial complex between London Road and Osmaston Road eventually occupied 128 acres.

In 1844 the North Midland, Birmingham & Derby Junction and the Midland Counties railways were amalgamated under the new name of the Midland Railway Co., with George Hudson, the 'railway king' as chairman. In 1868 the company opened a new line to London, via Bedford to St Pancras. A railway along the Erewash valley was opened in 1847 and extended northwards in 1862 to join the Midland line at Clay Cross. The Midland Railway's competitor, the Great Northern Railway, began a service between Nottingham and Derby, with a new station at Friar Gate, to try to capture some of the coal trade from the Erewash valley collieries. Both companies were surprised to find that passenger

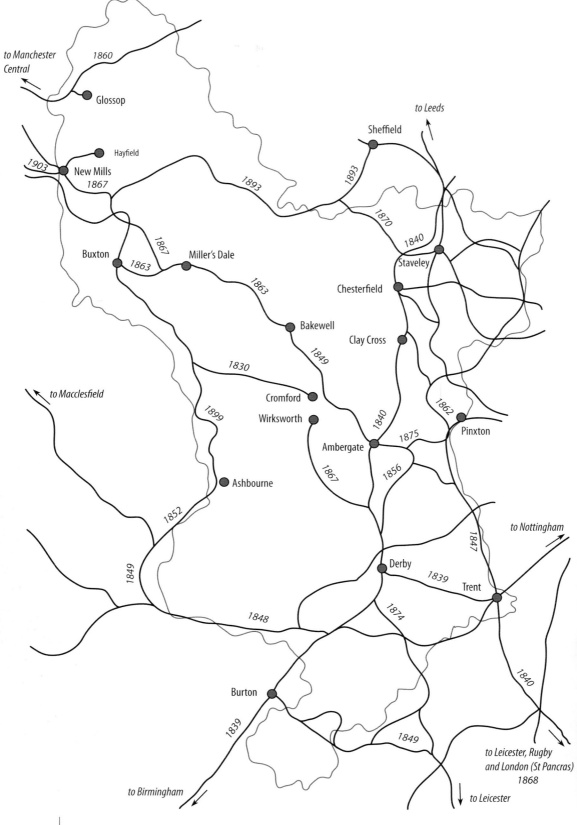

to Manchester Central

1860

Glossop

Hayfield

1903

New Mills

1867

1893

to Leeds

Sheffield

1893

1870

1840

Staveley

1867

Buxton

1863

Miller's Dale

1863

Chesterfield

Bakewell

1849

Clay Cross

1830

to Macclesfield

1899

Cromford

Wirksworth

1862

Pinxton

1840

Ambergate

1875

1867

1856

Ashbourne

1852

to Nottingham

1847

1849

Derby

1839

Trent

1874

1848

1840

Burton

1839

1849

to Leicester, Rugby and London (St Pancras) 1868

to Birmingham

to Leicester

traffic was larger than they had anticipated and was soon accounting for about two-thirds of their revenues. The next step was to cater for the tourist trade into the Peak District.

The first section of the Manchester, Buxton, Matlock & Midland Junction Railway was opened from Ambergate to Rowsley (where Paxton designed the station) in 1849. The Midland Railway Co. soon took them over, but failed to persuade the Duke of Devonshire to allow the line to continue through Chatsworth Park; eventually, the Duke of Rutland agreed to a tunnel behind Haddon Hall, with a station near Castle Hill, Bakewell. The line continued through small stations placed well away from the villages of Hassop and Great Longstone, across a spectacular five-arched viaduct over Monsal Dale and through tunnels at Cressbrook and Litton and in Chee Dale, and so on to Buxton, where a link to Manchester was available. The opening in 1863 was greeted by Ruskin's famous condemnation of the destruction of the scenery so that every fool in Buxton could be in Bakewell in half an hour and every fool in Bakewell could be in Buxton in half an hour. In 1867 the line was extended to New Mills, where another connection to Manchester could be made. When the Cromford & High Peak Railway was amalgamated with the London & North Western Railway in 1887 parts of the original track were realigned and in 1899 a new section was constructed between Ashbourne (which had been connected to Derby since 1852) and the isolated station at Parsley Hay and so on to Buxton.

Samuel Russell's
view of *c*.1840
looking south from
near Halfpenny
Bridge towards the
new North Midland
Railway line from
Derby to Leeds.
The viaduct spans
the Derby–Matlock
road and the river
Derwent. The
entrance to Longland
Tunnel is seen to the
right.

FAR LEFT
Monsal Dale viaduct.
The Midland
Railway line from
Derby to Buxton and
so on to Manchester
had no option
but to follow the
Wye valley once
it reached Monsal
Head. It crossed
Monsal Dale over
this spectacular five-
arched viaduct and
continued through
tunnels above
Miller's Dale and
and Chee Dale. This
section was opened
in 1863. In 1981 it
was converted into a
walkers' and cyclists'
trail.

ABOVE
Railway viaducts,
Miller's Dale.
Viewed from the
deck above, the
viaducts span the
river Wye at Millers
Dale on the line
from Derby to
Buxton. This section
of the line was
constructed by the
Midland Railway
in 1863. In 1905
a second viaduct
(*right*) was added
and the adjoining
station was given a
new platform. The
ironwork for the
viaduct was supplied
by the Butterley
Company. The line
was closed in 1967
and the older viaduct
(*left*) now forms part
of the Monsal Trail.
PHOTOGRAPH: CARNEGIE

Meanwhile, in 1870 the Midland Railway Co. had opened a line to Sheffield, which was routed to serve the collieries in and around Unstone and Dronfield. In 1893 the Manchester, Sheffield & Lincolnshire Railway connected Chesterfield with Annesley, and later (as the Great Central Railway) Nottingham and London Marleybone. The Great Central also absorbed the Lancashire, Derbyshire & East Coast Railway, which in 1897 had linked Chesterfield with Lincoln. Sheffield had been connected to Manchester via the Woodhead Tunnel since 1849, but in 1894 an alternate route (now the only one) through the Hope valley and New Mills was opened. The formidable engineering problems along this line included a tunnel that was three miles 950 yards long between Totley and Grindleford. Bulmer's *Directory* (1895) noted, 'By the construction of this line, the wild and romantic scenery of Peakland is thrown open to the admiring gaze of visitors and tourists'. Five years later, the Sheffield Clarion Ramblers caught the train to Edale and ventured on to the moors for the first time. The railways allowed a new form of recreation for working-class men and women.

Coal mining

The lower transport costs offered by the railways enabled the East Midlands coalfields to compete on equal terms with Northumberland and Durham. The Derbyshire coal industry expanded enormously during the course of the nineteenth century. By 1862, for instance, total coal output at the Butterley

Samuel Russell's view of Clay Cross station and matching tank house that were opened in 1840 on the North Midland Railway between Derby and Leeds. They were designed in an Italianate style by Francis Thompson, under the supervision of Robert Stephenson. The original station was replaced after Clay Cross became the junction with the Erewash Valley line in 1861–62.

Chesterfield's first railway station, c.1840. Samuel Russell's view of the station that was designed in Tudor style by Francis Thompson, when the Derby–Leeds line was opened by the North Midland Railway in 1840. The tank house is seen in the background. This station was replaced in 1870.

Company's collieries had risen to between 700,000 and 800,000 tons a year; by 1870 production at the company's 15 collieries was beginning to overshadow the ironfounding side of the business.

The Clay Cross Company became by far the largest supplier of Derbyshire coal to London. After George Stephenson's death in 1848, his son Robert sold his shareholding and the re-named company proceeded to build more houses, a school and a mechanics' institute for its workers. Clay Cross grew from a village of 564 inhabitants in 1831 into a thriving community of 1,478 people in 1841 and 6,347 by 1881. The four pits that had been sunk at Clay Cross by 1854 were followed by two at Morton in 1865 and 1874, the Parkhouse Colliery (Danesmoor) in 1867 and the Avenue Colliery (Wingerworth) in 1881. In 1871 Sir William Jackson MP became the sole proprietor of the company.

The Staveley ironworks that G.H. Barrow had re-established by 1840 were supplied by local collieries, whose surplus coal was exported down the Chesterfield Canal or along the new North Midland Railway. He was succeeded by his younger brother Richard, who sank a series of new collieries: Speedwell (1841), Hopewell (1843), Hollingwood (1843), Springwell (1853) and Seymour (1858), which by 1865 were producing 743,000 tons of coal per annum. In 1864, the year before Richard Barrow died, the business was transferred to a new joint-stock company, the Staveley Coal and Iron Co. Ltd, under the managing directorship of Charles Markham, a former Midland Railway engineer who had married the daughter of Joseph Paxton. Another entrepreneur who was actively involved in the Staveley company was an industrial chemist, Henry Davis Pochin, the founder of the Sheepbridge Coal & Iron Co. Ltd. By 1871 the collieries at Sheepbridge, Dunston, Nesfield and Norwood had a weekly output of some 10,000 tons. The workforce for the Sheepbridge company and the New Whittington ironworks, which Thomas Firth & Sons of Sheffield established in 1857, were housed in a new community about a mile below the village of Old Whittington. Another local company, the Grassmoor Colliery Co., was founded in 1846 by Alfred Barnes, who in the 1880s become the Liberal MP for Chesterfield and president of the Mining Association of Great Britain.

Branch lines connected collieries to the main railway network. When the line from Sheffield to Chesterfield was opened in 1870, branches to the Ramshaw, Unstone Main, Summerley and Dronfield Silkstone collieries were provided. The population of Unstone rose from 878 in 1861 to 2,368 in 1881. The boost from the railways was such that by 1870 16,405 miners were employed in Derbyshire pits and total output had reached 5,102,267 tons per annum. Derbyshire 'Brights' had a national reputation as excellent house coals and the 'Top Hard' seam was used for steam coal and for making hard coke for iron smelters. But demand for coal proceeded in booms and slumps. A recession in the iron trade meant that in 1877 many collieries were working only three or four days a week and some of the smaller ones were forced to close. In the long term, however, output from Derbyshire mines rose from nearly 8 million tons in 1880 to 18 million tons in the record year of 1913 and in the same period the number of miners increased to 48,486. The mining of coal had become the county's major source of employment.

Great fortunes were made from the coal industry by the owners of colliery companies and by those landowners who received royalties for the minerals on their estates. William Drury-Lowe collected Italian old master paintings for the house that he rebuilt on a 4,680 acre estate at Locko Park. The Miller

Mundays of Shipley and Heanor, the Palmer Morewoods of Alfreton Park and the Cokes of Brookhill also enlarged their estates and erected stylish new residences. Further north, the fortunes of the Sitwells of Renishaw were revived by mining coal beyond the park and the Hunlokes of Wingerworth and the Turbutts of Ogston benefited greatly from royalties paid by the Clay Cross Co. Proprietors of colliery companies such as the Markhams, Jessops and Wrights made enough money to join the ranks of country gentlemen. Indeed, in the late 1840s Francis Wright of the Butterley Company built an enormous country house at Osmaston near Ashbourne in a neo-Jacobean style inspired by Tissington Hall, the home of his wife, and fitted with an internal railway, a hydraulic lift and other mechanical devices. At the same time, he also rebuilt the village and paid for a new parish church.

As pits got deeper, the mining of coal became more hazardous. Although the disasters were not on the scale of those in the Dearne valley pits in South Yorkshire, they were still horrendous. Twenty-three men were drowned in a Clay Cross pit in 1861, 25 men and two boys died at Renishaw Park Colliery in 1871 and 45 miners were killed in a gas explosion at Parkhouse Colliery (Danesmoor) in 1882. In 1861 Derbyshire miners took the first step towards the formation of a trade union, when Chesterfield and Grassmoor miners started a branch of the South Yorkshire Miners' Association. Four years later, the Derbyshire and Nottinghamshire Miners' Association was founded. At first, colliery owners such as Charles Markham (at Staveley) and the Clay Cross Company were firmly opposed to trade unionism and bitter disputes broke out, as at Shirland in 1876 when wages were reduced by 15 per cent. By 1880 the trade union movement had become strong enough for the county's miners to create their own Derbyshire Miners' Association. The union's banner bore the biblical text, 'Bear ye one another's burdens'. Both the secretary, James Haslam, and treasurer, W.E. Harvey, were Primitive Methodist preachers, who disliked violence and industrial strife.

Many pit villages, such as Arkwright Town or Doe Lea Cottages, were uninspiring rows of parallel terraces, some of which had degenerated into slums by the end of the century. Epidemics such as typhoid swept through them and infant mortality rates were amongst the highest in the land. In 1901 the rate at Shirebrook was 236 per thousand births, compared with the national average of 151 and with the rural south-west Derbyshire rate of only 88; the new pit village was only a few years old, but it soon reached ten times the size of the old farming settlement that it had replaced. In 1910 the medical officer of health for Chesterfield Rural District Council deplored the housing conditions in the colliery villages of Mosborough, Eckington, Grassmoor, Killamarsh, North Wingfield, Stonebroom and Speedwell.

Some colliery companies, however, provided a better environment for their workers. The Staveley Colliery's Barrow Hill estate (1852–55) and the model villages built for E.M. Bainbridge's Bolsover Colliery Co. at Bolsover (1891–4) and Creswell (1896–1900) were the most ambitious schemes. The village of

Model village, New Bolsover. Between 1891 and 1894 the Bolsover Colliery Co. built 200 houses for its employees in a model village near their new colliery, below the castle and the old settlement on the escarpment. All the houses were made of bricks made in the company's coalyard. These semi-detached villas in Villas Road, overlooking the cricket ground, were set apart from the village and were superior in size and style, for they housed the colliery officials and administrative staff.

PHOTOGRAPH: AUTHOR

New Bolsover below the castle was provided with a village green, allotments, a co-operative piggery, schools, institute, a Methodist chapel, orphanage, co-operative stores and facilities for football, cricket, bowls and tennis. The houses recorded in the 1901 census enumerators' books began with those of the colliery company's secretary and cashier, the colliery clerk, the book keeper (who also acted as the local preacher), the under manager, the mechanical engineer, the farm bailiff and a few other clerks, followed by those of the school master, a teacher and her housekeeper, the co-operative stores manager, two blacksmiths, the butcher, saddler, carpenter, joiner, two horse keepers, the drayman, the gardener and two labourers. Nearly every other head of household worked down the mine or at the pit head. They included six deputies, a foreman, seven men in charge of the stationary engines, a plate layer, two lamp men and 78 miners, eight of whom were 'contractors' who employed a small team of hewers and 'stallmen'. If we include sons and boarders, 100 men worked at the coal face, 22 boys were pony drivers and another 37 worked on haulage and servicing the mine.

The recorded birthplaces of the men and women who had come to live in this new community reveal that on the whole they had not travelled far. The great majority had been born within 15 miles of Bolsover, in the towns, villages and hamlets of the Derbyshire, Nottinghamshire and South Yorkshire coalfields. Fifty-three of the male householders had been born in Derbyshire, 31 just across the border in Nottinghamshire and ten in South Yorkshire. Another six had been born in Staffordshire and three in Leicestershire and the rest had come from scattered places further afield. The birthplaces of their wives followed the same pattern, whilst those of their children show that families had moved around the local coalfields to find work. The mobility of the New Bolsover miners, however, was little different in scale from that of farm workers and other labourers. The Derbyshire–Nottinghamshire coalfield was the 'country' with which they were familiar.

Creswell model village. In 1896 the Bolsover and Creswell Colliery Co. continued its enlightened policy of providing superior working-class housing in spacious surroundings when it commissioned Percy Houfton, a Chesterfield architect, to design a model village at Creswell around a large oval green. The houses were finished by 1900. Seven years later, Houfton designed the model colliery village at Woodlands, north of Doncaster.

By 1906 Derbyshire's 176 pits were producing 16,250,000 tons of coal a year. The Miners' Federation of Great Britain had achieved its first success in the national lock-out of 1893 and in 1906 James Haslam, the secretary of the Derbyshire Miners' Association, was elected to Parliament as the Liberal-Labour candidate for Chesterfield. The following year, W.E. Harvey, the union treasurer, was elected on the same ticket for north-east Derbyshire, and in 1910 both men were victorious as Labour candidates. The years leading up to the First World War saw mounting unrest on the Derbyshire and Nottinghamshire and Derbyshire coalfield, with a major strike in February 1912.

Iron and steel

The coke-fuelled iron industry was at the forefront of the British Industrial Revolution. Until the great expansion of the steel industry in the second half of the nineteenth century, wrought iron was the metal that was preferred by architects and civil engineers, who appreciated its strength and its ability to resist shocks and corrosion. Wrought iron was used for farm machinery and power looms in textile factories, for the early railways and civil engineering projects and for a wide range of machine tools, which were sold around the world. But ironworks also made a wide range of domestic goods, particularly the stoves, fire ranges, fenders and pipes that did so much to improve the standards of comfort in homes across the land. The new companies commonly owned and worked coal and ironstone mines, coking plants, furnaces, foundries, rolling mills and other departments that were gathered together on the same site.

By 1848 the county's ironworks were producing about 95,000 tons of pig-iron per annum. Output rose steadily through the second half of the nineteenth century to a peak of 770,000 tons in 1900. The Butterley and Codnor ironworks led the way with a workforce of about 1,500 and an annual production of nearly

21,000 tons of pig-iron by 1848. One of its ironworks specialised in castings, the other in wrought iron and forgings. Under Francis Wright's direction, the Butterley company became an engineering firm of international renown. But as British ironstone seams became exhausted and new forms of steel captured national and international markets, the Derbyshire ironworks began to decline. When Leslie Wright became managing director of the Butterley company in 1902, he closed the blast furnaces and reduced the number of collieries before modernising them.

The Staveley company, too, grew enormously during the Victorian period. By 1864, when it became a limited company under Charles Markham, an engineer who had been assistant locomotive superintendent at the Midland Works in Derby, its annual output was 690,000 tons of coal, 13,000 tons of pig-iron and 19,000 tons of castings. Markham moved to Brimington Hall and later to Tapton House. Like his friends, Charles Binns of the Clay Cross Co. and Alfred Barnes of the Grassmoor Co., he was a liberal, paternalistic employer who had no time for trade unionism. The Staveley works exported coal, supplied the railway companies, and made iron pipes for the water and gas companies. In 1906 the Devonshire Works at Staveley opened with three blast furnaces, 100 of the latest Simplex coke ovens and a chemical plant which made sulphuric acid, benzol, sulphate of ammonia and other products.

By the end of the nineteenth century the Stanton Ironworks Company had blast furnaces, foundries, brickworks and collieries at Teversal, Pleasley, Silver Hill and Dale Abbey and a national reputation for its cast-iron pipes. Other Victorian ironworks were established on the coalfield near the new North Midland Railway line along the Amber and Rother valleys at Wingerworth, Grassmoor, Newbold and Unstone. Then in 1900 Bryan Donkin of Bermondsey amalgamated with the new firm of Clench & Co. of Chesterfield, specialists in high-speed steam engines; two years later, he moved north and began to expand the Chesterfield works and its range of products, including components for the gas supply industry. In Derby in 1848, the Britannia Foundry on the banks of the Derwent was taken over by Andrew Handyside, a Scottish engineer who had worked for several years in St Petersburg and had married a Ukrainian wife. His company built a brass foundry in 1868 and a malleable cast iron foundry in 1877. Thirty years later, Handyside's was the second largest employer in Derby with 1,200 workmen. The firm had become famous for the iron bridges that it built for the London, Brighton and South Coast railway, the Albert Suspension Bridge over the Thames in London, the Central Station at Manchester and two bridges in Derby for the Great Northern Railway. Bridges were also made for customers in Russia, India, Japan and South America. Other products included cast iron window frames, Post Office pillar boxes, ornamental fountains, garden vases, seats and lamps. But poor management and fierce competition made the firm bankrupt in 1910. Several other ironworks were based in Derby, notably James Haywood's Phoenix Foundry, manufacturer of bridges and cast iron mile posts.

Another engineer who set up home in Derbyshire was Joseph Whitworth of Manchester, designer of tools and machines to the highest standards of accuracy and the developer of a system of standard gauges and screw-threads. In 1854 the fortune that he had made in Manchester enabled him to buy and develop the Stancliffe estate and quarry in Darley Dale and in 1871 he came to live there. Although he was described as a 'monumental egotist' and an unpopular autocrat, he was a noted philanthropist who provided his workforce with superior housing by the standards of the time. Thanks to his generosity, the Whitworth Cottage Hospital was founded at Darley Dale in 1889 and the Whitworth Institute and park was opened in the following year.

The risks that were taken in establishing a business and the dire consequences of failure are illustrated by the rise and fall of Wilson Cammell's, Dronfield between 1873 and 1883. John Austin and Malcolm Ford have shown that this steel firm was established from Sheffield and that by 1881 some 500–600 men were employed. The census returns for that year show that 19 per cent of the workforce came from the Dronfield area, 12 per cent from elsewhere in Derbyshire, 12 per cent from Sheffield and 57 per cent from further afield, especially from Staffordshire, Cambridgeshire, Lincolnshire, Nottinghamshire and Yorkshire. Most families were housed across the river valley from the town, especially between Green Lane and Snape Hill, where the Dronfield Freehold Land Society built cottages and middle-class houses on a 19-acre site divided into 180 allotments; another group of 50 company houses known as Cammells Row were built close to the works on Chesterfield Road. The company flourished and Dronfield prospered until the home market for rails was saturated and the firm's land-locked position placed it in a uncompetitive position for overseas customers. On 'Black Friday', 2 April 1883, Wilson Cammell moved their entire business to the Cumbrian coastal town of Workington. Within a fortnight 221 houses were unoccupied, shops were closed and property values

Magpie Mine, Sheldon. Magpie Mine was worked from 1740 and closed for the last time in 1954, after previous closures and reopenings. The 800 tons of lead that were mined here in 1827 long remained the record for the annual output of a Derbyshire mine. Drainage was always a major problem for the deep main shaft. A Newcomen-type engine was installed by 1824, a Cornish engine replaced it in 1869, then between 1873 and 1881 a long sough was constructed to the river Wye at Ashford. Another problem that led to acrimonious disputes with other miners nearby involved the rights to mine this lucrative vein. The surface remains are the best for any nineteenth-century British lead mine. The chimneys, ore-crushing circle and circular powder house date from 1840, the Cornish engine house and the horizontal winding drum to 1869. The Agent's House and the adjacent smithy (erected in the 1840s) have been restored as the Field Centre of the Peak District Mines Historical Society.
PHOTOGRAPH: CARNEGIE

had collapsed. About a third of Dronfield's population moved away, many of them taking up the company's offer of employment in Workington, where the newspaper observed that, 'Never before had an almost complete community been transplanted into West Cumberland'. As Workington's population rose, Dronfield's fell, from 5,169 to 4,166. It took 40 years for the town to regain its 1881 level.

Lead

As Derbyshire's Victorian coal and iron industries boomed, the ancient lead industry withered away. By the 1860s most White Peak mines had closed because of the low price of lead, the exhaustion of seams, the mounting expense of drainage and foreign competition. The final blow came in 1885 when the

Broken Hill Proprietary Co. began to mine cheap lead-zinc ores in Australia. Derbyshire had 2,333 lead miners in 1861, but only 871 two decades later and a mere 285 by the end of the century. The depression of 1880–82 brought lead mining to an end in many districts and caused a dramatic fall in the local population. The Derbyshire lead industry was, however, a long time dying and a few mines bucked the trend. Most famously, the Mill Close Mine (Darley Dale), which had been worked by the London Lead Co., was reopened by Edward Miller Wass in 1859 and soon became profitable. By 1887 its output had risen to nearly 4,000 tons of dressed ore per annum, which accounted for 85 per cent of all the ore that was raised in Derbyshire. About 100 men were employed underground and about 50 on the surface. Most of the miners lived nearby at Darley, Wensley and Winster, though some had migrated from Cornwall when Cornish engines and pumps were installed at the mine. The ore was taken from the mine by horse and cart to Wass's smelting works at Lea, eight miles away. Mill Close Mine was not closed until 1940.

Textiles

Derbyshire had pioneered the Industrial Revolution in the cotton industry, but in the steam age the leadership had passed to Lancashire. However, the mills of north-west Derbyshire flourished on the fringes of this new home of the industry. The largest cotton mills in Glossopdale were those in Howardtown or New Glossop, surrounded by grimy rows of stone-built terraced housing.

Glossop became a mill town in the nineteenth century, with long rows of terraced houses built close to the cotton mills. Wren Nest Mills in High Street (shown here after the roof was destroyed in a disastrous fire in 2007) was built in the first decade of the nineteenth century and once employed 1,400 workers. It ceased trading in 1955 and was converted into apartments.

PHOTOGRAPH: CARNEGIE

The former Springfield Mills, Sandiacre. This four-storey tenement lace factory by the Erewash Canal in Sandiacre was built in 1888 by T. Hooley Ltd, a firm founded by Terah Hooley of Long Eaton. His son Ernest Terah Hooley (1860–1947) became a property dealer and company promoter, floating companies such as the Dunlop Tyre Co., Raleigh Cycles and Schweppes, and investing in land, particularly the Risley Hall estate, before he went bankrupt in 1898. Lace tenement factories such as this were divided into units occupied by small businesses. The mill has recently been converted into apartments and the site in the foreground awaits development. Rows of terraced housing once surrounded the mill.

PHOTOGRAPH: CARNEGIE

By 1851 the ancient and extensive parish of Glossop contained 60 mills and its population was soaring. At Dinting, on the outskirts of the town, the calico mill which had been built in 1825 was followed by others along the valley of the river Sett, using water power at first, then steam. Calico printing remained an important industry in this area until the 1960s. By 1846 the ample supplies of flowing water at New Mills powered eight cotton-spinning mills, four calico printing mills, four candlewick mills and two dyeing mills. Steam engines were introduced from the 1840s and engraving, printing and bleaching businesses were established.

The number of people employed in the hosiery industry in Nottinghamshire, Leicestershire and Derbyshire had risen to 43,900 by 1844. By then, steam-powered hosiery machines had been introduced and, although hand-frame knitters long continued to work on special types of hosiery, in general the numbers employed in the trade soon began to dwindle. Between 1860 and 1890 the number of Derbyshire silk mills fell from 42 to 14. Meanwhile, the weaving of tapes, webbings, bindings, braids and ribbons, which had begun in Derbyshire early in the nineteenth century, became concentrated in Derby, Ashbourne and Wirksworth.

The hand-made lace industry had spread from Nottinghamshire in 1825, when John Boden and William Morley built a lace factory at Castlefields, Derby. Three years later, Pigot's *Directory* named 11 lace firms in south-east Derbyshire, particularly at Heanor, Ilkeston and Long Eaton. In the 1840s and 50s the main occupation of the working-class women of Ashbourne was the poorly paid job of embroidering patterns on machine-made lace net; 73 women with this occupation were recorded in the census of 1851. The south-east Derbyshire lace industry attracted more small firms in the 1870s, when labour disputes in Nottinghamshire caused them to move across the county boundary, and then in the 1880s huge, brick-built tenement factories, where

'room and power' for machines could be rented, were erected alongside the canal and railway in the Erewash valley. The largest of these was Harrington Mills, Long Eaton (1885–87), which at one time had 26 tenants, the next largest were Victoria Mills, Draycott (begun in 1888 and completed in 1907) and Springfield Mills, Sandiacre (1888). As this Derbyshire industry continued to grow in the years leading up to the First World War, over 4,000 people in Long Eaton – one in four of its inhabitants – were employed in the manufacture of lace on large Leavers machines, each of which weighed 20 tons.

Other industries

STONE

In the second half of the nineteenth century the quarrying and burning of limestone expanded into a major industry. Harpur Hill had one of the biggest limeburning works in the country and the chimney of its Hoffman kiln, erected in 1872, soared 170 feet high. Another enormous kiln was erected at the Perseverance Works, Dove Holes and numerous kilns were built at Miller's Dale, Middleton-by-Wirksworth and other places besides the railway lines through the Peak District. Lime workers lived close to the quarries and works, especially those in Cowdale, Harpur Hill, Peak Dale and Dove Holes.

In Victorian times, millstone grit from the Stancliffe Quarry at Darley Dale was used in public buildings, notably St George's Hall, Liverpool, and for paving Trafalgar Square and the streets of London, while the quarries at Little Eaton provided stone for Derby Cathedral and Birmingham Town Hall. The villages of Birchover and Stanton-in-Peak acquired their present character alongside huge new quarries. By the late nineteenth century the Derbyshire millstone industry was in decline, for composite millstones, such as those made of carborundum grit, had become more efficient than Peak stones and roller milling at the ports had begun to replace most of the windmills and water mills in the countryside. The old Derbyshire millstone quarries were used increasingly for the manufacture of stones for pulping wood into paper or for grinding paint, crushing rape seed and grinding animal foodstuffs.

In 1899 the Derwent Valley Water Board was created by the joint authorities of Leicester, Derby, Nottingham and Sheffield to construct huge reservoirs in the narrow Upper Derwent and Ashop valleys on the border with Yorkshire. Between 1901 and 1916 farmsteads, hamlets and the small village of Derwent were submerged under the Howden and Derwent dams. The quarries that provided the stone and the railways that were constructed to take stones to the

Limekilns, Miller's Dale. In the late 1870s and early 1880s large limestone quarries were opened alongside the Derby–Buxton railway line and huge kilns were cut into the rock. These kilns were opened in 1878 and closed in 1930. Limestone and fuel was tipped into the top of the kilns and in each 'eye' a man and a boy had the unpleasant job of drawing quicklime, which was then riddled and graded and taken by barrow to the railway trucks. Large kilns such as these produced about 50 tons a day. Their firebrick linings had to be replaced every two or three years. Extensive quarries and slag heaps stretch behind the kilns, here and further up the line at East Buxton (1880–1944).

PHOTOGRAPH: CARNEGIE

dams have left a rich industrial archaeology. At Millstone Edge the quarry was extended along the skyline to Bole Hill and workshops and sheds were provided for 350–450 workers. The first task was to remove the heaps of debris left by the millstone makers, then railways, loading bays, workshops and sheds were constructed. During each working day of ten hours a hydraulic ram pumped 12,000 gallons of water from a stream below, steam-powered travelling cranes were used to place the newly cut stones into trucks, and cables connected to a self-winding drum lowered the stones by cables down a steep incline to the railway at Grindleford. The weight of each full truck pulled an empty truck back up the incline. In a working life of 7½ years, over 1.2 million tons of stone were sent from Bole Hill Quarry to the construction sites in the Derwent valley.

The navvies who built the dams moved from one public work to another. By 1908, at the height of this huge operation, the Derwent Valley Water Board employed 2,753 workers. Many found lodgings in Bamford, Bradwell, Castleton and Hope, but others were housed in a temporary village that the Derwent Valley Water Board constructed in 1901–03 mid-way between the two dams. This they named Birchinlee after a nearby farm, but it became widely known as Tin Town. It was laid out in three streets, with a school, recreation hall, two hospitals, a bathhouse, public house and shops. At its peak in August 1909, a total of 967 people, including wives and children, lived there. Most of the buildings were plain, corrugated iron huts, lined inside with wood for insulation. They were demolished after 14 years, upon the completion of the reservoirs.

Tin Town, Birchinlee, showing the arrival of Jesse Eyre's mobile butcher's shop. The two men on the far left stand in front of the Post Office and the Recreation Hall, the venue for dances, whist drives, concerts and cinema shows. The village has been completely demolished.

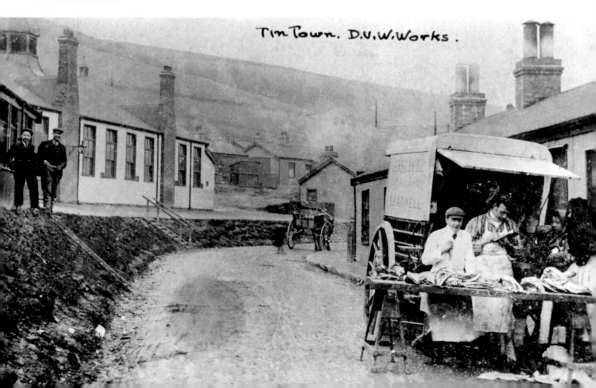

Tin Town. D.V.W.Works.

POTTERY AND BRICKS

The various Derbyshire potteries thrived in the Victorian period. In 1878 Edward Phillips and William Litherland, both formerly of the Worcester Royal Porcelain Works, moved the manufacture of Old Crown to the former borough workhouse in Osmaston Road and began to trade as the Derby Crown Porcelain Co. The potteries on the coalfield continued to produce their usual range of domestic wares for working-class houses and in the south of the county fireclay deposits proved an ideal raw material for the manufacture of sanitary wares and salt-glazed drainpipes in coal-fired kilns. Their products

Dismantling Hilltop Works Pottery, Woodhouse Street, Church Gresley. The potteries on Derbyshire's coalfields flourished in this period: the huge rise in the population meant high demand for cheap domestic and sanitary wares. The best-known firm in Church Gresley was that founded by Thomas Goodwin Green in 1864, specialising at first in kitchen earthenwares, then from the 1920s in the collectable Cornish Ware range. It is not certain whether this dismantled works was operated by T. G. Green or by H. R. Mansfield Ltd, who had clay pits and pipe works in Church Gresley.

In 1874 the Slater brothers bought the brick and sanitary pipe works at Denby from the local landowner, William Drury-Lowe. This extra large load of pipes, with a group of workers sitting on top, was carried on an Armstrong-Saurer motor lorry operated by F. H. Roper of Ripley.

were much in demand from the newly constituted local boards of health. The railways enabled the Swadlincote – Woodville – Church Gresley area on the Leicestershire border to became a major centre of sanitary ware manufacture between 1875 and 1914.

Clay for brickmaking was widespread in south and eastern Derbyshire and many small brick kilns had long supplied the local market. The brickmaking industry grew considerably in the nineteenth century, for brick clay could be mined with coal, and slack coal provided cheap fuel for firing the brick kilns. The Butterley, Staveley, Stanton and other colliery companies had their own brickworks, where bricks were made for their workers' houses and for other local buildings. In the White Peak, deposits of silica sand at Friden were first worked in 1892 for use in the manufacture of firebricks.

Great landowners

The Chatsworth and Haddon estates remained by far the largest in Derbyshire, but the history of the two houses in the Victorian era was completely different. While Chatsworth had been adapted to the fashions of the modern age, Haddon became a romantic ruin when the Dukes of Rutland concentrated instead on rebuilding Belvoir Castle. Having finished his great new wing at Chatsworth, the sixth Duke of Devonshire and his head gardener, Joseph Paxton, turned their attention to remodelling the village of Edensor and to restyling the gardens on the hillside east of the house. Between 1839 and 1841 most of the houses in Edensor were rebuilt in a variety of eye-catching styles taken from pattern books from many parts of Europe. The houses and cottages alongside the holloway that had formed the old road down to the crossing of the Derwent by the mill were removed, except for the one which was occupied by the family of the man who acted as the clerk of works for the new scheme. The entry for Edensor in Bagshaw's *Gazetteer* (1846) reads: 'Everything tends to show his Grace's taste, good feeling, and liberal disposition towards those in humble circumstances.' The population of the village fell from 748 in 1841 to 487 in 1901, partly because many other estate workers were housed in another village at Pilsley, but the population of Beeley also fell from 406 to 340 in the same period. When the medieval parish church was replaced in the late 1860s by a neo-Gothic building designed by Sir George Gilbert Scott that was large and imposing enough to serve a town, Edensor became the finest estate village in the land. These high-quality buildings were a world apart from the brick terraces that housed the industrial workers on the coalfield or the thatched cottages of farm labourers elsewhere. Census returns confirm that they were occupied by the estate's craftsmen, labourers and servants. These families were mostly of local origin; 14 of the 27 male heads of household in 1881 had been born in Edensor and seven others in neighbouring villages, though plenty of individuals had come from more distant places to work on the important jobs on the estate.

In 1844, in anticipation of a return visit from Tsar Nicholas that never happened, the Emperor Fountain (at that time the highest in the world) was constructed in the canal pond. The water was fed from a moorland reservoir down a channel and over a mock-ruined aqueduct. Paxton had already achieved fame through the great conservatory that he had built to receive plants from all over the world. He then designed a camelia house and, with the active co-operation of the duke, imported tens of thousands of trees to adorn the rather barren hillside. Great boulders were stacked on top of each other, waterfalls were designed, ponds constructed and two special areas became an arboretum and a pinetum.

In south Derbyshire the income of the Harpur Crewes of Calke Abbey came from agricultural rents and the quarrying and burning of lime at Ticknall. In Victorian times, they built up a substantial estate of 12,923 acres, much of it grouse-shooting moorland in north-east Staffordshire and adjoining parts of Derbyshire, where they employed ten gamekeepers by the 1870s. But the family became reclusive eccentrics with a strict regime under which, at meal times,

the junior servants were not allowed to speak until the housekeeper, butler and ladies' maids had retired after their first course. Their house has been preserved as it was in its final stage by the National Trust as a stark reminder of the declining fortunes of a landed gentry family that did not adapt to a new era.

The Peak District moors that had been enclosed for the shooting of grouse in the first half of the nineteenth century began to take on their modern managed appearance when shooting butts were introduced in the 1840s. These were built waist-high and their stone or wooden construction was disguised by turf. By the early 1860s the breech-loading shotgun was in widespread use and a loader or two helped the shooter to keep up the rate of firing. In the past birds had been shot as they flew away, but now they were driven towards the butts by beaters who were paid to rouse the birds by shouting, shaking rattles and firing guns into the air. The management of the moors, particularly the burning of sections on a rotation basis so as to provide fresh shoots of heather while preserving thick cover for nesting, now began in earnest in order to provide enough birds to shoot. Drains were dug in the wettest parts of the moors to encourage heather rather than cotton grass or bog-moss and purple moor grass; deep ditches helped to prevent the spread of fire; pony and cart tracks took the sportsmen on to the moors; and stone cabins provided shelter at lunchtime. In the 1870s the Duke of Rutland stopped sheep grazing on his Longshaw estate in the summer months so that the heather could be managed solely for the grouse. At the same time, he provided a diversion for the shooters by constructing a 70-acre rabbit warren that stretched for nearly a mile under Curbar Edge; the keeper's cottage, known as the Warren Lodge, was built about 1877. By the 1880s the 'bags' of grouse that were shot each day were enormous. The record annual 'bag' on this 9,270 acres of grouse moorland, together with the 'sporting rights' over 2,200 acres of adjacent farm land, was the 7,266 grouse shot in 1893.

The agricultural depression of the last quarter of the nineteenth century meant that landowners whose income was dependent on farming were unable to improve their country houses. The large, new buildings that appeared in the countryside were erected for men who had prospered in industry – often beyond Derbyshire – and who could commute by rail. Thornbridge Hall was built in a neo-Jacobean style in the 1870s for a Lancashire businessman, Frederick Craven, then partly remodelled for George Marples of Sheffield at the turn of the century, when the estate was enlarged to over 400 acres. The house at Lea Wood, which was designed in 1874 by W. E. Nesfield for Alfred Alsop, was one of Derbyshire's earliest examples of the Arts and Crafts Movement.

Farming

In 1851 James Caird, the agricultural writer, noted that in Derbyshire, 'Wheat does not, on the whole succeed well. Oats are more common and much more depended on. Nine-tenths of the county are in grass. It is a dairy and rearing district, the growth of corn being of quite inferior consideration.' He found Derbyshire a picturesque and pleasant county 'where the pastures are well managed, the ploughed land neatly cultivated, and the stock suitable to the soil and carefully tended'. This was the period of High Farming when farmers prospered. As prices for dairy products rose and Derbyshire was connected by quick rail services to London and to the industrial towns of the Midlands, the liquid milk trade gradually became more important than the manufacture of cheese. Both large and small farmers benefited when large dairies, such as the Express Dairy at Rowsley, organised the collection of milk and saw to its marketing.

The improvements made during the period of High Farming included land-drainage schemes and the cultivation of specialist crops. John Baker, a wealthy hosier who owned Litton Frith, grew watercress in what became known as Cressbrook Dale and lavender and peppermint on the slopes descending to the river Wye. Model farms included that built for Alfred Miller Munday at Shipley in 1860–61, one for the Burdetts at Foremark, and a third for James Oakes at Riddings. Meanwhile, the Peak District continued to offer good grazing ground. In 1840 the Tithe Commissioners noted that, 'it is the custom here, as in the whole neighbouring district, for the occupiers to take in great quantities of cattle to ley from May to November, from Yorkshire, Lancashire and other counties.'

The effects of the agricultural depression, which began in the 1870s when American wheat flooded the market, were less severe in Derbyshire than in corn-growing counties, for here land was mostly laid down to grass. Even so, the acreage under cereals dropped sharply and when refrigerated meat arrived from Australia and New Zealand the number of sheep and cattle fell too. Only the dairy herds remained unaffected. Farming was still in the era of horses, carts and hand tools, broken perhaps by the annual visit of the threshing machine. In the Edwardian era 92 per cent of Derbyshire farmland was tenanted and the average size of a holding was 42.2 acres, a situation which had hardly changed for over a century. Many farms had been tenanted by the same family down the generations.

Holmesfield Park boundary stone. The coppicing tradition in Derbyshire's deciduous woods continued up to the First World War. This internal boundary stone in Holmesfield Park Wood is the first of four that were erected between 1906 and 1910, when the wood belonged to the Duke of Rutland. Similar stones from the same period can be found in other Haddon Hall estate woods, such as Smeekley Wood in the Cordwell valley and Monk Wood, Barlow.

PHOTOGRAPH: AUTHOR

'... Nine-tenths of the county are in grass. It is a dairy and rearing district, the growth of corn being of quite inferior consideration.'

JAMES CAIRD, 1851

Distribution maps of surnames in the 1881 census reveal patterns that had not been altered much by the increased mobility opportunities provided by the railways. Most families stayed within the neighbourhood or 'country' that had long been familiar to their ancestors. Many still lived close to the place where their surname had originated back in the Middle Ages, particularly in the Peak District and other northern parts of the county. Some rare names such as Jeffcock, Memmott and Ronksley had moved to Sheffield and families that had produced numerous sons, like the Alsops, Bagshaws, Eyres and Heathcotes had spread much further. They were still recognisable as essentially Derbyshire names, however, as were such distinctive surnames as Blanksby, Boler, Bownes, Briddon, Burdekin, Buxton, Drabble, Froggatt, Glossop, Levick, Ollerenshaw, Outram, Padley, Raworth, Shimwell and Wildgoose.

Religion

A programme of church reform under Henry Ryder, the evangelical Bishop of Coventry and Lichfield, had provided increased accommodation for worshippers in the county's parish churches, old and new, or in licensed rooms or schools. Upon his death in 1836, the ancient see was divided and the archdeaconry of Derby (which covered the entire county) became part of the diocese of Lichfield. The retention of the medieval parochial structure hindered the Church of England's responses to the rapid growth of population. Glossop parish still covered 49,960 acres and Bakewell 43,020 acres. Such large sizes favoured the spread of Nonconformity in places distant from the parish church. In 1843 legislation was finally passed to enable the creation of new parishes,

THE INTERIOR, LOOKING EAST, BEFORE THE RESTORATION OF 1843

but these powers were not taken up for some time in most of Derbyshire. The Established Church was also racked by controversies over the payment of tithes and church rates and by arguments over doctrine.

The only ecclesiastical census ever taken for England and Wales was that on Sunday 30 March 1851. Its first finding was that most people did not attend any form of religious service; in Derbyshire they formed considerably less than half. This was especially true of the industrial districts. A report made five years later showed that of the 1,647 men employed by the Butterley Co. in Derbyshire and Nottinghamshire, only 18 were regular worshippers and 26 occasional attenders at the Church of England and only 45 regular and 150 occasional worshippers went to a Nonconformist chapel. The second finding in 1851 was that although the Church of England was by far the largest denomination, many more people went to chapel than to church. The statistics were not presented clearly, but if we take the highest attendances at services that day, we find that in Derbyshire 20,790 went to the Church of England, 46,213 to various Protestant chapels and 2,298 to the Roman Catholic church. The Protestant Dissenters included 17,903 Wesleyan Methodists, 11,965 Primitive Methodists, 4,178 members of the Wesleyan Reform Movement and 1,666 Methodists of other persuasions, together with 5,484 Baptists, 3,983 Congregationalists and 1,034 others.

These figures for the whole of the county mask a great deal of local

The interior of St Mary and All Saints church, Chesterfield. Before the restoration of 1842–43, the nave of Chesterfield church was packed with box pews and galleries and dominated by the organ. A stove provided some heating and a chandelier some light. The pulpit was topped by a canopy and reached by a winding staircase. Most of this clutter was swept away during Gilbert Scott's restoration.
PHOTOGRAPH: CHESTERFIELD CHURCH

Wesleyan Reform Chapel, Foolow. The Wesleyan Reform movement attracted a lot of support in Derbyshire when it broke away from the main Wesleyan church. The Peak District, in particular, has numerous small Wesleyan Reform chapels. This example by the village green at Foolow is inscribed: 'Foolow Chapel and Sunday School 1866'.
PHOTOGRAPH: AUTHOR

variation. Attendance at Anglican services remained high in estate and other small villages, whereas Methodism was strong in open villages with large numbers of freeholders and in the new coalmining and industrial towns. The Primitive Methodists appealed to farm labourers and the industrial poor and the new Wesleyan Reform Movement was strong in places not far from its national headquarters at Sheffield. Roman Catholicism persisted in its traditional strongholds, such as Hassop, Hathersage and Glossop, and attracted Irish immigrants in Derby.

Margery Tranter's edition of the 1851 returns for Derbyshire provide a snapshot at a particular point in time. In the second half of the nineteenth century many new churches and chapels were built and attendances increased, but they did not match the tremendous rise in the national population. Early

St Margaret's church, Wormhill. The rebuilding of Wormhill parish church in 1864 included the heightening of the medieval tower, described three years earlier by Sir Stephen Glynne as 'a small western steeple'. In a remarkable piece of ecclesiology for a remote part of the White Peak, the new tower was topped in the style of the late Anglo-Saxon church at Sompting (Sussex) or contemporary Rhineland churches.
PHOTOGRAPH: AUTHOR

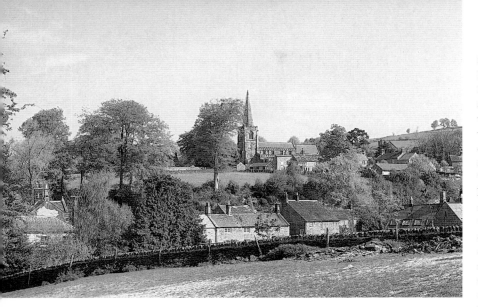

St Michael's church, Hathersage. St Michael dedications are often associated with hilltop sites, where the saint was depicted in medieval art fighting the devil. The church stands beside the Norman ringwork known as Camp Green, the original residence of the lord of the manor. Rebuilt in the Perpendicular Gothic style in the late Middle Ages, it owes much of its present appearance to Butterfield's restoration in 1849–52. Modern Hathersage developed in the valley below, along the turnpike road and around the needle mills that created a Victorian industrial village.

PHOTOGRAPH: AUTHOR

Victorian churches, such as Wensley (1841–43), Woodville (1846) and Rowsley (1855) favoured the Norman style, but then a variety of Gothic designs from the leading church architects of the day became the dominant fashion: Sir George Gilbert Scott's Edensor (1867), William Butterfield's Bamford (1856–60) and his restoration of Hathersage (1849–52) and Monyash (1884–87), J. L. Pearson's restoration of Steetley (1880) and Whitwell (1885–86), G. E. Street's work at Long Eaton (1868), and Norman Shaw's at Youlgreave (1869–70), Great Longstone (1872–73) and Upper Langwith (1877). The most prominent local architect was H. I. Stevens of Derby, the designer of numerous Gothic churches, including Osmaston (1845), the former St Alkmund's, Derby (1846), Belper (1849), Clay Cross (1851) and Alvaston (1855–56). Many other churches were built anew, improved or restored by local architects: Alfreton (1868), Alsop-en-le-Dale (1882–83), Barlow (1867), Borrowash 1899, Brackenfield (1856–57), Brassington (1879–81), Buxton St Mary (1914–15), Etwall (1881), Hognaston (1879–81), Holloway (1901–03), Morton (1850) and Wilne (1917–23). The Nonconformists, too, abandoned their early, unpretentious styles in favour of Gothic edifices with grand frontages. Some of the new chapels were not readily distinguishable from contemporary Anglican and Roman Catholic churches.

Religious bodies, notably the National Society (Church of England) and the British and Foreign Schools Society (Nonconformists), and private philanthropists, including lords of the manor and industrialists, provided scores of elementary schools and Sunday schools across the county and in 1850 Bishop John Lonsdale founded a female teacher training college in Derby. But at the time of the 1870 Education Act, which set up secular schools run by elected local boards where existing provision was inadequate, 8,828 Derbyshire children had no school to attend. In some places, such as Ilkeston, new National schools were built to prevent the election of a board, but within a dozen years, Derbyshire

All Saints church, Bakewell. By the early nineteenth century the ancient minster church at Bakewell was in urgent need of major repair. An architect's report in 1824 suggested that the old church should be dismantled and replaced by an entirely new one, but this was resisted by the parishioners. Five years later, however, they agreed to remove the bells and to take down the tower and spire. In 1840 a second report emphasised the alarming state of the building. Finally, all agreed with the solutions and costings offered by William Flockton, a Sheffield architect. In November 1841 work began on demolishing and rebuilding the Newark, the crossing and the north transept and in building a new octagonal tower and spire. In 1852 the nave was taken down and rebuilt. The churchyard was closed for burials in 1858.

PHOTOGRAPH: AUTHOR

had 42 school boards, mainly in the east of the county, where the population had risen rapidly, and elementary education had become compulsory. By 1888 six new board schools served 41 per cent of the borough of Derby's children.

Recreation

The contrast between the rapid rise in the population of the burgeoning industrial communities and the steady decline of the rural population throughout Britain in the second half of the nineteenth century stimulated interest in the folklore, customs, song, dance, dialect and vernacular architecture of a passing way of life. Two Derbyshire men, Llewellyn Jewitt and Sidney Odall Addy, were leading figures in the national movement to record and celebrate the survivals of a popular culture that they thought went back to time immemorial. Exaggerated claims were made for the antiquity of customs which thrive today as never before.

Derbyshire is now deservedly famous for its annual well dressings. The veneration of holy wells had been suppressed as a 'Popish superstition' at the Reformation, but a few gentry families had remained true to the Catholic faith. At Tissington the Fitzherberts either preserved or revived the custom. Our first evidence comes in 1748 when Nicholas Hardinge wrote that at Tissington 'we saw springs adorned with garlands; in one of these was a tablet inscribed with rhymes, composed by the schoolmaster in honour of the fountains, which, as Fitzherbert informs me, are annually commemorated upon Holy Thursday, the minister and his parishioners praying and singing over them.' The present custom of designing pictures from petals and other vegetation into soft clay spread on boards had developed by the early nineteenth century. A newspaper description of 1839 stated that:

Tissington Well Dressing, 2007. Tissington's six wells are decorated with scenes from the Scriptures for a week in early May, following Ascension Day. The annual dressing of the wells at Tissington was recorded in 1748 and was probably a survival of a medieval custom. It began to spread to other White Peak villages in the nineteenth century. The art of well dressing begins with the soaking of the boards on which the pictures will be mounted in the village pond. They are then plastered in locally dug clay, which has been mixed with salt and trod to the necessary consistency. The picture is then traced on boards with a pointer or toothed wheel and marked with alder cones or coffee beans. The painstaking task of completing the picture with flower petals and other natural materials then begins. The petals overlap to allow rain to run off the picture. A blessing ceremony in the church is held on Ascension Day, after which the minister blesses each well in turn. The dressings remain in place for a week and are visited by thousands of people from many parts of the country.
PHOTOGRAPHS: AUTHOR

> The stems and flowers are closely inserted, and a brilliant mosaic is thus
> prepared, forming as it were, a ground work for various ornamental
> designs, as crowns and stars, and appropriate mottoes, chiefly from
> scripture, which are most imperiously introduced.

This Tissington custom spread to other places in the White Peak when piped water was supplied in the 1820s: at Wirksworth (1827), Youlgreave (1829) and Tideswell about the same time. After the wells were blessed by the minister, a week's festivities and hospitality in pubs and houses began. Until recent times, all the designs illustrated biblical texts. The custom as we know it is very much a nineteenth-century one that has expanded greatly in recent years.

The Castleton Garland procession is another custom that has changed form over time. Nowadays, it is led to each of the village's six inns by a man on horseback bearing a three-feet high garland over his head, followed by a queen on horseback, a brass band playing a traditional tune, schoolgirls dressed in white and boys in scout and cub uniforms. The procession ends at the parish church, when the garland is hoisted on to a central pinnacle on the south side of the tower. Since the First World War, the ceremony has been followed by the playing of the last post and then by maypole dancing. The changes that have been made to the original, simple morris dance are well documented. Children

were not involved, the queen was described in 1885 as 'a man on horseback, dressed as a woman, who acts the fool', and the music was supplied by a pipe and tabor or a fife and drum. The king's costume (which is now in the village museum) was an old coachman's coat turned inside out, with a large rosette. The procession originally started from the house where the garland was made. It was led by a man on foot carrying a besom, who was followed by the king or 'The Man', then by morris dancers with two or three musicians, the fool dressed as a woman and a few others who rode behind the dancers to keep a space for them. In this earlier form it was a rare survival of one of the May Games, a traditional way of raising money for the church. These fund-raising activities were banned by the Puritans in the mid-seventeenth century but restored to celebrate Charles II's restoration on 29 May 1660. Various parish groups were expected to put on an entertainment and to collect money from the crowd. At Castleton the bell-ringers organised this particular May Game, which is why the garland is shaped like a bell and ends up on the bell tower of the church. The Castleton churchwarden's accounts for 1749 record the payment of eightpence 'for an iron rod to hang the Ringers Garland in'.

Similar processions once took place in other Derbyshire villages. In 1789 John Byng rode out from Chesterfield:

> We were upon our horses by half past nine o'clock and rode through Normanton, a village where the May Pole was, as others of this county, richly adorned by garlands, composed of silk, gauze and mock flowers; and around which (a woman told me) they danced in the Morris-way; but not in honor of the goddess Maia on the 1st of her month, but, rather in memory of the Restoration, upon the 29th of May.

Derbyshire's most famous folk song is 'The Derby Ram', which Llewellyn Jewitt noted in *The Ballads and Songs of Derbyshire* (1867) was set as a glee by

Dr Callicott in 1867 and sung at public dinners in the county town. The ballad was originally performed by farmworkers in pubs and houses as an annual plough-play between Christmas and Plough Monday (the public holiday on the Monday after 6 January). Such plays involved song, dance and ad-libbing foolery and their purpose too was to raise money for the local parish church. The young men either dragged a plough around the streets or carried a carved animal head or skull; in Derbyshire a ram's skull was used. Such plays date from the second half of the eighteenth century. An additional twist to the tale is that in 1858, during the Indian Mutiny, a ram was adopted as the mascot of the 95th Derbyshire Regiment and named Private Derby. As with all old ballads, various verses were sung, but Jewitt's printed version has become the standard.

'The Derby Ram'.

As I was going to Darby, Sir,
All on a market day,
I met the finest Ram, Sir,
That ever was fed on hay.
Daddle-i-day, daddle-i-day,
Fal-de-ral, fal-de-ral, daddle-i-day.

This Ram was fat behind, Sir,
This Ram was fat before,
This Ram was ten yards high,
  Sir,
Indeed he was no more.
Daddle-i-day, &c.

The Wool upon his back, Sir,
Reached up unto the sky,
The Eagles made their nests there,
  Sir,
For I heard the young ones cry.
Daddle-i-day, &c.

The Wool upon his belly, Sir,
It dragged upon the ground,
It was sold in Darby town, Sir,
For forty thousand pound.
Daddle-i-day, &c.

The space between his horns, Sir,
Was as far as a man could reach,
And there they built a pulpit
For the Parson there to preach.
Daddle-i-day, &c.

The teeth that were in his mouth, Sir,
Were like a regiment of men;
And the tongue that hung between
  them, Sir,
Would have dined them twice and
  again.
Daddle-i-day, &c.

This Ram jumped o'er a wall, Sir,
His tail caught on a briar,
It reached from Darby town, Sir,
All into Leicestershire.
Daddle-i-day, &c.

And of this tail so long, Sir,
'Twas ten miles and an ell,
They made a goodly rope, Sir,
To toll the market bell.
Daddle-i-day, &c.

This Ram had four legs to walk on,
  Sir,
This Ram had four legs to stand,
And every leg he had, Sir,
Stood on an acre of land.
Daddle-i-day, &c.

The Butcher that killed this Ram, Sir,
Was drownded in the blood,
And the boy that held the pail, Sir,
Was carried away in the flood.
Daddle-i-day, &c.

All the maids in Darby, Sir,
Came begging for his horns,
To take them to coopers,
To make them milking gawns.
Daddle-i-day, &c.

The little boys of Darby, Sir,
They came to beg his eyes,
To kick about the streets, Sir,
For they were football size.
Daddle-i-day, &c.

The tanner that tanned its hide, Sir,
Would never be poor any more,
For when he had tanned and retched
  it,
It covered all Sinfin Moor.
Daddle-i-day, &c.

The Jaws that were in his head, Sir,
They were so fine and thin,
They were sold to a Methodist
  Parson,
For a pulpit to preach in.
Daddle-i-day, &c.

Indeed, Sir, this is true, Sir,
I never was taught to lie,
And had you been to Darby, Sir,
You'd have seen it as well as I.
Daddle-i-day, daddle-i-day,
Fal-de-ral, fal-de-ral, daddle-i-day.

Despite their considerable interest in the past and the foundation of the Derbyshire Archaeological Society in 1878, Derbyshire antiquarians did not produce a hefty county history. Nor have they left us a glossary of its dialect. The speech of south and east Derbyshire was similar to that of Nottinghamshire and Leicestershire, but with recognisable local differences;. a Derby accent, for instance, was not quite the same as an Erewash valley one. Peak District speech was more northern, but again with much local variety. Accents placed people within the neighbourhood or 'country' that they had known since birth, but also identified them with a particular place within it. The sense of belonging to a small community that was distinct from its neighbours is evident from adverse comments on surrounding towns and villages, as in the verse:

Ashford in the Water / Longstone in the lice / Sheldon in the Nut Wood / And Bakewell in the Spice. Baslow for gentlefolk / Calver for trenchers / Middleton for rogues and thieves / And Eyam for pretty wenches.

Steve Bloomer, Derby County's most famous footballer. He joined the club in 1892 and in his long career scored 332 goals in 536 appearances in First Division games (some with Middlesbrough) and 28 goals in 23 appearances for England. He was the biggest star in English football in the 1890s and early 1900s and the top scorer in the First Division in five seasons. During his time with Derby County the club were FA Cup finalists on three occasions and runners-up in the First Division of the Football League once.

As the middle classes of Derby began to move into the suburbs in the last quarter of the nineteenth century the central streets took on the character of a shopping and entertainment district. The Derby Grand Theatre, for instance, was opened in 1886. The working classes too had higher wages and more time to spend them as their average weekly working hours fell. The railways enabled families to take day trips or even longer holidays to Cleethorpes, Skegness or Bridlington. More leisure time and better communications led to the formation of amateur sports clubs and a few professional teams. The Derbyshire County Cricket Club was founded in 1870 with grounds at Derby, Chesterfield, Buxton, Heanor and Ilkeston. In 1884 the Derby County Association Football Club formed a team that was known from the start as The Rams; they soon became one of the country's leading teams and reached the FA Cup Final in 1898, 1899 and 1903. The current Chesterfield FC dates only from 1919, but it followed three short-lived clubs, starting in 1867 when the Chesterfield Cricket Club formed a football team. Outdoor pursuits such as cycling, rambling, mountaineering and golf also took off in the late Victorian and Edwardian period and in the remotest part of the White Peak Flagg races date from 1892.

The horse-drawn omnibuses and trams and the services provided by country carriers began to be replaced at this time. In 1898 Thomas Barton started a public bus service in the Derby area and within ten years he had extended it to Long Eaton and Nottingham. Then from 1913 the Trent Motor Traction Co. ran services from Derby to Ashbourne, Chesterfield, Ilkeston, Melbourne and Burton-upon-Trent. Derby quickly adapted to the motor age, for it was in Nightingale Road in 1908 that Rolls-Royce (founded four years previously) set up a factory to build the car that was known later as the Silver Ghost; here 6,173 chassis were made until the line was discontinued in 1925. Meanwhile, in 1897 Herbert Frood of Combs in the parish of Chapel-en-le-Frith had developed a new friction material for brakes, which became an immediate success and eventually led to the construction of the large Ferodo brake lining and friction pad works which flourishes today.

The pace of change in the Victorian and Edwardian era was most evident in the county town and the industrial communities on the Derbyshire coalfield, though even there most women still bought their provisions in small family shops in the nearby streets. Life was still lived at the local level. Nineteenth-century England remained a horse-drawn society and many places were cut-off from the hustle and bustle of the new industrial era. The bicycle was becoming popular but as yet few cars travelled along the unmetalled roads. Ordnance Survey maps show that towns were still surrounded by small settlements, fields and woods, for suburbs had not yet spread far into the countryside.

The First World War to the present

When the First World War broke out in 1914, thousands of Derbyshire men volunteered for action. The county regiment, The Sherwood Foresters, quickly expanded to 33 battalions, the second of which joined the British Expeditionary Force to France, while the first was brought back from India for service in the trenches. Conscription was enforced in 1916, followed by the slaughter of thousands of soldiers in the trenches. The Sherwood Foresters were involved in all the major battles on the Western Front and 11,409 members of the regiment were killed. They are commemorated by a memorial, designed as a beacon on a high point at Crich, that is visible for many miles around. Other Derbyshire men fought in the Gallipoli campaign. War memorials in every town and village record the large numbers of soldiers who never returned from the four years of a war that had been fought on an unprecedented scale. In the whole of the British Empire, nearly 1 million men and women were killed and over 2 million were wounded.

No. 7

5th Battalion The Sherwood Foresters
(Nottinghamshire & Derbyshire Regiment).

'G' COMPANY ORDERS.

DRILL HALL, ILKESTON,
August 4th, 1914.

1. **Parade.**
   The Company is ordered to Mobilize. All ranks will report themselves at the Drill Hall at 9 a.m. on August the 5th.
   Dress : Marching Order (with rifle, bayonet, and bandolier).

2. **Medical Inspection.**
   The Company will parade for Medical Inspection at the Drill Hall at 9 a.m.

3. **Kit.**
   Kit bags will be brought to the Drill Hall at the same time as the men report themselves. Each bag must be clearly labelled with Regimental Number, Name, and Regiment, and should contain the articles enumerated on the " Notices to Join."

4. **Kit Inspection.**
   The kits of the men passed fit for service will be inspected by half-Company Commanders, who will make a list of deficiencies. These lists will be handed to O.C. Company.

5. **Accommodation.**
   Men, whose homes are at the Head Quarters of the Company, will be allowed to stay there for the night. The remainder of the Company will be accommodated in the Drill Hall.

6. **Messing.**
   Each man must bring food for one day with him. Tea and breakfast (next day) will be provided for those men who are accommodated at the Drill Hall.

7. **Passes.**
   No one is to leave the Drill Hall after 9 a.m. without written permission from the O.C. Company.

8. **Alarm Post.**
   The Alarm Post will be the Drill Hall.

9. **Fire.**
   In case of fire or other alarm the Company will parade on the Alarm Post in Company Column, facing the Drill Hall.
   Dress : Marching Order (with rifle, bayonet, and bandolier).
   The Company Buglers will sound the Alarm at the Drill Hall, and at Market Place, White Lion Square, and the Rutland Hotel.

10. **Duties.**
    The following duties will be found by the Company :—
    No.1 Section   1 N.C.O.   Guard on Drill Hall.
                       6 Men.
                       1 Bugler.
    To mount at 10 a.m.

11. **Detail.**
    Orderly Sergeant for the 5th inst., Sergeant Mackenzie.
    Orderly Corporal for the 5th inst., Corpl. Syson.

HENRY NEWTON, Captain,
Commanding "G" Company,
5th Batt. Sherwood Foresters.

The inter-war years

The economic boom that followed the war collapsed in 1921 and Britain soon plunged into the throes of depression. The nation's manufacturing industries had lost much of their competitive edge in the international market and during the rest of the twentieth century Derbyshire's importance in the national economy declined relentlessly. In the 1920s one in ten of the national workforce was out of work, but the world-

The Sherwood Foresters Regimental War Memorial, Crich. Designed in the form of a lighthouse, whose flashing beacon has a range of 38 miles, this memorial to soldiers who died in the First World War was built high above the quarry at Crich in 1923. Most of the soldiers were recruited from Derbyshire and Nottinghamshire. In 1952 the memorial was re-dedicated to include those who had died in the Second World War. Another memorial was erected in 2008 to commemorate soldiers who died on operational service since 1945 in Palestine, Korea, Northern Ireland and Afghanistan. Commemoration services are held every Armistice Sunday.

wide depression of 1929–31 raised this figure to one in five. At its highest point in 1932, Britain's unemployment level reached nearly 3 million people, or 23 per cent of the labour force. Districts such as east Derbyshire that relied on heavy industry were badly affected and unemployment levels rose well above the national average. Those who remained in work saw their standards of living rise a little in the inter-war years, but the many families who had no regular wage coming in had to struggle to make ends meet.

COAL

The years leading up to the First World War had been a time of considerable expansion in the coal industry. In 1913 the nation's mines had produced 287.4 million tons of coal and Britain's share in the world export trade in coal had amounted to 55.2 per cent. The future seem assured, but after the war the coal industry began to contract in face of foreign competition. The number of men employed in the nation's coal mines fell from 1,227,000 in 1920 to

827,000 in 1932. By the outbreak of the Second World War seven years later, Britain's share of the export trade in coal had fallen to 37.6 per cent. The mine owners' response to the world-wide depression was to offer lower wages. When Derbyshire's miners joined their union's refusal to accept these cuts they were locked out on 1 April 1921. By the beginning of July the hardship that their families had endured forced the miners back to work on the new conditions. A new era of bad relationships between owners and workers had begun.

Nevertheless, coal mining remained the nation's leading source of employment. In 1924 nearly 50,000 Derbyshire miners were employed underground. In that year, the Staveley Coal & Iron Co. began to develop its Markham collieries. They took on an extra 500 workers, whom they housed nearby in Poolsbrook and Duckmanton, and by 1929 output had risen from about 30,000 tons a month to over 50,000 tons. Conditions at the pit-head improved at the main collieries after 1920, when a levy on coal output, and then on royalties, provided amenities including baths, canteens, recreation grounds and health services. But inadequate housing was a serious problem, for much of the old stock was not up to standard and local authorities were reluctant to adopt new statutory powers to build council houses in the 1920s and 1930s because they knew this would cause the rates to rise. Little growth took place in Erewash valley towns such as Alfreton, Heanor and Ripley until the 1960s. Council inertia caused the Staveley and Butterley companies to continue their long-established policy of building houses for their workers. The new Hollingwood estate at Staveley, for example,

During the 1920s some 50,000 Derbyshire men worked in the coal industry.

COURTESY OF JOHN ROUGHTON
ON BEHALF OF MARGERY SMITH
AND WWW.PICTURETHEPAST.
ORG.UK

No. 111.]   [See No. 102.
 "FOR MEN MUST WORK."
 Getting and loading up the celebrated "C.X.C. Gold Medal" Coal in one of the Clay Cross Co.'s Pits, 300 yards below ground.

was planned as a garden city of 880 houses on 114 acres in 1920–27. But about that time, the opening of new, deeper pits across the Nottinghamshire border in the Dukeries tempted many mining families from the Heanor, Codnor and Alfreton district to migrate a few miles to the east. The Erewash valley coalfield was no longer one of the most prosperous mining areas in Britain.

In 1926 the depression worsened across the country and the mine owners proposed both a cut in wages and an extension of working hours from seven to eight each day. On 4 May widespread sympathy for the miners' cause brought British industry to a standstill in the only General Strike in the nation's history. But after nine days the other trade unions withdrew their support, leaving the miners to stay on strike alone until November, when they returned to work defeated as winter drew near. The bitterness of that struggle never left the memories of mining communities. The typical mining settlements were towns in terms of their size but villages in most of their facilities. Everyone who lived there either worked in the local mine or had a friend or neighbour who did. The dangerous nature of the job was all too evident. In 1938 an explosion at the Staveley Co.'s Markham Colliery killed 79 men and injured 38; the last major disaster in Derbyshire was in 1950 at Creswell, when 80 men were killed as a result of an underground fire. Pit villages and towns sprawled across the coalfield, unlovely and often monotonous to look at, very different in character from other places in Derbyshire, their inhabitants defiant and insular. Their social cohesiveness become legendary in the strike-bound years of the 1920s.

IRON

The iron industry too suffered from the slump that followed the First World War. Jobs were lost and companies tried to improve their competitiveness by amalgamating with others. As the demand for wrought iron contracted in favour of steel and because of the depression, the smaller ironworks went out of business. The Staveley works had blast furnaces and pipe shops that were as modern as any in the country and the Stanton Ironworks Co. had become Britain's leading manufacturer of pipes, but even they struggled in the inter-war years. In 1919–20 the Stanton company took over the Riddings Ironworks, then in 1926 the Butterley Co. closed down its Butterley blast furnaces. Worse was soon to come. Seventeen of Derbyshire's 35 blast furnaces were either demolished or ceased production in the two-and-a-half years after June 1928. Many of these furnaces had become outdated and their supplies of ore were vanishing. Even the companies which remained in business were forced to contract. The Stanton company closed its Riddings site in 1926 and the old works at Staveley had gone by 1930.

OTHER INDUSTRIES

In the inter-war years lead mining effectively came to an end. The last great venture was the Mill Close mine in Darley Dale, which closed just before the Second World War. But some old mines were reworked for other minerals, such

Advertisement for Stanton Dale refined pig iron, *c.*1946. The pictures on the advert demonstrate the various stages of the production of a large cast iron pot at the Stanton Works site at Riddings Foundry. They show the core being lowered into the mould, molten iron being poured into the mould, and the finished casting on the back of a lowloader.

as the white calcite which was obtained at the former Cromford Moor Mine in the 1920s; a large mound of waste by Black Rocks dates from that time. Another ancient Peak District industry in terminal decline was that of hewing millstones. Below Millstone Edge a huge pile of debris descends the hillside and scores of millstones of various sizes are stacked together at the side of the track, waiting for a customer who never came. These stones are different in shape from the ones that were used in the old, water-powered cornmills or windmills. Some were for grinding paint, others were made to pulp wood in the paper mills of Scandinavia and other parts of Europe, Canada and the United States; a few were sold to a Swedish paper mill as late as 1939, just before the Second World War brought this ancient industry to an end. But the quarries that produced high-quality building stones from the millstone grit measures at Stancliffe, Stanton and Birchover continued to flourish and to receive orders for such prestigious buildings as Sheffield City Hall, while the demand for limestone ensured the enlargement of the extensive quarries around Buxton.

In the late eighteenth century Derbyshire had led the way with the manufacture of cotton, but by the twentieth century this industry was of little significance, except in the district around Glossop and New Mills. The lace industry that had flourished in the tenement factories of Long Eaton, Sandiacre and Draycott in late Victorian times peaked during the first decades of the twentieth century, but in the 1920s demand for lace fell sharply and within ten years the industry had shrunk to half its size. Little lace was produced during the Second World War, but the industry survived.

Many parts of the East Midlands, however, fared reasonably well during the inter-war years. Derby grew from a provincial county town into a thriving industrial centre because of major new industrial developments, starting with Rolls-Royce and the opening of the British Celanese works at Spondon for the manufacture of synthetic fibres and chemical products. On the eve of the Second World War the borough's three major manufacturing industries were railway rolling stock, motor cars and aero-engines, and artificial silk. Together with engineering and electrical and mechanical engineering, these industries provided work for 48 per cent of the registered employed within the borough. Derby did better than many other places during the 1920s and 1930s.

A millstone loading bay. The largest set of abandoned millstones in the Peak District were stacked for collection between the quarries at Millstone Edge and Bole Hill. These stones were not used for milling corn but for pulping wood into paper, grinding paint, and other uses. They were exported as far away as Canada and Scandinavia until the years leading up to the Second World War, when demand ceased.

PHOTOGRAPH: AUTHOR

Town planning and housing

On the coalfields and in most urban districts the Labour Party made spectacular advances after 1918, when all men over 21 and all women over 30 were given the vote. The rural parts of Derbyshire, however, remained solidly Conservative. In 1919 local councils throughout Britain were made responsible for the planning and improvement of towns and villages. They now had the power to replace slums with new houses. The problem of the Victorian legacy of shoddily built terraced houses, blackened with smoke, lacking basic facilities and squeezed into every available space close to the works or mills had to be faced. Fortunately, the demand for new housing was eased a little by the national trend towards smaller families. The population continued to grow, but not at the rate at which it had expanded in Victorian times.

Improved transport encouraged people to move from the smoky, busy town centres to the peace of the suburbs. Derby's built-up area spread when both the council and private builders erected low-density residential housing. The borders of the borough of Derby had already been widened in 1877 and again in 1901, then in 1928 and 1934 more of the adjacent rural parishes were absorbed. At first, the borough council was reluctant to take advantage of the 1919 legislation and their initial modest proposal was for only 446 houses, but the Ministry of Health persuaded them to produce a new plan for 1,000 more. Eventually, 6,852 council houses were built in the borough between the wars and the centre of the town was cleared of slums. The borough council was also responsible for hospitals, schools, a technical college, a teacher training college, libraries, museums, art galleries, baths, the acquisition of Markeaton and Darley Parks, reservoirs, the supply of gas and electricity, sewage disposal, and a bus station that was one of the most advanced in the country. Meanwhile, in 1927 the Anglican diocese of Derby, covering the whole of the county, was formed out of the existing diocese of Southwell and the parish church of All Saints became Derby cathedral.

A similar picture of suburban expansion, though on a smaller scale, can be painted for Derbyshire's other towns. In 1938 Chesterfield got a fine new town hall on a prominent site beyond the market place and some handsome suburbs further west, but the county has few notable public buildings from this period. The county's other towns grew at a slower pace than before the First World War.

The countryside

The movement of families away from the countryside, which had been such a marked trend in Victorian times, continued well into the twentieth century until bus services and then car-ownership enabled people to commute. The 1931 census found that the population of 112 Derbyshire parishes that had more than 50 people had declined during the previous 50 years. Farming remained

Chesterfield Town
Hall. Designed by
Bradshaw, Gass &
Hope in 1937–38,
this imposing
building occupies
a commanding
position to the west
of the old town. It
replaced an earlier
town hall at the edge
of the market place.
Classical architecture
was still in favour
for public buildings
in the years between
the two world wars.
PHOTOGRAPH: CARNEGIE

depressed and the old rural industries no longer provided much employment. Most of the land that had been ploughed for cereals during the First World War reverted to grass in the depressed years of the 1920s until the threat of renewed hostilities in the late 1930s and then the home food production campaign of the Second World War favoured arable farming once again. For most of the time, Derbyshire farmers could not compete with the overseas mass-production of cereals; instead they concentrated on producing milk and beef and in some places on growing vegetables. Between the wars farming offered little financial reward for the long hours of labour. Capital investment was usually out of the question.

After the First World War aristocratic and gentry families throughout the land found that the prolonged agricultural depression reduced their income from both direct farming and rents to such an extent that a country estate was no longer a sound investment. Their problems were compounded by the payment of death duties. The Chatsworth estate was reduced and the Cavendish family

Grouse-shooting
butt, Derwent Edge.
After the First World
War, grouse-shooting
returned to its
Edwardian intensity,
with enormous 'bags'
recorded at the
height of the season,
but the decline of
the sport was soon
evident. The acreage
of heather moors
in the Peak District
fell by 36 per cent
between 1913 and
1980 and the grouse
population was
reduced substan-
tially. 'Bags' are
now increasingly
uncertain.
Nevertheless, half a
million grouse are
still shot in Britain
each year and
virtually all moor
owners rely on the
income derived from
grouse shooting to
cover the costs of
running their estates.
PHOTOGRAPH: AUTHOR

Kinderscout. Kinder is an ancient name for the highest place in Derbyshire that rises to 2,088 feet. The 'scout' ending is from a Viking word meaning a cliff or overhanging rock, probably the one known as Kinder Downfall, where the wind can be so fierce that the stream is blown back over the top. Once the scene of access battles, Kinderscout can now be roamed by all. On reaching the top, the walker finds a 15 square-mile plateau of peat bogs, intersected by channels known as groughs. When the National Trust acquired the Kinder Estate in 1982 it tackled one of the worst cases of upland erosion in the Peak District. Sheep were banned, derelict walls rebuilt, boundary fences constructed, effective fire-fighting methods introduced, firm surfaces provided for walkers on the Pennine Way, and light dressings of fertiliser and limestone dust applied to prompt indigenous seed to germinate. The improvement has been dramatic.

PHOTOGRAPH: AUTHOR

had to sell books, manuscripts and some of their art collection after the death of the eighth duke in 1908. In 1916 they sold Devonshire House in Piccadilly and in 1929 Chiswick House went too. In the 1920s large parts of the Haddon estate in north Derbyshire were sold, mostly in small parcels to the tenants as mortgagees. The Curzons too were hit by death duties in 1925, though the fortune brought by the American heiress who had married the marquess helped them to continue in the old manner for another half century. The Gresleys of Drakelow Hall, another of Derbyshire's Norman families, sold up in 1931 and their house was demolished seven years later, the same year that Doveridge Hall and West Hallam Hall were pulled down and the Rotherham-Cecils sold Dronfield Manor House to the local authority. Many another minor historic house, such as Cartledge Hall, began to crumble or was reduced to the status of a farmhouse or a group of cottages. Meanwhile, the gentry in the coalfield parishes, who had been made wealthy from their royalties and investments, moved away to more pleasant surroundings.

The hey-day of grouse-shooting continued into the 1920s, when enormous annual 'bags' were recorded; for instance, 6,004 birds were shot on the Duke of Rutland's Longshaw estate in 1921. But the cost of rearing grouse had become greater than the income from sales. In 1927 heavy death duties forced the Duke of Rutland to sell his shooting moors, after about a hundred years of use. Longshaw Lodge and its park went to the National Trust, the Yorkshire section was bought by Sheffield Corporation, and those parts of his Longshaw Estate that lay within Derbyshire were purchased by Chesterfield Rural District Council, who let the shooting rights to William Wilson, the owner of Stanage Moor, and who were even less tolerant of ramblers roaming the countryside than the duke had been.

In the years between the two world wars the chapel culture remained strong in both the towns and the countryside. Both Wesleyan Methodism and Primitive Methodism continued to attract large congregations. The Whitsuntide processions, Sunday School anniversaries and organised day-trips were still major events and in many places the churches and chapels were the focus of social activities as well as religious observance. During the 1930s, however, the old attachments weakened as the opportunities

The Mass Trespass in 1932 is widely regarded as a crucial event in the struggle to acquire the 'right to roam', but the campaign had actually begun much earlier and many ramblers thought that the event did more harm than good. It publicised the struggle, but did not lead to any immediate changes.

One of the earliest purpose-built cinemas in the country still in use, the Scala in the centre of Ilkeston can seat 400 people. It was built by James Parsons & Sons of Bulwell and was opened in 1913. The name (presumably from La Scala, the opera house in Milan) is typical of those taken from exotic locations abroad.

PHOTOGRAPH: CARNEGIE

Rolls-Royce Merlin engine. Work began in the 1930s on what is regarded as one of the finest and most successful piston engines ever built for aviation, and development continued during the Second World War, when it was used for Spitfires, Hurricanes, Lancasters and Mosquitoes. The engine was a vital component of the planes used in the Battle of Britain and its development transformed Rolls-Royce into a major aviation company.

PHOTOGRAPH BY CARNEGIE, WITH PERMISSION OF DERBY MUSEUMS AND ART GALLERY

for leisure pursuits increased. The steady rise in their standard of living of those who kept in work was reflected in more spacious houses and comfortable furniture, improved diet and better health, and enjoyable recreational activities either as participants or spectators at sports events, while even in small towns the cinema provided a new form of mass entertainment.

Since the Second World War

War memorials record the heavy casualties in the Second World War, though these were not quite on the same scale as those of 1914–18. This time, however, the civilian population sometimes had direct experience of the brutality of war through bombing. Derby suffered its first air raid on 19 August 1940 and its total casualties during the war were 74 people killed and some 350 wounded. Schools were evacuated to country houses, and factories were turned to the manufacture of munitions and aircraft components. The Rolls-Royce company converted their Derby works into a factory for building its 'Merlin' aero-engine, which was to play such a vital role in the Battle of Britain as the power unit for the Supermarine Spitfire and the Hawker Hurricane. Famously, the 'Dambuster' 617 squadron used the Ladybower, Howden and Derwent reservoirs to practise their assault on German dams in the Ruhr.

The population of Derbyshire has continued to rise at a slower rate than it had achieved in the nineteenth century. The county had attracted its share of Irish immigrants in Victoria's reign, though not as many as some other industrial regions further west and north. After the Second World War its population was made more diverse through immigration form central and eastern Europe. In the 1940s and 1950s Polish, Ukrainian and Hungarian refugees fled from the Soviet bloc and a new influx of Irish people arrived. Then from the late 1950s until the 1970s thousands of families from the new Commonwealth countries, especially India, Pakistan and the West Indies, came to find work, often on the night shift and on public transport or in the hospitals. They took over the old quarters of Victorian Derby, but were less evident in the county's other towns and hardly at all in the villages and hamlets of the countryside. In 2005 Derbyshire had an estimated population of 981,270, including 233,750 within the city of Derby.

A tableau of youthful innocence which is considered 'the secret of England's greatness', as the signs on the cart proclaim. Empire Days, coronations and the annual Whitsuntide celebrations provided frequent opportunities for dressing up and processing through the towns and villages of the county.

COAL

Derbyshire's coal mining and manufacturing industries had played an essential role in the Second World War and remained the dominant source of work long afterwards. Full employment seemed to be assured during the years of recovery from the war, but foreign competition soon threatened the old supremacy.

The nationalisation of the coal industry was a priority of the newly elected Labour government. On 1 January 1947 the National Coal Board took over

Ladybower reservoir. Between 1906 and 1916 the Howden and Derwent Dams had been constructed in the Upper Derwent valley to provide water for Derby, Leicester, Nottingham and Sheffield. The construction of the Ladybower Dam for the same purpose began in 1935 and work continued without interruption throughout the Second World War. The filling of the reservoir began in March 1943, it came into partial use in February 1944, and was formally inaugurated by King George VI and Queen Elizabeth on 25 September 1945. The new reservoir submerged the hamlets of Derwent and Ashopton, many of whose residents, together with water board employees, were re-housed in a new estate at Yorkshire Bridge. The fanciful name Lady Bower was recorded in 1584.

a workforce of 704,000 men who mined 184 million tons of coal a year in 958 pits in the British coalfields. In addition, open-cast mining had become a large-scale business. In 1955 over 30 pits were worked in north-east Derbyshire, with five in south Derbyshire and five others just across the Leicestershire border in the same coalfield. Markham Main became the largest colliery in Britain, employing thousands of men. The NCB operated in a seller's market until 1956–57 when the effects of cheap imported crude oil were first felt. Uneconomic pits were closed and in some mines machines replaced men until by 1976 the national workforce numbered only 247,100. The fortunes of the coal industry improved in the early 1970s, when the era of cheap oil came to an end. The bargaining power of the National Union of Mineworkers was strengthened and successful strikes restored the colliers to their premier position as industrial wage-earners.

Meanwhile, since 1945 the NUM had put forward its own parliamentary Labour candidates in the coalmining constituencies of east Derbyshire, where they were elected with huge majorities. In 1970 the Bolsover Labour Party rejected the national headquarters' favoured candidate in favour of Dennis Skinner, who has served as its MP ever since. For many years, the Derbyshire NUM headquarters in Chesterfield was the centre of political activity throughout the coalfield, but since the closure of all the county's mines that influence has declined. Six parliamentary seats are now held by Labour, Chesterfield has a Liberal Democrat MP and West Derbyshire a Conservative one.

The national miners' strike against pit closures in 1984–85 was the most tumultuous event in modern politics and one that divided the nation and indeed coal-mining communities. It received some strong support in the North-east Derbyshire coalfield, but little across the border in Nottinghamshire or in the South Derbyshire coalfield. The prolonged battle that lasted nearly a year ended in defeat for the miners and disastrous consequences for their communities. In the late 1980s and early 1990s Derbyshire's pits were closed one by one. When Markham Main ceased production in 1994 coal mining in Derbyshire came to an end. Since then, the landscape of the coalfield has reverted to its former character with the removal of pithead winding wheels and colliery muck stacks or it has been changed by regeneration schemes that have introduced 'light' or 'service' industries. The character of the coalfield has changed dramatically in the last two decades. We can now see that the so-called traditional pit villages existed only for a relatively short time in Derbyshire's long history, for they lasted only 100–150 years. The lasting legacy of the two coalfields is that they were responsible for a great shift of population so that a majority of Derbyshire's inhabitants now live in the eastern half of the county.

Another huge impact on the landscape came from the opencast mining for coal, which started during the Second World War. In many cases, the contractors did not replace all the topsoil that they had removed, nor the

Rolls-Royce Conway jet engine. The development of the world's first turbofan engine began at Rolls-Royce in the 1940s and was used to power Boeing 707s from 1954. Its success confirmed Rolls-Royce's leading position in the aviation industry.

PHOTOGRAPH BY CARNEGIE, WITH PERMISSION OF DERBY MUSEUMS AND ART GALLERY woods and hedgerows which they had destroyed and the land drains that they had damaged. The blighted, impoverished landscapes that were created by opencasting took decades to recover, but in recent years stringent planning conditions have ensured that opencasting is undertaken more responsibly.

IRON

By the late 1950s the companies that owned Derbyshire's ironworks were beginning to close down unprofitable parts of their business and to try to improve their competitive edge by amalgamation. The Clay Cross Co. closed down its blast furnaces in 1958 and the Butterley Co. closed its Codnor Park forge in 1965. The county's production of iron was now concentrated at Stanton (five furnaces), Staveley (four), Sheepbridge (two) and Renishaw (two). That same year, Staveley and Stanton were united into a single organisation, then in the following year the Sheepbridge works closed down. In 1969 production at the Riddings works came to an end and in 1974 both the Stanton and Staveley blast furnaces were shut down. Eventually, the remaining businesses of the Butterley Co., the Clay Cross Co. and James Oakes & Co. were each taken over by larger firms that had no connection with Derbyshire. Nowadays, neither pig-iron nor wrought iron is produced in Derbyshire, although iron pipes are still made. The Butterley Company was finally taken over in 1968 and only the brickmaking capacity was retained.

ENGINEERING

Engineering remains an important Derbyshire industry, although after the Second World War, Rolls-Royce's motor-manufacturing was transferred to Crewe and the expense of developing the Rolls-Royce RB 211 aero-engine led to the company's financial collapse and nationalisation in 1971. It became a private enterprise again in 1987 and merged with Northern Engineering Industries in 1989, since when it has continued to thrive as a world-class aero-engine and turbine manufacturer, commanding 25 per cent of the world market for civil aviation engines. The company's aerospace and industrial power divisions, which are based at Derby, are now Derby's largest single employer. Meanwhile, Derby remains the centre of British Rail's research activities.

Just beyond Derby and alongside the A38, the Japanese firm Toyota Motor Manufacturing (UK) Ltd has invested nearly £1.85 billion in a large car manufacturing plant on the site of the former aerodrome at Burnaston, where its two assembly plants employ some 4,900 employees to make 285,00 vehicles a year. Then in 2004 JCB Power Systems opened a multi-million pound state-of-the-art manufacturing plant and assembly line for diesel engines at Dove Valley Park on the A50 at Foston. Meanwhile, the Ferodo brake lining and friction pad works, now part of the T. & N. Group, continues as a major employer at Chapel-en-le-Frith.

Civil engineering skills have been in demand for the construction of motorways and upgraded trunk roads and in the creation of large reservoirs

In 1989 Toyota Motor Manufacturing (UK) Ltd began to develop this site at Burnaston, where the A38 crosses the A50 south-west of Derby. Their first cars were produced three years later. Toyota are now a major employer, with a commitment to environmental responsibility.

BY COURTESY OF TOYOTA UK

in many parts of the county, following the successful schemes in the valleys of the Upper Derwent, the Goyt and the Etherow; the largest of the newer reservoirs are those at Ogston and Carsington.

TEXTILES

Derbyshire's great days as a leading centre of Britain's textile industry are long since past, but various trades continue to play a significant role in the county's manufacturing economy. Brettle's of Belper became part of the Courtaulds group in 1964. In Derby, another hosiery firm, F. Longdon & Co., established about 1802, now specialises in knitted elastic fabric. Knitwear and hosiery are also still made by I. and R. Morley Ltd of Heanor (established 1874) and by John Smedley Ltd at Lea Mills (founded at Lea Mills by Thomas Smedley, the father John of Matlock Bank hydro fame, who installed new machinery). The market for lace fell sharply after the war, as fashions began to change, and many firms were made bankrupt. Nevertheless, those knitwear, hosiery and lace-making firms that have adapted to changing demand and have invested in new processes still flourish, albeit on a much reduced scale. The introduction of artificial fibres in the 1950s provided new opportunities and the British Celanese factory at Spondon (now part of Arcodis) employs over 800 people at its 360-acre site in the manufacture of textiles and rayon products.

QUARRYING

The quarrying of limestone in the White Peak has continued on a much bigger scale since the Second World War. In recent decades the demand for industrial limestone and high-quality lime has rocketed. When the Peak District National Park was created in 1951 it was given a strange shape, for the quarrying areas around Buxton, Matlock and Wirksworth were excluded. The incongruous sight of the tall chimney of Earle's Cement Works at Bradwell from many viewpoints within the National Park is explained by the decision to allow quarrying and the manufacture of cement to continue as a major employer in the Hope valley. The enormous Tunstead Quarry in Great Rocks Dale, which was opened in 1929, has a 1¼ mile working face. Its principal product is the industrial limestone which is valued for its chemical purity in industries where it is used as a basic oxide, a flux, a neutralising agent or a source of calcium, for instance in glassmaking and sugar refining and the reduction of sulphur emissions in coal-fired power stations. Many other processes use limestone that has been burned at high temperatures to make lime. Tunstead and the adjacent Old Moor Quarry produce about 5.5 million tons of limestone each year, the largest production of high-purity industrial limestone in Europe. Tunstead is also the biggest producer of lime in the UK and its cement plant uses almost

This huge limestone quarry, owned by Tarmac Ltd, is hidden from view along the 'White Peak Scenic Route', beyond the deserted medieval village of Ballidon. It is a major producer of limestone and concrete products.

Limestone works, Hindlow, near Buxton. The quarrying of carbon- iferous limestone in the White Peak is now at an unprec- edented level. Hindlow Quarry is owned by Lhoist UK Ltd, whose limestone crushing, screening and washing plant produces three sizes of limestone. They claim to make the purest lime in the United Kingdom.
PHOTOGRAPH: CARNEGIE

all the waste that is produced during the processing of the limestone. Some 400 people work at the site and a larger number are employed by contractors and local businesses.

Longcliffe's Brassington Moor quarry, which specialises in high purity limestone, was founded in 1927 by John Shields and is still family owned. The total output from Derbyshire's limestone quarries is now about 20 million tons a year, which represents about 15 per cent of national production. Since the Second World War Derbyshire has become the major fluorspar producer in the country, the mineral being used in the steel, chemicals and ceramics industries, while barytes is used in the manufacture of paint and paper. A modern company, Glebe Mines (Laporte Industries), has reworked old lead mines around Eyam for the fluorspar and barytes which had been thrown aside as worthless by the early miners but which are now more valuable than lead. Quarrying has replaced the mining of lead as the major employer in the Peak District but at the same time it has become a despoiler of the Derbyshire landscape and a generator of heavy lorry traffic on both wide and narrow roads. The Council for the Protection of Rural England are at the forefront of battles with quarrying companies who use old mineral permissions from before the creation of the Peak District National Park to extend their operations, in both the White Peak and on the gritstones, most notably on Stanton Moor. The proposed extension of the Backdale Quarry on Longstone Edge has provoked a Save Longstone Edge campaign and proposals to extend Dirtlow Rake quarry

Dirtlow Rake. The large-scale quarrying of limestone and the exploitation of old lead rakes for fluorspar and barytes has replaced lead mining as the major industry and despoiler of the landscape in the White Peak. The re-working and proposed expansion of Dirtlow Rake above Castleton and Bradwell is one of the contentious issues that have led to public enquiries and long drawn-out legal battles between developers and conservationists in the heart of the Peak District National Park.

above Castleton and Bradwell are being vigorously opposed by the Peak District National Park, the CPRE and other interested organisations.

Meanwhile, in south Derbyshire, the Trent and Derwent valleys have long been exploited on a large scale for gravel and sand. The monitoring of the work by archaeologists has led to a new understanding of the history and prehistory of this district and in the long-term the ecological benefits will be considerable. Demand from the building trade has also given a new stimulus to gypsum extraction in the Nottingham-Derby area, the most important area for gypsum in Britain and one that accounts for around 40 per cent of national production.

DERBY

Since 1945 industrial estates have been developed on a large scale around Derby and pre-war housing plans have come to fruition with the building of the Mackworth and Chaddesden estates. An outer ring road was constructed in the inter-war years and an inner one in 1967, then in the 1970s the A52 from Nottingham was re-aligned as a dual carriageway close to the centre of the town. Derby is now encircled by very busy through roads linked to the region's motorways.

Since the 1950s extensive clearance schemes have got rid not just of poor-quality housing but most of Derby's architectural heritage. The fine Georgian town seen in old paintings and prints has mostly gone; only Friar Gate and

the Wardwick retain much of their old quality. Buildings in Bridge Gate and most of Full Street were demolished to make way for the inner ring road; the Assembly Rooms were gutted by fire and its façade removed to Crich; and other parts of the historic core of the borough were replaced by undistinguished office blocks, stores, and shopping precincts. In 1966 the boundary was pushed forward into the suburbs and the countryside to form the County Borough (from 1977 the City) of Derby, covering 19,100 acres, then in 1998 Derby became a unitary authority, separate from the rest of Derbyshire, except for ceremonial purposes. The new facilities for the enlarged town included a civic centre, a large shopping complex and a theatre, none of them impressive buildings.

Derby's industrial structure is less diversified than Nottingham's but in recent years it has developed service industries that make it less reliant on engineering.

Since its replacement by Matlock as the administrative centre of the county, its influence has been restricted to those parts of south Derbyshire that are within commuting distance. The northern half of Derbyshire has little in common with the former county town and looks more towards Sheffield or Manchester; it does not regard itself as being part of the East Midlands. In the south, Derby is overshadowed by its ancient rival, Nottingham. The area that is now within the city's boundaries has become part of an urban sprawl that stretches across the Erewash valley into Nottinghamshire, a district that is constantly busy with traffic. All way down from the Yorkshire border, east of a line from Chesterfield to Derby, an urban belt covers much of what was once the concealed coalfield of Derbyshire and Nottinghamshire. This part of the county is typical of many other modern English urban regions where the population has left the town

Derby County FC, 1946. Derby won the FA Cup in the first final after the Second World War, beating Charlton Athletic 4–1 in extra time. Raich Carter and Peter Doherty, the club's famous international inside forwards, sit either side of centre forward Jack Stamps in the commemorative photograph.

centres for the suburbs and town boundaries have spread outwards in the last few decades to accommodate middle-class suburbs and council estates. In north Derbyshire, Sheffield exerted a similar influence to Derby in the south. Middle-class suburbs or large council estates covered the former countryside of Dore, Totley, Meersbrook, Norton, Mosborough, Hackenthorpe and Beighton, all of which were taken into Sheffield, and the private housing estate that was built in the 1970s in Dronfield's Gosforth valley was at that time the largest in Europe. Elsewhere in Derbyshire, some smaller towns, particularly the ancient market centres, have experienced only modest growth. In large part, this is because of planning restrictions that have sought to preserve the character of places in and around the Peak District National Park.

The reorganisation of local government in 1974 made minor alterations to Derbyshire's boundaries and created a two-tier system, with a county council based in Matlock and eight district councils. Thirteen towns have between 10,000 and 100,000 inhabitants, but three-quarters of the county's population live within a quarter of its area. Most of rural Derbyshire remains sparsely populated.

THE COUNTRYSIDE

The horse-and-cart era came to an end in the 1950s except on some small family farms in the uplands, where it survived until the 1960s. Rural parishes remained quiet, remote places, difficult to reach along unmetalled lanes and pitch dark at night time. Meals were still cooked over the fire in the main living room, hot water had to be boiled in pans, on Mondays clothes and sheets were washed in the corner 'copper' or 'set-pot', and on Fridays the tin bath was placed in front of the fire for the children. Many farmhouses and cottages were without gas, electricity or water closets. Even those country people who were not farmers did not travel far to work, though buses sometimes enabled them to go a

The tremendous spread of bracken, seen here at Stanage, is a vexatious problem on the moorland edges in the Peak District. Bracken was once cut as litter for horses and cattle, for fuel and thatch, and as a source of potash for the making of soap, glass or fertilisers, but it no longer has a use. Over grazing by sheep, whose numbers have trebled since the Second World War, has meant that bracken has encroached upon and eventually suppressed the heather. European Community regulations prohibit the aerial spraying of herbicides such as Asulam, where moors are close to drinking water (as they often are), so the control of bracken is an expensive, difficult and long-term task.

PHOTOGRAPH: AUTHOR

few miles. Near relations and distant cousins were mostly to be found within walking distance, for extended families still lived in the same neighbourhoods or 'countries' as their ancestors.

After the Second World War, Derbyshire farmers continued to send their milk by rail to London. The installation of piped water from the late 1960s lessened the reliance on the old dew ponds and enabled upland farms in the White Peak to increase their herds of dairy cows. The old methods of making hay in summer time were gradually abandoned in favour of silage; tractors and other machines reduced the need for hired labour, oil rapeseed was planted in the lowlands, and Derbyshire farms became increasingly owner-occupied and farmed as family units as many of the great estates were sold off in order to pay death duties. Falling profits and the catastrophe of the outbreak of foot-and-mouth disease made the need to diversify increasingly apparent. Tea rooms and bed-and-breakfast accommodation sprang up in the countryside and nowadays it is even possible to see alpaca and buffalo grazing in the Peak District. Meanwhile, the highly intensive and specialised market gardens at Melbourne, which depend largely on Derby for sales, and the long-established nurseries at Borrowash remain profitable.

Grouse shooting continues in the Peak District, but not at its old intensity. The heather moors were reduced by 36 per cent between 1913 and 1980 and the numbers of grouse fell substantially. Fortunately for those who love these landscapes, the National Trust and the Peak Park Planning Board now own much of Derbyshire's northern moorlands and manage them on traditional lines. A regular burning cycle of about 12 years promotes young heather, keeps down coarse grass and bracken, and prevents the spread of silver birch. The right to roam has given everyone the chance to appreciate this glorious scenery in summer time.

Hopton Hall. The twentieth century saw the demolition or conversion to other uses of many of Derbyshire's country houses and the break up of their estates. The Gell family held an estate at Hopton from at least 1327. They rose in status in the seventeenth century, when the present house was begun. The family connection with the house and estate ended in 1989. The grounds now attract large numbers of visitors in February to see the display of snowdrops.

PHOTOGRAPH: AUTHOR

COUNTRY HOUSES

Gladwyn Turbutt has calculated that of the 47 Derbyshire landowning families listed in 1876–83 by John Bateman as owning more than 2,000 acres, the majority of whom also owned country seats, only 17 of their descendants survive in present-day Derbyshire, all with considerably reduced acreages. The 13 who still occupy one of their original family seats are: Bagshawe (Wormhill), Chandos-Pole (Radburne), Kerr (formerly Cowper; Melbourne), Devonshire (Chatsworth), Palmer (formerly Drury-Lowe, Locko), Fitzherbert (Tissington), Stanton (formerly Harrison, Snelston), Rutland (Haddon), Shuttleworth (Hathersage), Sitwell (Renishaw), Thornhill (Stanton-in-Peak), Neilson (formerly Wilmot-Horton, Catton), and Scarsdale (Kedleston, which is mostly owned by the National Trust). Long-established families who were not in Bateman's list but who have continued to reside in their family seats include the Blackwalls of Blackwall, Coke-Steels of Trusley, Meynells of Meynell Langley, and Wrights of Eyam. He has also shown that only 15 of the 104 'Principal Seats in Derbyshire' that were listed in *Kelly's Directory* in 1936 are still owned by the same families. The decline of the power and influence of many of the county's old landowning families has been remarkable, though the Duke and Duchess of Devonshire still retain their prime position.

Sales of gentry estates and the demolition of country houses continued after the Second World War. The Ogston estate properties were sold in 1952 and Etwall Hall was demolished three years later. When Elvaston Castle and its 388 acres of grounds was sold to Derby Borough Council and the Derbyshire County Council in 1966 the contents of the house were dispersed and the estate was opened as a public park. Four of Derbyshire's greatest country houses – Calke, Hardwick, Kedleston and Sudbury – are now owned by the National Trust, while English Heritage have taken over Bolsover and Peveril castles and are repairing Wingfield Manor.

The determined preservation of Derbyshire's finest houses began in the 1920s, when the future ninth Duke of Rutland set about restoring Haddon

The Drawing Room, Calke Abbey. Sir Henry Harpur refitted this room in 1793–94 and changes were made between 1833 and 1856. This is the best room in the house, now that The National Trust has painstakingly restored the faded and tattered chintz covers and the silk curtains.

CALKE ABBEY ©NTPL/ANDREAS VON EINSIEDEL

Hall to its medieval splendour. In 1819 Edward Rhodes had written in his *Peak Scenery*: 'A gloomy and solemn silence pervades its neglected apartments, and the bat and the owl are alone the inmates of its remaining splendour.' The Dukes lived at Belvoir Castle, so Haddon Hall had remained unimproved through all the changing fashions of the eighteenth and nineteenth centuries and had degenerated into a romantic ruin. A growing interest in England's medieval heritage saved it from further decay. The first and major task was the construction of a new oak roof to span the hall; otherwise, the intention was to preserve as much as possible. But although the structure of the garden was intact, it had long been neglected. A huge effort had to be made to clear it before it could be replanted and redesigned to its present appearance.

A very different fate awaited Calke Abbey, which had long been secluded from public view in a hollow within an ancient deer park that had been landscaped in the 1760s and 1770s. The Harpur family, who had been resident here since 1622, had changed their surname to Crewe in 1808, then later to Harpur Crewe. Several generations of the family were collectors who never threw anything away, so the rooms are filled with cases of antiquities and silver, butterflies and stuffed birds, children's toys and minerals. Little had changed since late Victorian times. When Charles Harpur Crewe died in 1981, his younger brother, Henry, was faced with death duties amounting to £8 million. Four years later, the house was taken over by the National Trust, who made the decision to preserve the arrangement of the rooms as they were in the final days of the family's residence; only two rooms were re-decorated. An enormous amount of building work was needed to repair the structure, before the house could be opened to the public in 1989.

Heavy death duties forced other aristocratic families to transfer their houses to the National Trust in order to retain part of their estates. In 1967 Lord Vernon passed Sudbury Hall with its gardens and parkland to the Trust and built a new house nearby. The hall was opened to the public and a Museum of Childhood was created in some of the outbuildings. Then in 1987 Viscount Scarsdale transferred Kedleston Hall and its park to the Trust, with the arrangement that he and his family continued to live in one of the pavilions. The house remains much as it was when completed in the eighteenth century, though it was enriched by the treasures that George Nathaniel Curzon collected during his travels in Asia in between 1887 and 1894 and while he was Viceroy of India from 1899 to 1905. The Indian Museum was completed in 1927, two years after his death. Lord Curzon had served as Foreign Secretary in the Conservative government and might well have become Prime Minister had he not been in the House of Lords. He was created an earl in 1911 and a marquess ten years later. His marriage to the daughter of a Chicago millionaire enhanced the family's fortune at a difficult time for landed families and he became the most distinguished of the long line of Curzons, stretching back to Norman times. The levying of death duties in 1925 and 1977 had a devastating effect on the Curzon estate, but an unprecedented grant of £13.5 million by the National Heritage Memorial Fund, an investment of £1 million by the National Trust, and the raising of £2 million through a public appeal saved the house and its setting.

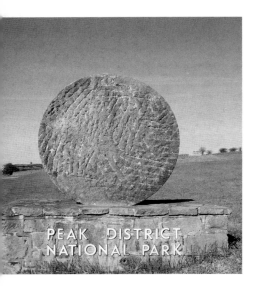

The Peak District National Park. When Britain's first National Park was opened in the Peak District in 1951, its boundaries were marked by distinctive signs made from abandoned millstones, one of the Peak District's traditional industries. This sign greets visitors from Sheffield and north Derbyshire at Owler Bar.

PHOTOGRAPH: AUTHOR

Chatsworth House has been open to large numbers of visitors ever since it was built; thousands of people came on railway trips to see it in Victorian times. It was not until 1908 that a small admission charge was made, with profits going to local hospitals. But when the Second World War broke out in 1939 the family left and a girls' school took over until 1946. Four years later, the estate was hit by huge death duties when the tenth duke died. The total acreage of the Cavendish holdings had to be reduced from 120,000 acres to some 72,000 acres as properties in Scotland, Eastbourne and the High Peak were sold. Chatsworth lost eight of its most valuable works of art and Hardwick Hall went to the National Trust. The final payment of duty and interest was made in 1974. Chatsworth House was maintained but was no longer the family home until the eleventh duke and duchess made the decision to return. They moved in from Edensor Lodge in 1959 and the duchess personally supervised the restoration of the house. The turn-around has been remarkably successful. Chatsworth has become a hugely popular attraction and can make reasonable claim to being the best-loved country house in Britain. In 1981 a Chatsworth House Trust was formed to avert the threat of future death duties.

Regeneration

Like all parts of Britain, Derbyshire has benefited from the establishment of the Welfare State and the great rise in the standard of living that has occurred since the late 1950s. Regional identities have lessened in a new era of rapid communications, cheap travel, popular culture, social mobility, the mass-production on a global scale of cheap, high-quality goods, increased leisure and changing attitudes toward morality and religion. In all these aspects, Derbyshire has conformed to national trends. The death of the coal industry had reduced the

David Mellor's Cutlery Works, Hathersage. David Mellor, renowned metalworker and designer, moved from Sheffield to Hathersage in 1990 when he bought the old gas works and commissioned the Michael Hopkins Partnership to design a circular cutlery factory on the foundations of the gas holder and to convert the ancillary buildings into a home and offices. In 2006 a visitor centre, including a design museum, was opened alongside the tea room and shop.

Marsden   Meltham
Butterley Res.
Holmfirth
Barnsley
Greenfield
Saddleworth Moor
Holme
Penistone
Dunford Bridge
Crowden
Stocksbridge
Manchester
Bleaklow
Glossop
Snake Pass   *Howden Res.*
Derwent Res.
R. Loxley
Kinder Reservoir   ▲ *Kinder Scout*
Hayfield   Edale   Ladybower Res
Sheffield
Hope
Bamford   *Redmires Res.*
Castleton   Hathersage
Chapel-en-le-Frith   Bradwell   R. Derwent
Peak Forest   Great Hucklow   Grindleford
Kettleshulme   Dove Holes   Foolow   Eyam
Pott Shrigley   Combs   Stoney Middleton   Curbar
Ernwood Res.   Tideswell   Litton   Calver   Baslow
Rainow   R. Wye   Chesterfield
Lamaload Res.   Buxton   Ashford in the Water
Macclesfield   Taddington   Bakewell
Chelmorton   Sheldon   Chatsworth House
Wildboarclough   Flagg   Monyash   Haddon Hall
Bosley Res.   Flash   Hollinsclough
Wincle   R. Dane   Youlgreave   Darley Dale
R. Churnet   Longnor   R. Dove   Middleton   Birchover
Rudward Res.   Hartington   Elton   Winster   Matlock
Biggin   Bonsall   Matlock Bath
Tittesworth Res.   Warslow   Cromford
Leek   Alstonefield   Middleton
Wetton   Parwich   Wirksworth
Grindon   Crich
Tissington
Ilam   Thorpe
Fenny Bentley   *Carsington Res.*   Ripley
Stoke on Trent   Belper
Ashbourne

– – – *Pennine Way*
——— *Boundary of National Park*

separate identity of the eastern parts of the county and its southern tip. Today, Derbyshire's chief claim to fame amongst outsiders is the attractive scenery of the Peak District National Park, which is visited each year by millions of people.

The protection of this scenery has been a constant battle that continues to this day. Back in the 1930s the Council for the Preservation (now Protection) of Rural England was formed, with a headquarters in Sheffield, to stop the encroachment of suburbs and uncontrolled building in the countryside and to fight the extension of quarrying. Reliable public transport and the growing ownership of motor cars had hastened the movement away from towns, reversing the trends of the previous century, but it had also enabled urban dwellers to ramble in the countryside and to appreciate that its beauty could be destroyed if rigorous planning regulations were not enforced. Environmental groups such as the CPRE, which advocated the creation of national parks and of green belts around towns, were joined by local and national rambling associations that argued for the right to roam on what were still private moorlands, staffed by gamekeepers who were instructed to keep the public out. The most significant step towards the achievement of these objectives was the creation of the Peak District National Park – the first such park in England – in 1951. The Peak Park Planning Board has played a vital role in ensuring that new buildings or rebuildings conform to the style and materials of the older houses in the neighbourhood and in restricting the spread of industry and housing. One of its chief concerns in recent years has been to allow modest schemes for cheaper houses for young local families who would otherwise be unable to match the escalating prices paid by those wealthy enough to be able to live in the countryside. In the last few decades, the conversion of old buildings, under strict planning requirements, has been an astonishing and welcome

Derby Silk Mill Museum. Many of Derbyshire's former industrial sites are now popular museums. The Silk Mill on the banks of the river Derwent at Derby has been converted into the Derby Industrial Museum. Little of the original early eighteenth-century silk mill remains, for it was destroyed by fire in 1910. The tower survives in altered form.

development for those who can remember the time when farmhouses had no gas or electricity, when cooking was done over the fire, and barns and other outbuildings were becoming derelict. The CPRE has rewarded the best of these adaptations by its annual awards for good practice. The most outstanding achievement has been David Mellor's conversion of an abandoned gas holder and other buildings at Hathersage into a cutlery works and visitor centre at the Round House.

Another landmark was the Town and Country Planning Act of 1947, which required local authorities to prepare development plans for their districts. Designated areas were earmarked as zones for light industries or for new housing estates and plans were made for relieving traffic congestion by ring roads or other schemes. Councils were given powers of compulsory land purchase and control over private development and the central government provided funds to demolish slums, preserve buildings of historic and architectural interest, designate green belts, build new bus stations and multi-storey car parks, and convert streets into pedestrian precincts. The downside of all this was that separate local identities were reduced by a new environment of glass and concrete buildings and dreary multi-storey car parks, and the replacement of old family-run shops and businesses by national or multinational department stores and supermarkets, so that every town centre began to look the same. Chesterfield only just managed to save its open-air market, which had given the town its distinctive appearance since Norman times, after a vigorous campaign against redevelopment by local protesters. The most astonishing and welcome change of all was the transformation of grimy Victorian towns by the vigorous application of the 1956 Clean Air Act and the later use of government grants to clean public buildings.

Derbyshire has no New Towns and few high-rise buildings. Sir Nikolaus Pevsner found hardly anything of national note when he surveyed the county's buildings in 1953, nor did his successors. But while they may lack architectural

Cauldwell's Mill, Rowsley. A corn mill and a fulling mill occupied this site alongside the river Wye during the reign of Queen Elizabeth I. In 1874 John Cauldwell took a lease from the Duke of Rutland and built a large mill powered by two water wheels, for grinding flour and animal feed. In the late 1880s he replaced his millstones with roller mills and then installed a water turbine in place of the water wheels. The present turbine was installed in 1914. The mill closed in 1978, but was soon reopened and operated by the Cauldwell's Mill Trust as the only complete Victorian roller mill powered by a water turbine in the country. The opening of a craft centre and coffee shop has helped to make the mill a popular place to visit.

PHOTOGRAPH: CARNEGIE

Rutland Mills, Ilkeston, with the parish church in the background. Built about 1881 for C. and F. Sudbury as a hosiery and glove works, it was known later as Rutland Garments. Since its recent renovation and conversion into offices and other purposes for a variety of organisations, the building has been re-named Rutland Mills.

distinction, the county's public buildings including hospitals, schools and the new University of Derby serve their purposes well and some of the new industrial buildings stand out amongst the numerous warehouses and giant sheds that have sprung up alongside the modern road system in every English county. The Derbyshire section of the M1, which was opened in 1969, was the first of the county's motorways and new, upgraded trunk roads which provided fast communications with other parts of Britain. Meanwhile, the opening of the East Midlands Airport in 1965 as a joint venture between Derbyshire, Nottinghamshire and Leicestershire helped to make foreign travel quicker and cheaper for everyone.

The closure of the remaining pits was a devastating blow to the economy of the Derbyshire coalfield. Regions which were dependent on mining and heavy manufacturing industries have fallen behind the rest of the country in relative terms even though their inhabitants have shared in the unprecedented rise in national standards of living since the 1950s. Official surveys of consumer trends place Derbyshire well below the national average in purchasing power. An environment of huge colliery muck stacks, broken down buildings, and an all pervading sense of decay was unattractive to investors. New light industries did not need to be tied to sources of power and raw materials; proximity to markets and rapid communications were their main concerns when choosing a new site. Generous financial inducements from the national government and the European Community were needed to regenerate the old coalfield districts and huge amounts of cash had to be provided for clearing derelict landscapes and providing attractive environments. The process began with the construction of industrial estates on former colliery sites, including those at Alfreton, Clay Cross, Codnor, Ilkeston, Dronfield, Pinxton and Tibshelf. Thorntons, a leading manufacturer and retailer of chocolate and other confectionery products, took the opportunity to move from Sheffield to Somercotes. The proposed Markham

Vale Development is currently one of the largest regeneration schemes in England that hopes to create thousands of jobs. The scheme includes a road system linking with the M1 at a new Junction 29A, rail freighthead facilities, the greening of former colliery tips, and a Technology Centre with workspace units for small companies.

The landscape of the former coalfield has been transformed by the demolition of pit-head buildings and winding engines, by the levelling or reshaping of the muck stacks that dominated the skyline, and by the greening of abandoned opencast sites. Country parks and designed walks through former colliery districts or along the towpaths of the canals have made the environment much more attractive. Perhaps the most dramatic and welcome change of all has been the replacement of the dreary terraced rows of the old pit village of Arkwright Town by a much more pleasant and imaginative estate across the road.

On the north-western border of Derbyshire the closure of textile mills left a huge problem of what to do with the massive buildings that had dominated the landscape and economy since the early Victorian era. The Glossop mills closed in the 1950s and 60s and the paper mills that Edward Patrington had founded there in 1873 closed in 1963. Glossop Hall, the home of the Duke of Norfolk's agent, was demolished in 1956 and its grounds were purchased by the local council and turned into Manor Park. The old, two-up, two-down back-to-back houses with an outside privy and a tin bath hanging in the yard at Gamesley were demolished and replaced by an overspill estate in 1968. Changes to the environment and the opening up of former industrial areas to the public for recreational uses have been particularly successful in and around New Mills. The public were allowed into the Torrs area in 1974, the Torrs Riverside Park was created in the late 1990s, the Torrs Millennium Walk provided spectacular access and views in 2000, and the Goytside Meadow Local Nature Reserve, managed as a traditional pasture without the use of chemical fertilisers, was opened in 2004. The Sett Valley Trail follows a former railway line for 2½ miles and more energetic walkers can ramble along the Goyt Way, a ten-mile, easy access walk from Whaley Bridge to the Etherow Country Park. Other local attractions include the canal basins at Bugsworth and Whaley Bridge.

The railways across the White Peak that were closed in the 1950s and 60s have been converted by the Peak District National Park into long-distance walking, cycling and horse-riding trails. The line of the Cromford & High Peak Railway has become the High Peak Trail and the connecting link from Ashbourne to Parsley Hay is now the Tissington Trail. Edale is the starting point of the 268-mile Pennine Way along 'the backbone of England' to Scotland, whose first section was opened in 1965. Another notable long-distance walk is the Limestone Way from Castleton to Rocester, an initiative of the Derbyshire Dales District Council. Local branches of the Ramblers' Association have been active in persuading councils to signpost rights of way and in designating new routes and in 2000 the Countryside and Rights of Way Act established the right to roam and finally opened up thousands of acres of rough moorland. Meanwhile, railway enthusiasts have re-opened short stretches of lines between Matlock and Darley Dale and in the Golden Valley near Ripley, volunteers have restored stretches of canals, and in 1959 Crich quarry was acquired for what has since become the popular attraction of the National Tramway Museum.

In 2001 the area designated as the 'Derwent Valley Mills and their Communities' received the highest recognition of its contribution to world history by its addition to the list of UNESCO World Heritage Sites. Interest in the county's heritage has risen to unprecedented levels with the creation of the Derbyshire Record Office, local history libraries at Matlock and Chesterfield, museums such as that at Bakewell Old House, heritage centres, and local and family history societies. The Derbyshire countryside is protected as never before. The county has numerous Environmentally Sensitive Areas, Sites of Special Scientific Interest, and Areas of Outstanding Natural Beauty. The Forestry Commission are reducing their production of conifers in favour of more diverse deciduous woodland and they have become more receptive to public access; the Upper Derwent valley, in particular, has become very popular with visitors. The new National Forest, extending over 200 square miles in south Derbyshire, Staffordshire and Leicestershire, has a massive programme of woodland creation for the benefit of local communities and wildlife. The Woodland Trust now owns several woods in Derbyshire, the Derbyshire Wildlife Trust manages 40 nature reserves throughout the county, and a privately owned wildlife and Conservation Park, near Chapel-en-le-Frith has been opened as the Chestnut Centre. Throughout the county, but particularly in the Peak District, both public and private bodies, such as The National Stone Centre near Wirksworth or the Peak District Mines Historical Society at Matlock Bath, offer interpretations of the county's diverse history and industrial archaeology. Popular interest in Derbyshire's past is at a higher level then ever before.

Bibliography

S. Ainsworth, 'Prehistoric Settlement Remains on the Derbyshire Gritstone Moors', *Derbyshire Archaeological Journal*, cxxi (2001), pp. 19–69

S. Ainsworth and J. Barnatt, 'A Scarp-Edge Enclosure at Gardom's Edge, Derbyshire', *Derbyshire Archaeological Journal*, cxviii (1998), pp. 5–23

C. B. Andrews (ed.), *The Torrington Diaries*, 2 vols (London: Eyre & Spottiswoode, 1935–38)

P. A. Ardron, 'Peat Cutting in Upland Britain with Special Reference to the Peak District: Its Impact on Landscape, Archaeology and Ecology', unpublished Ph.D. thesis, University of Sheffield, 1999

J. Austin and M. Ford, *Dronfield and Wilson Cammell, 1873–1883* (Sheffield: Scarsdale Publications, 1983)

S. Bagshaw, *History, Gazetteer and Directory of Derbyshire* (Sheffield: 1846)

C. Ball, D. Crossley and S. Jones (eds), *Houses in the Derbyshire Landscape: The Moss Valley* (Sheffield University, Division of Adult Continuing Education, 1996)

J. Barnatt, 'Neolithic and Bronze Age Radiocarbon Dates from the Peak District: a review', *Derbyshire Archaeological Journal*, cxv (1995), pp. 5–19

J. Barnatt, 'Taming the Land: Peak District Farming and Ritual in the Bronze Age', *Derbyshire Archaeological Journal*, cxix (1999), pp. 19–78

J. Barnatt, 'To Each Their Own: Later Prehistoric Farming Communities and their Monuments in the Peak', *Derbyshire Archaeological Journal*, cxx (2000), pp. 1–86

J. Barnatt and A. Dickson, 'Survey and Interpretation of a Limekiln Complex at Peak Forest, Derbyshire; and a Review of Early Limeburning in the North-west Peak', *Derbyshire Archaeological Journal*, cxxiv (2004), pp. 141–215

J. Barnatt and K. Smith, *The Peak District: Landscapes Through Time*, 2nd edn (Bollington: Windgather, 2004)

J. Barnatt and T. Williamson, *Chatsworth: A Landscape History* (Bollington: Windgather, 2005)

K.M. Battye, *Unstone: The History of a Village* (privately published, 1981)

J. V. Beckett, *The East Midlands From AD 1000* (Harlow: Longman, 1988)

J. V. Beckett and J.E. Heath (eds), *Derbyshire Tithe Files, 1836–50*, Derbyshire Record Society, xxii (1995)

J. V. Beckett and J. P. Polak (eds), 'The Scarsdale Surveys of 1652–62', *A Seventeenth-Century Scarsdale Miscellany*, Derbyshire Record Society, xx (1993), pp. 3–72

D. Bell, *Memories of the Derbyshire Coalfield* (Newbury: Countryside Books, 2006)

G. Beresford, *The Medieval Clay-Land Village: Excavations at Goltho and Barton Blount*, Society for Medieval Archaeology monograph series, 6 (1975)

J. M. Bestall and D. Fowkes (eds), *Chesterfield Wills and Inventories, 1521–1603*, Derbyshire Record Society, i (1977)

J. M. Bestall and D. V. Fowkes, *History of Chesterfield*, Chesterfield Borough Council, 2 (1984) and 3 (1978)

J. M. Bestall and D. Fowkes (eds), *Chesterfield Wills and Inventories, 1604–1650*, Derbyshire Record Society, xxviii (2001)

B. Bevan, *The Upper Derwent: 10,000 Years in a Peak District Valley* (Stroud: Tempus, 2004)

M. Biddle and B. Kolbje-Biddle, 'Repton and the Vikings', *Antiquity*, 66 (1992), pp. 36–51

A.H. Birch, *Small Town Politics* (Oxford University Press, 1959)

I. S. W. Blanchard, 'Economic Change in Derbyshire in the Late Middle Ages, 1272–1540', unpublished London University Ph.D. thesis, 1967

I. S. W. Blanchard, *The Duchy of Lancaster's Estates in Derbyshire, 1485–1540*, Derbyshire Archaeological Society Record Series, 3 (1971)

W. Bray, *Sketch of a Tour into Derbyshire and Yorkshire*, 2nd edn (London: White, 1783)

T. Brighton, *Royalists and Roundheads in Derbyshire* (Bakewell and District Historical Society, 1981)

T. Brighton, *The Discovery of the Peak District* (Chichester: Phillimore, 2004)

T. Brighton, *Bakewell: The Ancient Capital of the Peak* (Tiverton: Halsgrove, 2005)

T. Brighton, 'Haddon Hall Gardens: Facts and Fancies', J*ournal of Garden History*, 6, no. 3 (1986), pp. 232–64

T. Brown, *General View of the Agriculture of the Count of Derby* (London: Board of Agriculture, 1794)

D. Brumhead and R. Weston, 'Seventeenth-Century Enclosures of the Commons and Wastes of Bowden Middlecale in the Royal Forest of Peak', *Derbyshire Archaeological Journal*, 121 (2001), pp. 244–86

T. Bulmer & Co., *History, Topography, and Directory of Derbyshire* (London: 1895)

T. A. Burdekin (ed.), *A Victorian Farmer's Diary: William Hodkin's Diary, 1864–66* (Derbyshire County Council, 2003)

K. Cameron, *The Place-Names of Derbyshire*, 3 vols (Cambridge University Press, 1959)

A. M. Chadwick and H. Evans, 'Reading Roystone's Rocks: Landscape Survey and Lithic Analysis', *Derbyshire Archaeological Journal*, cxx (2000), pp. 101–22

S. D. Chapman, *Stanton and Staveley: A Business History* (Cambridge: Woodhead-Faulkner, 1981)

S. D. Chapman, *The Early Factory Masters*, 2nd edn (Newton Abbot: David & Charles, 1992)

M. Chatfield, *Churches the Victorians Forgot* (Ashbourne: Moorland, 1979)

R. Clark, *The Derbyshire Papist Returns of 1705–6*, Derbyshire Record Society, occasional paper, 5 (1983)

J. C. Clifford and F. Clifford (eds), *Eyam Parish Register, 1630–1700*, Derbyshire Record Society, xxi (1993)

B. E. Coates, 'The Origin and Distribution of Markets and Fairs in Medieval Derbyshire', *Derbyshire Archaeological Journal*, lxxxv (1965), pp. 92–111

R. W. P. Cockerton, 'The Wirksworth Slab', *Derbyshire Archaeological Journal*, xxcii (1962), pp. 1–20

J. Collis, *Wigber Low, Derbyshire: a Bronze Age and Anglian Burial Site in the White Peak* (Sheffield University: Department of Prehistory and Archaeology, 1983)

J. C. Cox, *Notes on the Churches of Derbyshire*, 3 vols (London: Bemrose & Sons, 1875–79)

J. C. Cox, *Three Centuries of Derbyshire Annals* (London: Bemrose & Sons, 1890)

J. C. Cox (ed.), *Memorials of Old Derbyshire* (London: Bemrose & Sons, 1907)

M. Craven, *A Derbyshire Armory*, Derbyshire Record Society, xvii (1991)

M. Craven and M. Stanley, *The Derbyshire Country House* (Ashbourne: Landmark, 2004)

D. Crook, 'The Forest between the Erewash and the Derwent, 1154 to 1225', *Derbyshire Archaeological Journal*, 103 (1990), pp. 98–106

D. Crook, 'The Development of Private Hunting Rights in Derbyshire, 1189–1258', *Derbyshire Archaeological Journal*, cxxi (2001), pp. 232–43

D. Crossley and D. Kiernan, 'The Lead Smelting Mills of Derbyshire', *Derbyshire Archaeological Journal*, cxii (1992), pp. 6–47

R. R. Darlington (ed.), *The Cartulary of Darley Abbey*, 2 vols, Derbyshire Archaeological Society Record Series (1945)

D. Defoe, *A Tour through the Whole Island of Great Britain* (London: Everyman edn, 1962)

The Derwent valley Mills and Their Communities (The Derwent valley Mills Partnership, 2001)

V. S. Doe (ed.), *The Diary of James Clegg of Chapel en le Frith, 1708–55*, parts 1–3, Derbyshire Record Society, ii (1978), iii (1979) and v (1981)

Duchess of Devonshire, *The House: a Portrait of Chatsworth* (London: Macmillan, 1982)

D. N. Durant, *Bess of Hardwick: Portrait of an Elizabethan Dynast* (Cromwell: The Cromwell Press, 1998)

D. N. Durant and P. Riden (eds), *The Building of Hardwick Hall*, 2 parts, Derbyshire Record Society, iv (1980) and ix (1984)

M. Edmonds and T. Seaborne, *Prehistory in the Peak* (Stroud: Tempus, 2001)

D. G. Edwards (ed.), *Derbyshire Hearth Tax Assessments, 1662–70*, Derbyshire Record Society, vii (1982)

D. G. Edwards (ed.), *Derbyshire Wills Proved in the Prerogative Court of Canterbury, 1393–1574*, Derbyshire Record Society, xxvi (1998)

T. Elkington (ed.), *The Nature of Derbyshire* (Buckingham: Barracuda Books, 1986)

J. Farey, *General View of the Agriculture and Minerals of Derbyshire*, 3 vols (London: Board of Agriculture, 1811–17)

G. Fellows Jensen, *Scandinavian Settlement Names in the East MIdlands* (Copenhagen: Institut for Navneforskning, 1978)

R. S. Fitton and A. P. Wadsworth, *The Strutts and the Arkwrights, 1758–1830: A Study of the Early Factory System* (Manchester University Press, 1959)

T. D. Ford and J. H. Rieuwerts (eds), *Lead Mining in the Peak District*, 4th edn (Ashbourne: Landmark, 2000)

D. V. Fowkes and G. R. Porter (eds), *William Senior's Survey of the Estates of the First and Second Earls of Devonshire, c.1600–28*, Derbyshire Record Society, xiii (1988)

E. Garner, *The Seven Canals of Derbyshire* (Ashbourne: Landmark, 2003)

H. J. H. Garratt, *Derbyshire Feet of Fines, 1323–1546*, Derbyshire Record Society, xi (1985)

D. Garton, 'Buxton', *Current Archaeology*, 103 (1987), pp. 250–3

M. Gelling and A. Cole, *The Landscape of Place-Names* (Stamford: Shaun Tyas, 2000)

R. Gem, 'Melbourne, Church of St Michael and St Mary', supplement to *Archaeological Journal*, 146 (1989), pp. 24–30

A. Giller, 'The Surnames of Scarsdale Hundred', unpub. Ph.D. thesis, University of Sheffield, 2001

M. Girouard, *Robert Smythson and the Elizabethan Country House* (Yale University Press, 1983)

M. Girouard, *Hardwick Hall* (London: The National Trust, 1989)

C. Glover and P. Riden (eds), *William Woolley's History of Derbyshire*, Derbyshire Record Society, vi (1981)

S. Glover, *The History and Gazetteer of the County of Derby*, 2 vols (Derby: 1831 and 1833)

A. R. Griffin, *Mining in the East Midlands, 1550–1947* (London: Cass, 1971)

D. Hadley, *The Northern Danelaw: Its Social Structure, c. 800–1100* (London and New York: Leicester University Press, 2000)

C. Hart, *The North Derbyshire Archaeological Survey to A.D. 1500* (Chesterfield: North Derbyshire Archaeological Trust, 1981)

N. B. Harte, *History of George Brettle and Co. Ltd, 1801–1964* (London: Courtaulds, 1973)

E. Heaf, *Tideswell Tracks* (privately published, 1999)

J. Heath, *The Illustrated History of Derbyshire* (Buckingham: Barracuda Books, 1982)

A. Henstock (ed.), *Early Victorian Country Town: A Portrait of Ashbourne in the mid-Nineteenth Century* (Ashbourne Local History Group, 1978)

D. Hey, 'The North-West Midlands: Derbyshire, Staffordshire, Cheshire, and Shropshire' in J. Thirsk (ed.), *The Agrarian History of England and Wales, V:I, 1640–1750* (Cambridge University Press, 1984), pp. 129–58

D. Hey, 'Yorkshire's Southern Boundary', *Northern History*, xxxvii (December 2000), pp. 31–48

D. Hey, *Packmen, Carriers and Packhorse Roads: Trade and Communications in North Derbyshire and South Yorkshire*, 2nd edn (Ashbourne: Landmark, 2001)

D. Hey, *Historic Hallamshire* (Ashbourne: Landmark, 2002)

D. Hey, 'Barlow: The Landscape History of a Peak District Township', in R.W. Hoyle (ed.), *People, Landscape and Alternative Agriculture: Essays for Joan Thirsk* (British Agricultural History Society, 2004), pp. 1–29

D. Hey, *A History of Sheffield*, 2nd edn (Lancaster: Carnegie, 2005)

D. Hey, *A History of Yorkshire: 'County of the Broad Acres'* (Lancaster: Carnegie, 2005)

H. Hill, *Freedom to Roam: The Struggle for Access to Britain's Moors and Mountains* (Ashbourne: Moorland, 1980)

R. Hodges, *Roystone Grange: 6000 Years of a Peakland Landscape* (Stroud: Tempus, 2006)

A. M. Hopkinson (ed.), *The Rolls of the 1281 Derbyshire Eyre*, Derbyshire Record Society, xxvii (2000)

A. Hopkinson, V. Hopkinson and W. Bateman (eds), *The Derbyshire Church Notes of Sir Stephen Glynne, 1812–1873*, Derbyshire Record Society, xxxii (2004)

B. Hutton, *Historic Farmhouses Around Derby* (Cromford: Scarthin Books, 1991)

B. Hutton, 'Sudbury Home Farm in the Parish of Doveridge, Derbyshire', *Derbyshire Archaeological Journal*, 117 (1997), pp. 86–96

C. Kerry, 'A History of Peak Forest', *Derbyshire Archaeological Journal*, xv (1893), pp. 67–98

C. Kerry, 'Leonard Wheatcroft, of Ashover', *Derbyshire Archaeological Society*, xviii (1896), pp. 29–80

C. Kerry (ed.), 'The Court Rolls of the Manor of Holmesfield, Co. Derby', *Derbyshire Archaeological Journal*, xx (1898), pp. 52–108

P. Kettle, *Oldcotes: The Last Mansion Built By Bess of Hardwick* (Whitchurch: Merton Priory Press, 2000)

N. Kirkham, *Derbyshire Lead Mining Through The Centuries* (Truro: Bradford Barton, 1968)

D. Knight and A. J. Howard, *Trent Valley Landscapes: The Archaeology of 500,000 Years of Change* (Great Dunham: Heritage, 2004)

D. Kiernan, *The Derbyshire Lead Industry in the Sixteenth Century*, Derbyshire Record Society, xiv (1989)

D. Kiernan (ed.), 'Lawrence Oxley's Accounts, 1672–81', *A Seventeenth-Century Derbyshire Miscellany*, Derbyshire Record Society, xx (1993), pp. 121–82

M. Langham, *Buxton: A People's History* (Lancaster: Carnegie, 2001)

D. and S. Lysons, *Magna Britannia, V: Topographical and Historical Account of Derbyshire* (London: 1817)

R. Meredith, 'The Eyres of Hassop, 1470–1640', Derbyshire Archaeological Journal, lxxxiv (1964), pp. 1–51, and lxxxv (1985), pp. 44–91

R. Meredith, *Farms and Families of Hathersage, Outseats, Derbyshire*, 2 parts (privately published, 1981–83)

J. Moreland, 'The Bradbourne Cross', *Current Archaeology*, 179 (2002), pp. 456–60

C. Morris (ed.), *The Illustrated Journeys of Celia Fiennes, c.1682–c.1712* (London: Macdonald, 1984)

S. C. Newton, 'The Gentry of Derbyshire in the Seventeenth Century', *Derbyshire Archaeological Journal*, lxxxvi (1966), pp. 1–30

F. Nixon, *Industrial Archaeology of Derbyshire* (Newton Abbot: David & Charles, 1969)

Old Dronfield Society, *Local History Trail* (Dronfield: 1978)

M. R. Palmer and P. Neaverson, *Industrial Landscapes of the East Midlands* (Chichester: Phillimore, 1992)

Sir N. Pevsner and E. Williamson, *The Buildings of England: Derbyshire* (Harmondsworth: Penguin, 1978)

J. Pilkington, *A View of the Present State of Derbyshire* (Derby: 1789)

J. D. Richards, 'Excavations at the Viking Barrow Cemetery at Heath Wood, Ingleby, Derbyshire', *The Antiquaries Journal*, 84 (2004), pp. 23–116

D. Riden (ed.), 'The Autobiography of Leonard Wheatcroft of Ashover, 1627–1706', *A Seventeenth-Century Derbyshire Miscellany*, Derbyshire Record Society, xx (1993), pp. 73–120

P. Riden, 'The Origin of the New Market of Chesterfield', *Derbyshire Archaeological Journal*, xcvii (1977), pp. 5–15

P. Riden, 'The Population of Derbyshire in 1563', *Derbyshire Archaeological Journal*, xcix (1978), pp. 61–71

P. Riden (ed.), *George Sitwell's Letterbook, 1662–66*, Derbyshire Record Society, x (1985)

P. Riden, *The Butterley Company, 1790–1830*, Derbyshire Record Society, xvi (1990)

P. Riden, 'The Charcoal Iron Industry in the East Midlands, 1580–1780', *Derbyshire Archaeological Journal*, cxi (1991), pp. 64–84

P. Riden (ed.), *Derbyshire Directories, 1781–1824*, Derbyshire Record Society, xxxiii (2006)

P. Riden and J. Blair (eds), *History of Chesterfield, V: Records of the Borough of Chesterfield and Related Documents, 1204–1835* (Chesterfield Borough Council, 1980)

A. Rimer, *The Cromford and High Peak Railway* (Ligfield: Oakwood Press, 1967)

A. F. Roberts and J. R. Leach, *The Coal Mines of Buxton* (Cromford: Scarthin Books, 1985)

B. Robinson, *Wall Across the Valley: The Building of the Howden and Derwent Dams* (Cromford: Scarthin Books, 1993)

D. R. Roffe, 'An Introduction to the Derbyshire Domesday', *The Derbyshire Domesday: Introduction and Translations* (Alecto, 1990), pp. 1–27

A. Saltman (ed.), *The Cartulary of Dale Abbey*, Derbyshire Archaeological Society Record Series, 2 (1967)

R. B. Schofield, *Benjamin Outram, 1764–1805: An Engineering Biography* (Merton Priory Press, 2000)

R. Scollins and J. Titford, *Ey Up Mi Duck!* (Newbury: Countryside Books, 2000)

S. Scott and C. Duncan, *Return of the Black Death* (Chichester: Wiley, 2004)

S. Scott and C. Duncan, 'The Destroying Angel', *Ancestors*, 26 (October 2004), 52–56

P. C. Sidebottom, 'Stone Crosses of the Peak and The Sons of Eadwulf', *Derbyshire Archaeological Journal*, 119 (1999), pp. 206–19

D. Sissons (ed.), *The Best of the Sheffield Clarion Ramblers' Handbooks: 'Ward's Piece'* (Tiverton: Halsgrove, 2002)

H. Smith, *The Sheffield and Chesterfield to Derby Roads* (privately published, 2003)

H. Smith, *The Guide Stoops of the Dark Peak* (privately published, 1999)

J. H. Smith and J. H. Garlick (eds), *The People of Glossop in 1851 and 1881* (Glossop & District Historical Society, 2002)

R. Somerville, *History of the Duchy of Lancaster*, I, 1265–1603 (London, 1953) and II, 1603–1965 (London, 1970)

R. Somerville, 'Commons and Wastes in North-west Derbyshire – the High Peak "New Lands", *Derbyshire Archaeological Journal*, xcvii (1977), pp. 16–22.

J. Spavold and S. Brown, *Ticknall: Pots and Potters* (Ashbourne: Landmark, 2005)

P. Stafford, *The East Midlands in the Early Middle Ages* (Leicester University Press, 1985)

J. Stetka, *King Edward's Burh* (Bakewell & District Historical Society, 1997)

J. Stetka, *From Fort to Field: The Shaping of the Landscape of Bakewell in the 10th Century* (privately published, 2001)

B. Stone, *Derbyshire in the Civil War* (Cromford: Scarthin Books, 1992)

B. Sykes, *Blood of the Isles* (London: Bantam, 2006)

C. Taylor, 'Ravensdale Park, Derbyshire, and Medieval Deer Coursing', *Landscape History*, 26 (2004), pp. 37–57

H. M. Taylor, *St Wystan's Church, Repton: A Guide and History* (Repton Church, 1989)

R. Taylor, *Wheston Cross, Derbyshire* (privately published, 2003)

F. Thompson, *A History of Chatsworth* (London: Country Life, 1949)

M. Tranter (ed.), *The Derbyshire Returns to the 1851 Religious Census* (Derbyshire Record Society, xxiii, 1995)

G. Turbutt, *A History of Derbyshire*, 4 vols (Cardiff: Merton Priory Press, 1999)

G. Turbutt, *A History of Ogston* (Higham: The Ogston Estates, 1975)

G. Turbutt, *A History of Shirland and Higham* (Higham: The Ogston Estates, 1978)

G. Ullathorne, 'The Surnames of the High Peak Hundred of Derbyshire', unpublished Ph.D. thesis, University of Sheffield, 2002

G. Ullathorne, 'Recording the Plague', *Ancestors*, 18 (February 2004), pp. 15–21

H. Wheeler, 'Excavation at Willington, Derbyshire, 1970–72', *Derbyshire Archaeological Journal*, 99 (1979), pp. 58–220

J. E. Williams, *The Derbyshire Miners: A Study in Industrial and Social History* (London: Allen & Unwin, 1962)

M. Wiltshire, S. Woore, B. Crisp, and B. Rich, *Duffield Frith* (Ashbourne: Landmark, 2005)

A. Wood, *The Politics of Social Conflict: The Peak Country, 1520–1770* (Cambridge University Press, 1999)

R. Wood, 'The Romanesque Church at Melbourne', *Derbyshire Archaeological Journal*, 126 (2006), pp. 127–68

S. M. Wright, *The Derbyshire Gentry in the Fifteenth Century* (Derbyshire Record Society, viii, 1983)

The Victoria History of the County of Derby, 2 vols (London: 1905–7)

E. M. Yates, 'Map of Ashbourne, Derbyshire', *Derbyshire Archaeological Journal*, lxxx (1960), pp. 124–8

J. P. Yeatman, *The Feudal History of the County of Derby*, 6 vols (London: 1886–1907)

Index

Entries in *italic* type refer to the illustration captions.

Acknowledgements

We would like to thank all those who have helped in the picture research for this book. A project of this scale and ambition incurs debts of gratitude to many people, without whose help and support it would not have been possible. Those who kindly provided images or who helped in their research include Catherine Kendall of Museums Sheffield; Matt Edwards and Francine Smith of Derby Museums and Art Gallery who kindly provided several images and allowed me to photograph objects in their collections; the staff at the National Monuments Record, Swindon; Nick Tomlinson of Picture the Past for collating the material that we selected from www.picturethepast.org.uk and for liaising with the copyright holders on our behalf; Dr Trevor Brighton for allowing us to reproduce lithographs by Samuel Rayner from his personal collection; Dae Sassitorn at www.lastrefuge.co.uk for the aerial image of Arbor Low; Joe Stack at W.W. Winters of Derby for the portraits of Steve Bloomer and Derby County FC; Nick Tully at Chesterfield College for sending us the image of Tapton House; the staff at Haddon Hall Estates for the photograph of the Long Gallery; Malcolm Dolby for the photographs of Minning Low and the aerial views of Bolsover Castle, Barlborough Hall and Hardwick Old Hall; Christopher Charlton and the Arkwright Society at Cromford; Sheila Edwards for her images of Tideslow Rake, the bridge across the Bar Brook on Big Moor and Whalley Bridge Canal Basin; Anna Betts from the Air Photo Library, Unit for Landscape Modelling, University of Cambridge, for locating and helping us to acquire the aerial views of Melandra Castle, Barton Blount and Bonsal Moor; Fran Halsall for the images of the Barbrook II barrow and Nine Stone Close stone circle; Diane Tranter from the Peak District National Park Authority for sending us an image of Chee Tor; Emma Thomas and Steve Carter of Toyota UK for the aerial photograph of the Toyota factory, Burnaston; Robert Jones at the Government Art Collection for guiding us through process of acquiring the paintings 'Matlock Church', 'Valley in Derbyshire' and 'Haddon Hall'; Margaret O'Sullivan and the staff at Derbyshire Record Office for their invaluable help and for allowing me to photograph images from their archives; Creswell Crags Heritage Trust, with thanks to John Scott; Chris Smith, Twenty Trees Photography; John Barnatt for the image of the Eaglestone Flat Bronze Age cremation urn; Hampden Maps for a map of Derby, from *The Beauties of England and Wales* (1806); Brian Sprakes for the use of his photograph of Norbury manor house; Peter Shelton for his images of the medieval stained glass at Dronfield church; Renishaw Hall; Katherine Oakes of The Landmark Trust; Jonathan Webb of www.webbaviation.co.uk for several aerial images, including the frontispiece; Tom Vine from the Science and Society Picture Library for researching and scanning images of Derby railway works for us to choose from (and all at the last minute!); the National Trust Picture Library for images of and from their properties at Hardwick Hall, Kedleston Hall and Calke Abbey; The National Archives for the image of the sixteenth-century map of Ashbourne and the seventeenth-century map of Wormhill; Roger Hull of Heanor District Local History Society.

The exact source of each illustration is given in a credit line at the end of the captions.

Many of the modern photographs were taken by the author over many years, and we are most grateful to David for access to his vast collection of slides and, latterly, digital photographs. Meanwhile I, as publisher, was lucky enough again to have the job of scooting around on my motorbike to photograph items of historical interest in most corners of Derbyshire. My thanks go to all the many people who helped with directions to out-of-the-way places. Technology has moved on since I took photographs for David's *History of Yorkshire*; back in 2005 it was still better to use medium-format film, but now in 2008 all of my images for this book were taken using a Canon Eos 5D digital camera. However, I still use the same, huge old tripod (the very sight of which helps to perpetuate the illusion that I know what I'm doing), which my father-in-law picked up at a car-boot sale for 50p a few years back … it is heavy and solid enough to hold the camera rock steady even at the 35–40 second exposures at f22 which are needed to give plenty of depth of field in low light, such as with the alabaster tombs or the stained glass images. Some antiquated things are still better than the most up to date!

Finally, my apologies to the proprietor of the Castleton hotel where I stayed in February 2008. Intent on capturing Peveril Castle at sunrise I tried to leave by the front door at 6 a.m., but succeeded only in setting off the burglar alarm!

Alistair Hodge, Carnegie Publishing, September 2008